Democracy at Work

A Comparative Sociology of Environmental Regulation in the United Kingdom, France, Germany, and the United States

Richard Münch with Christian Lahusen,
Markus Kurth, Cornelia Borgards,
Carsten Stark, and Claudia Jauß

Westport, Connecticut
London

Library of Congress Cataloging-in-Publication Data

Democracy at work : a comparative sociology of environmental regulation in the United
Kingdom, France, Germany, and the United States / Richard Münch . . . [et al.].
p.   cm.
Includes bibliographical references and index.
ISBN 0–275–96840–5 (alk. paper)
1. Environmental policy—Social aspects—Europe.   2. Environmental policy—Social
aspects—United States.   I. Münch, Richard, 1945–
GE190.E85 D46   2001
363.7′056—dc21   00–029842

British Library Cataloguing in Publication Data is available.

Library of Congress Catalog Card Number: 00–029842
ISBN: 0–275–96840–5

First published in 2001

Praeger Publishers, 88 Post Road West, Westport, CT 06881
An imprint of Greenwood Publishing Group, Inc.
www.praeger.com

Printed in the United States of America

The paper used in this book complies with the
Permanent Paper Standard issued by the National
Information Standards Organization (Z39.48–1984).

10 9 8 7 6 5 4 3 2 1

Contents

Preface

The capacity of democracies to be open to new problems, as they are articulated by new social movements, and to carry out policies in order to solve these problems and to allow for the sustainable development of society has been thoroughly tested everywhere since the 1970s. The articulation of new ecological challenges by new social movements has become a test case for the ability of democracies to learn and improve their capacities for innovation, inclusion, conflict management, and consensus formation. Based on an empirical research project, this book tries to give an answer to this question using the clean air policies of four countries to explore how democracy works when it is confronted with such challenges. The countries under investigation are the United Kingdom, France, Germany and the United States. Each of them has established a specific type of democratic culture and practice that implies different forms of conflict settlement and regulation of society with different sorts of advantages and disadvantages.

There is a growing interest in learning from the practices and experiences gathered by different countries all over the world in order to master new problems. Learning about how democracy works in different cultural and institutional settings is certainly an important aspect of this worldwide learning process. Insofar as the European societies are transformed into more multilevel and more pluralistic democracies in the process of European integration, the American model of a multilevel competitive and pluralistic democracy is of utmost importance for comparative reasons. This is why we compared three European countries and the United States. Drawing this comparison, we discover the transformation that the European democracies will undergo in the European integration process with all its consequences, what they can gain, and what they will have to give up. In this perspective, we learn something from the comparison of three European democracies with the United States about their ongoing and future transformation in the European integration process, which cannot be established when studying the European countries only. At the center of this comparative study is the capacity of different types of democracy for conflict management and consensus formation, especially their capacity of innovation and including new problems articulated by new social movements in the political process. In this sense, it is not political science, but a comparative sociology of democracy. The focus is not on governance and administration but on innovation, conflict settlement, social integration, and consensus formation. Because political science has specialized in questions of governance and effective policy making, there is even more need for sociology in studying democracy and politics with regard to the fundamental questions of societal innovation, political conflict settlement, social integration, and consensus formation. This book wishes to contribute to the revitalization of the sociological study of democracy and politics. It is a comparative sociology of democracy at work.

Policy research as a branch of political science has been separated far too much from questions of politics and polity and also from questions of social transformation in the broader sense of social theory. Further, the theory of democracy in political science lacks embedding in the broader context of social theory. It is the particular purpose of this book to reestablish those links between different branches of social science. What we look for is a theory of democracy that is rooted in social theory as well as comparative empirical policy research and thereby bridges the gap between those two opposing fields of discourse and research. We hope that such an approach will bear fruitful results for social theory, the theory of democracy, and empirical policy research. The aim is to bring back sociology to the study of politics and not to leave it to political science only, because we think that sociology has something to say that is not completely covered by political science.

According to its purpose, the book should not be read as a report on clean air policies describing a series of legislative acts and political events. Such more descriptive studies are already available (Murley 1995; Cooper and Alley 1994). The book aims, however, at a farther-reaching theoretical interpretation of the facts described. Our emphasis is particularly on this theoretical interpretation. It starts with the elaboration of the theoretical framework in Chapters 1 and 2. The next step is the application of the framework to interpret the structures and processes of clean air policies in the four countries under investigation theoretically in Chapters 3 to 6. Thus, even the case studies concentrate on theoretical interpretation. The four case studies then provide the basis for the comparative theory of democracy, which is elaborated in Chapter 7. The conclusion looks at the perspectives of democracy in a future, that will be fundamentally shaped by the further development of European integration and global sociation. Readers who are interested in more detailed information regarding the individual cases can be referred to our research report to the *Deutsche Forschungsgemeinschaft*, which can be ordered at http:\\www.dfg.de. The case studies on Germany by Carsten Stark and on the United States by Claudia Jauß have been completed as dissertations at the University of Bamberg and have been published in German (see Bibliography). We are proud to mention that Claudia Jauß was awarded the 1999 Fulbright dissertation prize in Germany for her work.

We are grateful to Susan C. Madiedo and Brigitte Münzel for doing the translation from the German original. All quotations from German and French books or interviews have been translated by Susan Madiedo and Brigitte Münzel.

Abbreviations

ACBE	Advisory Council on Business and the Environment
ADEME	Agence de l'Environnement et de la Maîtrise de l'Énergie
APPA	Association pour la Prévention de la Pollution Atmosphérique
BATNEEC	Best available technique not entailing excessive costs
BDI	Bundesverband der Deutschen Industrie
BimSchG	Bundesimmissionschutzgesetz
BPEO	Best practicable environmental option
BPM	Best practicable means
BUND	Bund für Umwelt und Naturschutz Deutschland
CASAC	Clean Air Scientific Advisory Committee
CCIP	Chambre de Commerce et d'Industrie de Paris
CDF	Charbonnage de France
CIRED	Centre International de Recherche sur l'Environment et le Développement
CITEPA	Centre Interprofessionnel Technique d'Etudes de la Pollution Atmosphérique
CNPF	Conseil National du Patronat Français
CSIC	Conseil Supérieur des Installations Classées
DETR	Department of the Environment, Transport and the Regions
DoH	Department of Health
DRIRE	Direction Régionale de l'Industrie, de la Recherche et de l'Environnement
DTI	Department of Trade and Industry
EDF	Electricité de France
ENA	École Nationale d'Administration
EPA	Environmental Protection Act (U.K.), Environmental Protection Agency (United States)
EU	European Union

FoE   Friends of the Earth
GDF   Gaz de France
HMIP   Her Majesty's Inspectorate for Pollution
HoC   House of Commons
IEHO   Institution of Environmental Health Officers
IPC   Integrated pollution control
KRDL   Kommission Reinhaltung der Luft
LAI   Länderausschuß für Immissionschutz
LCPP   Laboratoire Central de la Préfecture de Police, Paris
MAFF   Ministry of Agriculture, Fisheries, and Food
NRDC   Natural Resources Defense Council
NSCA   National Society for Clean Air
RCEP   Royal Commission on Environmental Pollution
Reg-Neg   Regulatory negotiation
S3PI   Secrétariat Permanent pour les Problèmes de la Pollution Indus-
            trielle
SAB   Science Advisory Board
SNCF   Société Nationale des Chemins de Fer
SRU   Sachverständigenrat für Umweltfragen
STIIC   Service Technique Interdépartementale d'Inspection des Instal-
            lations Classées, Préfecture de Police
UBA   Umweltbundesamt
UFIP   Union Française des Industries Pétrolières
UIC   Union des Industries Chimiques
VCI   Verband der Chemischen Industrie
VDI   Verband Deutscher Ingenieure

Chapter 1

Introduction: Democratic Politics and Ecological Challenges

Christian Lahusen and Richard Münch

Clean air is a key issue of the national environmental policies of most industrial-ized nations. Risks and damages to people and nature such as occurred, for in-stance, as a result of London's smog in 1952 or the acid rain's impact on forest decline in the 1970s and 1980s exerted a substantial influence on both the emer-gence and development of this policy field. Industrial plants and road traffic were blamed, above all, for being the main polluters and were consequently subjected to a whole series of pollution abatement measures. A series of regulatory instruments from the field of environmental policy (e.g., monitoring and permit-granting procedures, prohibition of products and additives, environmental fees and taxes) was developed also in regard to clean air. The experiences gathered with these measures were rather mixed and gradually raised an awareness for the complexity of biochemical processes, societal causes of environmental degradation, and the difficulties of finding quick answers and simple policy solutions. Many of the regulatory measures that were initially used to address environmental problems such as summer smog, the greenhouse effect, acid rain, and forest decline (most of them "command and control" measures) were increasingly complemented or replaced by a wider range of policies (market instruments, voluntary agreements, alternative dispute resolution, among many others), some of which had been de-veloped and tested in other countries before. At the same time, the public debate on clean air policies became more contentious because the established regulatory priorities and means were criticized for being deaf to cost-benefit considerations, on the one hand, and for transparency, accountability, and democratic legitimacy, on the other.

Clean air regulation in the realm of both stationary and mobile sources conse-quently forms an interesting topic of research. As far as the policy issues of this research are concerned, we have to point out that we forwent both a coverage of atmospheric air pollution in connection with climate changes and the considera-tion of air pollution inside buildings.[1] When we, therefore, talk about air pollution in the following text, we refer first and foremost to tropospherical pollution but, above all, to all those phenomena that are discussed and regulated in context with smog or ozone close to the ground, acid rain, smell-related nuisances, and toxic substances. Mobile and stationary sources, which are at the center of analysis, represent two of the main causes of air pollution (a "technical" level) and are part of at least two distinct policy fields and communities that are affected by environmental regulation and/or have to be aligned with its programs (the political level). Each of these regulatory fields is characterized by different target groups and actors with their specific needs, interests, norms, knowledge, and belief systems (the societal level), which have to be coordinated and incorporated in order to arrive at a comprehensive set of cross-sectoral clean air policies.

A COMPARISON OF NATIONAL POLICY STYLES

A comparative study is particularly appealing for our research purpose since it allows us to look into the question of how different countries respond to these varied, intertwined challenges of clean air policies. Countries such as the Federal Republic of Germany, France, Great Britain, and the United States of America developed differing forms of regulation, which are undoubtedly amalgamating and approaching each other (Jänicke and Weidner 1997b). However, differences are not eroded completely, as many of the national regulatory styles tend to re-produce themselves under new circumstances. The four countries were chosen as cases for our comparative analysis, as they made it possible for us to work out different styles of regulation in a particularly striking manner. The country comparison was based on four ideal typical models that were formulated according to analytic and heuristic considerations, on the one hand, and empirical insights into national policy styles to be found in scholarly literature of the last two decades, on the other. According to these ideal types, environmental policy is handled either in the form of a technicist synthesis or consensus model (Germany), a pluralistic competition model (United States), a technocratic model of etatism (France), or a consultation-based compromise model (U.K.). In our research, these models served as heuristic tools for describing, explaining, and evaluating the different policy and regulation styles.

This study adopts the concept of policy style in order to stress the identity and continuity of clean air policies specific to each country beyond individual problem areas (traffic, stationary sources) and measures (regulative rule-making, market instruments, etc.). This concept helps to point out the specific features of each country, while undoubtedly engendering the risk of simplifying the reality of environmental regulation too much. Indeed, regulatory styles are conceived in this study as models or ideal types. Portrayed in this manner (Münch 1996), they become a *heuristic* instrument of social research, according to which specific characteristics are integrated into a theoretically consistent ideal type while, at the same time, attention is being paid also to a clear-cut separation between the different models (Weber 1972: 3–10). Therefore, these ideal types serve as a useful *analytical* tool for a comparative analysis of society, as they supply assumptions and "yardsticks" for the empirical case analyses and country comparisons (Heidenreich 1991). In this sense, however, ideal types can never represent the full reality of a country, and policy styles can help to underline only dominant aspects of national regulation. This is to say also that the main interest in developing and using these heuristic and analytical concepts is a theoretical one: these ideal types or models can raise awareness for the relationship between particular causes and effects, and they help to highlight the dynamics, constraints, and opportunities specific to a particular type or style of regulation. Countries are used in this context as cases representing specific theoretical arguments and empirical constellations of facts in a particularly bold and clear manner. This is the special strength of ideal types as devices of scientific research and policy learning.

The concept of "policy style" has been criticized not only for exaggerating or caricaturing reality. It was also complained that scholarly writing on policy styles generalize findings of individual cases unduly by disregarding the specificity of each issue and policy field (see a survey in Richardson, Gustafsson, and Jordan 1991). In fact, the policy style argument usually tends to start from the assumption that particular forms and structures of political regulation are relatively independent of the issues and policy matters dealt with, and this argument is recurrently supported by reference to the fact that different policy fields are regulated in a similar manner within one country (Vogel 1986, 1996). Moreover, it is assumed that regulatory action unveils a certain resistance to change. These assumptions are contestable, however, yet also quite fruitful as regards the potential gain of findings, for it is precisely in a research area where globalization and the crisis of the nation-state have become the keywords, and international convergence and common learning processes an essential structural argument that it is worthwhile taking a closer look and asking whether this convergence or change might not be superficial phenomena and whether specific national policy styles are reproducing themselves in their latent structures under changed frame conditions.

Both the definition and operationalization of the concept of policy style refer to specific structural features and factors. For Richardson, Gustafsson, and Jordan (1991: 2), policy styles are "different systems of decision making, different procedures for making societal decisions. By policy style we perhaps, more cumbersomely, really mean policy making and implementation style." When doing research it is then important to work out "standard operating procedures," "legitimising norms for policy activity," and so on. The present study uses a similar research agenda. Starting from the aforementioned four heuristic regulation models, we distinguished between four central levels of analysis, which are all used in different research contexts and with different intentions. First of all, we have to mention the networks between the state, interest organizations, and science, which are, first and foremost, based on strategic considerations, exchange relationships, and interest alliances and which try to influence and guide policies consciously in their goals, contents, and procedures. Second, a series of professions (engineers, lawyers, physicians, etc.) is tied into the formulation and implementation of environmental policy. In each country, a proper "system of professional division of labor" is established, which impinges heavily on the forms and structures, opportunities and constraints of national politics and policies. Third,

institutional rules and normative standards are referred to as important components of environmental regulation in that they define common "rules of the game"
and/or normative guidelines by obliging politics, for instance, to hierarchy or
cooperation, expertise or participation. Last but not least, political culture plays a
role, too, since it affects the perception and definition of environmental problems
and the formulation of priorities and reasonable measures as well as the legitimation of political action in the form of common values and belief systems. Hence,
our research agenda moves a structural analysis of policies to the foreground.
Moreover, it tends to put particular emphasis on political cultures, which establish
common points of orientation and "leitmotifs" and thus lend consistency and
identity to national policies. In this way it argues for the existence of latent structures that tend to reproduce "standard operating procedures" under changed conditions.

In our research, these factors are included in a progressing chain of argumentation that starts from policy and network analysis in order to arrive at the sociology of knowledge and culture, for only on this level can the (latent) structures and
dynamics of national policy styles be reasonably dealt with. As we said before, the
existing study enjoys the benefit of building on a well-developed state of research.
In this context, we would like to mention, above all, the research done by
Knoepfel and Weidner (1985) and Héritier, Knill, and Mingers (1996), who provided important insights into, and inspirations for, a comparative research of
clean air policies, even though this was done only in the field of stationary
sources. The first research, above all, was of particular importance for the theoretical delimitation of our study and offered invaluable insights into the practical
side of comparative research whose farsightedness and honesty represent a virtue
that can be rarely discovered in published research reports and prevented us from
several (though not all) wrong decisions and problems. The focus of this comprehensive study was on the efficiency and effectiveness of regional implementation
systems and on a corresponding international and interregional comparison of the
benefits and successes of clean air policies. Our project, in contrast, was less focused on the research of regional implementation systems and more to national
regulations. In fact, we did not carry out our own implementation research but
rather used the existing results as far as necessary. At the same time, we were less
interested in an explanation and assessment of the quality and success of regulatory action (the so-called outcomes) and more in an explanation and evaluation of
country-specific forms of regulation and policy styles (the so-called outputs).

As a result, our study does not deal with the question as to how successful different countries or different measures are in the field of air pollution abatement
(Jänicke and Weidner 1995) and as to what societal conditions of success can be
outlined in order to arrive at efficient solutions to the problems (Jänicke 1990;
Jänicke and Weidner [eds.] 1997b).[2] We were less interested in these practical
matters but, instead, eager to better understand and explain national policy styles
as to their common features and differences. This means that our research is more
theoretically oriented and tries to show why environmental policy is handled in a
specific way in regard to its capability of taking up societal grievances, settling

conflicts, and arriving at consensually supported solutions while respecting social integration, democratic legitimacy, and public welfare. In this context, we were particularly interested in demonstrating how policy making, regulatory action, and implementation are marked by networks, professions, institutional rules, and (political) cultures and what strengths, weaknesses and dilemmas of political problem solving that result from these realities. To this end, we had to penetrate more deeply into the practice of political regulation and the inherent political philosophy than this had happened before in the field of environmental policy analysis. We consider this our specific contribution to the broader research context. From this point of view, the practical relevance of our findings can be answered: we may ask questions as to the innovation potentials and the direction of political change anew, we may determine the possibilities of developing or reforming established policy repertoires, and we may circumscribe the factual chances of transferring successful instruments by referring to the structural conditions of the policy models in question. An instrument such as a mediation procedure, for instance, may be successful in one policy context but may fail in a second one, since the introduction of the instrument may be rejected, or the instruments may be diluted, lose their innovative potentials, or become a mere piece of symbolic politics.[3] At the same time, individual instruments may also have nonintended effects on the functioning and structure of domestic policy by integrating conflicting instruments or by reorienting the established regulation style partially into a different direction. Yet, an appraisal of these practical conditions and effects of successful policy change can result only from systematic research oriented to describe and explain the underlying regulatory models and policy styles.

Alongside the investigation mentioned earlier, the study of Adrienne Héritier's research team (Héritier, Knill, and Mingers 1996) was of use for our own work, even though her focus is on the development of European clean air policies (see also Héritier 1993, 1997). In view of the former project by Knoepfel and Weidner, this study approached the question of national forms of regulation within the European context, thus trying to filter out the specific features of national styles of regulation as a preliminary step to the proper object of research. This study is also based on a multidimensional explanatory strategy; that is, Héritier carries on a policy network analysis that repeatedly refers to exchange relationships, institutional settings, and regulatory philosophies so as to fill blind spots of a rationalist actors' theory.

Our own research agenda was not focused on European environmental regulation and the interaction of national and international politics. Through the addition of the United States we opted for an exclusively comparative research agenda. This focus made it possible for us to look more closely and in a more encompassing way into the structural features, dynamics, and consecutive problems of political regulation in general and the various policy styles and models in particular. This kind of questioning required a specific theoretical framework. The aforementioned frame of reference is based on the sociology of knowledge and culture, which not only changes or extends the factors taken into consideration but also gives more unity and stringency to the multidimensional explanatory pattern as such. Therefore, our starting point is the question as to how societies structure and organize interests, norms and rules, knowledge and expertise, symbolical interpretations and values (the explanans), how they mediate and interrelate them politically and thus guide the regulatory practices (explanandum). The advantage of this is that the identity of national cultures of regulation can be highlighted more precisely and that the continuity of *latent* policy styles can be recognized beyond visible (and possibly superficial) changes. Our framework of analysis thus postulates a dialectic relationship between change and continuity.

POLITICS IN THE SOCIETAL CONTEXT

Politics takes place in a societal context that involves much more than the mobilization and application of power. A comprehensive interpretation and explanation of what is going on in a particular area of policy making have to go beyond the inner structure and dynamics of that process and put it into the overall context of society and culture. This requires looking at the networks of actors involved in policy making, the institutional rules of that process, the role played by professional experts, and the relevant cultural tradition as an overall background not only within a specific policy process but also in its linkage to the wider society. Policy analysis in this sense is societal analysis and needs not only political science but also sociology. What we are doing here is policy analysis from a sociological point of view. This intention calls, above all, for an interpretive sociology that starts with some basic concepts and assumptions in order to obtain a frame of analysis but is directed to the continuous qualification, specification, concretization, and revision of the preliminary frame in the process of investigation in order to approach a satiated interpretation and explanation of the reality under review. In doing so, we take up and specify Strauss and Glaser's (1967) model of the discovery of grounded theory according to our intentions. We start with an idea of policy making in general, specify types of regulation analytically, begin the interpretation and explanation of policy making of a particular country with an analytical type, go on with a closer description of the policy process in that country, and end with a concretization of the analytical type for the country, which results in an empirical case with a unique structure and dynamics. In this empirical case, we interpret and explain certain features of policy making—particularly problems of conflict settlement—by the style of policy making, which is made up by the specific character of networks of actors, institutional rules, professions involved, and ideas of legitimation. In doing so, we aim at a sociology of democracy as it works in the political regulation of society on the example of clean air politics.

In a political science perspective, policy making is studied in terms of governance. It is asked whether and how the structure of governance allows for the political regulation of society in a democratically legitimated way under the structural conditions of the society and the economy in a certain historical epoch. Political regulation is a matter of the generation and application of governmental power in an effective and democratically legitimated way. Thus, it is investigated, for instance, whether the government has the capacity to reduce environmental pollution in an effective and democratically legitimate way and what problems of effective and democratically legitimated program formulation, implementation, and enforcement occur. In a sociological perspective, the same process is addressed as a problem of broader societal conflict settlement in the zone of interpenetration between government and society, concentrating on the question as to the way in which conflicts can be articulated and settled, new values, political goals, and interests are included in the arena of conflict settlement, societal innovation can take place, new social movements can be included, and new consensus can be generated. Policy making is not interpreted as a problem of governance and effective, democratically legitimated political regulation of society but as a problem of social change and social integration in the sense of the society's capacity of conflict settlement in accordance with societal innovation, inclusion of new social movements, and consensus formation.

Our model of analysis thus tries to work out the network of actors, the professions that define the situation and elaborate problem solutions, the institutional rules of the policy process, and the cultural ideas of legitimating decisions that are interdependent and constitute the framework and style of political regulation. This framework and style result in specific capacities of political regulation with regard to (1) societal innovation, (2) conflict settlement, (3) inclusion and (4) consensus formation, which are also interdependent. The different elements that form the framework and style of political regulation are not related to one another in simple and monodirectional causality but in mutual shaping and constitution. Thus, the network of actors *opens* or *closes* the access of professions to political regulation, opens or closes access to establishing and applying institutional rules and to defining the legitimacy of decisions. The professions *determine* who is competent and who is to be accepted in the network, which institutional rules are appropriate, and how legitimacy is constructed. The institutional rules *channel* the acceptance of actors in the network, the decision making, and the referring of decisions to legitimating ideas in a binding way. The cultural ideas *give legitimation* to the acceptance of actors in the network, to the attribution of competence, and to institutional rules. The same mutually constitutive and shaping relationship holds true for the consequences of the framework and style of political regulation. Societal innovations open the space for action, reorganize conflict settlement, inclusion, and consensus formation. Conflict settlement via power *determines* innovations, inclusion, and consensus formation. Inclusion channels innovations, the exercising of professional competence, and the legitimation of decisions in a binding way. Consensus formation *redefines* the network of actors, professional competence, and inclusion. There is a primary relationship, and there are secondary relationships of the elements of the framework and style of policy making to the elements that build up the capacity for political regulation. The primary relationship of the structure of networks refers to the potential for innovation: the more open the network, the more chances for innovation. In a secondary way, the network determines more or less *open* conflict settlement, institutional rules, and legitimating ideas. The primary effect of professional work is the more or less *effective* conflict settlement; its secondary effect is more or less effective innovation, rule constitution, and application and definition of legitimacy. The primary effect of institutional rules is the binding channeling of inclusion; its secondary effect is the *binding channeling* of access to networks, conflict settlement, and legitimation. The primary effect of cultural ideas of *legitimation* is the legitimation of a consensus; its secondary effect is the legitimation of innovation, conflict settlement, and inclusion. There is not a monodirectional causality either from the constitutive elements of the regulation framework and style to innovations, conflict settlement, inclusion, and consensus formation, because the latter have repercussions on the former. They reset networks, professions, institutional rules, and cultural ideas of legitimation (Diagram 1.1).

Diagram 1.1
A Sociological Framework for Studying Political Regulation

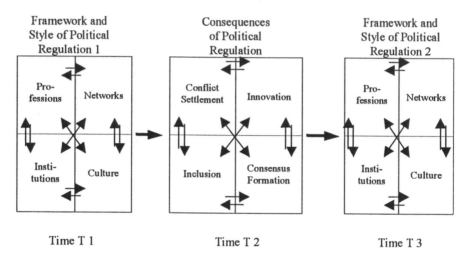

Policy making and/or regulation of society can be conceived neither as a one-sided hierarchy of orders nor as a mere provider of stimuli whose effects are completely outside political control. For both views, the actual political process appears as a black box that cannot be observed more closely. What type of policy is made with the help of what resources and with what sort of impact is decided, however, precisely within this black box of political theory's both hierarchical and systems-theoretical approach (Luhmann 1989; Scharpf 1989; Windhoff-Héritier 1987). To make a collectively binding decision on programs of society formation and regulation, political power is required first and foremost. Yet, political power is shaky when it rests merely on the monopoly upon the instruments of power. Only when an agreement is reached about the legitimate access to this monopoly of power, on the legitimate power of decision making and the legitimate use of power, will politics be a peaceful process involving legitimate and collectively binding decisions. In this case, power will remain a matter of the ultimate sanction against resistance in individual cases. Only when the citizens share common ideas about what values the political decision making process should adhere to and within what institutional rules of the political process these values should be realized will politics move along in such a peaceful way. Politics will then be embedded in the structure of institutional rules and the horizon of political culture. If we want to gain an understanding of the political process and of policy making in particular, we will have to investigate just this structure of institutional rules and the horizon of political culture. In fact, they mirror how policy is made legitimately. As far as this concerns democratic politics, political culture and institutional rules express common ideas of living democracy.

Yet, policy making is also a dynamic process that mobilizes resources in the framework of political institutions and political culture and transfers them into collectively binding decisions. To implement collectively binding decisions, political power must be mobilized. To this end, democracies require majorities. Political power involves an access to the monopoly of the legitimate application of force. The smallest unit of political power in a democracy is the vote. In parliamentary elections, the elector gives his or her vote to an MP who, in turn, votes on laws. These laws are then implemented via legitimate executive and bureaucratic power and via legitimate police power if necessary, possibly after having been examined by the courts. Should political decisions not only be accomplished through power in the sense of implementation against resistance but also be supported by the citizens' cooperation, a particular resource must be mobilized. This resource may be called influence. It concerns the ability to make other people support and cooperate in the realization of a political program. Other than political power, influence does not rest on access to the stately monopoly of power, but rather on solidarity, esteem, respect, reputation, loyalty, or recognition of a claim to leadership.

Political decisions may, however, be more or less correct substantially and, consequently, meet with more or less substantial approval. In order to secure this consent, the necessary expertise must be mobilized when legal programs are to be conceived. In their assessments, at best, experts give a seal of truth to the conception of a law; at worst, they provide it with a seal of untruth. Only if a program can undoubtedly make a claim for truth will it experience the necessary substantial approval. What is understood by truth and how it can be proven differ from one culture to the other. The culture-specific understanding of truth and the corresponding commitment to the value of truth will decide on whether a political program will witness sufficient substantial approval. Beyond the substantial correctness, political decisions may gain in legitimacy only when they prove compatible with the basic values and basic norms (basic rights) anchored in the culture and make a contribution to their realization. That means that political decisions must be borne by general value commitments in order to be regarded as legitimate.

As a rule, political programs cost a lot of money after all. Either they imply direct expenses—as for social or educational programs—or they cause indirect expenses when authorities have to be maintained, for instance, to control environmental standards. The state does not receive its funds on a silver platter but, instead, has to absorb them from the economic cycle by way of tax revenues. The degree to which these tax resources are available depends on the economy's prosperity. To secure this prosperity, governments have to supply favorable frame conditions and provide stimuli for investments through their economic policy.

For systematic purposes we may locate the interlacing of politics, economy, civil society, and culture presented so far within a social space of action. This space of action can be formed by the combination of two integral parts of action: the complexity of the symbolic world, which serves as an orientation for the actions and the contingency of action, that is, the number of different ways of acting (Münch [1982] 1988: 81–96). In the social scope of action, the ways of acting are limited actually by political decisions, although they remain represented symbolically. The economical mobilization of resources increases the possibilities both of imagination and of action at the same time. In civil society, traditionally evolved norms limit the possibilities of imagination and of action simultaneously. In cultural reflection, the symbolic world is reduced to a limited number of basic values by way of abstraction, which, however, leave a wide scope of possible alternatives open for action. Politics is the place to exercise power, while economy is the place to create money; the civil society is the place to generate influence, and culture is the place where to mobilize value commitments such as the commitment to the value of truth. Politics, economy, civil society, and culture must not be regarded as functional systems, but rather as fields of action having their own rationality: the collectively binding finding and making of decisions for politics; the mobilization of resources for the economy; solidarity for civil society; and (self-)understanding for culture. The concretization of these rationalities, which guide the actions, is made by the emergence of institutions of politics, economy, civil society, and culture.

The institutions help to refer the particular rationalities to guiding ideas. In modern societies, the consented formation of the future has become the driving force behind politics in order to realize a fair social order and a good life; the growth of the gross domestic product (GDP) guides the economy; the welfare of the entire population determines the civil society; and the progress of knowledge is the central idea of culture. The institutions of democracy and rule of law, of social market economy, of the welfare society and of education, science, and art serve for the realization of these central ideas. When we say that policy has to mobilize resources in the form of power, money, influence, and value commitments (truth) in order to form society, this implies that the required resources can exclusively be gained where they are at home, and only in line with the particular institutionalized rules: political power inside the institutional complex of politics itself; money in the economy; influence in the civil society; and value commitments (truth) in culture (science). It should have become clear by now that we follow a definitely action-theoretical approach (Diagram 1.2).

Diagram 1.2
Politics in the Societal Context

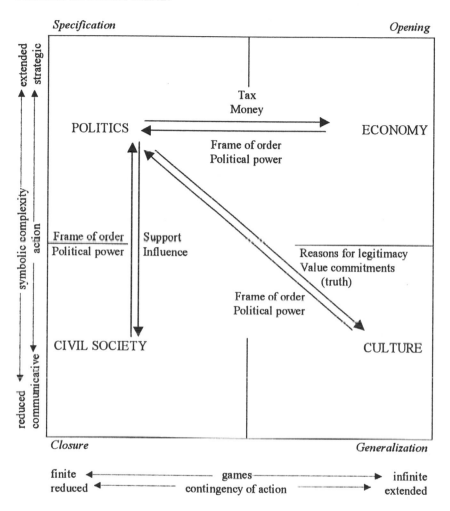

IDEAL TYPES AND "THICK DESCRIPTION"

Our country surveys on clean air politics regarding stationary sources in the United Kingdom, France, Germany, and the United States work out the aforementioned structural components of the policy process: the networks, the professions involved, the institutional rules, and the political culture. We selected these four countries as they—each in its specific way—had the most sustained influence on modern Western culture, producing their own ideas of state and democracy, knowledge, technology, and truth. As far as these countries are concerned, we may, moreover, follow up a comparative study conducted before regarding the culture of modernity as well as a first sketch of various models of risk politics (Münch [1986] 1993a, 1996). The four countries in question are particularly apt for establishing ideal types of politics whose starting point rests in the analytical differentiation of compromise, conflict, competition, and consensus as four independently definable forms of the coordination of actions within networks that cannot be reduced anymore. They complement each other and, together, result in a complete entity. We do not claim, in this context, that historically, concrete politics in one of these countries is represented fully by one ideal type, but we rather believe that a certain country presents a greater proximity to one particular ideal type than the others so that it is particularly suitable for research into the specific features and causal effects of an ideal type. We suppose that when conducting a cluster analysis, Great Britain prior to Margaret Thatcher's government would most widely correspond to the compromise type, France mostly to the conflict type, Germany to the synthesis type, and the United States to the competition type. We may also assume that a cluster analysis conducted in 1960 would have shown these differences more markedly than in 1995. Meanwhile, the countries have approached each other more closely (Jänicke and Weidner 1997b: 312), mainly by moving toward the competition model. This applies, above all, to the United Kingdom after the Thatcher reforms. Nevertheless, France and Germany, too, have moved somewhat in this direction; this is attributable to the rising number of political actors and political stages coming to the fore as a result of the decentralization on the inside and the linkage to the European level on the outside. However, the countries have to accommodate the new facts from their specific traditions, demonstrating thus also a certain resistance to change (Weale, Pridham, Williams, and Porter 1996). As a consequence, ever new problems and dilemmas particular for the country in question will arise. To reach a sufficiently large understanding of this procedure, it was, therefore, indispensable to link the internal European comparison of the development in the European countries with the external comparison of the development in the United States. Without including the United States, the internal European comparison would lack the exemplary presentation of the structures, processes, and problems of a politics that is largely determined by pluralism of interests, multifarious levels and various stages, and tough and open competition as well as the extensive inclusion of the public. Here, a politics is shown to us whose individual structures and dynamics are of a pioneering importance for politics in the European multilevel system. Unfortunately, the internal European comparisons frequently neglect this glance across the Atlantic so that the analyses lose clearness and are limited as to their explanatory power.

The countries involved in our survey do not show their tendency toward one particular ideal type because of an isolated discussion of an individual case, but rather as a result of their comparison with the other countries. Therefore, the United Kingdom prior to Margaret Thatcher served, in particular, as a field of research for the ideal type of compromise. The inclusion of countries being considered examples of a "consociational democracy," such as the Netherlands, Switzerland, and Austria, would bring these countries closest to the ideal type of compromise. Then, however, the United Kingdom would have to be transferred some distance away from these countries and more toward the ideal types of the struggle for power and of competition due to its concentration of power with the government, which works with a reliable parliamentary majority, and due to its industrial relationships, which tend more toward an open settlement of conflicts when compared to the neocorporatist arrangements (Lehmbruch 1967; Lijphart 1968; Lehmbruch and Schmitter 1982) (Diagram 1.3).

Diagram 1.3
The Countries' Position in the Space of Action

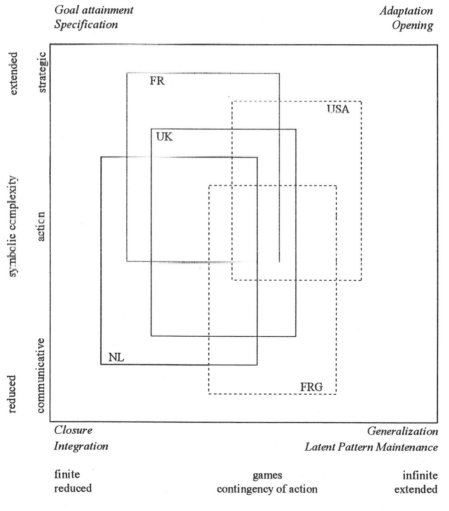

Our country surveys start with a general and comparative presentation of the problems and instruments of clean air policy. The surveys themselves were carried out by way of a secondary analysis of existing studies, analysis of newspapers and documentations, and interviews of important actors from the policy process (approximately 40 interviews per country).

The results of the different case studies are subject to a comparative examination. Last but not least, the results of the different case studies and their comparison are interpreted against the backdrop of exemplary texts from political philosophy, which have pointed the way in the different countries' history regarding the understanding of democracy, state, government, and politics as well as knowledge, technology, and truth.

As deep as possible an understanding of the particular features and specific problems and dilemmas of the political regulation of society in the individual countries should be created. In doing so, the analysis should raise the question as to how far and in what form conflicts can be processed and a political regulation of society is possible while maintaining social integration, that is, how a consensually supported political formation of the future can be made. The conclusion will refer this question to the challenges of the present time, which can be described by terms such as pluralization of the structure of interests, individualization of the conditions of life, medialization of politics, scientification of problems, Europeanization, and globalization. Last but not least, our comparative study on clean air policy wants not only to describe this sphere of politics but to deepen our understanding of the various political systems to such an extent that we become aware of the problems and dilemmas that will most probably arise when coping with the new challenges under their specific structural, institutional, and cultural conditions.

The analysis of past politics and their inclusion in a historically evolved environment of networks, institutional rules, professional-scientific associations, and political cultures should not be an end in its own but should help us follow the path into the future with a better knowledge of the specific problems and dilemmas to be coped with. Our research of the policy process of clean air serves the establishing of ideal types of politics that are most markedly discovered in the countries under review (Weber 1973: 190–212). What results most striking during the comparison is put into the foreground; what is less striking is left in the background so as to make the impact of the striking features as strong as possible. We do not want to get lost in detailed historical descriptions of "how it was like" but want to develop a sociological analysis capable to work out specific problems and dilemmas of politics based on ideal types.

Certainly, the ideal types do not say everything about what is happening in a country, yet at the same time their features and causal effects are of a cross-border significance, ultimately even of universal importance when referring them to the modernization process. This means that the problems and dilemmas of a competition democracy, which we can observe most markedly in the United States, are, of course, also significant for the other countries insofar as they have borrowed elements from this ideal type and/or will do so in future more than before. There are many indications for this. The same applies to the other ideal types. The specific effectiveness of "dominance by virtue of knowledge," which we seized in its ideal typical form in Germany—the gap between technical discussions and an emotion-alized public—makes itself felt in the other countries, too, due to the generally growing scientification of politics. The same goes for the selective concerting between the administrative elite and the large-scale industry in France. It pushes interests that have not been covered onto the street. Of course, this development can also be observed in other countries. The paralyzation of politics by the bonds of a strong civil society, which was demonstrated to us in Great Britain prior to Margaret Thatcher, is in no way irrelevant for the other countries, where similar elements can be discovered. Thatcher's coup of liberation shows the significance of the rigorous use of the majority power, which is necessary to dissolve such fossilized structures, but, at the same time, points out the price of a lost consensus.

Compared to the historical presentation of a country's variedness, the ideal types offer a sharper and deeper understanding of specific, generalizable features and causal effects of politics. Through these ideal types we may explain why specific political problems and dilemmas are so distinct in one country, while others are less marked. We may, however, also transfer the ideal type worked out for one country by way of a case study to other countries insofar as it shows what problems and dilemmas can be found in comparatively less striking aspects of politics but may develop more strongly in the course of time. This ideal-typical strategy is the decisive difference between sociological comparison and historical research. Both strategies are, however, legitimate and complement each other.

We do not want to disregard the counterpart complementing the elaboration of ideal types. Instead, the thick description, according to Clifford Geertz (1973), and the formation of ideal types in Max Weber's sense (1973: 190–212) should be kept in a tight relationship that is productive for both parts. The empirical case studies are designed to supply a thick description of the policy process of clean air and, at the same time, relate it to the corresponding ideal type. The result will be an empirically significant description of our individual subjects of research while at the same time pointing out specific ideal-type connections of general significance.

In this sense, we are following a praxeological approach (Bourdieu 1972) in working out the logics of the specific political practice. Under the form of a historically concrete practice it is our task to unveil the in-depth logics behind the decisions, which produces contexts of effectiveness pointing beyond the individual case. From these practices, which repeat themselves in various individual cases, the particular practice dominating a society is worked out. Its logic, in turn, includes features and causal effects appearing always and everywhere under the same conditions. In our strategy, the question as to the capability of generalization of empirical descriptions does not arise in its usual form. We do not start from the particular world of ideas of particular actors and groups to conclude a cross-actor and intergroupal national culture that would not live up to the differentiation into completely different cultures. Instead, our description of the policy process of clean air mirrors a practice representing a social fact for both actors and groups beyond their individual perceptions and normative ideas. In addition to this, we not only describe cultural ideas. The description of political practice unites action, structures, and cultures. Networks, institutional rules, professional communities, and political cultures form the frame of reference for political practice to develop. Networks determine the structure of chances excluding particular actions and making others possible; on the one hand, they act as a constraint and, on the other, as an empowerment (Giddens 1984: 5–28, 297–304). Institutional rules determine the forms of conflict settlement and agreement. Professional communities define the situation, the inherent problems, and the possible solutions to these problems. Political cultures supply the legitimate ideas for the currently used political practice.

Networks, institutional rules, professional communities, and political cultures create the frame of reference to practice, on the one hand, but, on the other, are continually reproduced and transformed within this practice. Seen from a methodological point of view, our interviews of deciding political actors are designed, above all, to take up the close connection of these basic aspects of political practice alongside the entanglement of culture, structure, and action within political practice. Since political practice represents the common *field* where actors of completely different origin, ideas, and preferences have to work together, we believe that we are able to make a binding statement for the political field of clean air regarding the politics and democracy model applied in this field.

The usual question as to whether national cultures exist at all in view of the cultural heterogeneity is superfluous in this approach. Political practice reduces even the widest cultural heterogeneity to what happens in fact. This includes, for instance, that the political practice in one country may differ from that in the others by a greater heterogeneity, a greater antagonism, or pluralism of the incoming cultural ideas, which, in turn, marks its character with the corresponding features and causal effects.

It would be naive to suppose, however, that the current political practice can be fully understood from the momentary situation. Each practice has a history. This applies, in particular, to legitimate ideas that are at the basis of this practice and that are referred to when the actors reflect about the meaning and purpose of their actions, when they dispute and agree. The history of ideas is a reservoir used in this case, depending on how deeply the reflection, the dispute, and/or the agreement should go. Each country has its own tradition of more or less sustained contributions to this history of ideas. In addition to this, there are connections and discussion flows *between* the different traditions that, in turn, have an impact on their continuation. Because of the particular condensation of discussions and political practice in the different countries reaching far beyond the discussion contexts *between* them, it may be assumed that even in view of their crossing context of discussion, traditions do not change so much that they will lose their character completely, thus becoming unidentifiable (Vogel 1986, 1996; Weale, Pridham, Williams, and Porter 1996). This applies especially insofar as political practice offers particularly good chances for survival to its corresponding contributions to the history of ideas and, at the same time, is legitimated by these contributions. We might say that both sides have entered a symbiotic relationship and stabilize each other. We therefore anticipate that we will be able to deepen our understanding of empirically established practice by looking closely at it from the point of view of historic contributions pointing the way to the particular country's political philosophy. In doing so, we reach that deep structure of practice that makes it possible for us to raise and answer more basic questions regarding the capability to process conflicts and form consensus for social integration and to form the future in a comparison of the countries under review. This includes the reflection on the change of the political practice resulting, on the one hand, from the changes of the societal sideline conditions of politics and, on the other, from a country's political learning when looking at other political cultures. Such insights are supplied neither by the pure construction of ideal types nor by getting lost in empirical descriptions, but only by their constructive connection in ideal-typically led empirical descriptions and empirically saturated interpretations aiming at basic questions.

If we look beyond the political field of clean air researched in this book, it is certainly not exaggerated to assume that the practices used in other political fields cannot be completely different since they take place, at least to a large extent, under structural and cultural conditions that they share with clean air policy. Of course, each political field has its own particular special conditions involving deviations between the different fields. Yet the common cultural and structural conditions keep these deviations within close confines so that the practices used in the different fields of politics in one and the same country are much closer to each other than to the political fields of other countries. Certainly, there is some adjustment pressure beyond the national borders due to the subject matter and to cross-country consultations. In the framework of the European Union (EU) this adjustment even goes further and deeper due to the increasing common European regulations in a political field. This is established, above all, in the field of clean air policy. Our country studies show, however, that the common European regulation subjects the established political practice in the different countries to a learning process yet does not make its typical character disappear completely (Majone 1996a; Héritier, Knill, and Mingers 1996). Adjustments frequently seize the surface of regulation *instruments* only, but not the regulation *philosophy* behind them, while the regulation *practice* is taken up only insofar as it has to be renewed under changed conditions. Of course, this renewal of the regulation practice is not made by its being replaced by an identical cross-European practice, but rather by a reproduction of the country's specific practice under changed conditions. The very fact that the transfer of the EU legislation is fully in the hands of the member countries' administration necessarily implies the inclusion of EU legislation into the countries' specific practice. This means in no way, however, that nothing will change in this practice but rather that the problems and dilemmas of the countries' specific political practice will remain effective in the framework of the European Union and require a careful research.

The transfer of the political events to Brussels and the practice developing there are a completely different story. This development supports the trend toward the policy model of a negotiation democracy, thus approaching the American model. As a result, the American competition democracy offers starting points to understand the evolving pluralistic negotiation democracy on the European level. The opening of European politics to the pluralism of interests is made under the sign of unequal approaches to the centers of decision. It is true that the short cycles of everyday practice boast a clear opening to most different interests. Yet the long cycles of basic decisions are determined by the cartel-type cooperation between the European Commission and the representatives of the governments and of the long-established, powerful organizations (Lahusen and Jauß 2000). In complementary studies to our project we have carried out research into how far this development proceeds, what forms it will take, and what problems and dilemmas it will produce (cf. Münch 1993b: 133–181; 1998: 325–344).

NOTES

1. A research of clean air politics consequently ignores the other environmental media such as soil and water, although these are closely intertwined with the problem of clean air. In fact, the principle of "integrated pollution control" has been formulated as a future-oriented model and has been introduced into national environmental policy, at least verbally. In this research, however, this principle can be taken into account only insofar as it has substantially changed national environmental policies in general and the regulation of air pollution in particular. Nevertheless, this is the case only to a very limited degree. In the U.K., where this principle was taken up programmatically, it is interesting to point out that the practice of clean air has traditionally already taken into account local circumstances and the causal relationships. Consequently, its logic tended more strongly toward the concept of an integrated survey. This means that the concentration on clean air will by no means prevent us from clearing the view to underlying national styles of regulation consistently.

2. We would basically say that the success of individual measures (as well as the direct and indirect influence of politics in general) can hardly be assessed and considered independently of other parameters (such as climate, geography, economy, demography, etc.). Therefore, studies of this type mostly work with evidences and arguments of plausibility. One might also use, as in our case, the development of air pollution and its effects merely as a background information and a point of reference for one's own theoretical arguments, its explanations, and assessments.

3. The examination of "new" regulation instruments will help illustrate this point. In fact, the strong attention that social sciences have paid to these innovations is not matched by the practical relevance of the measures under consideration. This applies not only to mediation processes and other tools of alternative dispute resolution (Zilleßen and Barbian 1992; Daele 1991) but especially also to market instruments (e.g., bubbles, allowance systems, etc.), which have hardly ever inched to the fore in Germany so far. Our research project also covers these questions, since it tries to work out the structural features and framework conditions of control repertoires as a whole.

Chapter 2

Political Regulation in Sociological Perspective: A Multidimensional Framework of Analysis

Christian Lahusen

INTRODUCTION

According to Max Weber, "Very frequently the 'world images' that have been created by 'ideas' have, like switchmen, determined the tracks along which action has been pushed by the dynamic of interest" (Weber 1958: 280). One could thus certainly explain the speed and direction of political attempts at problem solving in the area of environmental pollution by a reference to the interests of those affected and by the negotiation and decision making processes triggered by these interests. Action guided by interest refers to, and builds on, however, cultural and cognitive foundations that encompass the value of the natural goods to be protected, knowledge about the actual problems and situational conditions, and the normative validity and legitimacy of politics. Let us assume that one can call this system of values and judgments, meanings and interpretations "culture." That means, then, that one needs to study the cultural basis of political action to better understand the structure and dynamics of the politics of modern societies. This assumption is theoretically discussed in this chapter following a cultural perspective. For this purpose, the current debates within political science and sociology are critically discussed. It is argued that the political processes of various countries are structured according to specific organizational forms and strategies that can be seen as an aggregate of these cultural and cognitive foundations. Only in this way can the comparison of regulatory and political styles be accomplished advantageously.

NETWORKS OF SOCIETAL INTERESTS

Policy research, especially in the Anglo-Saxon world, has a special preference for interorganizational networks. Historically, this theoretical perspective is doubtlessly to be appreciated as progress since it generally led to a change especially in the conception of government and in general in the conception of the structures and dynamics of governance that explicitly allow the relationship between politics, the state, and society to be defined anew. Although these newer research debates clearly carried interdisciplinary characteristics, they developed in political science and sociology with their respective assumptions and approaches.

In political science, these discussions were primarily represented by a research approach that was oriented toward rational-choice theories (e.g., Hanf and Scharpf 1978). According to these scholars, politics cannot be adequately described by "top-down" approaches, since such approaches examine primarily socioeconomic, legal, and political macrostructures and reduce the analysis of politics to formally specified responsibilities and mandates and institutional procedures and platforms and thus come to a formalistic conception of politics. In contrast, the "bottom-up" approach concentrates on a microsociologically inspired analysis of interorganizational patterns of relationships, which today still makes up a considerable portion of the relevant research on politics. This approach has to be approved for directing the empirical eye to the diversity of participating actors, their mutual relationships, and coordination problems. The strategy of analysis used by this approach refers first to the conception of government, since the state is also seen as a complex, interorganizational network of relationships—even in the case of states organized in a hierarchic and centralist way. This applies, then, especially to the policy making process, which always includes a wide sphere of governmental and nongovernmental actors. Governance depends, therefore, on the solution of underlying problems of coordination, motivation, and the supervision of interorganizational action. Successful governance was essentially explained by exchange relationships that arise from interorganizational dependencies and/or interest coalitions. As a result microeconomic explanation was favored, and macrostructural contextual factors were neglected.

This interest in microsocial exchange relationships was increasingly integrated in the following years into an approach that emphasized the importance of the context of collective action (Toonen 1985). Sabatier and Hanf (1985: 307) made an argument for "a causal model that includes both the aspects of strategic interaction among multiple actors with their individual goals, interests and strategies, and the broader situational factors (socio-economic, political and legal) which set the context and define the parameters for individual actions and interactions." The subsequent game-theoretical reformation limited the reductionist "bottom-up" perspective and introduced the situational context of the analyzed interorganizational exchange relationships. According to that approach, interorganizational systems of negotiation (Scharpf 1993b) are always based on exchange processes, but within political, economic, and cultural constraints. The latter are elements of the structure of the political system, the national economy, and the value system of society, which predetermine different "games." Scholars who apply this approach then analyze implicitly and/or explicitly external structural conditions in order to derive analytically different game situations, define the possible and probable game strategies of the individual actors, and determine the consequences that arise from such strategies.

The exchange and game theory perspectives are to be appreciated for having put hierarchy into question as the sole structural principle of governance and for pointing to markets or interorganizational networks as possible alternatives (Scharpf 1993a; Thompson, Frances, Levacic, and Mitchell 1991). Although each of the alternatives has its own advantages and limitations, exchange and game theory facilitated putting into question the ability of the state and the political system to effectively regulate public problems and grievances by addressing internal obstacles and external conditions. This criticism of traditional ideas of governance and state regulation was amplified by a primarily sociological debate about the ability to politically govern and regulate modern societies. The background of this sociological debate was modernization theory's occupation with the (functional) differentiation of modern societies. Particularly, the functional systems theory of Niklas Luhmann put the skepticism about the ability to regulate autopoietic systems on the agenda. Politics becomes a Pandora's box because policies (e.g., of environmental protection and employment, culture and the development of technology) are always directed at societal subsystems (law, science, economy, education, religion, etc.), which function according to their own codes and programs. Even if the antagonism between the government and the opposition (as the binary code of the political system according to which politics operates) allows for, and brings about, political decisions, it is still completely open as to if and how policies have an effect and resonate within science and economy (to name only two examples), since the latter operate solely according to that which can be scientifically proven or that which is cost-effective and profitable. Therefore, policy outcomes always turn out more or less as actually intended, but always in a different form than politically intended.

The functionalist systems theory no longer considers the state to be the head of society; rather, it is a "specialist among specialists, an equal among equals" (Willke 1992b: 63), because society is a heterogeneous body with many centers. Political regulation can, therefore, operate (if at all possible) only as a "decentralized regulation of contexts" (Teubner and Willke 1984), since it can deliberately change only constraints and contextual structures within which the involved partial systems operate and evolve according to their own functions and logic.

The position of Luhmann is to be acknowledged for discussing the problem of the *societal* conditions necessary for the success of political regulation. As a result of this discussion, criticism about the (in-)abilities of politics (e.g., lack of political will, opportunism of politicians, coordination problems among state agencies and interest groups) wins a broader view for the systematic problems of the regulation of functionally differentiated societies. This occurs, for the most part, with an implicit warning not to endanger the evolutionary gains of functionally differentiated societies and their autonomous subsystems by an excessive regulatory impetus. Within policy research these proposals are readily accepted, often because they support already existing research agendas. Thus, policy research increasingly turned to the variety of possible instruments beyond the legal command and control approaches (Jänicke and Weidner 1995; O'Riordan and Cameron 1994). At the same time, the concept of "private interest governments" (Streeck and Schmitter 1985) was utilized for discussing societal differentiation processes (Mayntz 1993), since neocorporatist assumptions could be applied to the autonomous self-regulation of societal subsystems by interest groups.

Critics of Luhmann's systems theory, however, have also argued that the autopoietic radicalization of differentiation theories improperly limits research areas and questions (among others, Münch 1992; Scharpf 1989). As a reaction, scholars dedicate themselves more decisively to policy successes (Jänicke and Weidner 1995) in order to identify factual conditions for a successful politically intended and conceived regulation. At the same time, though, other underlying problems of political regulation are coming closer into view, such as the topics of power, culture, and legitimacy (Offe 1985; Eder 1990), the power of experts and the dependence of policy making on scientific evidence (Kwa 1987; Jasanoff 1987), and the self-blockades of collective bargaining due to generalized rational calculations (Scharpf, 1993a), among others. Finally, the problems of political regulation that arise directly from systemic interdependencies need to be considered as well. Scientific debates, for example, influence and affect policy making, inasmuch as political debates influence and affect policy-relevant science, thus endangering institutional boundaries and the functional division of labor between the subsystems: the political need and use of scientific evidence might endanger the credibility of consensus formation within science, and the latter might expose policy making increasingly to scientific reasoning and debates on conclusive scientific evidences, which could thus hamper political decision making and implementation. In this case the failure of the state to respond to its mandate is not explained by the autopoietic blindness of the subsystems and their inability to coordinate their functioning, but rather by the interdependencies of the systems (Münch 1994, 1995).

As a recent development in the social sciences, network analysis made important proposals for the further development of theoretical assumptions and the explanation of characteristic structures of politics (Moore and Whitt, 1992). Network analysis promised to integrate the different theories within political science and sociology in a meaningful way and to profitably combine the research questions and strategies of both disciplines. The term "network" means here the "combination of the most varied executive, legislative and societal institutions and groups involved in the creation and enforcement of a particular policy" (Windhoff-Héritier 1987: 45; Cook and Whitmeyer 1992). The definition of this term is, first of all, a description or diagnosis of political conditions and corresponds to the previously mentioned observation that governance is not to be conceived of solely as a hierarchy (Scharpf 1993b). On the contrary, new forms of organization are developing that include "relatively stable patterns of interaction between actors, groups and/or organizations" (Benz 1993: 169) and in which the relatively autonomous actors can no longer be moved by directives, but only by the incentive to coordinate (Scharpf 1993c: 9). Network analysis, therefore, turns to interorganizational patterns of relationships, whereby it appropriately conceives of the structure of politics and allows the policy process with its dynamics that arises from the relations and interactions of the actors involved to be clearly understood. The internal structure of politics first comes to light when the processes of policy making and the previously mentioned interorganizational networks are studied, not the structures of the political system. Policy processes include a series of tasks and responsibilities (Windhoff-Héritier 1987) that integrate different societal institutions and professions in the sense of the sociological theory of societal differentiation. It can be argued, then, that policy processes integrate a (scientific) definition of the problem, agenda setting processes of the mass media, (political) program planning, (technical) standard setting, (legal) codification and validation, and (administrative) program specification and implementation, among others. Even the case of a "purely political" decision making process thus creates a vast array of demands for organizational work in the realm of science, technology, law, public communication, and so on. As a result of this, the work areas of the diverse actors (particularly of the state administration) open up for the respective symbolic claims and institutional orientations toward (technical-scientific) truth and (political) majority, (moral) imperatives, (economic) cost-effectiveness, and (administrative) efficiency and practicality, among others.

Scholars conventionally use the term "network" to describe the actors (populations) and their relations (structures) involved in the policy processes. If this term is to keep explanatory worth, though, the quality of social links and interactions must be theoretically specified. If we draw on the many different network theories for this purpose (Cook and Whitmeyer 1992), a basic consensus is shown, which has not advanced the theoretical debate considerably. Interorganizational relationships are defined, for the most part, as exchange relationships. Here, then, money, knowledge, reputation, and power are exchanged as scarce and unequally distributed resources. Consequently, the increase in value of economic undertakings, power struggles, the search for truth, the attainment of reputation, collective learning processes, and discursive argumentation, community building, and legitimization is reduced to exchange processes.

As already described, this exchange theory perspective has been broadened by game theory within policy research. This is apparent when Scharpf (1992b) analyzes game orientations, when Ostrom (1989) deals with institutional and constitutional choices, when Benz (1993) looks at cognitive or normative aspects of collective actions, and when Héritier, Knill, and Mingers (1996) speak about cultures and mentalities. These factors were, however, introduced only ad hoc as external constraints of rational choices and interactions. A cultural sociology is, however, interested in these factors as a prerequisite of policy making itself. "Game" situations, interests, goals, and means are first defined on the basis of institutional structures and rules, knowledge and truth, norms and values, communities and identities. These aspects not only function as a stabilizing, order-giving context for negotiation systems (Benz 1993; Scharpf 1993a) but can also generate their own problems, such as symbolic struggles about the dominant definition of the situation and conflicts over accepted and valid truths, values or identities—problems that are symptomatic of the environmental policies from the 1970s to the 1990s.

INSTITUTIONS AND NORMATIVE RULES

In the last few years an interest in political institutions has arisen that opens up the one-sided microsociological orientation and brings to discussion the importance of the societal context of interorganizational interactions. The institutional structure of state administrations, their responsibilities, and routines, the spectrum of political parties, and the opportunities for democratic participation are identified as elements of the political system that have effects on policies, because they define not only the existing points of access to the decision making process and the existing power structures but also the procedures and means (not least of all, the content and goals) by which policy making has to take place.[1] Determining factors, then, are identified independently from the actors involved, which helps to explain how policies are made: the openness of the political system (e.g., electoral system, weight and role of the elite), the form of government (e.g., federalism vs. centralism), forms and responsibilities of legal proceedings, and so on (Mény 1993; Lester 1995a). As the previous discussion has made clear, this formal characterization of the structure of the political arena has necessarily to be seen from the point of view of the actors. An "open" system does not say anything about if and how actors also use the system to discuss specific problems and to meet demands. The particular differences between U.S.-American and European politics, for example, are not based primarily on the formal structure of the state since a system of checks and balances is guaranteed in principle, even if in modified form, in all countries. Thus, it can be said that the institutional arrangements arise out of political practice—that means out of the structures and dynamics of the specific interorganizational interactions, which, however, are themselves influenced by institutional structures.

The concept of strategic action is of interest here since it attempts to capture the interrelation between action and contextual structures. Strategies are action sequences that strive to deal with external constraints—whether the latter are external factors attributed to the actions of other "players" or to macrosocial structures. If we use the game metaphor, the actions of other actors and the structure of the political system are points of reference for the generation of one's own tactics and strategies. They are consequently—and necessarily—used for one's own purposes. This use of external constraints treats political systems as "political opportunity structures" that offer an amount of opportunities and constraints for autonomous, organized actions (Moore and Whitt 1992).

This approach has a very practical appeal in research since it can be tied to the rhetoric of the actors themselves. The "institutional" perspective, though, has to be pushed ahead another step in order to be able to determine the underlying structures and dynamics of the regulatory style specific to a country. For this, the postulated relationship between structure (state administration, networks) and actions (strategies) has to be more precisely responded to. For exchange and game theories, it is a matter of two complementary, but discrete and separate, figures. Structures are external to actions; that is, government and networks form an external opportunity structure that actors strategically use. Here, it is argued that the relationship between structure and action is rather to be conceived of as an interdependence. According to this view, the actors' relationships and strategies, which have a structuring influence on the political system, are prestructured themselves by institutional contexts in regard to their goals, orientations, and rationales. A detailed analysis of policy processes reveals that the strategies of political action are based on axioms and rules (e.g., in regard to the definition of the problem, the given arena, valid goals, legitimate means), which can be defined as institutional rules or principles.

The discussion about institutions (Göhler 1994; March and Olsen 1989) is extremely helpful in the discussion of this problem. In their reception of the sociological term "institution," the scholars who engage in this debate do not just emphasize that political institutions *organize and order* politics by providing a framework of rules and procedures for the production and enforcement of generally binding decisions. Instead, the institutions *symbolically orient* the policy processes by the institutions' proper cognitive and cultural system of values and judgments, meanings and interpretations, political models and ideas (Göhler 1994). Democratic competition as a principle of pluralism implies, for example, that politics functions according to rules of fairness (nominal equality of all actors) and with an orientation toward the public (transparency, accessibility, etc.); policies arrived at by agreement between state and associations are a characteristic reference point of neocorporatism and institutionalized rules of (informal) cooperation and collaboration with a particular regard for the appropriateness and feasibility of means. These rules, then, are able to be evaluated according to their efficiency and effectiveness and are able to be legitimated with regard to political values and ideas. In this respect, institutional rules are explicit points of reference or implicit foundations of political action. In both cases, though, they are a structuring factor of politics.

In this context, five central institutional rules can be identified that appear in all of the countries as a structuring factor of political action. *Hierarchy* is one such rule. It does not simply mean the power relationship between the state and society established by the constitutionally guaranteed monopoly of power. Much more, hierarchy as an institutional rule also refers to the decision making and directive structure within the state and the political system. The picture of interorganizational relationships previously depicted makes clear, however, that hierarchic principles of decision making and implementation are supplemented by rules of *cooperation*. From the governmental actors' viewpoint, cooperation allows for the tapping of resources of the other societal actors and brings them together in the decision making process at the level of program planning and implementation as well. The involved interest groups, first and foremost the industrial enterprises and associations, are interested in conjoint solutions in policy planning and implementation since this offers them the chance of greater influence and control. On this strategic level, cooperative network structures are established where, due to hierarchic rules, they are not welcome or even explicitly excluded.

If we speak about cooperation as the best strategic option, then we also have to add that cooperation is explicitly named as an institutional rule. Cooperation is

introduced in order to temper strictly legal control and command policies and can
also be observed beyond formal procedures of public hearings and collective
bargaining. The hierarchic relationship between the state and the polluters, where
regulation is a matter of commands and controls, turns then into a partnerlike
relationship where both sides contribute to the managing of commonly recognized and defined problems—each in accordance with one's possibilities, compe-
tencies, and interests. This institutional rule is especially important when precautionary action is to be taken. According to the principle of prevention,
environmental damage should be avoided before it is caused—even in the case of
uncertainty about causes and consequences, adequate means and costs. Precautionary action would increase regulatory initiatives (measurement and monitoring
procedures, technical norms, and quality standards), if action is not transferred to
the polluters (whether a company or a consumer) and their potential self-
surveillance and self-regulation. The more that cooperation is fallen back on, the
more distinctly the state can concentrate on leading, supervising, or simply coordinating tasks (Cooper 1995). The same is also true, then, for the principle of
cost-effectiveness and practicality, according to which political decisions are to
reflect the specific, situational conditions. The search for cost-effective and practicable means often becomes a product of cooperation in that the definition of
best options requires constant negotiations between the state and the societal
interests.

If cooperation is a characteristic rule of regulation, then it remains tied to hierarchies. Cooperation adapts itself to the hierarchic structure of intra- and interorganizational relationships. On the level of the practice of permit granting, there
are, for example, contacts between the specialists of the state offices and those of
the enterprises, mostly technicians and engineers. The management of the enterprise takes action, then, when needed in order to negotiate with administrative
chiefs and decision makers. In the context of program planning, interests are
represented by the leadership of industry in the ministry of the environment, but
also if possible via the ministry of industry, the cabinet, or the head of government. This means that cooperation and the interest intermediation of associations
have to be differentiated accordingly. Technical agreements, which are then introduced on the basis of expert information or decision making criteria, take
place on a subordinate level. Politics in the classic sense of the determination,
implementation, and surveillance of collectively binding decisions, goals, and
priorities becomes established, then, on a higher authority level. The hierarchic
organization of interest intermediation is, therefore, a logical strategic option.
These hierarchic structures create political inequalities since they give advantages
to nationally operating associations. The grouping together of industrial interests,
for example, allows for more consistent positions to be formulated, for the exertion of influence to be concentrated, and, finally, for the exploitation of the
power potential that depends on the economic significance of the represented
branches, the reputation of the large associations, and the established contacts at
the top levels. The hierarchically arranged practices of cooperation are not developed, then, due only to strategic considerations but also because hierarchic struc-

tures represent a quality of national politics per se. Certainly, federal and unitary-centralist states are different with regard to the form in which national politics and policies are set up and generated (Hanf and Toonen 1985; Lester 1995b). Nevertheless, the national arena maintains a relatively autonomous, distinctive position since politics here has to be carried on according to the general welfare, or the *volonté generale*. Societal interests have to demonstrate national relevance in order to influence politics because national politics refers to society and its common good as a whole. Politics cannot simply be the result of the aggregation and addition of local politics.

In addition, *effectiveness* and *efficiency* are mentioned repeatedly as rules and assessment criteria of clean air policies. Effectiveness and efficiency have an impact, then, on a whole series of politically relevant aspects. For instance, they refer to the questions of whether a public problem is solved effectively and whether a policy contributed to the solution in an efficient and cost-effective way. The rules of effectiveness and efficiency are then often in a tense relationship with the questions of the *legitimacy* of politics. Courts, for example, are indispensable for the (positive and negative) sanctioning of binding decisions, and their practice also legitimates the policy process (Majone 1996b; McSpadden 1995). Nevertheless, litigation can block policy making and implementation due to purely formal criteria and thereby accelerate the legal professionalization of the actors—even if this distracts them from the content of litigation and of effective and efficient problem solving (O'Leary 1993). This is also true for the permit-granting procedures, which require transparency and public participation. Hearings and the disclosure of data and documents consume time and resources, and institutions have to argue with the positions taken by the experts and representatives of interests even if the positions do not appear to be expertly or politically founded. The same is true for media coverage, which is an indispensable arena of modern democracies in that it guarantees the public transparency of policy making but which appears troublesome as soon as the coverage distorts or simplifies problems. Finally, politicians are the final decision makers. They need to weigh the pros and cons between agendas and interests and carry on politics with regard to the public welfare and the adequate solution to the specific issue. From the viewpoint of administrative effectiveness, though, there is the repeated complaint that politicians would always rely too much on momentary opinions and public issues and too strongly on short-term successes, whereby difficult problems and technically necessary steps would frequently not occur, and other (nonsensical or false) measures would be taken (Majone 1996b).

It now becomes clear that administrative effectiveness and efficiency refer to sound evidence or *expertise* as an underlying criterion of evaluation and rule of political action. Within politics, experts play an important role (Jasanoff 1990, 1995; Renn 1995). They are commonly given two functions. On the one hand, they should advise those in politics in regard to research and the definition of the problem. On the other hand, they should develop concrete measures and procedures for the implementation of political guidelines and for the solution of environmental problems. Especially in the area of monitoring, standard setting, and technological advancement, a scientific and technical infrastructure is established that supports and advises the political arena.

On both levels of the inclusion of scientific-technical expertise, a fundamental ambivalence is institutionally established. On the one hand, all actors pay explicit attention to a clear differentiation between scientific-technical advice (as *an* input into politics) and the final political decision making process and its outputs. Indeed, all actors insist that it is the responsibility of the politicians to reach generally binding decisions. Scientists and technicians can achieve their validity and legitimacy as advisers and experts only by a functional separation (Jasanoff 1987), whereby their actions help exclusively to ascertain the truth and not, for example, politically or economically opportunistic considerations. The same is true for politicians, then, who cannot barricade themselves behind the "final evidence" of scientific research since they have to take various interests and values into consideration in order to fulfill their formally established task. Even technical norms and standards are, therefore, always political products as soon as they no longer correspond only to the actual "state of technology" but have gone through a political negotiation and decision making process and have taken on the form of political decisions. However, the more that policy making depends on scientific counseling and policy-relevant "trans-science" (Majone 1984), the more that the differentiation between expertise and politics and the many disjointed procedures that coordinate science and politics and safeguard the integrity and autonomy of both spheres are obliterated (Jasanoff 1987). In this regard regulatory agencies and science advisers exert increasing influence on political regulation, thus establishing as a "fourth" and "fifth branch of government" (Majone 1996b; Jasanoff 1990). Nevertheless, the *institutional* differentiation is maintained as a (myth or) means to legitimate policy making, the aim being to generate and reproduce autonomous political institutions and procedures of decision making. This fixation on political decisions, however, reveals a formal understanding of politics since the policy process comprises a "pre-" political sphere of technocratic expertise and a "post-" political sphere of administrative implementation in which the political decision deteriorates into a "proclamatory" episode. Politics are infused by expert and administrative discourses, whereby correct and good policies no longer result from a successful specification of common and collectively binding goals alone but are the result of an efficient and effective regulation of technical problems and thus of the adaptation of politics to the objective constraints of technical and administrative structures.

PROFESSIONS AND THE DIVISION OF REGULATORY LABOR

In the previous section it was argued that expertise is a structuring rule of the policy process in all countries. From the perspective of the sociology of knowledge it can be argued that politics needs a definition of the problem, goals, and means that allows the causes of the emerging problems to be identified and the long- and short-term goals to be set as well as instruments and measures for problem solving to be determined. Politics in modern, liberal democracies becomes a question of "governability" in the sense of Foucault (1988), which requires the basic allegiance of the citizens and the political manageability of the issues to be regulated. In this regard, policy making is dependent on knowledge and corresponding techniques and skills in order to tackle three problems: define the underlying problems according to their causes and consequences; construct political issues as a means to tackle and manage them accordingly; and thus identify the relevant tasks and accomplish the factual work. The particular significance of professions can be attributed to this interest in the "governability" of public problems (Johnson 1993). Here, professions claim to have the relevant knowledge and skills, proper qualifications and professional ethos, which they try to institutionalize as a politically disinterested, objective expertise (Larson 1990). Their influence is more systematic the more that the professions introduce themselves into the different organizations involved in the policy making process and define common positions and strategies for environmental protection. In this respect, the professions contribute to the formation of policy networks and to the coordination and integration of regulatory tasks in the various societal areas (economy, politics, science, etc.).

Their influence in politics can be implicit, whereby a professional approach and its particular problem definitions and problem-solving strategies are shared by their members and maintained organizationally through the internal network of university departments, technical publications, conferences, and professional training, among others. Or the professions explicitly intervene, when, for instance, professional associations participate in political decision making procedures to offer their expertise and advice and/or to carry on political lobbying. This influence does not just depend on the organizational "infrastructure" of the professions, which supports and guides the interorganizational relationships and interactions across the different societal areas and subsystems. More than that, professional work is explicitly institutionalized within clean air policies. On the one hand, this inclusion increases the power of professionals and experts, not because it opens up new opportunities for professions to introduce the interests of their associations but more fundamentally because it introduces specific epistemic definitions of the problem and related problem-solving strategies. On the other hand, political regulation benefits from the reputation of the professional communities, which can socially support and legitimate policies (Larson 1984; Majone 1996b). Right here is where internal solidarity functions as a structuring principle of collective action, especially if the authority and legitimacy of the profession is questioned (Jasanoff 1990). Environmental associations play an interesting role in this context, because as a part of the ecology movement they often criticize the epistemic basis of politics and its underlying conception of nature and environmental protection. It is noteworthy that the environmental associations did not maintain a fundamentally oppositional stance and, therefore, develop objectives and methods of work suited to the political arena (Yearley 1992). They even tend to professionalize by recruiting professionals or acquiring professionally recognized expertise, even if their particular issues and claims are opposed to those of the establishment (Christmann 1992; Lahusen 1996).[2]

Within environmental regulation, natural scientists and technicians as well as lawyers play a crucial role. Economists, too, stand out as gaining in influence. Therefore, it is possible to speak about a division of labor between the professions that takes on the technical, legal, societal, and economic dimensions of the problem –a division of labor that certainly has no definite internal boundaries but that is the object of several disputes about the relevance, validity, and effectiveness of the various professional definitions of the problem, their skills, and strategies. In this sense, Andrew Abbott (1988) argues that no individual profession but rather the system of professions and the professional division of labor altogether need be studied. Professions bring "jurisdictional claims not only to classify and reason about a problem but also to take effective action towards it" (Abbott 1988: 38). This division of professional labor results, then, from the different specialty areas and "jurisdictional claims" of the individual professions. However, it is also the object of the explicit regulation by the state, which intervenes by way of professional and educational policies, the recruitment practices of the state's administration, the financial support it gives to professional institutes and agencies, and commissioning professionals to provide evidences and statements. If professions have a structuring influence on political regulation, then the state participates in the indirect regulation of this professional influence (Rüschemeyer 1986; Collins 1990).

The explanatory value of professions becomes, therefore, evident only when the structure of the division of professional labour is taken into consideration (Boehmer-Christiansen and Weidner 1995: 120 – 124). Technicians, for example, play an important role in all of the countries and can substantiate this position on the level of formal responsibilities as well as on the level of regulatory practices. Although there are substantial differences between the countries analyzed, the importance of technology-based emission control policies reinforces the role of engineers, not only for the given policy instruments but also for the regulatory process altogether. This profession can defend its position and even expand on it as the profession tries to take on additional tasks and skills. Engineers strive to have a say in the definition of practicality and cost-effectiveness, in legal questions of the day-to-day regulatory work, in the management of resources, and in public relations as a part of their routine work. A similar statement can be formulated with regard to lawyers. Particularly in the early days of environmental policies this profession played a crucial role in the formulation and judicial control of general goals, procedures, and means of environmental regulation. However, they often increased their influence by specifying and prescribing legal requirements and procedures with regard to the determination of technological standards, practicable and cost-effective means, resource management, and others.

A transformation of environmental policies and regulatory styles is not likely to occur under these conditions. A change can be observed only in countries in which other professions can institutionally establish their position in the policy making process. This is the case in those countries where the monopoly of engineers and/or lawyers is broken up primarily by economists, in part also by social scientists. In this way, they alter traditional policies, introduce new instruments, or even transform the whole policy style. As we will see, these developments depend on collective learning processes that try to remove the flaws of traditional policies and/or try to go new ways. These learning processes are, however, not random but socially structured, especially due to (competing or antagonistic) professional discourses. Consequently, the political debates about the improvement of environmental regulation increasingly entangle themselves into the jurisdictional claims and disputes of (competing) professions.

Professions, consequently, have a two-pronged influence on the structure of political regulation. On the one hand, it can be pointed out that the professions have an integrating and coordinating effect on negotiation systems (Benz 1993) beyond systemic boundaries. In our research we also obtained repeated indications of the importance of informal contacts, long-term acquaintanceships, and cliques. A shared professional career and common professional orientations are especially important in the development and reproduction of professional communities with their structuring effect on the environmental policies of the respective countries. On the other hand, professional groups (as a means of social exclusion and identity formation [cf. Murphy 1988]) have their own discourses about professional skills and knowledge that are institutionalized within the area of environmental protection. This development increases the depoliticization of policy making and implementation because the distinctive characteristic of professional discourses is precisely their explicit apolitical nature: expertise asserts a privileged and purely rational access to "objective" truths (Larson 1990). The power of the professions is based, then, primarily on the disinterestedness of professional labor, on its *useful* knowledge, *proven* skills, or *recognized* expertise. Even in the case of explicit lobbying, professional associations rely on a strategy of disinterestedness, much in tune with the early scholarly debate about the societal function and role of the professions (Haskell 1984; Collins 1990). Expertise, then, can undermine politics in a technocratic way and degrade politically legitimated decision making processes into mere proclamatory procedures of symbolic politics (Edelman 1971).

CULTURE AND MEANING

The preceding section made clear the need to explain the previously identified factors. Whereas political science approaches in general and game theory studies in particular treat interests as "objective" and external factors, the sociology of culture considers interests themselves as objects in need of explanation. According to Pizzorno (1990, 1993), the identification of interests has an explanatory and enlightening function if political action and speech are not to be understood by themselves but are to be explained in relation to "something" behind them. What this approach overlooks, however, according to Pizzorno, is that interests themselves have to be analyzed with regard to cultural factors. Culture plays a special role here in which not only values are taken into account (a narrow definition of culture), but symbolic representations, interpretations, and definitions, too (a broad understanding of culture). This cultural perspective defines social action as a cultural phenomenon per se, since social action in general and politics as a specific form of collective action are always tied to particular interpretations and assessments, to social meaning (Weber 1958). For such purposes, it is necessary to analyze politics in an interpretive manner and to ask about the "culture of the political action," that is, about the underlying system of signs and symbols, interpretations and assessments.

This cultural perspective also does justice to the interdependence between the issue and the form of political action, precisely because it disputes that the environment is an "objective matter" that objectively predetermines possible policies and their structural problems—as if environmental problems (pollution, use of resources and its consequences) would automatically predetermine political interests, which would then predetermine the range of possible policies. The "environment" is not external to politics but is inherently in interaction with it. This is so, first of all, because environmental problems always have to be perceived and defined before they can be the grounds for collective action. This perception and definition of problems depend, then, on cultural values and interpretations, which not only have to do with the general value of this public good but also imply particular assumptions about the kind of action that should be taken, as will be shown later. It is argued that we cannot say anything about the subject of political regulation (the "environment") that is not, first of all, perceived through the glasses of our culture as a symbolic system of values and meanings. Thus, an intervening variable is placed between the issue and the remedial political action that predetermines the tempo and direction of policy making and implementation.

This conception of culture as intervening factor or system needs to be developed further, though. It is emphasized that the process by which environmental problems are perceived and defined cannot be separated from the organization of politics itself. Thus, it can be argued that the perception and definition of environmental problems are in a close relationship with the way in which politics is organized and the way in which the regulatory practices are structured. If one understands politics as a sphere of collective action, then one has to ask about the organizational forms (Douglas and Wildavski 1982) or the strategy of collective action (Swidler 1992) that shape the practice of politics as well as the perception and definition of the topic at hand. These organizational forms and strategies are carriers of cultural systems of meaning, which not only have to do with values that then assess the priority and the effectiveness of environmental policies but include underlying meanings and symbolic representations that clarify which environmental policies are conceivable, appropriate, and sensible. The way in which politics is organized, then, has an effect on the perception and definition of the environment, and vice versa. This argument needs to be clarified.

In all of the countries, clean air policies are part of *environmental* regulation, that is, the policies that are geared toward the human environment. In all of the languages, environment means not merely nature but also involves the habitat shaped by human hand (forms and density of settlements, the agricultural and other use of land, protected areas, etc.). The idea of a socialized nature, of a symbolically and mentally as well as materially and objectively constructed nature (a "Vergesellschaftung"; cf. Eder 1990) characterizes the modernization process of the Western industrial nations nicely. This particular relationship of modernity to its environment is based on a two-pronged, anthropocentric orientation that is also currently reflected in environmental policies. On the one hand, human needs have an unlimited priority in the identification of problems and goals. Environmental protection serves, above all, humanity. In this respect, human health has to be protected from harmful environmental effects, the natural basis for the survival of humankind has to be managed rationally, and human needs for relaxation and aesthetic refreshment have to be met accordingly. In this sense, effective environmental regulation is not concerned with the protection of nature per se, since nature is not an end in itself, but a mere means, and environmental protection is, therefore, an effective intervention in the environmental problems that are harmful or disturbing to people (e.g., volcanic eruptions, floods, epidemics). Modernity is thus interested in nature only as a socially constructed environment of society. On the other hand, humans are actively involved in the shaping and making of their environment. This is at the same time a cause and mandate for further action. Demonstrable, damaging effects always lead to a broader, often precisely formulated intervention, whereby the social construction of nature does not diminish but instead leads to a constantly revised intervention. Environmental regulation, therefore, reproduces itself as a twofold protection: the protection of humans from harm by the environment and the protection of the environment from *harmful* human interventions. Environmental regulation, then, is concerned with a *more rational* contriving of the natural habitat. National policies illustrate that societal intervention is not put in question but is "rationalized" instead; that is, the intervention into, and the use of, nature are to become more methodical and systematic, more appropriately and effectively structured. This claim to rationality determines, then, the political relevance of research and development, of expertise altogether, since rational use and planning require a systematic and methodical research on ecosystems, on the one hand, and on the ways in which interventions have a demonstrably causal effect on humans, on the other hand.

Although a similar process of rationalization can be seen in all of the countries, there are, nevertheless, differences among the political cultures (e.g., Short 1991; Nash 1992). In the United States, for example, nature is spoken of in legislation as a resource that needs to be managed more effectively. Environmental policies, therefore, have to enable and assure an effective and efficient resource management and thus maintain the natural habitat for use by future generations. In this sense, nature is a *collective good,* whereby it is always understood with regard to its utility and subjected to utilitarian regulation. Even the appraisal of wilderness and the ecological critique of this exploitative way of dealing with nature have not changed; rather they have rationalized the dominant discourse that appropriates wilderness as a scarce and valuable resource (e.g., reservation parks) and aims to adapt its policies to the interdependencies of various areas of regulation (water, air, soil), thus increasing the complexity and flexibility necessary for coherent resource management. In Germany, nature constitutes a distinct *objective matter* that can and must empirically and analytically be distinguished

from its societal alter ego, also in order to submit it more effectively to an "objectified" regulation. The political debate about the "death of the forest" reveals,
for instance, a less utilitarian stance and a more analytic stance that departs from
an idea of a proper objective matter. The sensitivity to the intrinsic value of this
"animate object" has grown due to the ecological discourse but has changed the
actual work on the matter very little because it continues to be handled in a primarily detached and technical way. In Great Britain the preservation of nature has
a historical significance that accompanies industrialization, and some of the oldest
nature reserves and conservationist associations in the world exist there. Conservation is entrusted to traditional associations, as a result of which the orientation
toward traditional conservation predominated for a long time. In a culture of
gardening, nature was not dissociated from society, and traditional conservation
had the idea of a safeguarded habitat yet *civilized habitat*. The discourse of the
new, political ecology has certainly taken up and politicized the idea of environmental protection, which is different from that of the nature reserves. However,
nature is still predominantly conceived of as a civilized environment; protection
is thus geared toward coordinating the preservation of nature and the societal
cultivation of nature as two complementary sides of a common process. In France
conservation and environmental protection are without a doubt less explosive
topics than in other countries, which is certainly due to less pollution and the size
of the country. However, the understanding of nature is much less oriented toward the idea of an untouched environment but instead is committed to the idea
of a *worked-on environment*, in regard both to a traditional, agrarian use and
modern technocratic planning. The environment is conceived of less as an untouched good, environmental protection is determined less as an independent
task, and environmental policies are defined less as an autonomous policy field.
This is so because environmental protection is, if at all a proper policy issue, part
of a transcending, rational project of modernity, particularly when considering
national policies. The greater sensitivity to the environment, which arose in
France following the national and international waves of mobilization of the
ecology movement, has improved the position of environmental issues within the
overarching modernization project of national politics, but only to underline the
technocratic rationalization and administration of environment protection.

    This claim to rationality is, as previously mentioned, not unchallenged since
in all countries ecology movements have developed to fundamentally criticize the
way humans have dealt with nature and the way environmental policies have
institutionalized this approach. Even if it is not easy to characterize *the* discourse
of the ecology movement, a few central positions that are of interest to us can,
nevertheless, be determined (Brulle 1996; Devall 1992: 51–61; Eder 1993). On
the one hand, a moderate discourse formulates the demand for a more effective
environmental protection. This position revolts against the overexploitation of the
earth, which not only destroys nature but also directly endangers humanity and
its future generations. However, the position is not fundamentally against the
appropriation and use of the environment. This ecological position was included
in the majority of the political agendas over time and now makes up a broad

portion of institutional environmental regulation. Environmental associations see themselves here in the role of representing environmental interests as opposed to other competing interests and groups. They advocate wider-ranging goals and monitor the implementation of binding measures. Another discourse within the ecological movement, which has lost weight since the institutionalization of the first position, puts the justification of a rational appropriation and use of the environment in question. The environment in this case stands for a value of its own, which is worth maintaining irrespective of the value of nature for human-kind. Due to the fact that this discourse is in blatant contrast to the dominant discourse, it is dismissed as an emotional-hedonistic reaction, and its systematic criticism is thereby disqualified. Although romantic ideas have undoubtedly ex-isted, this position touches on a particular argumentation, a rationalizing dis-course even, that tries to obtain an understanding of nature and complex ecosys-tems. This position even endeavors into the rationalization of modern societies when it demands the ecological reorganization of industrial society. Ecosystems are models for the reorganization of all societal facets of life, which answer the question not only about the maintenance of creation but also about the sustain-ability of modern society. Although this position is belittled by those forming the dominating political conception, the position, nevertheless, acts at times as the quarry of innovative ideas for the evaluation of the existing policies and the con-ception of new models.

This critique of the dominant concept of nature systematically focused the re-lationship between nature and society and, in doing so, also criticized the com-plex, interconnected system of actors and interests, institutional arrangements and structural principles, professional divisions of labor and routines, claims for validity and legitimization, that is, the inherent interaction between the "objec-tive" issues and the strategies of political action. In every country the reaction to this ecological debate was and is equally clearly pronounced. Rationality is at-tributed only to the moderate project, which means that one does not really get involved in the actual ecological discourse. Counterarguments are measured by their own criteria, interests and institutional arrangements, normative rules and professional routines of the established regulatory practices and as a result are dismissed as impractical, exaggerated, questionable, or simply ridiculous. That is equally true in every country with regard to the denigration of the "fundamental-ists" or "Jusqu'à boutistes", who do not make an appeal for real changes but for a simple rejection of the status quo. The fact that this strategy of disqualification is effective also points to the dominance of the prevailing conception of nature and the corresponding rationality of the project.

STYLES OF POLITICAL REGULATION

As was argued, the definition of the problem and its management are structur-ally intertwined with each other. That is true not only because a specific problem definition predetermines or gives rise to corresponding strategies for problem solving but also because environmental issues are often defined from the view-point and perspective of the regulatory institutions and practices. Thus, a technocratic regulation is complementary to a conception of nature in the sense that a wilderness area awaits a rationalization and administration by modernity, whereas a policy of pluralistic interest coordination supports the idea of wilderness as a collective good that should be managed rationally. A causal relationship between the individual elements of the political processes (problem definition, program planning, implementation, etc.) and the structural factors introduced (interests, institutions, professions, culture) can, therefore, be spoken of only with reservations. It is more meaningful to ask about the underlying strategies of collective action as a whole, as Ann Swidler (1992) did in another context. In the following, four of these strategies are introduced. They aim to discriminate between national regulatory styles by highlighting analytical differences and specific features: strategies of compromise (United Kingdom), a state-centered strategy (France), and strategies of consensus and synthesis (Germany) and of pluralist competition (United States). When arguing that these strategies describe political styles, this is not meant to say that one strategy prevails in a country at the cost of the others—for example, in the United States pluralist competition would prevail at the cost of consensus formation, state interventionism, and integrative compromise building. This characterization would overstate the political style too much. It is argued, rather, that these strategies identify structural principles of collective action that help to characterize the political style of a country in all of its dimensions and orientations (Richardson, Gustafsson, and Grant 1991; Vogel 1986). Using the same example, competitive structures would characterize not only the democratic articulation and coordination of interests but also professional guidance and the use of scientific evidences, governmental activism and interventionism, the settlement of problem-specific compromises, and the formation of a political consensus. These latent strategies or structural patterns of collective action emphasize the identity and continuity of the political style because the interorganizational networks, institutional rules, the systems of professions, and the political discourses are interrelated in a compatible and/or mutually reinforcing manner.

In Great Britain a *strategy of compromise*—and a complex process of consultation that underlies it—can be regarded as a structuring principle of the political process (see Chapter 3 in this book). These systems of consultation are functional, as in Great Britain no legally codified and formalized system of policy making and implementation exists (Boehmer-Christiansen and Weidner 1995: 115–124). As opposed to the United States, where a strongly formalized legal system of institutional responsibilities and guarantees of public participation exists, in Great Britain a complex system of consultations between governmental and nongovernmental organizations plays this integrative and structuring role. These systems of consultation are based on an interconnection of the state and society that propels what has been named "bureaucratic accommodation" of societal groups and interests (Richardson and Jordan 1983), but only to give testimony to a civil society with a long history of voluntary and public associations. That means that in British politics, the state can and must fall back on societal interests, as a result of which a clear separation of politics and society hardly seems to be possible. Compromise forms the point of reference of this consultation practice, and thus societal interests, institutions, professions, and discourses are introduced into these consultation-based compromises. This strategy not only promises to coordinate and harmonize conflicting interests but is also evaluated as the best option to effectively handle the underlying problems and issues. Generalized legal codifications, such as prescriptions, definite levels of admissible emissions, and prescribed technical standards, seem to be impractical and pointless, since they do not account for situational conditions and concrete constellations of interests in which problems appear and solutions are pending. The specificity of each case, the changing natural situations, and the particularism of interests involved can be fruitfully used and integrated only in a complex system of mutual consultations and compromise-building. Only such a strategy of political action can produce such a pronounced orientation toward the practicality of policies. This refers, on the one hand, to the appropriateness of the chosen regulatory options in regard to the problem at hand—whereby the appropriateness rarely refers to narrowly conceived problems but refers rather to overlapping problems and their situational specifications at the local level ever since the concept of "integrated pollution control" (Weale 1996). On the other hand, practicality is oriented to the feasibility of policies and includes, therefore, explicit considerations about (local) power relationships and the constellation of interests, as well as taking into account the practices and skills of the local authorities and industrialists involved. As opposed to the principle of cost-effectiveness or "Verhältnismäßigkeit," which considers the specificity of each situation and its circumstances when determining emission standards and technical norms, the politics of "practicable means" tries to respect the specific issues and situations in each case and to activate and use the knowledge and skills onsite. In the British case, policies are not oriented toward general characteristics but instead ask about specifics relevant to practice, which allows for the activation of specialized knowledge, practical experiences, and "sound science" (Boehmer-Christiansen and Weidner 1995: 120–125). The consultation system can, consequently, fall back on the most diverse actors who can introduce their own particular, but already put-into-practice, knowledge. In principle this strategy of problem definition and solving is open in the sense that even without legal guarantees, diverse societal interests, institutions, and professions might provide the necessary inputs for a practicable regulatory option. In principle, decision making procedures are not standardized, and, consequently, room is made for a variety of positions as well as evaluation and decision making criteria. Decisions themselves are always specific configurations of various values and interests, interpretations and options.

If compromise appears as a flexible strategic option of political action, it must also be clarified that this strategy of policy making and implementation is itself prestructured. Conditions for access are evident in the British case, since a network that is not legally, but socially, constituted operates on the basis of social relations and rules generated and reproduced to bring about compromises. Therefore, compromises (and the underlying systems of consultation) are the means to reproduce a policy-community and validate, legitimate, and thus strengthen its conditions for access. The agreement on practicable options is integrative and closes off the policy-community, since it involves the actors in a common decision making process and generates their compliance and loyalty. At the same time, only those are heard who can contribute to the practicality of policies and who have the necessary resources—a matter not only of money, power, and knowledge but also of reputation. Recognition, however, is accorded only to those who introduce needed resources and to those who have a mastery of the rules of informal cooperation and of the predominant language of professional relationships. Political participation cannot, therefore, be legally enforced but has to be socially obtained and granted as a distinct privilege. Consequently, politics is constituted along the lines of complex, but closed, networks. It tends to integrate even dissenting opinions, but this integration is accompanied by moderation and often even demands it. Moreover, political regulation is open to the specificity of the individual cases and situations but has difficulties moving the broader general line of conduct beyond the established common sense.

In France politics is still organized along a state-centered (or etatist) strategy (see Chapter 4 in this book). This certainly does not mean that the state has an unlimited autonomy and monopoly with regard to political action. Also in France negotiations and bargaining play an important role, and the societal orchestration of policies is an important goal and medium of political planning and implementation. According to the state-centered strategy, politics strongly orients itself toward safeguarding the functioning of the state and its mandate, and the policy process is thus strictly structured according to the organization of the government administration. That means that political decision making is founded on hierarchic-centralist structures, as a result of which politics becomes a matter of the special responsibility, authority, and legitimacy of the political decision makers and their administrative bodies. This structure is valid for the national as well as for the regional levels, whose responsibilities are clearly divided between policy making and implementation. These political decision making structures are certainly democratically grounded since even the final decision makers have to answer to the public. The weakness of environmental policies, then, is to be attributed to the lack of the public's will to consistently enforce existing environmental policies and to the weakness of the public mobilization of the Green movement—as unanimously stated by our interviewees. Without a doubt (potential) majorities have a decisive influence on the political agenda, the staffing of governmental offices, and the appointment of corresponding public figures. However, issues, policies, and politicians and functionaries are tied together in a package at the top of the government, even against the pressure of the streets and the fluctuations of the popularity scale—just as, for example, the public mobilization against the Chirac administration since the fall of 1995 demonstrates. It is especially true for environmental regulation that national politics is more than the sum of all of the local politics, that national policies have to achieve more than just being responsive to the sum of all of the local interests and demands. National interests and common welfare are a qualitatively distinct and higher level of regulation and can be determined only by extrapolation by the governmental heads and their advisory elite. As a result, a separation of national and local politics and a leading role of the former can be seen. This also means, then, that local environmental problems need to be positioned into a national context and that environmental policies have to be positioned in a larger political framework (industrial and energy politics, for example). Therefore, ministries obtain their own room for political activities only in accordance with their respective position in the cabinet and the reputation and weight of the appointed ministers. The different laws and decrees, political initiatives and projects highlight that this scope of action is also used by the ministers, who are the final decision makers. At the same time this policy making process underlines the relative independence of the national decision making process. There is less reference—also according to the arguments of the interviewees—to the practice of implementation and local political realities than there is to the top of government and its national elite, on the one hand, and to the efforts of political public figures to strengthen their position and public image in the national arena, on the other hand.

On the level of implementation, a similar structure is repeated. The French prefects are the heads of the regional administration and represent the central state. They are the ultimate decision makers with regard to implementation. Without a doubt, the prefects are bound to a context of negotiations with local politicians and locally affected interests, which can severely limit the independent scope of action in decision making. However, in spite of the moderate decentralization of the French administration and the stronger position of regional councils and parliaments, it is still the responsibility of the prefect to formulate priorities for the respective region in regard to the implementation of national interests and policies. On both levels, therefore, we find a structural similarity that organizes politics according to hierarchic-centralist structures. This hierarchy vertically connects the various levels of decision making with each other and assures state-centered strategies. Nevertheless, this is not the only and not the most characteristic feature of this political style.

The hierarchic and centralist structures force the horizontal integration of various societal sectors and areas of action. This is expressed by the explicit regulation of interest intermediation, institutional responsibilities, professional jurisdictions, and public discourses according to a state-centered functional setting. It is particularly the case with the "technical services" within the policy making and permit-granting practice, as these services are institutionally subordinated to, or associated with, the state administration. Similarly to Germany, technical expertise is directly linked to the political decision making process, though the relationship of the two elements to each other is reversed. The emphasis is less on (independent) professions as an infrastructure of an "objectified," good policy. Instead, correct and good policies need to be brought about by governmental action first and last. In this sense, the state does not transfer expertise to professional associations and professions, organizations and associations but rather binds them to itself through the recruitment of its staff and the foundation and financing of corresponding agencies. Although a number of independent and industry-sponsored agencies are active in this area as well, the state aims to maintain its autonomy and leading role by assigning specific functions, for example, the provision of scientific evidences and professional guidance. A similar statement can be formulated in regard to panels and procedures of societal deliberation and cooperation, because on this procedural level the state aims to assign them a merely preliminary and preparatory function.

However, at this procedural and institutional level a tight horizontal interconnection of the state and the society is established across the different societal interests, institutions, and professions. The establishment of the political class and technocratic elite on the national and regional levels not only seems to be, then, the consequence of a strategic reinforcement of interest alliances but is also founded on the state-centered administrative settings themselves. In other words, interests, professions, institutions, and discourses are functionally tied to, and utilized by, the state but, at the same time, submit the state to an emerging political class and professional elite with a distinct interest structure and rationalist discourse. This class and its technocratic elite are explicitly reproduced according to common professional backgrounds, recruitment and career strategies, and solidarity and loyalties and thus intermingle the higher state administration, finance, and industry with a discourse that legitimates its state-centered strategy of political regulation with reference to the higher rationality of its modernization project (Bourdieu, 1989).

It is precisely the structural similarity of both levels that seems, then, to determine the frequently complained of friction between policy making and implementation, since not only are independent responsibilities and decision making procedures established, but so are the discourses and negotiations, the political class and administrative elite for each one. An integration of the various regional politics into national politics is neither desired nor possible; a commitment to local and regional negotiations is possible in national politics only if regional institutions and public figures have access to the national (i.e., Parisian) arena.

In the case of Germany, a consensus model is repeatedly spoken of in the scientific and public discussion (see Chapter 5 in this book). This *consensus- or synthesis-oriented strategy* is evident already when considering the stipulation of general goals at the national level. The goals set forth in the Federal Ambient Air Quality Protection Law attempt to establish a consensus that has a politically integrative effect and consequently prescribes a first framework for the further business of daily regulation. As a result of this, the claim is strengthened that in the regulatory practices, that is, in the corresponding rules and prescriptions, technical standards, admissible levels of emissions, and permit-granting procedures, a consensus between, and a syntesis among, the diverging interests, professions, institutions, and discourses is kept as a goal and principle of regulatory action. Undoubtedly, the reality of environmental regulation is characterized by a number of conflicts, which are effectively pacified on the level of the federal framework law and its broad goals but which erupt on the level of specific prescriptions and procedures. However, negotiations and compromises are enshrined in a "highly legalistic regulatory system" (Boehmer-Christiansen and Weidner 1995: 119).

Politics organizes around three structural features that enable the maintenance of the underlying strategy of collective action. First of all, consensus-oriented policy making and implementation need a lot of time in order to check the correctness and validity of the individual articulations of interest and positions and to establish a societal consensus out of the multitude of conflicting positions. Consequently, policies are seen to be valid and legitimate only if the respective laws and practices can stand the test of time; hence, they have to be formulated with careful consideration and calmness. Thus, there is the tendency to separate policy making from the political pressures of the daily business of politics and from the urgency of public agendas and debates. Second, the consensus strategy is geared toward the integration of diverging positions. For this purpose, it does not orient itself primarily toward the determination and specification of time-bound compromises but rather toward deliberation and the ascertainment of an "objective" truth. Hidden behind the search for a consensus is, therefore, the attempt to integrate various particular interests, institutional functions, professional discourses, and societal values into a common, generally valid solution; thus, politics is carried on as a generalized synthesis of particular articulations. Compromises are only individual steps on a long road toward a synthesizing consensus and are guided in their identification by this claim, too. However, a long-term extension of the political process (i.e., the reference to the durability of policies and the needed time for the elaboration of policies) is but only one possible and conditionally realizable strategy in light of daily political pressures and demands for action. The consensus strategy can much sooner fail due to the diversity of existing interests and actors, values and expertise, and a durable regulation would block itself with time, if it constantly requires an integrative solution made by consensus. Consequently and third, procedures made by consensus can persist only if they are made immune not only to daily political business but also to pluralist competition. Thus, the conditions for success of this strategy put a limitation on the circle of participants integrated into the deliberative policy making and implementation processes (Vobruba 1992). If the state, acting for the common welfare, has a mandate to tackle public problems, then it needs only the knowledge and the views of those actors affected by state intervention to be able to consider the political consequences (i.e., the appropriateness and feasibility of the policies) of its intervention. This orientation establishes a permit-granting cartel between government officials and industrialists, an "ecological corporatism" (Jänicke and Weidner 1997a: 308) that in other countries would surely be criticized and seen as a conspiratorial power alliance (Boehmer-Christiansen and Weidner 1995: 123–124). In Germany, however, this policy community is obligated to an objective or technical discourse abstracted from the societal interests involved. Only this "objective" abstraction can assure the effectiveness, durability, and legitimacy of political regulation. In this respect, politics has to be liberated from particular interests in its core and become a place of objective discussion, a discussion, then, that does not entertain the irrationalities of emotional reasoning and the egoism of particular needs but that allows itself to be guided only by the issue itself. This claim to an interest- and value-free policy making and implementation process is successful only by linking up with professional communities whose ethos commits them to a rational and "objectified" approach toward public needs and policies. The state, which would have the mandate, monopolizes neither this policy deliberation nor the participating professional expertise. The state rather shelters these discourses and often delegates them even to professional associations, as, for example, the national association of engineers in the case of clean air standards and technical norms. Professional discourses and expert panels act then as fiduciaries of a broader public policy deliberation, as the (purely "technical") synthesis of diverging interests into a consensus and evidence is restrained and entrusted to them. This not only prestructures the political debates and negotiations within environmental regulation but at the same time obligates political action (not least of all, interest intermediation) to conform to this strategy of consensus and synthesis.

In the United States, politics is structured according to a *strategy of pluralist competition* that covers all aspects of the political process. It submits societal interests, professions, institutions, and discourses to a generalized competition that is geared toward a fair settlement of competing positions (see Chapter 6 in this book). This is true for the organization of the government, where the system of checks and balances between the judicial, executive, and legislative branches, on the one hand, and the (often overlapping) responsibilities between the federal and state governments, on the other hand, establish a multitude of interconnected institutions and arenas that tend to monitor each other with regard to problem definition, policy making, and implementation (Lester 1995b). The explicit orientation toward the public is also characteristic of this system (Dunlap 1995; Ingram, Colnic, and Mann 1995). Legislation, the administration of justice, and the permit-granting practice not only assure the public transparency of decision making procedures and the decisions themselves but also formally guarantee the general participation of societal actors. Next to the judicial branch, the legislative and the executive consider it their task to maintain these affirmed rights. This is especially true for the regulatory agencies. They have a political mandate that is precisely and ambitiously formulated, by which they can be legally obligated (Majone 1996b; Bryner 1987; McSpadden 1995). Moreover, they have to proceed completely unbiased in the gathering, assessing, and evaluation of all positions, objections, and demands if they do not want to be sued. Certainly, the governmental institutions reserve the right to make the final decision themselves, since they are formally legitimated to do so—in contrast to the many interest groups or experts heard. However, a policy strategy results that is the opposite of the German and French case. In the former country the circle of participating actors is limited with reference to the necessarily "objectified" consensus among diverging positions. This procedure is legitimated by entrusting policy deliberation to "disinterested" professional discourses. In the United States, political decision making is founded on a guarantee of public participation (Costain and Lester 1995), which not only has legitimate functions but is geared also toward mobilizing the necessary expertise. What is considered to be a fixed reference point of political decision making in the other countries becomes blurred here under the conditions of public competition. The objectivity of expertise vanishes as soon as conflicting positions and claims are introduced within the individual professions and/or in the political process (Bryner 1987; Jasanoff, 1990, 1995). Competition within the system of professional work, about which we just spoke, undermines, then, the possibility of politics by consensus altogether because it questions the validity and reputation of professional expertise. On the other hand, different from the French case, even if governmental institutions reserve the right to make the final decision themselves, this formal right is eroded in practice. This is due to the system of checks and balances itself, by which the societal actors have the opportunity to question or block decisions. Moreover, it is due to the practice of informal consultation and arbitration, which has established itself parallel to the formal decision making procedure and is aimed at overcoming the problem of the administration's scarcity of resources as well as the blockade of the decision making process. However, it turns out that efforts are made to win back this fixed point of political decision making—under the observance of a competitive strategy: for example, peer review as a means of validating and "objectifying" scientific expertise (Jasanoff 1990), and regulatory negotiation procedures as a means of consultation and coordination and of interests (Weidner 1996). Competition reproduces itself, therefore, as a latent structural principle, first of all, because it legitimates politics. Competition assumes equal opportunity and individual freedoms, just as impartiality and fairness are established as maxims of the decision making process. Institutional rules of competition, therefore, form the actual consensus of U.S.–American politics, through which all conflicts regarding individual matters should, in principle, be able to be resolved or to which all parties involved in the conflict can, in principle, be obligated. This foundation constitutes an integrative frame of reference for an otherwise highly conflictive arena of changing lines of conflict, demands, and alliances. In the politics of competition, all decisions appear, however, as provisional and first have to provide proof of their objective and societal validity. Moreover, in a situation of competition in which politics has to remain committed to prompt action by its orientation toward the public, the pragmatism of "just do it" is the optimal strategy for action by which alternatives are tried out, gauged by, and evaluated in, practice, generalized to broad recommendations, and integrated into a comprehensive, yet patchworked, concept—a "disjointed incrementalism" specific to pluralist models of democracy. Accordingly, short-term demands and pressures for action can be complied with without sacrificing the opportunity for pragmatic correction in the long-term process of reaching a broad, yet always partial, consensus. Hence, a competitive strategy submits politics to a constant process of "trial and error" and disintegrates it into provisional and situational bargains and compromises, compensatory instruments and solutions that prevent policy making and implementation from becoming an otherwise unavoidable, systematic blockade. Hence, competitive politics is responsible for a high degree of openness and fragmentation (Andrews 1997) and a high potential of innovation with equally high resulting costs (Kraft and Vig 1994). Moreover, a schism between formal or "symbolic" pluralist guarantees and informal networks of influence and power and the related schism between legitimization and efficiency or effectiveness become the more evident.

CONCLUSIONS

Comparative research professes to equally bring out commonalities and differences between the individual countries, that is, to identify a "theme" with general validity and determine the "variations" of the theme within each country. Comparative research is, therefore, a method that allows for the verification of existing theories (Ragin 1991; Oeyen 1990). In this sense, theories are not sufficiently complex if they unjustly generalize the specifics of individual cases or if general statements are not consistently enough traced back to specific cases (Rüschemeyer 1991). In this chapter the attempt was made to determine the structure and dynamic of national politics from an encompassing, sociological perspective. It was argued that interests, professions, institutions, cultural values, and symbolic representations are important structural features. National politics integrate, organize, and structure these elements according to a specific strategy with a particular code: the strategies of etatism, of pluralist competition, of compromise, and of consensus and synthesis. It was argued that these strategies emerge from the structure of national polities and politics but also from the societal contexts specific to the various countries. In this regard a sociological approach seems crucial for better understanding the structure and dynamic of national styles of regulation. Moreover, this perspective allows to shed some light on the recurrently debated question as to the persistence and change of national policy styles. In this sense it was argued that continuity and change are dependent not only on regulatory reform, the features of the established policy repertoires, and the structure and adaptability of the political system alone but also on the societal factors and contexts portrayed in this chapter. Hence, national styles of regulation are not immune to change. Indeed, scholarly writing has been arguing that national policy styles are moving closer to each another, for instance, through a less legalistic and more cooperative orientation under the Bush and Clinton administrations and the Republican-led Congress (Kraft 1996: 186–192) on the one side of the Atlantic and a more formalistic and restrictive approach under the Thatcher, Major, and Blair administrations on the other side (Lowe and Ward 1998). In all countries there is a certain trend toward "cooperative environmentalism" (Switzer and Bryner 1998: 303–306) and the cooperative state (Lahusen 2000). However, in this study it is argued that these changes evolve from different points of departure and that these obvious transformations might be misunderstood if the contextual factors are disregarded. The latter are to be conceived of as societal paths that direct and channel policy changes in a certain manner. Certainly, these paths may change themselves the more that the underlying societal context factors (e.g., institutional rules, professions, discourses) alter. As shown in this chapter, however, these changes are far more conditional and slow than many proponents of regulatory reform would expect. Sociological insights might thus be helpful for those who wish to work on realistic and lasting improvements.

Apart from these observations of the dialectic relationship between persistence and change, the present chapter aimed at highlighting the cultural dimension of environmental politics and policies. This culturalist perspective might irritate when considering that politics and policies are submitted ever more to political bargains, legal codification, formal procedures, regulatory rule making, and scientific review with the explicit aim to increase the rationality of the policy making and implementation. Indeed, regulatory action of our societies seems to be exposed to the rationalization process specific to Western modernization (Weber 1958). However, this is not to be conceived of as a pure "disenchantment" that strips politics of collectively shared cultural values and meanings, as theories of the bureaucratization, functional differentiation, or generalization of interest-oriented exchange relationships argue from very different perspectives. It is rather assumed that the rationalization of politics propels the reconstruction and reproduction of social meaning and cultural orientations and deepens the interrelation between meaning and interests, institutions, professions, and public discourses. Political power and authority thus become constantly infused by a symbolic "reenchantment" that rationalizes and veils at the same time the political nature of power and authority.

For instance, it was observed that modernization founds itself on a rational appropriation and use of the natural environment, which is even intensified through environmental protection, as it increasingly socializes the environment mentally and materially. The ecological critique has itself been appropriated by the dominant discourse only to rationalize the "socialization" of nature and, at the same time, the symbolic "naturalization" of political regulation. The more that environmental protection moves away from a curative reaction to environmental damages and toward a proactive maintenance of the functioning of natural ecosystems, the more that policy making and implementation will be oriented by the (scientifically or ethically, in all cases symbolically determined) essence and logic of natural ecosystems, on the one hand, and the more the environment will be constructed mentally and materially by these symbolically structured political interventions, on the other hand.

In this sense, political regulation makes itself dependent on the "manageability" of public problems and thus on existing expertise and knowledge, related skills, and working routines. Consequently, a professional infrastructure with a proper division of labor is established as a supportive instrument of policy making and implementation. In this regard, the rationalization of political regulation takes the form of a (conflictive) learning process that entangles itself ever more with (competing) professional discourses and thus becomes ever more strongly molded by the knowledge systems, working routines, and ethos of professions. Finally, governments and state administrations become more dependent on contributions and resources from a variety of societal actors, of which professions are but only one. Politics operates then within broad networks with a variety of corporate actors and interorganizational relationships. Consequently, policy making and implementation repeatedly break the institutional procedures and arenas and are rationalized then according to broader social rules and principles (precaution, cost-effectiveness, cooperation, among many others) that aim to order, control, and guide the broader arenas and contexts of action. On each level or argumentation, power and authority are not disenchanted by an instrumental rationale that constantly formalizes and/or functionalizes decision making procedures and arenas but are rather constantly reenchanted by the very submission of policy making and implementation to social meaning and the symbolic definition and construction of the issues and problems at stake, of the rules, principles, and criteria that guide interorganizational decision making and the tasks, skills, and working routines upon which the daily regulatory practices are based.

NOTES

1. Héritier, for example, argues in regard to the "regulatory competition" on the European level that negotiation processes between the participating actors are limited and made possible by institutional guidelines (e.g., formal organizational structures or legal regulations). Thus, a federal constitution and a second house, in which the sub-national units are represented on the central level, offer opportunities for action and possibilities for exchange for sub-national actors who are closed in a unitary system (Héritier, 1993; Héritier, Knill, and Mingers 1994). See also Scharpf (1993b), Laumann and Knoke (1989), or O'Toole (1993). Here the institutional arguments of game and exchange theory are introduced with the limitations still to be identified.

2. Gabriela Christmann (1992: 478) states in this sense: "To be able to reach the goals of the movement, the actors of the local 'eco-scene' actually fall back on those means which are considered as having a great potential for success in the modern industrial society: the most institutionalized protest possible and the—most scientifically substantiated as possible—rational argumentation. One can . . . very well formulate that *'romantic'* individualism in social movements—at least in the ecology movement—functions in our time in a *less* radical form."

Chapter 3

United Kingdom: Rule by Virtue of Convention and Consultation

Markus Kurth

INTRODUCTION

The characteristic features of the political regulation of environmental risks in the United Kingdom (U.K.) and its unique institutional forms as opposed to those found in the United States and in continental Europe are especially appropriate for demonstrating how culture can explain the development of modern political systems. In light of the uniqueness of the patterns of political regulation in the United Kingdom, explanatory variables that do not ask about the specific cultural features of the interaction between politics and the society appear to be unsatisfactory from the start. Especially with the example of Great Britain (GB), it can be shown that political culture, which covers the whole of ideas, values, and convictions as well as their meaningful realization in the practices of the actors, acts as a corset for the policy process that, on the one hand, stabilizes and reduces conflicts (i.e., works toward integration) but, on the other hand, can develop into a considerable constraint for maintaining the status quo.

INSTRUMENTS OF REGULATION

A look at the patterns of regulation, be it legal standards and principles or the behavior of the actors, reveals a remarkably uniform and historically stable structure of the political process in Great Britain. Superficial observations tend to equate this constancy with immobility and do not see that the historic stability is based on movement between the poles of stagnation and innovative continuity (i.e., innovation without wasting resources). The invisibility of norms and safeguards in the United Kingdom's political system appears incredible to almost all of the other Western countries, where positive law, constitutional jurisdiction, and established principles suggest a more rational exercise of political power. Clichés about the old-fashioned English and persistent prejudices about "Europe's dirty man" obscure the fact that in Great Britain there have been and still are irregular phases in which the policy community of the political field "environment" has developed new forms of the societal treatment of environmental risks, which also in a worldwide comparison earn the rating of innovations. At present, Great Britain is in such a phase again: The political project of "integrated monitoring for environmental protection," new instruments such as the "Eco-Auditing" that transform the economic logic, the interdisciplinary debate about "Agenda 21,"and a societal change of consciousness that is reflected, for instance, in the exorbitant number of members of environmental associations compared to the rest of Europe have started a lasting process of change. In light of this radical change, it can be astonishing that the basic values and ways of functioning of the political regulation in Great Britain continue to remain stable. This chapter portrays the permanent parameters of the United Kingdom's policy process and describes it as a very specific and demanding form of political regulation.

NETWORKS OF ACTORS: INFORMAL FORUMS AS A LEADING PRINCIPLE OF COMPROMISING

A multitude of discursive procedures and a wide range of actors grouped around the political center turn out to be a necessary concretization and an inevitable, institutional extension of deficits found in the political system. The balance between an unlimited abundance of governmental power and a restricted exercise of power was and still is kept by the authority that has been granted to established groups, agencies, and formally subordinated governmental institutions. Although these are formally completely dependent on governmental decisions, they act autonomously in fact. As a result, political power appears to be divided and sometimes even split up. Political power spreads out from the center to hierarchically structured, interwoven centers of action, conglomerations, and coordination points. The hierarchy, however, does not or only formally represent an organized arrangement of institutions and organizations that are subject to the strict principle of the division of power and representation. "Relations in Whitehall are complex and fluid, and the lines of division are more often than not to be found between the political and bureaucratic elements in government but within them as alliances of ministers and officials compete with each other to advance particular goals or defend common interest" (Smith, Marsh, and Richards 1993). The particular pattern of political dynamics, especially as regards the influencing of the political center from the outside, exists in the casting of specifically tailored spheres with the societal actors. I'd like to characterize these meeting places of actors as forums. These forums act as vestibules to reaching a compromise in which "compatible" actors (i.e., those with the ability for mutual understanding and negotiation), are brought together. They channel and reduce political conflict without suppressing it completely by making participation possible, on the one hand, and limiting it, on the other. As successive springboards from the periphery to the center, they offer marginal actors, such as protest groups, the perspective of moving forward. "The relative permeability of Britain's system of 'bureaucratic accommodations' of environmentalist concern, with its elaborate system of public consultation on planning matters, has thus absorbed a lot of environmentalist energy which in other, less open systems might have found an outlet in radical politics" (Rootes 1995: 183). At the same time, radical viewpoints are toned down with each step forward that is accompanied by integration and order. Opposition currents and protest groups, which are presented defiantly as alternatives to the system, are practically not found at all and could never win lasting support.

As a component of the system of forums, historically established nongovernmental organizations (NGOs) play an important preparatory role. In the area of environmental politics, central, renowned organizations such as the National Society for Clean Air (NSCA) represent a kind of "universal community of participating actors." Regular conferences and meetings of experts of the NSCA not only allow for an exchange of opinions and information. Research as well as hearings can, to a certain extent, be tested and carried out in advance. Here contacts between ministers, municipalities, the industry, and environmental groups can be prepared and fostered. In addition to the NGOs, which cover a broad spectrum, smaller organizations offer a kind of training ground with their events. The task of selecting topics as well as people is spread out among various spheres. However, there is the precondition that the procedure of open discussion should always be in the center of the meeting place inside the forum. The quality of a contribution is measured by the degree to which it can be understood by everyone. NGOs are an important place where political conflicts are preliminarily worked out in the way outlined earlier and then latently maintained. Larger, near-to-the-state, independent committees and permanent research commissions work in a similar fashion. As an example of a forum that clears the policy path completely without formal authority to act is the high-ranking, industrially staffed Advisory Council on Business and the Environment (ACBE). The opinions of the council regarding expectations and possibilities in relation to future regulations are separated from daily conflicts in that the people coming together there are not involved in the classic lobbying of an enterprise, a branch of industry, or an organization. Furthermore, the participants are chosen according to the environmental performance of their enterprise (i.e., they are the forerunners of environmental protection in their companies and make alterations not only in limits of emissions). Seemingly nonbinding recommendations reach out of this circle into the power centers and create expectations there about possible horizons and levels of acceptance of political regulation of the economy. At the same time, these recommendations given by the ACBE, as opposed to those of the Department of the Environment, Transport and the Regions (DETR),[1] show the "stragglers" and "interrupters" among the enterprises which regulatory means and goals they can expect in the long run.

The opportunity for "advancement" offers the central state organs the possibility of integrating potential protests and raising their own legitimacy. Thus, each group that primarily makes up the industrial and political center—oligarchies such as the city, departments of key ministries, heads of enterprises, and economic organizations—can extensively influence the profile of the political community without being involved in a general counterdefense of demands of other societal groups and sectors. At the same time, less powerful interest groups can gradually allow their issues to seep into the power centers in this way. The necessity to facilitate the negotiation and, ultimately, integration of all viewpoints without exposing exclusive vested rights to direct confrontation and immediate demands initiated this dynamic and is its driving momentum. The entanglement of governmental and societal groupings essentially promotes the state's embedding in society and the common perception of a broad unity of the state and the societal community.

The DETR is in the center of the political field of environmental protection. In light of the increase of nongovernmental regulatory procedures and consultation "outside of politics," the DETR represents only an intersection in the clean air policy network. Yet, no other actor within the British clean air policy community has so many and such diverse connections to other actors and simultaneously occupies such a central position of power. The DETR makes suggestions and takes up legislative initiatives. It has the responsibility for municipalities (i.e., it determines their budget as well as the essential features of local planning and administration). It communicates the principles of implementation to the regulatory officials. It manages the negotiations within the European Union (EU), implements EU guidelines and directives, and presents political initiatives there. Last but not least, it appoints scientific advisory committees and finances environmental research, the results of which become the basis of discussion for air quality standards. The overall environmental strategy of the government, its political goals within and outside the responsibilities of the DETR, and the progress achieved in their implementation have been published in the annual "white papers" since 1990. Expressly made up of a cross-section of different policy areas, the DETR can and does exert influence on the authorities of other departments, especially the Department of Trade and Industry (DTI), the Ministry of Agriculture, Fisheries, and Food (MAFF), and the Department of Health (DoH). The transition from an interconnection of responsibilities in common programs to a gradual takeover is blurred.[2] In spite of a relative abundance of formal power in the hands of the DETR, its decisions represent the result of external initiatives, internal processing, external safeguards, and interministerial agreements. The network spun around the intersection represented by the DETR can be roughly depicted in the form of concentric circles. Around the DETR or next to its special departments is a functionally differentiated internal network of departments that includes a gray area of semigovernmental agencies and actors. A detailed description following the formal hierarchies would break up the framework of this chapter. It would also conceal the fact that innumerable specialized relationships of the societal and political actors with the subdepartments of the DETR cause a different distribution of autonomy to act than what it first appears to be. An examination of the way the actor network functions—the interplay between societal actors and government that is passed on through the forums—can be carried out using the example of the Royal Commission on Environmental Pollution (RCEP).

Set up by the government as an independent, standing body, the RCEP met for the first time on 20 February 1970 "to advise on matters, both national and international, concerning the pollution of the environment; on the adequacy of research in this field; and the future possibilities of danger to the environment" (RCEP 1984: 2). Its members are appointed by the Crown based on the suggestions of the prime minister but are free to choose their own topics, manner of working, and their concluding remarks: "We have no specific or restricted task. We are authorized to inquire into any matter on which we think advice is needed" (RCEP 1971). The self-conception of the RCEP's role and function in the political process developed and became more concrete in irregular phases after it had definitively established itself as a lasting body:

> The existence of a standing Royal Commission with such broad terms of reference implies a judgment that pollution will continue to raise issues of such consequence to the nation as to justify an independent "watch-dog" body. . . . We expect . . . to concern ourselves with the principles that relate to pollution control and abatement and to deal with matters which may escape the attention of the official bodies having more narrowly defined responsibilities than those of the Commission, but which may nevertheless be of considerable importance for the future protection of the environment. (RCEP 1974)

While this statement, taken from the 4th report, justifies the aspired role of a "watch-dog," the position taken in the 10th report is more aggressive in accordance with reports published in the meantime that received much attention: "we would not rule out the possibility of our acting as a long-stop to draw attention to any striking weaknesses in our institutional arrangements" (RCEP 1984: 5). The reports of the RCEP encompass (1) current individual problems (lead in the air, water pollution by oil, etc.); (2) the general principles of pollution control such as the "integrated pollution control" (IPC); and (3) the resulting principles of regulation (such as the "best practicable environmental Option"—BPEO). While research oriented toward harmful substances looked back on debates, the reports under the latter categories present political concepts that—even if with a considerable time delay—were essentially adopted by the government. In connection with the problem of clean air, the report published in 1976, *Air Pollution Control: An Integrated Approach*, can claim to be the first elaborated concept of integrated environmental protection and conservation that includes concrete suggestions for administrative implementation. At the same time, the RCEP harshly criticized the informal practice of regulation and the secrecy practices of the national regulatory officials at that time, the Alkali and Clean Air Inspectorate. Eleven years later, the institutional conditions for an integrated system of environmental protection and conservation were created with the reorganization of the monitoring bodies and the creation of Her Majesty's Inspectorate for Pollution (HMIP), and the necessity of a new fundamental, legislative regulation was obvious. In 1988 the RCEP was again able to define principles and terms with the well-developed report on the *Best Practicable Environmental Option*. The IPC as well as the concept of BPEO have represented the core elements of the British regulatory regime since 1990. The definition of BPEO developed by the RCEP was almost adopted word for word; based on this, the HMIP developed a corresponding methodology for practical use.[3]

Why can the RCEP be considered the prototypical characteristic of the political culture in GB? The official and nonpartisan nature of the RCEP as an independent correspondent to the Crown and as not only the moral but legal obligation of the government to express an opinion about the recommendations of the RCEP unfolds its potential to have an impact, first of all, in connection with its members. The approximately 20 members, who change irregularly and at varying times, overwhelmingly boast scientific, political, or economic careers. They mostly occupied and still occupy various leadership positions in professional and technical associations and in this way bring a storehouse of contacts with about 100 organizations and the corresponding knowledge into the RCEP. This background is also reflected in the RCEP's way of working. It makes an effort to include the whole spectrum of relevant actors in its research. For the 10th report, *Tackling Pollution* from 1984, 186 institutions, organizations, and private individuals were asked to take a written or verbal position. For the report published in 1994, *Transport and the Environment*, 255 actors were consulted, and in addition 63 foreign institutions and organizations as well as 10 domestic ones were visited by members of the commission. On the basis of this "submitted evidence" the RCEP formulates its reports and concrete recommendations. The RCEP focuses the topics like a corrective lens that has been polished through pragmatic experience and scientific methods and has also remained untouched by daily political constraints. It supervises a kind of political hearing procedure through which viewpoints not only come to the attention of the center of the government but are also characterized as worthy of consideration and are thus authorized or even popularized. The reputation of the members, based on their origin, thorough research and lack of involvement in a scramble for political jobs, allows the RCEP to carry out precisely these tasks even without a mandate for political representation. I'd like to emphasize that the interplay of the factors that make up the reputation is important. It is the product of institutional position (independent, but without a mandate), a wealth of expertise, and the approach (broad analysis under the inclusion of many contributions), which make the RCEP an especially effective vestibule to the political center and an ideal forum for the passing on of ideas for political regulation oriented toward compromise.

INSTITUTIONAL RULES OF POLICY MAKING: CONSULTATION AND PRACTICALITY

Cultural dispositions on the general level of the political system and in the processing chain of the forums are also, in principle, established in laws and regulatory procedures. It can be demonstrated that the common point of reference in the form of the "common good" manifests itself concretely in permit-granting procedures as a binding orientation toward the value practicality and in corresponding actions as a search for appropriate solutions. Accordingly, British clean air politics is based on a very specific form of regulation that does not use universal levels of emissions based on formal criteria as an instrument of political regulation. Fixed emission levels have not been seen as a negotiable option to push into either the political or the administrative arena. In the strategy paper of the Deparment of the Environment (DoE) *Air Quality—Meeting the Challenge* this principle is given particular emphasis: "National policy on air quality is firmly based on effects—centering on air quality as opposed to emissions" (DoE 1995: 17). This has also hardly changed due to recent pressure from the outside, more precisely, from the EU. The Environmental Protection Act (EPA) passed in 1990 offers the possibility of a regulation oriented toward emissions, but the law is used only to be able to give a legal framework to the inevitable adaptations that arise from the continental regulating philosophy of the EU. In spite of the emphasis on air quality, the preparations for binding air quality standards and the accompanying regulatory instruments oriented toward ambient air quality are still not finished. The idea of regulation oriented toward effects and goals excludes inflexible regulations that are not pragmatically tailored to specific situations. The principle of regulation (BPEO) covers this situation especially well and exposes that feature of environmental regulation that, according to the British viewpoint, the formal regulations on the continent hide: that the regulating decision represents a choice of different options, a compromise found by different problems, issues, viewpoints, and value decisions, which—as it cannot solely arise from scientific truth or economic interests—has to be simply "practical" in order to work.

Regulatory Principles: BPM, BATNEEC, and BPEO

The Alcali Works Regulation (WAR) Act of 1906 institutionalized the regulatory principle, which the Health and Safety at Work (HSW) Act of 1974 explicitly strengthens and which consequently has been the authoritative regulating principle in GB for most of this century: best practicable means (BPM). Section 34 of the Clean Air Act of 1956 defined "practicable": "'Practicable' means reasonably practicable having regard, amongst other things, to local conditions and circumstances, to the financial implications and to the current state of technical knowledge, and 'practicable means' includes the provision and maintenance of plant and the proper use thereof" (quote taken from Weidner 1987: 70). Since 1990 the BPM principle has been replaced by the principles best available technique not entailing excessive costs (BATNEEC) and BPEO. The BAT in BATNEEC reflects the continental European (especially German) view that has penetrated the EU's legislative framework. This view holds that admissible levels of emissions should be based on the emission levels achievable with the best possible technology. The additional NEEC seems to suppose that in the final relevant assessment of economical feasibility, the British view found within the BPM principle and the continental European view do not deviate too much from each other. Ultimately, the principles of the earlier system of monitoring have hardly changed. The principle of appropriateness should comprehensively be covered in the context of the construction of BPEO, upon which BATNEEC is based. It refers to the IPC and the mixture of pollution of air, water, and soil. It is the result "of a systematic consultative and decision making procedure which emphasizes the protection and conservation of the environment across land, air and water. The BPEO procedure establishes, for a given set of objectives, the option that provides the most benefit or least damage to the environment as a whole, at acceptable cost, in the long term as well as in the short term" (RCEP 1988: 5; DoE 1989).

A characteristic feature of the regulatory principle is that the fixing of the legislative guidelines, as set up principally in the IPC, lays down neither the area of monitoring nor the profit-and-loss account. Most decisive is the idea that regulatory decisions, which materialize as a permit first in light of concrete circumstances, can be communicatively reached between the participants only as decisions for each specific case. With the legislative introduction of environmental media (air, water, soil), processes, methods of work, and assessments of damage as elements of the concrete regulatory decision, the area of compromise not only is broadened but is first completely set up as such. "Technology" and "costs" as sole elements permit only a limited choice of options, whereas spheres of compromise live directly from the diversity of negotiating possibilities.

Rules and the Practice of Granting a Permit

The special feature of BATNEEC, as well as of BPM before, is the possibility to be expressed both in technological terms (i.e., concrete facilities) and in the form of emission standards. As a hybrid, BATNEEC takes on the role of a "performance standard" (i.e., a technically identifiable option "x," which makes possible the emission levels "y"). The drawing up of "Guidance Notes" for operators takes place, for the most part, in cooperative collaboration between those just mentioned and the regulating authority.

> HMIP circulates it [draft guidance] for comment within Government and to the representatives of the industries and other bodies affected. . . . If major questions about standards emerge, there may need to be fuller discussion. This draft guidance note again is issued for final consultation within Government, with industry and with other affected parties; and following any changes arising from the comments received, the guidance note is issued. In this way, the Chief Inspector canvasses a broad spectrum of views at what he considers appropriate guidance for each process. (DoE 1994: 14)

The whole problem of enforcement is, in principle, put off on the process of the construction of guidelines. Since the regulating authority acts in close cooperation with those regulated when exercising the legislative components (i.e., the drafting of the "presumptive limits" or "release levels" and the "notes on BPM" or the "Guidance Notes," which fulfill the legally established principles of BPM or BATNEEC and BPEO), problems of implementation and enforcement are already solved before the application of rules and the recourse to formal procedures have begun. Due to the unique, hybrid position of the Environment Agency, the analytical separation of program planning and implementation cannot be made. If the inspectors have to be seen as helping assistants instead of watchmen, it is not astonishing that prosecution and the threat of punishment play a subordinate role.[4] In the wake of the law passed in 1990, the DETR attempted to arrive at a permit-granting practice similar to the German and U.S.–American procedure. This could not be implemented as planned and was abandoned. Instead of an abrupt change, the historically evolved procedures and ways of behavior continued in newly created institutional structures. This remarkable resistance of the regulating regime in relation to the political initiative of the government is discussed in more detail later.

In regard to cultural patterns, we can recognize the following: the procedural rules of BPM, BPEO, and BATNEEC have the purpose of assuring the agreement of the state and society on a small scale. During the process of implementation, only the units "pollution control authority" and "plant operators" represent state and society. However, "statutory consultants" and the possible exertion of influence by environmental groups are hypothetically additional ways of establishing a decision to grant a permit, although the Environment Agency and the permit applicant are normally the only ones who negotiate. The special feature is that procedural forms dominate in the establishing of the contents of arrangements. The regulatory authorities act more as consultants than enforcers, and the context of the discursive regulation serves as an anticipated monitoring. Thus, a broadly defined, legal, protective understanding of environment can claim to be generally accepted since it is determined in advance that in the context of practical discussion it is to be worked on in detail and broken down into negotiable pieces.

Rules and Principles of Political Regulation

Which practical rules underlie the described procedures for coordination and reaching a consensus? Which principles of regulation within the rounds of coordination effectively mediate between the actors, so that a compromise can develop as a stabilizing condition for trust, acceptance, and effectivity?

Appropriateness and Reciprocity

Even a form of rule oriented strongly to compromise cannot prevent that time and again—practically constantly—the situation arises where a "loser" emerges from among the participants. In GB, there is an attempt to prevent the breaking up of the consensus coalition. The "winners" try to give the "losers" trust in the appropriateness of their actions. In light of the fragility of the mechanism for compromise, the expectation of every actor with regard to the others has to be confirmed before, during, and after the decision making process that their actions are mutually applicable to each other. This attitude concretizes the otherwise rather shapeless term of fairness: within the circle of those cooperating it is considered to be inadmissible to pressure inferior or weaker participants (i.e., to exploit situational but also structural, advantages as much as possible). In a comprehensive study about the relationship between interest groups and parliamentary committees, Ian Marsh came to the conclusion that even in procedures that act as a preparation for cooperation, the principles of "accommodation" and "fairness" are considered to be of the utmost importance: "Participants need to believe the system is fair in an abstract sense, that evidence relevant to the issue under review has been adduced and fairly weighed, and that the behavior of other members of the relevant policy community will conform to the actions proposed" (Marsh 1986: 471f.). Rhodes calls this moment of adaptability "accommodation": "Where agreement is not possible, the 'loser' is not antagonized, a special case of the British love of the underdog, and pains will be taken—through consultation over details—to minimize losing over the principles of policy" (Rhodes 1986: 391; in Richardson 1990: footnote 26).

Reliance

A condition for the assurance of trust, as important as reciprocity and accom-modation, is reliability. "Access to discussions, secret and otherwise, and effec-tiveness in . . . discussions hinge on the assessment of reliability—if and only if a group is deemed reliable, as in the case of the associations, will it command an entrée and attention" (Rhodes 1986: 391; in Richardson 1990: footnote 26). The actors—especially the interest groups—are constantly aware of the aspect that controls access, which here is emphasized as a function of reliability: "We have influence, we don't have power. We have no power at all. But you're only influen-tial if what you're saying is credible and authoritative" (Interview AA). In con-nection with rules, such as "practicality," that determine the permissible pattern of argumentation, the element "reliability" can contribute decisively to the elimina-tion of fundamental criticism. The effectiveness of reliability as well as that of the other rules, such as practicality, hinges on the willingness of each participant to stick to this code of behavior. Since the willingness cannot be tested repeatedly in every round of consultations, the participating parties have to have earned an appropriate reputation (e.g., in the conferences of the NGOs or by their contribu-tions to public hearings). Next to trust, reliability also directly leads to the goal of procedural effectiveness. In the area of implementation, reliability gives those regulating the confidence—it even almost assures—that those regulated will carry out the rules. The latter, in turn, can be sure that those regulating will act "in due course" and pursue their goal without great deviation. Therefore, it would be the equivalent of a betrayal to disregard an arrangement that has the character of an agreement. The relationship that in general is characterized by reliability is re-flected directly in the low costs of monitoring.

Coordination of Mutual Expectations and the Promotion of Mutual Under-standing: Predictability, Comprehensibility, and Internal Transparency

Prior to mutual recognition and the willingness to agree on appropriateness is the coordination of mutual expectations and the promotion of mutual understand-ing. On the level of implementation, for example, the talks held before the official permit-granting procedures serve this purpose: "Pre-application meetings develop an understanding of the process, understanding of the position of the operator, and a dialogue over what should be in an application" (Interview HMIP PPD). During implementation as well as in the definition of the problem and in program formulation, it is not important to reconcile conflicting positions. The participants are well aware of the opposing interests: "I mean, by sitting around the table we always knew which side of the table we were sitting on" (Interview HMIP RSD). This corresponds to the position of the industry: "But primarily, we would expect government to set the standards" (Interview with the environmental manager of a large chemical company). It is to the fore that there is the possibility for each individual to present the plausibility of his or her viewpoint and in return to re-construct the plausibility of different or even opposing positions. The task of the regulating authorities does not begin with the application of already existing rules: "The regulatory role of the inspectorate is to hold the discussions and a dialogue with the people it's regulating so that there can be a full understanding between both sides of the position we are coming from. We can understand what their constraints are and they can understand what our regulatory role is" (Interview HMIP PPD). The genesis of viewpoints, demands arising from them, and ways of behaving have to be comprehensible. Mutual understanding requires the internal transparency of interests and reasoning. The further course of negotiations becomes more comprehensible and predictable so that gains and losses are anticipated, which allows the establishment of "a look at the appropriateness of the actions of the others" at an early stage and prevents disappointments: "But, as far as I am being disappointed with organizations concerned, I think 'disappointed' implies your failure of expectations, doesn't it? And I think, if you really know the organizations involved as those of us who have been in the business for a long time, then it is very rarely that your expectations lead to disappointment" (Interview HMIP RSD). The establishment of comprehensibility and predictability results perfectly in the assurance of reliability and durability. The exchange of interpretations of the laws, the explanation of perceived practical constraints, and the discussion of environmental observations blend into a dialogue of compromising and result in a mutual understanding of the meaningfulness of collective action and its outputs.

Practicality, Pragmatism and Factualness

Reliability, coordinated expectations, and predictability not only stabilize each other but are also based on another rule that gives points of view their negotiable form. Although this rule intervenes in a very concrete way in the interactions, it is hard to define. Almost every actor refers to it explicitly or implicitly, without being able to explain exactly in an abstract way what this rule involves. Obviously, this has to do with a special routine behavioral pattern that needs to be applied in concrete practice and, not least of all, needs to be perceptible by the senses in the communication process in order to really take form and become effective. The core rule is named practicality. Practicality represents the central, mutual point of reference of most of the actors. A collectively preferred term among a great variety of actors, practicality includes the subjective component of the feasible selection more precisely than the term pragmatism which is used by Rhodes, for example. Practicality refers to a closeness to reality and a rooted objectivity that take up the concept of general satisfaction. Entirely in agreement with the principle of accommodation, practicality gives greater significance to the honest consideration allotted to existing relationships than the usually somewhat sloppy, conventional German "feasibility" (Machbarkeit). With the recognition of the existing conditions, the term conveys "practical constraints" in such a way that their establishment in the surrounding political, personal, and societal conditions is constantly visible. Of course, the significance of sound scientific data is emphasized by most of the actors, especially by those who have to defend themselves publicly. Criteria for economic and political efficiency, which are substantiated with scientific reasons and data, are likewise included in the argumentation. However, it is striking that no single component—be it economic or scientific, technical or social—can dominate the term practicality. Practicality avoids the metaphysical aura of objectivity that is attached to German "factualness" (Sachlichkeit) (even if both rules have the same intention of restricting the opportunities for change). As practicality brings about the commitment to a given reality of interests and historically evolved procedures, it prevents the introduction of extreme positions. Under these conditions, practicality limits from the beginning the spectrum of possible options and negotiable matters, so that conflicts are reconcilable in the forums. This requires, though, that the actors internalize this rule and not just pay lip service to it in order to obtain access to the forums. Practicality serves as a guiding principle fostering the internalization of reasoning by the actors. If practicality is embedded in each actor's mind, a considerable part of reasoning will be carried out individually by each actor and in advance.

Hence, practicality as a common term of reference helps to promote negotiating discipline. Expectations have to be created with the help of the rule practicality so that the subsequent mechanism of consensual change of expectations (i.e., the accommodation) can take effect. The high status of practicality becomes more obvious if one considers that this term is the only one among the principles presented here that can be found in law: including the word practicable, best practicable means, and best practicable environmental option clearly express that not only the state of the art, but also the modus operandi of a process, including its nontechnical milieu and local conditions, are worth thorough consideration. It now seems less amazing that in the time of the BPM principle, the component "practicable" was never legally or judicially taken up. It was rather adapted to changing conditions in the course of 100 years of practice by practicality. It should be clearer now than before that limiting the flexibility of the definition of practicality by binding legislation would have led the principle itself ad absurdum. The coordination of expectations with the tool "practicality" is that much easier since it is able to carry out another function: because negotiations about permits and political goals are directly connected with the visible, tangible world of individual facts, the potential for conflict is restricted, and its depoliticization becomes possible. "Practicality" helps to dissolve a complex of problems, full of conflict, into practical, workable disputed issues. Eventually, conflicts of interest simply appear to be different conceptions of practicality: "They [industry] lobby and put forward their view and they say, what the act requires you to do is this, and we interpret that in this way, 'we want you to regulate us in this manner.' And we will counter how we see it. And then, on a site by site basis you will get individual discussions on specific matters" (Interview HMIP PPD).

Without going into the topic of professions itself, it should be noted that, especially on the level of implementation, a mutual understanding of practicality is made possible by common education and mutually shared professional experiences. The ability to cooperate on the basis of a common understanding, which is understood as professionalism by the actors and which is expressed in the term "professional relationship" in interviews and documents, straddles customary ways of behavior and the common value system based on education and professional experience. The recruiting practice of the regulatory body, which requires various years of experience in industry of every inspector, falls into place here as the fitting together of the patterns of interaction and professional ethics. It's no accident that in the context of an IPC field study conducted by the Environmental Data Service, the concrete willingness of the inspectors to help on-site was rated higher by industry than the advice given through Guidance Notes. Since the recruiting practice makes a standard conception of practicality possible in the permit-granting procedures, it becomes practical itself and makes up the specific practical component of the political process (i.e., it consolidates its own determination of rationality).

Reconciliation through Compromise: Restrictions on Access and Pressure to Conform

We seem to have finally come to the core of the "typically British" regulatory style and to see the evidently most important pair of concepts, consensus and compromise. It must be emphasized here, though, that environmental legislation and its implementation in Great Britain are in no way casual, communicative events. The more concretely that an issue is treated in a vestibule, the more closely that the opinions of the participants have to stick to the rules of reaching a compromise. The more that a vestibule is involved in the preparation of actual decisions, the more that the rules serve as a selection criterion determining those authorized to exert influence. Informal barriers to access, which produce pressure to conform by the selective recruitment of persons and ideas and which should assure the functioning of the mechanism, can be illustrated through the example of interest groups—especially those in the environmental movement. Mainly, the interest groups have to fight against the procrustean bed of game rules. Even at the end of the 1970s no alternative to conformity to the code of behavior existed. In 1977, in the *Conservation News*, R. D. Harrison emphasized that the Conservation Society has to adopt a conforming strategy: "The Society must not be, or seem to be, merely a vehicle for anti-establishment agitation. The Society must beware of even appearing to be associated with those who are simply agitators or protesters. A reputation for obstructionism will inevitably prevent the Society's case from being heard" (Rothgang 1990: 90). This strategic recommendation was made at a time when new types of environmental protection groups, like Greenpeace, were arising. These new groups were not interested in being recognized as a partner of the government and focused on campaigns to evoke public reaction. Since then the situation has changed: With increasing success, the pressure from within as well as from the outside has grown to influence the political process not only on the level of problem awareness and definition but also in program formulation. A dilemma then arose: internal cohesion, the political ability to form alliances, credibility, and the ability to act became conflicting goals.

Indeed, with its own limited responsiveness Greenpeace tries to oppose the equally limited willingness of the government to consult. Greenpeace does this in order to avert the danger of being abused as the creator of legitimation. "We've said that we think that it (Round Table on Sustainable Development and Agenda 21) will just be a talking shop with a lot of us there, unless they are given a specific remit, and specific powers to take decisions on things that will have an environmental impact or affect the environment" (Interview Greenpeace). However, in order to not be pushed aside as a complete dissident, participation is not turned down under the condition of "guaranteed authority." But "guaranteed authority" to any member of the forums would degrade "accommodation" from being mutually passed on reciprocity to a mere act of mercy. The demand for "specific powers to take decisions" is completely contrary to the character of the British principle of consultation. While the demand for preferential treatment of one's own organization is presented as a condition for consultation that is to be considered legitimate, it is (intentionally?) not noticed that the realization of the demand would, in effect, abolish the principle of consultation. In this case, rejection of the rule restricts access not necessarily the position itself. The vestibules themselves, even if they are dominated by sympathizing actors, refuse to give opportunities to participate under such circumstances.

The inherent constraints of the logic of compromising and the unavoidable unity of the pressure of accommodation and the restriction to access will become even more seizable if we take a closer look at the rule of reliability: the requirement of reliability confronts interest groups, which claim to play a role as a driving power (i.e., primarily environmental protection groups), with substantial problems. As soon as their demands or some of the demands are under consideration and eventually integrated into the individual vestibules, the interest groups have actually fulfilled the function that they intended to take up, namely, the promotion of their ideas. In the context of the existing forums, other actors take up these ideas (in a modified form) as their own. Reliability in the sense of a gradual development and generalization of a political position within a group of actors threatens, though, the profile of such interest groups and their ability to be distinguished from each other, as well as their self-perception and their own legitimacy as actors who give the process dynamism. This has a direct effect on their ability to form coalitions. One of the interviewed experts worked as a campaigner for Friends of the Earth (FoE) before he switched to an automobilist's association. Therefore he could describe both sides: "Their [FoE's] role is to move the agenda forward. They will never agree with us [the automobile association] publicly because if they do that they seem to be agreeing with the establishment, which will undermine their ability to get members. Even though a lot of what we say is actually the same, they would never admit it. . . . Once we achieved one thing it's their job to move on to the next debate."

Special campaign-oriented groups like Greenpeace equate constancy mostly with stagnation and hardly care about the slow routines of everyday life in which long-term, concrete political development requires a relative tenacity. Due to the special significance of reliability in GB, activist and eye-catching strategies for problem definition mainly run the danger that their protagonists will lose a share of the forums as well as the support of the members and sympathizing actors. The latter then see themselves confronted with new demands while they are still pushing ahead the newly negotiated offers for compromise in the direction of the political center at the beginning of program planning through the vestibules. For example, the previously-mentioned automobile association might be considered not very progressive by the environmental protection groups. In contrast with environmental protection groups, the automobile association has access to the forums of program planning for the issue "traffic." The positions of this particular association, which are again weakened propositions of the environmental groups, are considered debatable, radical points of view at the political center:

We do have problems when we say things that are right in our view and are what they [environmental protection groups] have been saying with us, and they say suddenly: "No, no, that's not right." And there will come a stage when some of the more reactionary members of the road lobby will say: "Enough is enough. We've been trying to do all this and the environmentalists have been telling us we've got it wrong. We are never doing what they wanted us to. If they are going to keep moving the goal post, we are not playing anymore." And I think that will happen, there will be a backlash. (Interview with a representative of an automobile association)

From the viewpoint of the automobile traffic lobby, the offered "accommodation" in the form of a small concession is not picked up by the environmental protection groups in the interest of their own development in this case and is made into a starting point for further rounds of negotiation. As the environmental groups take away negotiable matters and constant points of reference from their opponents, they take the wind out of the rules of reaching a compromise and creating trust—reliability and accommodation. However, representatives of the groups recognize and admit that turning down participation in the negotiations is often difficult to justify to members and supporters. As long as the forums for consultation continue to be accepted—and in the perception of the public, there is always an appropriate sphere available within which the involvement in a public search for collective values is worthwhile—the rejection of the participation in this search seems to be, at best, a lost opportunity to the sympathetic observer and, at worst, a social defeatism. Thus, the government can try to force the framework of reaching a compromise on interest groups just by the setting up of forums for consultation. The pressure to adapt and to conform derives from the clientele of the interest groups, which expects the opportunities for talks to be taken.

Especially the last example should have clarified the ambivalent effect of the rules of compromising: On the one hand, the rules close the scope of action, as they do not permit any fundamental negotiation of the politics of the policy process or arguments over principles. "Bedrock values," closed worldviews, and all-embracing structures for ideas can be neither the issue nor the basis for reaching a compromise. Instead, individual problems broken down by discussion are negotiated, a process that often produces partial solutions with a limited range. Forcing one's way into broad and powerful constellations of actors, which have joined forces under a standard model or a grand strategy, is practically out of the question. On the other hand, the principle of willingness of the actors to enter into an exchange relationship with each other allows for a broad mutual acceptance and a structural, all-around ability to form coalitions as soon as it is important to reach a pragmatic solution. This is due, in part, to the fact that even if the actors' exchange does not result in an agreement, at least the respective interests and patterns of reasoning are presented. Reaching a compromise around practicality requires flexible formations of alliances with regard to the issues and opens up the scope of action in this way.

THE ROLE OF THE PROFESSIONS: EXPERIENCE AS A BASIS FOR POLITICAL ACTION

Personal Experience as a Reputation and Its Establishment in the Policy Process

If one recalls that many of the formalized ways used in other Western democracies to introduce and pass on particular interests and competing concepts are not available in Great Britain, it becomes clear that the acting individual gains significance as an actor. This does in no way mean that in GB individual people have a greater scope of action available than in comparable countries. Yet, the hierarchies of compromising need personalities to support their stability. These personalities have to have internalized the customary procedural forms and the unwritten political rules and be able to pass this on to the outside. This is especially true for forums that are hardly or not at all able to be supported by formal authorities and are dependent on other forums for the continued conveyance of their programs. Let me illustrate this by means of an example. The first criterion of the House of Commons Environment Committee in the selection of topics is the ability of a problem to stand a discussion and the possibilities to be expected to come to a unanimous result through a pragmatically oriented discussion. The selection of invited participants among the members of the parliamentary committee is decided by including the widest possible spectrum of viewpoints. In the determination of the representative of a viewpoint, technical qualifications are not the only crucial factor. Attention is also given to the fact that the representatives of viewpoints take on more than just one function. A representative of an association who is exclusively a public relations specialist or a scientist who has no interests outside his or her subject lags behind his or her colleagues who, for example, have represented various associations or, in the scientific area, are members of conservation and environmental protection groups.

A polyvalent qualification through participation in various sectors of the political, scientific, economic, and public life is, therefore, not least of all important because hearings and studies are not merely lectures and question-and-answer sessions. The lecturers are also able to enter into the discussion. The introduction of evidence is carried out by continually placing each fact presented into a context during the process of comparing and weighing the pros and cons; that is, it is immediately integrated into the total context of a policy process. This means that the amount of interests and the specific perception of facts of an area of regulation, expressed in their contributions to the process, have to take the equivalent definition of reality and interests of other areas of regulation usually concretely and, in oral procedures, usually immediately. To reach a mutual understanding and, not least of all, the success or the persuasiveness of a contribution, it is important to be able to play the song on many different instruments and in many different keys. Here the cultural principle of "common sense" and the rule of reciprocal implementation come to light directly in the form of people and their biographies. "Common sense" needs to be established in a manifest way in "heart and mind" alongside personal and professional experience as general foundations, which is able to be obtained only through concrete action and experience. Considerably more than other cultural patterns, common sense is attached to real contours and the life world backgrounds of characters. Common sense originates from them and, at the same time, is directly oriented to them. Every member is usually the product of a combination of several different organizational memberships, offices, and careers, which in the end form a conglomeration of experience. It is of no consequence whether it is a matter of a standing body of national significance like the RCEP or whether it concerns local commissions convened once only such as the Kent Transport Forum.

Empirical Examination and Experience as a Mode of Operation and the Spirit of the Law

The mixture of knowledge gained through experience and pragmatism, which is often summarized under the term "common sense," has its own tradition and validity within the necessities of the political system. The BPEO, like the previous BPM, claims knowledge gained through experience as a prerequisite, and the dialogue between the inspectors and the operators has this practical experience precisely as its goal. "So, it's a fairly pragmatic process with a lot of debate going on between the operators and the enforcement agency" (interview with the environmental manager of a chemical company). The closer the dialogue is to concrete cases, the more fruitful the process appears to the participants and the more it is perceived as a learning process instead of an authorization, that is, permit-granting procedure: "HMIP and inspectors are learning at the same time" (Keith Giles, Zeneca, quote taken from ENDS and Allot 1994: 145). In the area of committees and commissions, excursions work in the same way as the element of professional experience and education. Visits of the House of Commons' (HoC) Environment Committee to Sweden and Norway in 1984, which provided the opportunity to observe damage resulting from acidity in the lakes there and the accompanying discussion with Scandinavian scientists, are essentially responsible for a complete change in opinion, according to the concurrent opinion of the participants (compare with Boehmer-Christiansen and Skea 1991: 212). The RCEP took no less than eight excursions to foreign countries for its report *Transport and the Environment* in 1993/1994. These excursions included visits to model transportation systems (among others, the Tokyo subway system) as well as areas with chronic problems (Los Angeles). Since 1977, the Industry and Parliament Trust has run a fellowship programme for members of Parliament to take 12–18-month study courses. They include various several-day stays of the MPs in industry (Judge 1992: 57).[5]

Thus, we can see that the foundation of common sense in combination with (1) personal qualifications and diverse (self-) education and training as well as professional experience and (2) the hierarchic, institutional components that make a gradual synthesis of positions and their representatives possible arises and develops to fulfill in the end the vital conditions for the functioning of the policy process, that is, the recognized values of accommodation, appropriateness, reliability, and, finally, confidence.

THE CULTURE OF CLEAN AIR POLITICS

The particular nature of the British political system is traditionally characterized by the relationship between particular societal groups and a central concentration of political power. In contrast to almost all other states in the world, values and practices of the political system have developed without massive, violent upheavals since the seventieth century. As a symbol of continuity and a symbolic, fixed point of governmental sovereignty, the Crown remains both the formal source of executive authority and its guardian. The principle of trust is found in its most general form in relation to the Crown: the government and its staff, the Department of the Environment, Transport and the Regions (DETR), and the inspectorate are in a contractual relationship with the Crown—they are "Her Majesty's." Therefore, at least in nonmaterial terms, the government doesn't pursue its own interests but acts as an advocate of the monarch. The significance of such a personalization of the idea of state is perhaps best understood by a quick look at the United States. There, the principles of political power in their formulation in the amendments to the Constitution and the system of checks and balances represent the decisive counter-balance to an otherwise free unfolding of power of the election winners; the government and its staff are one part of the system of checks and balances. The constitutional guarantees by themselves mark off the area of the common good that is legally recoverable provided that one can apply this term to a basic right at all. By contrast, in GB the national community, state, and society form a unity. As a cultural sediment, there is an image of the subjects, whose well-being has to be looked after ("Nanny knows best"). In this way—and mostly implicitly—the legitimate reference to the common good as a standard of political power (beyond purely propagandist ends) is, in principle, made possible.

The difference between the U.K. and the other countries examined in this book is even more obvious if one recalls that GB does not have an elaborate, written constitution and that the government's power is practically not subject to any restrictions. If one measured the maturity of a parliamentary democracy alone on the degree of differentiation of its formally established system of checks and balances, one would have to state that many of the components of a complete liberal democracy are underdeveloped in GB. The fact that this unique concentration of power is unconditionally accepted is explainable only if the interests of those in authority—theoretically having nothing in their way—do actually restrain themselves. Otherwise, they would endanger the acceptance of, and the trust in, the political system. The value of the common good, and, with it, the willingness of every government to subjugate itself to it, represent an indispensable metaorientation without which the cohesion of the political system would be severely threatened. Here is the gateway to understanding the political system in GB: since no formally established fences in the form of a catalog of rights restrict the power of the government, both a procedure acting as a framework and prescribed values are needed that effectively regulate the use of political power. The common good, as, first of all, a largely undefined quantity, can genuinely promote integration in regulation only if it does not act as the legitimating idea for particular interests but is actually taken up and transformed into an identifiable point of reference for different interests.

Essential and primary elements of the political culture in GB, the pragmatic compromising, and the negotiated production of a consensus are consequently presented as the foundations of the legitimation of the political system.

The slow, but continual, process of democratization and both the broadening of participation and the growth in negotiable items have not allowed a virulent dichotomy between the state and the civil society to arise. While, on the one hand, the impression of the abuse of power could mostly be successfully avoided and, on the other, the demands for participation are not expressed in a frontal collision, the balance between trust and confidentiality was maintained, a relationship that can be characterized as symbiotic.

POLITICAL REGULATION: CHANGE AND STABILITY

During the 1980s, the British consensus experienced a series of changes. For the first time since World War II, a governmental administration massively intervened in societal and political structures without first providing a complete, societal safeguard. In some political areas—namely, industrial and social policy—only the end of the British tripartite system can be noticed. The important element—newly put to use or, better yet, for the first time displayed without reservation—in the repertoire of political regulation is the open use of political power as a coercive method and as the only method. That means that the power potential of the central government situated in the political system was rigorously activated, while additional political measures through the support of societal groups shrank to a minimum. Voluntary self-restrictions and accommodation—principles that up until then even the British prime minister felt subject to—were no longer valid as rules for the government. Although since the replacement of Margaret Thatcher by John Major in 1990 a gradual turning away from the methods of fierce confrontation could be observed, the element of "use of coercion" has firmly established itself in the repertoire of regulating instruments. To avoid misunderstandings, coercion was also known before the Thatcher administration. Its seldom use was generally based, though, on a broad societal understanding or was legitimated at least by such an understanding, which means that at least that much societal support had to be mobilized and that much resistance had to be absorbed as these were necessary to maintain the impression of a comprehensive consideration of interests. "Government-group bargaining appears to re-assert itself at some stage in the process. Thus, in policy areas where groups have been challenged directly by the government, those very same groups have been consulted and bargained with over the practicalities of policy implementation. Providing the main policy thrust remains intact, the government has been prepared to accommodate group pressures" (Richardson 1990: 26).

Coercion is oriented mainly toward continuously marginal deviants and in this way helps to seal smaller leaks in the consensual structure. The crucial difference of the Tory politics of the 1980s was that coercion was now deliberately put to use without exogenous reasons as an offensive power. While until the middle of the 1980s the predominant understanding of governing among the political elite regarded political power as a complement of organized group interests whose concurrence was considered to be a stabilizing condition and an important opportunity to maintain power equally, the "New Right" implemented a new strategic orientation. Moreover, it considered political power as an independent, by and large separate resource that could be arbitrarily used for the dismantling of selected organizations and interests. The prime minister emphasized regularly: "For me, consensus seems to be the process of abandoning all beliefs, principles, values and policies" (Thatcher 1981, taken from Kavanagh 1987: 7). The opportunity to maintain power was deliberately sought after in confrontation and in the selective granting of privileges to individual classes of voters. The repeated change of constituent boundaries gives a good example of the open willingness to exhaust all of the opportunities possible to regain a parliamentary majority without having to win much more than 40% of the vote.

On the other hand, a dirigiste style outside the symbolic places of struggle cannot be so clearly implemented. In environmental politics there is no clear preference for a specific political style: the Tories' traditional opponents, the trade unions, harmonize with their classic allies, the industry, and their arguments of competitiveness and job opportunities complement each other. Due to its wide-ranging nature, the problem of pollution also touches on such topics, which the conservatives preferentially cultivate out of ideological reasons, such as consumer interests and consumer awareness. "The British landscape," a furtherance of national identity, constitutes, as one of the few mechanisms left for integration, an important component of the conservative commitment to values. Landscape conservation issues link up the part of the environmental protection movement that criticizes the system with the part that holds conservative values. In the prospering regions of southern England, where the stronghold of the Tories is found, the well-off middle class promoted a restriction on the increasing automobile traffic, which they regarded as a nuisance. Alternatives to individual motorized transport, however, shrank drastically due to the government's pushing ahead the privatization of public transport. All in all, a complex picture showed and shows that a classification of interests according to the, up until then, dominating standard was no longer possible. A simple classification of good and evil as well as the corresponding polarization through labeling, which represented a practical as well as legitimating condition of the aggressive political style of Thatcherism, could no longer be carried out. Since the actors are not so easily classified in the simplified worldview of "shared convictions as to what is right and wrong" (Thatcher), the purposefulness of coercive measures and their general use is made difficult.[6] In this respect, the political field "environment," when compared to the politics toward the trade unions, is lacking in ideology and represents more the normal case of political regulation. This provides a good opportunity to observe the range of the new regulating element, coercion, and its adaptation to the existing rules and structures without having to take ideological distortions into consideration.

The corresponding element in the area of clean air was the so-called "arm's-length approach." When the introduction of the new IPC regime began in 1990, the reorganization of the Inspectorate in 1987 had led neither to the hoped-for increase in efficiency nor to a stringent practice of permit granting and monitoring. "What we are witnessing in the case of pollution control is a process by which a newly structured organization seeks to adapt the standard operating procedures it has inherited in a manner that retains the core elements of its inheritance and traditional client allegiances" (O'Riordan and Weale 1989: 280). In light of the organizational difficulties in the changeover and especially due to the scarcity of staff, keeping the old rules was seen, first of all, as completely reasonable by the Inspectorate and as having no alternative. Then the Inspectorate found itself at the lowest point ever in its 100-year history in relation to work performance as well as in the public perception. This situation threatened to compromise the whole IPC project. In addition, it was to be expected that a lax permit-granting practice due to the newly set up public register would quickly become the target of campaigns by environmental protection organizations. In 1990 Frank Feates, the chief inspector at that time, announced the new line: preapplication meetings had to be abandoned since they opposed the principle of operator responsibility established by the EPA in 1990. "It's also very difficult for us to properly document telephone calls, when strictly speaking these should be entered on the public register. Neither am I in favor of informal meetings that are then quoted back at me" (Frank Feates, taken from ENDS and Allot 1994: 16). This new line ended the meetings that had been most important for the creation of predictability, internal transparency, and the coordination of expectations. This approach clearly signaled the end of the old regime. Coercion and monitoring on the level of implementation as well as less cooperative rule making in program planning should from then on clearly demarcate the boundary between political and economic areas.

After only a few months the first criticism came from industry: the businesses did not know which information to give in the new applications for the authorization of a permit and would have to spend more time on it than they had before. In April 1991 as the first batch of applications for the processes, now regulated according to the principle of the IPC, arrived, the strictly formalized development of the permit-granting procedure soon proved to be simply impossible. Industry turned out to be partly unable and partly unwilling to carry out the required analysis of the flow of emissions and to associate it with a selection of technical options. Imprecise generalities and nonexisting, specific instructions for the generation of a BPEO intensified uncertainty and protests from industry. The HMIP and especially the inspectors, who were responsible for local regulation, had their hands tied. They could only turn down incomplete applications, and it took a lot of effort to find out in detail which plan the businesses pursued in the regulated processes so that the inspectors could finally let the businesses know which information was still needed. The time that passed between applying for, and receiving, a permit was considerably longer than the goal of four months. The animosities between the field inspectors and the political administration of the HMIP as well as those between the HMIP and industry threatened to block the whole regulation business. In the IPC study of ENDS, Jeff Hulse from BASF described the situation at that time as one in which he was very concerned about "the emerging relationships between the bureaucrats in the DETR and a now notorious group known as the Regulatory Standards Division in some dark corner of HMIP head office and the inspectors in the field, whom we had to deal with on a day-to-day basis" (ENDS and Allot 1994: 145). Since 1992, a return to the old orientation began to impose itself that, first of all, had to do with the removal of the time delay, which arose due to the formalized treatment of mutual ignorance and uncertainty: "It isn't an arm's-length relationship saying: 'It's unacceptable.' It will be advice-giving on what is necessary to allow us to assess it properly" (Interview HMIP PPD: 9). During 1992 the original conception of "arm's-length" failed altogether, and in May 1993 it was officially buried: "In order to save time and effort for ourselves and the operators we had to have these discussions before they made the application, so that we didn't waste all the administrative and professional time when going around it more than once. Of course it became clear that that ["arm's-length"] wasn't a sensual new system. And I think, at the end of the day the common sense prevailed. . . . We went back to the professional system" (Interview HMIP RSD: 5). According to the opinion of the industry, the element "coercion" is now serving primarily symbolic purposes. Coercion characterizes, first of all, the relationship between HMIP and the operators. An interviewed environmental manager of a chemical company said: "I don't think it was ever really going to work efficiently as a totally arm's-length target. But the sentiment must be that the enforcement agency has to be seen completely independent and credible, and that is important. . . . Arm's-length is important to us that the public see the Inspectorate as a credible body and not as toothless. So, it's important that we're seen to have credibility and independence, and yet we need to have a working relationship with them."

Although the boundaries of the exercise of power, which are primarily defined by the government in Great Britain, should be determined for the time being, one cannot assume nor observe that the instrument of coercion will remain on the back shelf. Pandora's box has been open for a long time. The synthesis of the Victorian value system and Keynes' padding is outdated as a stabilizing paradigm of British politics. Even Tony Blair's ruling New Labour Party gave up long ago the hope of being able to revive what's left of it. Therefore, the acting groups and organizations of the policy network as well as the sociologists who observe it must no longer, now and in the future, consider only the latent possibility of an independent initiative of a government that solely depends on political power but should also consider the latent existing real willingness of the government to include this power in its plans and to use it. The "shadow of power" (Scharpf 1993d) in which negotiations take place has grown longer and darker. Nevertheless, it would be exaggerated to proffer a dirigiste paradigm as the new guideline of political regulation in Great Britain. The great struggles of Thatcherism, which have been able to be generalized all too easily as the symbolic turning point, indeed plowed up the battle fields, but were not able to level off everything (Weale 1996; Mitchel 1990).

The synthesis of the English system of power administration showed itself as continuously stable with the rational concept of common sense. The two elements make a condition for each other: the searched-for point of reference, a decision that is seen as a uniting bond of a general nature, obstructs the dividing up of responsibilities and an appropriation of the setting of standards by exclusively technical authorities. Agreement about a permit, but also a political compromise, cannot be found in the context of a debate about basic principles. A generally accepted solution has to deal with abstract norms guided by ideas mostly as mere orientation points, which in the end only palely color the explicit compromises that are anchored in the material reality with the help of that momentum that carries out the merging of state and society. The requirement to negotiate where political power is used, where boundaries do not exist or are extremely blurry, prohibits the fixation on a "true" solution from the start.[7] When possible, a too-detailed establishment is avoided in the discussion of general questions, and the issues become the subject of specialized forums that are mostly removed from principles. The proclamation of a general will, the *volonté générale*, is rarely more than just the indispensable theatrical thunder of the political stage. Behind the scenes, though, there is a rehearsed search for the general will, for a basis that brings the least amount of impositions possible for the greatest number of participants. In spite of Thatcher's attempt to "Rambo-ize" politics, the significance of political power as a regulating resource in Great Britain is more restricted than in other countries. Particularly there, in spite of the hypothetical abundance of power available for use, the persons in command of the power centers of the governmental administration cannot arbitrarily, as an independent entity, use this power to put through a vision according to one's own "objective criteria." Such a strategy has to fail in the long run in a political system that depends on fine-tuning, adaptation, and consensual platforms for the use and reproduction of political power and communal obedience. This latent pattern of politics in Britain has neither completely dissolved in the Thatcher and Major eras, nor will it dissolve in the era of Tony Blair's New Labor.

NOTES

1. The DETR was created in 1970 from a merger of the Ministry for Housing and Local Affairs, the Ministry of Transport, and the Ministry for Public Buildings and Businesses. The responsibilities encompass almost as much as the English term "environment." As a "super ministry" responsible for all areas of national, regional, and local development and for the administration of planning laws and building regulations from structural planning to conservation as well as for housing construction and real estate property, the DETR is in no way comparable to the Ministry of the Environment of continental Europe.

2. The clearest example of a gradual takeover can be seen in the case of the DoH: the publication of the Policy Planning Guidance Note 13 (PPG 13) has to be evaluated as an attempt to weaken the planning authority of the DoH for road construction and represents the first political instrument that takes on as a political goal the overlapping of urban deve-

lopment planning and traffic flow as its main purpose as well as the reduction of automobi-le traffic.

3. Of course, the RCEP was helped by the pressure of public opinion with the publica-tion of the BPEO report. The government showed acknowledgment only later, after the report had been ignored for years.

4. Customarily, it is considered to be sufficient to warn a facility that it has not fol-lowed its authorization by means of an infraction letter which refers to BATNEEC. If that is not successful, formal conditions in the form of an improvement notice or even an en-forcement notice are imposed. The polluter has to pay a fine, if these are disregarded. The fines are so low, though, that one can consider them to be only symbolic punishments. However, this has almost never happened in the last decades.

5. The orientation to common sense and its counterpart, the ability to be empirically experienced, are found everywhere and determine in a stubborn way the relevance of is-sues in the public debate and in the public evaluation of regulation. The nuisance regula-tions in communal environmental law have a high public standing, and environmental damage in the form of a concrete nuisance represents an important, if not the dominating, way of discussing the problem of pollution. Routine and local pollution is in no way less of a priority than "invisible" pollution, which is long-term and has indirect effects, or than complex chains of reaction and exponentially developing environmental risks. Former problems can be combined with latter problems, and their solution provides evidence of competence and credibility: "Rats in someone's beautiful house, squirming around do concentrate the mind, global warming doesn't concentrate the mind. . . . If you as an au-thority can't clear a dog mess and kill rats, how are you going to deal with climate change? You've got to share problems, and you've got to get confidence of people" (Interview Nicholas Wilson, Institution of Environmental Health Officers [IEHO]). Being personally and immediately affected by something as a kind of empirical experience also leads to health risks representing a central topic of political campaigns. The demand for the intro-duction of catalytic converters was essentially made in GB by actors united together in the alliance for action, CLEAR. The predominating argument of the national debate was the nuisance of lead to people. In Germany, on the contrary, the dying forests predominated the discussion; the harmful chemical that could be reduced with the help of the catalytic con-verters was nitric oxide.

6. For the conservatives, that kind of complexity was naturally confusing and concern-ing and ran profoundly against their nature. Two solutions, which represent both of the main currents of the conservatives, appear to be suitable: either the return to the "good old times" and the persistence of existing arrangements or the modernization of the "New Right." Increasing environmental problems, the strengthened pressure of the public from inside as well as by the EU from the outside, and the political pattern of radical changes of existing regulatory arrangements propagated now in GB make the second possibility seem to have no alternative. As already stated, rushed solutions, which had fabulously proved themselves in the struggle against the trade unions, are out of the question. The problem arose that the ideological determination of values of the conservative modernization did not really intend to take hold of: (1) industry stands opposed to the majority of market-economy instruments of regulation (accusation of the simplification: ICI), (2) as a problem of collective goods, environmental protection extracts itself from the idea of market regula-tion through competition (externalization), (3) the required changes, which are necessary for a quantitative reduction of harmful substances, have to be reached through qualitative steps (technological improvements, change in consumer behavior, etc.) that are not eco-nomically programmable, and their implementation is hindered, rather than promoted, by the principle of competition (social state economy), (4) the time-frame that is valid for the

production of environmental risks, for the time when the effects of these risks take place and for their individual predictability, is completely different from the one that is effective in the production of goods and in the shaping of prices through markets, and (5) more than in the economy, the societal allotment of value plays a role—after all, the environment is a collective good. In addition, there is incomplete knowledge about the precise effects of the harmful substances and their cumulative effects.

7. Anyway, this exists only as a social structure of closed contexts of actors, which have an agreed-upon semantic that has been developed over the long term and is much too full of requirements to make broadly based platforms of compromises possible.

Chapter 4

France: Rule by Virtue of Elite Position

Cornelia Borgards

INTRODUCTION

In the course of the trend toward internationalization and the supragovernmental formation of politics, the examination of national patterns of politics again takes on increasing importance. The knowledge of the distinctive features of a nation's political style can lead to understanding strategies, political behavior on international political stages, or blockades specific to a country in their own peculiarity, and, should it be necessary, it helps to identify possibilities for a change in style.

The term "national political style" is understood here as an umbrella term for the interplay of a series of political, legal, and administrative institutions whose contents depends on the democratic structures of a country. The political system, various structures of access to the political stage, and various forms of participation and strategies of the various societal powers, as well as the production and use of scientific expertise, shape problem-solving strategies specific to a nation and impede efforts toward harmonization on a higher level. Thus, the significance of the public and the position of the citizens in the political process vary considerably in the countries under review.

Democracy as a governmental form and democracy as politics, as a principle of political decision making, are traditionally poles apart in France. The question of compatibility of these two sides is relevant, above all, for those actors who suffer from unequally distributed opportunities to realize their interests in the context of a substantial understanding of democracy. Thus, France serves as an especially good example of the exercise of power that, on the one hand, is *etatistic*, that is, centered on the government, and, on the other hand, is technocratic and in which the functional-technical rationalism of the societal philosophy of problem solving finds expression: "In no other country has a similarly great enthusiasm for the technical implementation of science for the formation of society been developed" (Münch 1993a: 554). This becomes apparent mainly in environmental politics, the political regulation of which is completely in the hands of a technical elite that has been educated by the state for these tasks. A technocratic formation of politics usually implies a certain arrogance toward the, for the most part, poorly organized civil society (cf. van Waarden 1993), an argument that is especially supported by Michel Crozier. For Crozier (1970), the specifically French combination of anarchistic individualism in the powers that are critical of society with the centralism of bureaucracy inevitably leads to a *société bloquée* (blocked society), where change can be experienced only as the result of fundamental crises. Therefore, the chance to be able to pursue effective bargaining lies in a stronger organization of simultaneously de-ideologized societal groups.

Following Crozier, Wilsford's (1988) concept of state-dominated pluralism takes on a somewhat altered perspective. Wilsford also assumes that the strength of the state in France simultaneously involves some kind of weakness. One of the tactical advantages of the centralist French state results in having a relatively arbitrary opening and closing of the policy arena to determine the structure of access to the political stage for certain interest groups.

Wilson used a similar argument, "In France the government clearly controls the use of corporatist forms. It has formed statutory bodies to promote 'concertation' among groups and government representatives, but it has refused to give these bodies decision making or other powers" (Wilson 1983: 909). This does not hinder actors to be powerful, but they have to assert their power in informal ways. According to Wilsford, the strength of the state is threatened to change into vulnerability if it forces the groups that are not accepted out of the official political sphere and, thus, to act without supervision. The dilemma from this perspective is not that there are too few organized interests but rather that these interests are either absorbed by the system or pushed into the periphery. Through the politically undesirable increase in the power potential of certain societal groups, according to the model, more flexibility can, in turn, flow into the political process. Just as in Crozier's argument, societal change according to this approach also begins as a by-product of political actions.

The position is not undisputed. The discussion about pluralism in regard to France has been extremely controversial up to the present. Supporters of the pluralism model, who theoretically follow the thesis of the strong state as well as the historical tradition of France, namely, that governments do not pursue any particular politics of special interests but instead recognize *the volonté générale* and attempt to implement it, confront a series of authors who support rather corporatist models of politics (Suleiman 1987). Whereas in the pluralistic model, access to the political stage depends on the resources of the respective interest groups, and these resources, in turn, determine the kind of influence that can finally be asserted on specific policies, corporatist decision making structures have the distinguishing feature that, next to the state, societal actors organized into associations with divergent interests are also involved in the policy process on the instructions of the state. According to the model, all interests should, in principle, be represented in this way. These relatively ordered and stable interconnections between the state and associations help to relieve the state of some of its work.

The specific kind of relationship between the state and society also forms the background of this chapter, in which the political regulation of the emissions from stationary sources is chosen as a representative topic. The question is how society (i.e., on the one hand, the interests of industry and, on the other hand, the interests of the environmental protectionists) is involved in the process of political planning. It should be more precisely determined if and in which way culturally distinctive features are recognized in the development of political institutions and, finally, how these features would be taken into account in a model of national policy style.

The constellation of actors within the field of clean air politics, the institutional rules of the political decision making process, the role of the professions, and finally the cultural background involved in the political process are examined as explanatory variables of the political system.

I start with a short description of the current situation of the political arena of clean air protection in France.

INSTRUMENTS OF REGULATION

The totality of the data on which this study is based can roughly be summarized in relation to the current problems in the area of French clean air protection as follows. At the present, environmental politics holds a minimal status in comparison to other societal and sociopolitical matters (unemployment and housing shortage).[1] Within national environmental politics, the main focus is on garbage and clean water politics, which predominate over the area of clean air politics. In the context of clean air politics itself, a trend away from the topic of the emissions from stationary sources toward the topic of mobile sources can be observed in regard to the perception of the problem.

The regulation of emissions from stationary sources was mainly discussed in France in the 1970s and the beginning of the 1980s. During this time period, the important clean air protection laws were passed. Since then routine has come to this political area. The emissions of the harmful chemical substance sulfur dioxide (SO_2), mainly caused by domestic fuel and industrial processes, decreased by 70% between 1980 and 1993, whereas the emissions of nitrogen oxide caused mainly by traffic decreased by only 20% over the same period. The levels have even increased in the area of mobile sources, if they are examined in isolation. The same is true for the emission of dust, which has also decreased in all areas with the exception of traffic. This development, which can also be seen in the other countries reviewed in this study, has political roots in the areas of traffic and energy in France. Because France fosters the use of diesel-powered vehicles through a lesser taxation of diesel fuel, their share in the total number of vehicles has steadily increased since the early 1980s. In 1994 these vehicles made up 47.6%, almost half, of all vehicles sold for private use. In comparison, the European average is 19.8%.

On the other hand, France has worked consistently on a transition of the energy sector from petroleum to nuclear energy since the first oil crisis in 1974 and the price increases that accompanied it (cf. Héritier, Mingers, Knill, and Becka 1994: 121f.). Thus, before 1974 two-thirds of the entire energy needs were covered by the importation of petroleum. In 1994 three-fourths of the electricity pro-

duced in France had nuclear origins (cf. CITEPA 1994: 113). This shift is especially reflected in the area of domestic fuel: Between 1960 and 1993 the use of
the main air polluter, coal, decreased in this sector from 59% to 1.5%; in the same
time period, the use of electric energy increased from 16% to 54%. Nuclear energy, therefore, has become one of the biggest and most controversial environmental problems in France. In the area of air pollution from stationary sources,
however, it has clearly contributed to relieving the problem.

The traffic problem as well as air pollution from stationary sources appear to
be limited to certain regions in France, according to the opinion of many actors.
On the one hand, a good geographic location is responsible: "France exports considerably more harmful substances than it imports from neighboring countries"
(Héritier, Mingers, Knill, and Becka 1994: 116). On the other hand, France demonstrates a strong tendency toward industrial centralization, which has a corresponding effect upon the structure of the residential areas (Héritier, Mingers,
Knill, and Becka 1994: 120f.).

The Parisian region, Ile de France, takes on a special position in every respect.
Ten million residents produce 25% of the total gross national product in service
industries, as well as in electronics, chemical, automobile, and aircraft construction industries. This causes considerable traffic problems: the greater Paris area
accounts for approximately 10% of the nationwide air pollution, according to the
estimates of the regional network responsible for such measurements, AIRPARIF.
This problematic syndrome can, in most cases, be carried over to the other
population centers.

Leaving aside these centers with heavy traffic and industry, the west and
southwest of France are agriculturally structured, above all, and so are relatively
spared air pollution. This led to a regional or local perception of the problem,
which hindered a strict national regulation and the development of a broad ecological awareness.

The regional way of looking at the problem was reflected in the concrete
measures of political regulation. A central feature of French clean air politics
related to stationary sources was the diversity of regulating instruments. Policy in
this area combined measures regarding facilities (procedures for granting a permit, procedures for declarations, and industrial contracts), measures regarding
products (e.g., sulfuric content in fuels), financial measures (tax-like fees, subsidies and credits, especially tax write-offs), and, finally, of an overriding significance, regional measures (protected and endangered areas). Within the facility-
related measures for ambient air quality protection, the principle of BATNEEC
(best available technique not entailing excessive costs) acquired great significance, so that the state of technology for the individual enterprises was always tied
to the aspect of economic viability. Diversity of guidelines that cannot, as in Germany, for example, be subsumed to one law was also typical for France.

In the 1990s, however, French clean air politics was set in motion more
strongly. In this context, we refer, for instance, to the law "Loi Barnier" of 2 February 1995, which established the precautionary principle, the polluter
pays'principle, and the participation principle as binding guidelines for clean air

politics. Above all, however, the general framework law "Loi sur l'Air" trod new paths in a dual respect. On the one hand, it is an attempt at giving higher priority to clean air politics and, at the same time, systematizing the various tools and measures more strongly that, so far, were at the roots of the more or less incremental growth of legislation.[2] On the other hand, the law originated from a large-scale concertation organized by the then-minister of the environment, Corinne Lepague. It not only accompanied the entire legislative process but stretched right through to the compiling of the decrees of application. In addition, we can recognize here an attempt at focusing both a systematic concept and cooperation and/or concertation as a reasonable entity.

NETWORKS OF ACTORS: STATE, ADMINISTRATION, AND PRIVILEGED SOCIETAL GROUPS

Type of State

The political system in France seems to be comparatively transparent due to its generally hierarchic structure. Nevertheless, experts argue over whether it is a semipresidential or a parliamentary system (Brickman et al. [1985]) speak of a presidential system). According to the constitution, it can clearly be classified as a parliamentary type; however, this constitution gives the president and his or her government overruling power and decision making rights, whereas the Parliament in comparison exercises a clearly subordinate influence on the activities of the government (cf. Kempf 1989).

Thus, the president, who is elected directly by the people for seven years with the possibility of reelection, presides over the Council of Ministers (Art. 9) and is in supreme command of the armed forces (Art. 15). He or she has the authority to hold a referendum (Art. 11), to disband the National Assembly (Art. 12), and to decide how to declare a state of emergency (Art. 16) as well as to appoint the prime minister (Art. 8), who as a rule appoints the cabinet–the individual ministers– in agreement with the president (cf. Duhamel 1993).

The prime minister and the government determine the political guidelines (Arts. 20, 21) and rank directly behind the president with regard to political power potential. This power is naturally much more comprehensive if the president and the head of state come from the same political camp, which has been the case as a rule, with the exception of two phases of cohabitation.

Parliament is made up of two houses: the National Assembly (Assemblée Nationale) and the Senate. The latter's most important task is to pass legislation, whose significance, however, is considerably limited in France due to the long way decrees have to pass through.

The course of a legislative bill formally runs through the following stages. First of all, appropriate projects are discussed in the respective ministries in order to reach a unified position within the ministry. An interministerial discussion ensues on the level of the administrations and offices. Afterward, all of the respective ministers are brought together under the chairmanship of the prime minister to reach an agreement. From here the bill goes to the respective Commission

Permanente of the Parliament, which is made up proportionally according to the political distribution of power. If no agreement has been reached, a commission composed of representatives of both houses is set up. If these negotiations are not successful, the National Assembly is asked by the government to decide on the matter. Laws and decrees are checked by the Conseil d'Etat (advisory council for legislation and administration) for their legal validity. With the signature of the prime minister and the other respective ministers, they become legally valid.

The entire legislative process (laws and decrees) is consequently established on the national level. The concrete implementation which follows is partly decided interministerially, that is, nationally (e.g., Arrêté Intégré) and sometimes in an inter-prefectorial way, that is, regionally (e.g., Arrêté d'Information et d'Alerte d'Ile de France). Procedures for the granting of a permit usually take place on the level of the départements.

Electoral System

With regard to the national representation of relatively young and less established interests such as the area of environmental politics, the electoral system plays a decisive role. The representatives in the National Assembly are directly elected according to the principle of absolute majority, which suggests a coalition of big political parties and makes the entry of smaller, perhaps ecologically oriented parties difficult. Thus, for the first time in its history, the Green Party (Les Verts) achieved concrete representation in the reelections of June 1997 with seven seats in the National Assembly and is now able to initiate environmental activities of a political nature on a central level. The members of the Senate are indirectly elected by the representatives of the National Assembly and by the representatives elected to the regional, general, and local councils in the départements. On the level of the regional councils, though, the system of proportional representation is used in elections. Consequently, at certain times and in ecologically polluted areas, the Green Party is able to enter into the local parliaments with several seats (cf. Große and Lüger 1993: 94; Martinot-Hoffman 1993: 15ff.).

Administration

On the administrative level, France is divided into 26 regions, 100 départements, and over 36,000 municipalities, of which 33,000 have fewer than 2,000 inhabitants. All in all, the French municipalities are only one-fifth the size of the European Union (EU) average (cf. Kukawka 1993: 22). "The ratio between the most densely settled (département Nord: 2,532,000 residents) and the least densely settled département (département Lozère: less than 73,000 residents) is 1:34.7" (Kistenmacher et al. 1994: 55).

Up until the beginning of the 1980s, state control reached through all political areas down to the local level by means of the prefects appointed by the central government. Only through the course of decentralization in 1982/1983 did the regions receive the status of autonomous political bodies like the long-established *départements* (Kukawka 1993). The rights and obligations handed over to the regional level by the state include, for example, the regional implementation of "planification," the promotion of regional economies, and professional education and further training. The *départements* are in charge of the general administrative budget as well as broad areas of the social and public health services.

The previous executive supervision by the state took the character of an "ex-post legality control." Supervision is now the responsibility of the presidents of the respective regional and *département* councils and the responsibility of the mayor in municipalities. Although the viewpoints concerning goals and uses of decentralization differ widely, the *départements*, which have been powerful, anyway so far, seem to have once again won with regard to financial expenditures as well as the transfer of additional authority. For the municipalities, which are closer to the citizens, the reform had negative, rather than positive, consequences, according to some authors: "Decentralization brought advantages for the elite of the intermediate levels such as the mayors of big cities. . . . The political and cultural basis of French centralism in contrast was left untouched and so was the position of the citizens in the decision making process as well" (Becquart-Leclercq 1989: 207).

Besides the opaqueness of the new system, the reform brought an abundance of laws and regulations with it as well as a growing bureaucracy of decision makers that intensified the traditionally rooted system of the accumulation of posts in France instead of reducing it. The dependence of the local authorities shifted from the arbitrary decisions of the state to decisions in favor of "important political notables" without losing stability in the process; altogether, a system in which its critics claim to have identified "tribal" structures (cf. Meny 1992: 19; Grémion and Muller 1990).

In the area of environmental politics, decentralization did not bring any changes with it that are worth mentioning. With the exception of the principle of regionally shared responsibility for environmental protection introduced in the law of 7 January 1983 regarding the new distribution of authority, all of the important possibilities for control remained on the side of the state (cf. Kistenmacher et al. 1994: 175).

The Policy Network

Clean air politics is based on a manageable and stable political network that has hardly changed over the years. Structures and constellations already described by Knoepfel and Weidner (1985) are still valid today. The state's clean air politics has the special feature that only a few, very generally worded laws are enacted, which are subsequently made more precise by a multitude of ministerial implementing orders (*décrets*) and ministerial or administrative decrees (*arrêtés*) (cf. Rest 1986). Responsibilities as well as procedural rules are established in these implementing orders. Beyond that, there are so-called *circulaires* in French law, which correspond to German administrative guidelines (cf. Rehbinder 1991: 129). It is noteworthy that none of the global laws prescribe national air quality norms. In France, emission norms are regularly found in the decrees of special, protected areas that are made at the request of the prefect or by an interministerial resolution. Therefore, standard setting procedures, which determine air quality standards, take place in France on a regional level. Every type of concretization, for example, the conditions for the commissioning of an industrial facility, is established on-site in the context of a permit-granting procedure. This strict political division of labor between national legislation and regional implementation is characteristic of French politics. That is why it seems to be a good idea to construct different networks with regard to the actors involved on both levels of political regulation.

The Actors' Network on the Level of Program Formulation

The area of program formulation is characteristically made up of a small circle of actors in the center of which a weak ministry of the environment is found.[3] Overall control is held by the Minister of the Environment and the cabinet, his or her closest technical advisers. On the administrative level, the ministry is currently divided into four central areas of management to which a series of departments and subdivisions is assigned: the Bureau de l'Atmosphère, de la Maîtrise de l'Energie et des Transports is a subdivision of the Service de l'Environnement Industriel, which belongs to the Direction de la Prévention des Pollutions et des Risques. A change in government, that is, the exchange of ministers, is the time when the employees of the different divisions try to exert influence on future politics (Interview Ministère de l'Environnement, Bureau de l'Atmosphère).

The characteristic French political style is again emphasized in the area of environmental politics. Environmental politics is an interministerial politics, and in the area of clean air, the Ministry of Industry plays a considerable role, and the Ministry of Health, a minor role. The influence of the Ministry of the Environment, therefore, seems to be very limited by the strong presence of the industry in the context of the political decision making process regarding the environment. This argument is confirmed in principle by all actors involved.

Close cooperation between the industry and the national administration for the environment developed only during the the last few years, according to a statement by the representative of the mineral oil company, TOTAL. This cooperation is due to the politics of individual personalities. In France, the industry is powerful enough to do without the public's inclusion when exerting its influence on political decisions. What is practiced is a so-called institutional promotion, which means that the politicians are influenced directly in the ministries and in Brussels (Interview TOTAL). This influence is guaranteed and channelled by large and powerful industrial associations, such as the Conseil National du Patronat Français (CNPF), the Union des Industries Chimiques (UIC), the Union Française des Industries Pétrolières (UFIP), and the Chamber of Industry and Commerce. They are involved in all of the clean air political committees, such as the Conseil Supérieur des Installations Classées (CSIC), which is involved in the introduction and revision of all legislation, decrees, and implementing orders in the area of clean air politics with regard to stationary sources.

The UIC played a decisive role in the working out of the *arrêté intégré* (a cross-sectoral, integrated ordinance). In France, this takes on the character of a directive, since it focuses the rules applicable, above all, to the chemical sector and updates. French industry exerted an enormous pressure to make the price–performance ratio be taken into consideration (Interview SHELL-CHIMIE). Moreover, it consolidates the orientation to individual cases as a central element of French clean air policy. As regards the development of the market for environmental technologies, France lags behind other comparable industrialized nations (cf. Héritier, Mingers, Knill, and Becka 1994: 127f.). "We do not necessarily want to use an avant-guard technology" (Interview SHELL-CHIMIE). If any classical technology allows for progress, it is used.

When negotiations fail, the Ministry of Industry is often brought in to put pressure on the Ministry of the Environment. The bigger the company, the closer its direct connection with the government and single ministries. Along with state concerns, such as Electricité de France (EDF), Gaz de France (GDF), and Charbonnage de France (CDF), which are present in negotiations, the big national and international companies directly take part in negotiating processes about regulating instruments. Smaller industrial companies, by contrast, are seen as "the real" troublemakers since they cannot afford any expensive environmental technologies, often do not have any lobby, and are poorly informed (Interview CITEPA).

The Ministry of the Environment cannot benefit from the political pressure of ecological parties or from an increased awareness of environmental problems from within the political party setup. Ecologically oriented parties have previously not participated in national politics due to the electoral system's preferential treatment of big parties. The dreadful financial state of the Green Parties is also a reason for this lack of participation since compensation to roughly cover one's costs is granted only to those having at least 5% of the votes (Interview Les Verts). Instead of a politically necessary consolidation, disagreements have led to only stronger differentiation within the Green Parties themselves. There are three Green Parties in France: Les Verts, Géneration Écologie, and Mouvement Écologiste Indépendant. There is no broad ecological alliance from which the Green Parties could benefit. Neither environmental associations nor leftist and ecologically oriented media support the Green Parties. There is rather no communication between ecological groups and parties. "For the political parties, the organizations do not exist, quite apart from the green parties. If something is undertaken, then it is in the field of a unification of the work of the associations in France" (Interview Bulle Bleue). Contacts with the ministerial level seem to be affected by the Green Parties' weak position, too: "There is no connection whatsoever with the centre of power. . . . The formulation of programs? No, that's a secret, nothing is known at all" (Interview Les Verts).

The Ministry of the Environment, on the other hand, states that "the eco movement suffers from the quarrels at its head, whilst we suffer from the weakness of the eco movement. The ecologists do not serve us, they don't make work easier for us" (Interview Minstère de l'Environnement, Bureau de l'Atmosphère). It has therefore hardly been possible in France so far to establish environmental themes not only as a strategic (election-related) element but as a stable element of the policies of the other parties.

Besides the industrial associations, environmental associations (e.g., Les Amis de la Terre, France Nature Environnement) that have been recognized through a process of "agreement" (evidence of at least three years of nonprofit activity) also form part of the commissions of the Ministry of the Environment, without, however, implementing their interests in fact. Although meetings and committees often bring about decisions that comprise the demands of environmental groups, in practice this is avoided by deviations (Interview Les Amis de la Terre). Smaller groups that are not acknowledged, such as Bulle Bleue, which is located in Paris, do not receive any financial means and are, therefore, isolated: "There are no contacts. We are practically cut off" (Bulle Bleue).

The scientific basis of environmental politics in France is guaranteed by in-house-expertise (cf. Brickman et al. 1985) through the addition of agencies. The Agence de l'Environnement et de la Maîtrise de l'Énergie (ADEME) emerged from the joining together of three smaller environmental protection agencies, among which is the Agence pour la Qualité de l'Air. ADEME is an organization incorporated under public law with a commercial nature whose task is to "prepare, support and extend legislative and regulatory measures for the authorities on a technical level" (Legrand et al. 1987: 60). ADEME has the responsibility of administering fees of an environmental and taxlike nature; it awards subsidies and credits and in this way is considerably involved in the development and testing of new techniques for the reduction of emissions as well as for the systems that monitor the air. Beyond that, it is active in the area of research and the promotion of information, which it either does itself or supports financially. In this way, ADEME is the supplier of scientific information as well as the enforcer of the policies of the Ministry of the Environment: "We are an arm of the Minister of the Environment," and according to the information that we received, it does not follow any independent political strategy (Interview ADEME). Its contacts are widespread and they include practically the whole range of actors in the area of clean air protection.

In France two large nonprofit organizations are exclusively active in the area of clean air protection: the Association pour la Prévention de la Pollution Atmosphérique (APPA), which has specialized its research in health aspects, and the Centre Interprofessionel Technique d'Etudes de la Pollution Atmosphérique (CITEPA), which is rather technically oriented and more or less corresponds to the German Verband Deutscher Ingenieure (Association of German Engineers). Its members are representatives of various industrial associations, energy producers as well as oil and mining companies. Neither APPA nor CITEPA is a standing member of the ministerial work group. They do not exert any direct pressure on legislative measures, just like the research departments of the large, state-run energy producers (e.g., EDF, GDF, CDF, and ELF-AQUITAINE); rather they have a purely advisory function.

The Actors' Network on the Level of Program Implementation

The procedures for granting a permit are found on the regional level. As a governmental representative, prefects grant permits for running a stationary facility or for changes in the facility. In this procedure an *arrêté* is enacted in which all of the conditions for the opening of the facility are cited. The conditions have to be at least in accordance with the national regulations; however, they can turn out to be stricter when adapted to the regional conditions, which is usually the case. A copy of the dossier prepared by the management of the facility is sent from the prefect to the administrative court, where an independent (often retired) engineer or high official is appointed as the head of the commission, who is then responsible for the concrete procedures of the Inspectors' Office.

Prefects and mayors are decision makers, but they are not necessarily experts in the area of clean air protection. That is why the procedure's concrete arrangement is determined by the technical services of the regional administration. Complete confidence is placed in these services (Préfecture de Police, STIIC [Service Technique Interdépartementale d'Inspection des Installations Classées], De Kerdaniel).

Since the technical authorities are not subordinate to any political office, they are, to a certain extent, independent of public opinion: "We are civil servants; ultimately, we are unable to exert public pressure. It is not possible to administer properly, when public opinion has steadily to be taken into account" (Interview Laboratoire de la Préfecture de Police [LCPP]).

On a regional level, clean air protection falls under authority of the Ministry of Industry, which, however, since 1992 has received all of its instructions from the Ministry of the Environment. The DRIRE (Direction Régionale de l'Industrie, de la Recherche et de l'Environnement)[4] is subordinate to the authorities in charge of the facilities requiring a permit. The inspectors are mostly technicians and engineers who carry out the procedure for granting a permit on-site through close cooperation with industry.

The inspectors of DRIRE are involved in the process of program formulation as long as there is an institutional exchange between the ministry and the implementing authorities. Every two months representatives of all regional offices meet in a Groupe du Travail sur l'Environnement Industriel, where legislative bills and projects are discussed as well as problems in the implementation of the laws. Besides these official contacts, there is regular, informal communication, according to statements by representatives of both ministries.

DRIRE or STIIC also takes over control of the conditions that were negotiated in the procedure for granting a permit. According to many actors interviewed, the real problems of French clean air protection seem to lie in these conditions. "First of all, regulations that exist already would have to be applied. . . . 400 engineers for 500,000 registered plants, of these 50,000 liable to authorisation. And what is even worse: 50,000 big plants which we would have to visit several times a year" (Interview CITEPA). In contrast, the process of granting a permit itself is seen by the administration as free of problems and well organized. "It is a concertation; the industrialists know us. They come and see us prior to preparing the dossier, and we tell them exactly what is expected from them. Therefore, they know the rules of the game, and that proceeds very smoothly" (Interview Préfecture de Police, STIIC).

The industrial companies interviewed by us also assess the French system as basically logical and well organized when compared to that in other countries. Regular, independent contacts with the engineers of DRIRE and the mayor of the municipality play a very decisive role. Normally, DRIRE assigns one inspector to exclusively look after the dossiers of a large enterprise. Contacts with the administration, with the prefects, and with political levels are systematically made and promoted. Since the ones running a facility invest a lot in good contacts, the exchange of inspectors is a loss-making deal for them (cf. Interview SHELL-CHIMIE). Because the administration has more power in its hands with regard to delaying a subject or to imposing stricter regulations, companies try to maintain smooth relationships with the inspectors.

The local public gains increasing importance on the level of the procedure for granting a permit. Ecological matters that could potentially bring about protests can be divided between political parties and environmental protection groups: whereas Green Parties, such as Les Verts, are currently very actively involved in problems caused by mobile sources, the environmental protection groups and citizens' action groups are active on a local level in the procedures for granting a permit (Interview DRIRE, Ile de France). In the context of public hearings, these parties and groups have the right to complain about the opening of a facility in the name of the environment. This causes at least a delay in the procedure since the administration is obligated to block the dossier and to study the case again. This possibility, which can be repeated as many times as needed,[5] is indeed used a great deal. That is how, for example, at the beginning of the 1990s a neighborhood action group was able to block the authorized expansion of a Shell branch operation in Lyon, which was ready for production, for well over two years (cf. Interview SHELL-CHIMIE).

In order to institutionalize contacts between the actors, the Council of Ministers founded for the first time in November 1971 in the industrial venue of Fos-Berre a Secrétariat Permanent pour les Problèmes de la Pollution Industrielle (S3PI).[6] These offices do not intervene directly in the procedure for granting a permit, but they do offer the ones who run facilities the opportunity to exchange views with all of the important actors on-site such as mayors, DRIREs, prefects, environmental organizations, representatives of the local population, and other administrations such as water, electricity, Gaz de France (GDF), and Société Nationale des Chemins de Fer (SNCF). "If one has good contacts with these authorities and a good lobby, if one has a dossier for a new plant ready for exploitation, and when all proceeds rather smoothly, then the dossier will progress almost completely on its own" (Interview SHELL-CHIMIE). For the administration as well as for the industry, such work groups raise the hope that conflicts can be resolved in advance and possibly without costly legal proceedings. In addition, the S3PI play an important role in the determination of the levels of harmful chemicals allowed within endangered areas (cf. Knoepfel and Weidner 1985).

This specific structure, namely, the very constricted form of national policy making and, on the other hand, the regional diversity, is found again in the institutional rules of the political processes, which are described next. Thus, state politics always appears cooperative when it serves the state's (frequently economic) interests. If this is not the case, the right to participate in the political process is given, but a substantial exertion of influence is not guaranteed at all actors alike.

INSTITUTIONAL RULES OF POLICY MAKING: HIERARCHY, CONCERTATION, AND TECHNICAL EXPERTISE

The French policy process can be described by the principles of hierarchy, concertation, and technical expertise.

Hierarchy

Central decision making structures are, first of all, found in the state machinery. National and regional levels are structured according to the same principle; the function of the prefect is reflected in that of the prime minister. Both are responsible for the accommodation of interests articulated in the political process. Hierarchic structures also stand out, though, in the practice of cooperation itself, which, as an established political rule, allows only persons of equal rank to communicate with each other (Chambre de Commerce et d'Industrie de Paris [CCIP], Vaudois; LCPP, Alary).

The political system makes a clear division between the areas of program formulation and implementation. On the national level, only national and international associations have a chance to articulate their interests. That is true for environmental associations as well as for the industry. On the stage of program formulation, politics has to be run in the sense of the *volonté generale*, and since this is conceptualized not as federal "bottom-up" politics but as centralized "top-down" politics, two criteria for selection result with regard to political participation by interest groups: First of all, the political actors on this level (1) have to be represented and (2) have to show the corresponding means and competence to be able to get things done. These circumstances put the small parties at a great disadvantage. They are often too weak and fragmented to appear as nationally organized actors. Besides that, not only do they lack the financial means to be able to run intensive research and to provide information, but they also often lack the legitimating effect that the active support of the public gives.

The large, capital-intensive industrial associations can do without public support since they can rely on the political influence of their members with regard to the comprehensive mobilization of power. The focusing of various interests allows the associations to form consistent positions, to concentrate on exerting influence, and, finally, to take advantage of their power potential, which can exert pressure at the top levels in the economic interests of the branches represented through the reputation of large associations and established contacts.

Hierarchic structures are not only established by the Constitution; rather, they represent a characteristic of the whole society in political decision making. Consequently, societal interests have to carry national relevance in order to shape politics. In France, though, national politics is not just the sum of local and federal politics. Therefore, the principle of hierarchy is also reflected in the type of relationship that the state has toward society.

Concertation

At first, hierarchy and cooperation seem to be institutional rules that oppose each other. Besides shaping the formal *systèmes de concertation*, as already described, the informal contacts also directly shape the face of politics. Meetings between industry and politics, which exclude environmental and citizens' groups, play an important role. Not the legislative process but a vast portion of prenegotiations passes by the public in informal circles to which only a few actors have access. Thus, the Greens and the environmental associations complain that there is a set alliance of politicians and industrial representatives and that there is an uncontrollable interconnection of interests that dominates politics. Some pressure groups such as farmers or forwarders are excellently organized. They are overrepresented everywhere, while others more or less go unnoticed.

Whereas the informal agreements are always based on mutual trust, the cooperative committees in French politics have only an advisory position. The concertation principle consequently becomes noticeable on a national level only as long as the interests of the state are not infringed upon. At any rate, the state retains its monopoly over the decision making process so that occasionally, in spite of a broad agreement in the respective committees, divergent decisions are made in the end. In this way, the state ignores the results that were worked out by the community and operates according to its own agenda. Not only the environmental associations but also the industry can be exposed to this arbitrary use of power, if it does not belong to the industrial branches preferred by the state. The broad guidelines of national policies, which determine the priorities, goals, and the opportunities for the collaboration of societal actors, are defined by the heads of state and politics. The practice of cooperation is used one-sidedly here in the service of the state's regulatory monopoly, whereby a legitimation of the accommodation of societal interests is guaranteed according to democratic theory but which has (controversial) consequences itself. Thus, the leading role of the state often does not appear precisely as the *volonté générale*, but as partisanship. "The French administration has a so-called Jacobinian tradition, . . . there is not really a common construction of texts where the interests of the particular are taken into account, where a compromise or a consensus are looked for. Such a construction does not correspond to the mentality of the French administration" (Interview TOTAL).

This particularistic use of a universal principle occurs in program formulation as well as in implementation. Informal contacts and routine agreements also ensure that the permit-granting procedure will go smoothly. They belong to the routine activities of the management of an enterprise.

On the regional level the decision making processes are increasingly more complex. Although extensive negotiations precede both the national and the regional level and are strongly marked by the particular power constellation, Lascoumes believes that there is a "system of double legality" that depends on the redistribution of competence in the wake of decentralization and in favor of the elected representatives. These different types of legality maintain a "formal" one in the sense of Max Weber, which is strongly conceived by legal texts, and a system of "horizontal legality" (Interview Lascoumes). This horizontal legality is the result of agreements that the prefect has negotiated with all the representatives of the territorial community, the general and regional councillors who are, in fact, the notability of the *départements* and regions. There is a system of mutual dependence between the interests of the prefect and the interests of the local politicians. As a result, the direct translation of national politics to a regional and local level is influenced by the interests of the elected politicians, and since every measure for the protection of the environment results, first of all, in expenses but in return mobilizes only few votes, the interest in political measures on behalf of the environment is very low at the moment.[7] A result of this accommodation of the prefects to the interests of the respective representatives is that the regulatory practice in the different regions and *départements* varies greatly. However, if the cooperation principle conflicts with the interests of the state, the prefects are the final authority in the implementation of the law. From the point of view of environmental associations, laws and decrees can, in this way, fizzle out or be stopped on the level of implementation.

The authoritative priority of the state is not formally touched by this one-sided cooperation, even if it is exposed on the regional level to greater political pressure. The legitimacy of the practice of cooperation seems, therefore, to be questioned in two ways: as a principle, it puts the decision making bodies in question provided that in the end they can be circumvented; as the structure for the integration of unequal societal interests, it has the stigma of preferential treatment of sociopolitical interests. The formalization of this (informal) practice fulfills, therefore, the function of channeling cooperation legally and politically.

Technical Expertise

In France as in other countries, technical expertise represents one of the most important foundations of environmental politics. All of the important technical and administrative occupations aid in the decision making process of the state; all of the advisory committees and consultations are utilized as help and preparation for decision making. Accordingly, the offices responsible for the area of clean air protection of the Ministry of the Environment employ technicians almost exclusively. Research institutions for the state and agencies commissioned by the Ministry of the Environment are turned to for scientific expertise. "Science plays an important though not always decisive role. It is our task as scientific researchers to supply information and scientific data on the risks and effects of pollution to the politicians" (Interview ADEME). The predominance of technical experts in almost all areas of administration in France is a result of the overall confidence in the technical formation of society. Particularly in environmental politics, predictability and the ability to quantify are considered values in themselves.

Whereas the German use of the term "environment" is generally associated with nature in public discussion, in France the society has always been an integrated part of nature. The environment is never a value in and by itself; rather, it is always connected with pollution, and pollution of the environment is harmful to people's health and diminishes the quality of life. Particularly in the area of clean air protection, the measurements clearly show that it is not a matter of the general, blanket protection of nature but always one of the preservation or restoration of the partial diminution of the quality of life.

Just as the protection of the environment is attached to the interests of humanity, the term "nature" can also be understood as the human wish to shape the environment. This predominant French understanding of nature is an integral part of the theoretical basis for subordinating environmental politics to human interests. The idea that nature is a product of human activities depends on France's marked agricultural structure. The primarily technical way of looking at problems and the corresponding philosophy of problem solving are also based on this very interventionist understanding of nature. As a result, the protection of nature is not seen as reasonable "in and by itself" but only as necessary where nature actually seems to be threatened. The commitment to technical rationality is, therefore, another reason that transregional measures still seem to be politically unpopular in France.

The role of science in the political process is perceived as important but not as decisive. On the contrary, scientists themselves make a strict division between politics as a decision making context and science as the provider of information (Interview ADEME). The rule of technical expertise, just like the one-sided practice of cooperation, also splits society into those with the power to shape politics and those with the power to define the problem. Technical know-how that is obtained through practice in an industry is one of the most necessary requirements for gaining access to the political stage. All the other professions, whose knowledge cannot be immediately utilized, are not politically involved in a strict sense. In this way, technical expertise is a requirement for access to the political stage of environmental politics just as it is the key to understanding the powerful meaning of certain professions that are traditionally involved in these politics.

THE ROLE OF THE PROFESSIONS: TECHNOCRACY

Due to the traditional French educational policy, professions play a prominent role in the staffing of state offices. The entire leadership of politics, administration, and industry is recruited from the governmental elite schools, called the Grandes Ecoles (see, e.g., Kessler 1986). After strict entrance requirements, a degree from such a school is a guarantee for a steep career. The area of clean air protection in France is handled on a national as well as a regional level completely by engineers and technicians educated in these Grandes Ecoles.

The Hard Sciences

Technical professionals are clearly overrepresented within environmental politics. This is true for the entire area that regulates environmental pollution, especially for clean air protection. In the Ministry of the Environment, the office responsible for clean air protection is staffed exclusively by mining and civil engineers and those with a polytechnical education.

The levels of implementation and program formulation are already linked to each other in educational training: The Ecole des Mines, which was attended by the ministerial staff that we interviewed as well as by the supervisory authorities, involves at least three years of theoretical as well as practical training in industry (Cohen 1988). "Inside these Corps, the ecological sensibility is currently very low. The technicians grasp environmental problems piece by piece, but in an extremely technical way" (Interview Centre International de Recherche sur l'Environment et le Développement [CIRED]).

An engineer's first job is usually in a regional supervisory office, where he or she is comprehensively entrusted with the practical problems of industrial firms. "Before leaving school at last, the young Corps members have to choose their first administrative allocation. Formally, their first position is necessarily a job in a DRIRE. . . . The engineers learn quickly and in a very practice-related way about how to handle the various tools, about the regulated and accepted norms. Right from the start, they possess a certain authority since they may order all those who contradict their rulings to close their plants" (Elie 1988: 598). Right from the start, the engineer is given full authority and responsibility up to and including the closing of a firm. The rotation of staff from regional administration into national politics is one of the foundations of the mutual understanding between industry and the administration. Engineers play the role of a mediator between private and public interests in which the protection of the environment should also find a place next to technical security (cf. Lascoumes 1994: 155).

The entrance to the distinguished Ecole des Mines is strictly limited. As a result, it is almost unavoidable that most of the later colleagues will have already met during their education. "I think that this hits the inner core of organization. In France, it is a very restricted area, an area of intimacy, where everyone knows each other personally" (Interview AIRPARIF).[8] The change from administration to industry practiced in training is replicated again in the biographies of industrial managers. Just the perfect knowledge of internal procedures and the logic of decision making make the formal inspectors indispensable to the companies.

Consequently, the entire area of problem solving within clean air politics in France is covered by the technical elite. In this way, the educational system reproduces a technical perception of the problem that predominates in the environmental area and that logically seems to require an answer based solely on the technical rationality of the experts. The discourse of the highly respected Grandes Ecoles is totaly sealed off from the public. For example, only France, in contrast to other European nations, was able to produce nuclear energy without any public discussion of the effects on the environment (Interview Roqueplo).

The Humanities

The purely technical administration of clean air protection also has its disadvantages for the industry. Neither national politics nor the implementation of clean air policies is shaped by lawyers in France. However, this could be an advantage in regard to the permit-granting procedure within which the examination of environmental impact is often formally and legally contestable. "These impact studies are conducted by research offices where engineers have the say. You don't meet any legal people in these studies" (Interview Ministére de l'Environnement, Bureau du Contentieux). This disadvantage for industry leads to a relatively high number of law-suits, which can at least cause a delay in the procedure. That is why large enterprises have started to maintain their own legal departments (cf. Interview SHELL-CHIMIE).

Dossiers that have been attacked in the context of permit-granting procedures can be attributed to the respective engineer handling the case. This leads to a sensitization of technicians in regard to legal problems because the matter becomes a professional (political) problem for the engineer. The engineers become not really "strict legalists" but "pragmatic legalists" (Interview Lascoumes). Consequently, legal questions are of interest only insofar as they are related to the technicians' career and not with regard to the protection of the environment. "The core of the problem is that in French environmental law there are too many procedures and that it is, ultimately, ineffective since it does not actually create any tools to protect the environment. It only brings about a lot of procedures" (Ministère de l'Environnement, Bureau du Contentieux, Carlier).

The diversity of legal instruments, which is regarded positively by Héritier, Mingers, Knill, and Becka (1994) from the point of view of adaptation to European politics, is conceived of differently here: many and diverse instruments do not inevitably lead right to effective environmental protection. Not the lack of legal instruments but their actual implementation constitutes the specific problem of the clean air politics in France.

With regard to the diagnosis of the problem, the public discourse is described by most of the actors from politics and the industry as nonobjective and poorly informed. Since the perception of environmental problems as being complex and multilayered is by definition automatically oriented toward a technical solution to problems, neither journalists nor citizens' action groups are attributed the authority to assess the issue correctly (Interview Ministère de l'Industrie). A newspaper analysis carried out by Lascoumes (1993) seems to confirm this trend. The analysis unveiled three ways of processing environmental information: a natural-anecdotal, a politically result-oriented, and a technical/economical-political way. The first two ways still predominate. Accordingly, a large gap exists between the very technical discourse of the experts, as, for example, in the periodical *Pollution Atmosphérique* and the "rudimentary level of ordinary communication."

Because environmental problems do not have the benefit of a stable and enduring lobby, sensational events and catastrophes are often used as a reason to argue about the problems related to the environment. Thus, the planning and authorization of garbage incinerators and nuclear power plants cause the biggest and most persistent protests in France. The technical point of view results in judging the public, from the start, to be an actor that is not to be taken seriously and that is to be excluded from the political process. Against the background of its complete power of definition, technical expertise wins in political decision making.

THE CULTURE OF CLEAN AIR POLITICS

The topic of clean air politics regarding stationary sources has a subdued public. In France political involvement in the area of the environment has developed differently and far more weakly than in Great Britain, Germany, and the United States. According to the French Ministry of the Environment, many of the directives from the EU would have had no chance to be implemented if they were introduced as national decrees. Except for sensational events and procedures, the political process of clean air protection seems to go along without any problems from all sides. Especially characteristic is the specific duality of a relatively rigid national political framework and its flexible regional implementation.

Central Administration and Regional Variation

It is shown that French politics is very strongly shaped by structures for access, which, however, by themselves do not say anything about the effectiveness of the realization of interests. On the level of program formulation, the boundaries of the actors' network are closed and impermeable. The French electoral system of absolute majority rule has resulted in the Green Parties' not being represented in the National Assembly until a short while ago. Legislation is prepared in the respective ministries. The Ministry of the Environment can be seen as the main actor; its range of activity, though, is limited by the much more powerful Ministry of Industry and the traditionally very influential large industries and their associations. The large, recognized environmental organizations also take part in legislative committees.

The scientific basis for environmental politics is provided by the agencies and research institutes commissioned by the Ministry of the Environment. These agencies and research institutes pursue no political strategy of their own. In matters that involve scientific expertise, technical sciences appear to be utilized entirely for political purposes. Lawyers, social scientists, and scholars in the humanities, in contrast, play no role in France on the political stage of clean air protection. The discussion of the technical and engineering professionals, who are authoritative in clean air protection and educated in the Grandes Ecoles, completes the picture. On all levels of the national administration, as well as in the environmental department of the large enterprises, a technical elite is employed who, due to their education and their societal role, bring a similar worldview and similar problem-solving strategies into politics. The rotation of staff in both industry and administration intensifies this effect and is the cornerstone for the mutual understanding and willingness to cooperate between those regulating and those regulated. The entanglement of staff in government, politics, and industry in the field of clean air politics is also reflected in the responsibilities held by the administration, for example, the DRIRE and the ADEME, which are in charge of controlling as well as promoting the industry.

Regional politics have a relatively wide scope of action in the interpretation of the general laws. On a regional level, close cooperation between the prefecture, the mayor, the industrial firms, the administrative offices, and the local environ-

mental protection groups can be observed. The negotiating process between industry and politics can be described as informal and usually cooperative. French politics makes an effort to integrate environmental organizations into the context of
permit-granting procedures, thus attributing to them an active part in the political
process. Where a conflict of interests comes up, and integration into the political
procedures is not possible or is not successful, legal proceedings take place, which
at least result in a delay of the permit.

Against the background of the relatively strict separation of program formulation and implementation, it does not seem to make sense to summarize national
and regional or local political processes and to verify France altogether as *"etatism,* adversarial, contemptuous and distrustful of organizations for special interests"* (van Waarden 1993: 207). On the contrary, the conclusions of our study in
regard to France lead to a differentiation of the political levels, which also has to
have an effect on the theoretical conception of the political style. Whereas the
process of program formulation follows an established hierarchic, centralistic
logic, which is oriented toward formal elements such as authority, structures for
access, legislation, and so on, the process of implementation is characterized by a
stronger orientation toward results. These two levels and their relationship to each
other are discussed next with the help of the concepts of vertical and horizontal
rationality.

Vertical and Horizontal Rationality

The idea of describing national and local decision making procedures in
France with regard to primary hierarchic and interactive structures seems to be
more or less uncontested. Pierre Lascoumes, for example, uses the terms of vertical and horizontal structures to differentiate two types of "legality." For Lascoumes, the question in the course of the organization of the new regional environmental offices (Direction Régionale de l'Environnement [DIREN]) is how the
predominantly decentralized and networklike structures in the local areas could be
validated on a central level (Lascoumes 1994).

Using the term "rationality" has the effect of pushing the analysis closer to the
intentions of actors, because there are not only two different kinds of legal structures but, more broadly, two kinds of legitimization of actions. The concept of
vertical rationality describes the structural principles of politics. Horizontal rationality describes the processes and results of the negotiations between the individual and collective actors who are on-site. Accordingly, vertical structural features are characterized by a high degree of formality, whereas horizontal
structures refer to more informal patterns of interaction and strategies. Although
the concepts of vertical and horizontal rationality as analytical tools do not perfectly fit the levels of national and local politics, the comparison makes an important trend visible: the passing on of interests on a national level follows the law of
lobbying and is primarily dependent on the economic and political power of the
intervening interest groups. The articulation of interests on a regional and local
level is, on the contrary, strongly oriented toward the political public.

Vertical Rationality

The passing on of interests in the legislative process is, as described, characterized by work in interministerial committees and commissions. The way industry exerts influence on the political process can be described as direct and effective. Unlike any other interest group, the large industrial organizations, the CNPF and the UIC, influence the shape of legislation. The preparation of the *arrêté intégré* provides an example of the concrete representation of interests. In France, this instrument provides a framework for more specific legislation because it packages the existing regulations for the chemical industry and brings them up to the state of the art. Representatives of industrial enterprises characterize the *arrêté* as a successful compromise because—just like the law for classified facilities and its implementing order—it authorizes the orientation toward individual cases as the central element of French clean air protection. Industry's tactic is aimed at both levels: national laws are central but make up only one side of politics. Concrete political intervention in the form of specific regulations and standards is enacted in the context of the permit-granting procedure. The generality and vagueness of national legislation give the authorities on-site the possibility of adapting the respective regulations to local conditions. The widespread appearance of the "exception to the rule" is not an unintentional consequence but rather a programmed component of national legislation. The industry's division of labor strategy consists of pushing ahead "nonbinding" legislation on the national level in order to be able to assert itself in the context of the orientation to individual cases in the permit-granting procedure. The possibilities for this strategy are informally checked. As far as France is concerned, the term frequently used in this chapter, "implementation," underestimates the possibility for political maneuvering on the local level because it suggests that the actual political process has ended a long while ago and must only be transformed into actions. This political practice also affects the "state of technology" to be used. In regard to the protection of the environment through measures regarding the emissions from stationary sources, cost considerations are absolutely first priority. The industry can exert influence on political decisions without the public.

This direct exertion of influence is practiced less on the highest level of ministers but more on the level of the staff employed in the various administrations of the ministries who keep their positions even when the government changes. Whereas industry lobbies act in this way so that they can have long-lasting contact and in doing so, operate right behind the public's back, the environmental organizations use the opposite strategy, namely, the mobilization of the public.

The representation of environmental interests on the national level turns out to be problematic due to many reasons. "French state officials have employed a variety of means to 'distort' the dynamics of interest representation" (Keeler 1987: 215). One of these means is the procedure for recognition, which the environmental protection groups and organizations have to go through in order to be allowed to sit on a ministerial committee. This procedure can represent a central means of pressure because, on the one hand, it offers the possibility to establish relationships with the state administration level and to be informed about legislative bills, and, on the other hand, because the receipt of subsidies depends on them. But participation is no guarantee for the realization of interests. Environmental protection groups recognized by the Ministry of the Environment, such as Les Amis de la Terre or France Nature Environnement, are involved in the commissions of the Ministry of the Environment without being able to effectively represent their interests, according to their own statements. Very often, the content of a law supports environmental protection groups. The actual policies, though, are characterized by "exception to the rule" regulations that open up to certain enterprises the possibility to pollute for years (Interview Les Amis de la Terre). This might be the other side of what the representative of the chemical industry meant by the "stage of improvement."

The opinions of environmental protection groups in the process of program formulation seem to be purely used as alibis. Thus, representatives from industry as well as the staff of various ministries judge the influence of French environmental protection groups on national politics to be extremely low. Their reputation on the ministerial level varies strongly with their readiness to allow for economic arguments within environmental protection. "Jusqu'au Boutistes," who practice ecology for its own sake and not in "the service of humanity," do not have a chance to pass the criterion recognized by the Ministry of the Environment and thereby push into the circles of those environmental protection groups worthy of subsidies (Interview Ministère de l'Industrie, Secrétariat Général des DRIREs).

The way environmental protection groups exert pressure in the process of program formulation is not based, therefore, on official participation in legislative commissions but is linked to protests on a national level. But the topic of clean air politics, in contrast to nuclear power, for example, is not of national interest. So, if environmental groups can exert any influence at all, then it is carried out very indirectly and is subject to economic fluctuations, which strongly correspond to the political presence of Green politicians. Even if it rarely happens that the Green Parties and environmental protection groups cooperate directly, this mandate offers the only possibility for the introduction of environmental topics with a political nature into public discussion in an enduring and politically legitimate way.

The structures accommodate to the interests of industry. In regard to legislation, all important interests can be realized. In the context of program formulation, it is important for the ones who run facilities that the legal regulations are oriented toward (1) the economic situation of the individual enterprises and (2) the ambient air quality situation of the region. Strict national emissions standards were rejected by the industry. Both demands have found their way into national legislation: The principle of BATNEEC is mentioned for the first time in the Law for Classified Facilities (1976), is then taken up again in the Arrêté Intégré (1993), and was finally firmly established in French environmental law in the Loi relative au renforcement de la protection de l'environnement (1995). The industry makes an effort to take environmental measures into its own hands and with its own staff. Accordingly, the principle of self-supervision of the output of harmful chemicals is very welcome by the large enterprises. The tax-like fees are also met with little defense on the part of the industry. On the other hand, all environmental protection groups interviewed complain that the fees are too low and cannot really motivate industrial firms to invest in new environmental technologies. In France the orientation toward ambient air quality in the form of "special protected areas" and "endangered areas" has a tradition; air quality has been regulated since 1961 in the Law against Air Pollution and the corresponding implementation decree (1974).

In summary, we can establish for the national political process that the guidelines for clean air politics are not produced by all societal groups that the procedures for coordination, compromise, and consensus encompass. Rather, they are produced in close cooperation between the governmental administration and the industry, represented by the Ministry of Industry, the industrial organizations, and direct representatives of large enterprises. Although the political institutions exist for a more comprehensive process of coordination and agreement, they do not seem to have any influence on concrete policies.

Whereas industry asserts its influence almost exclusively through lobbying with the exclusion of the public and thus acts politically on the level of program formulation, the environmental organizations are successful on the national and international levels in the area of problem definition and in the area of implementation on the regional level. In this way, they embrace the process of program formulation, from which they themselves are excluded. They use protests and the mobilization of the public on both levels. The effect of the protests is short-lived in that specific campaigns or legal suits are always linked to specific events. The legislative process is not touched by this. Environmental protection groups and the Green Parties, which often do not work with each other but instead work against each other, consequently are not part of the national agenda setting.

The regional way of looking at problems in the area of clean air politics is a two-sided coin for the environmental protection groups: On the one hand, this point of view prevents the strengthening of environmental groups nationally so that they cannot participate more actively in the legislative process. On the other hand, the environmental organizations are actually able to mobilize interests locally within the process of implementation precisely due to this regional viewpoint.

Horizontal Rationality

In the course of the afore-described reforms, the political actors and their problems certainly acquire a greater significance on a local level. The representatives of the local councils, as well as the mayors, have a concrete integrating function due to their dependence on the goodwill of the voters. The more that they can convert the goals of the industry into votes for themselves, which is the case in times of high unemployment, and the weaker that the environmental movement is locally, the smoother the negotiations process between industry and politics. This relationship, according to the Greens and the environmental protection groups, can be observed regardless of the political party and is not dependent on a government that is oriented to the left or right. The reverse is also true. The flexible realization of the law on a regional level can be described as a kind of crisis management from the viewpoint of the decision makers and not as a long-term rational strategy. As a rule, environmental protection groups are always involved in the political processes then, if there is unrest in the population and if conflicts are starting to develop. Whereas national political protests can at least temporarily be answered with no attention (with the exclusion of broad crises), the interests of the citizens are more directly affected on a local level, which then reach into the political process through the elected representatives. The decision making authority of the state is also valid here, but it is far more unstable than on the national level.

A possibility for the channeling of different interests is offered by the S3PI, which have already been described in the section on networks. These offices have different departments, such as air pollution, water pollution, industrial risks, or the transportation of dangerous substances, depending on local necessity. They formalize previous ad hoc arrangements between the participating actors on-site. Since then, such offices have been set up in eight areas that are particularly affected.

From the industry's point of view, the S3PI offices help to avoid costly legal proceedings; from the administration's point of view, they facilitate everyday routine to a considerable extent. With the help of the S3PI, lines of conflict can be more closely supervised and firmly controlled. Finally, the environmental organizations have at least the chance to be comprehensively informed.

POLITICAL REGULATION: PLURALISM, CORPORATISM, OR "CONCERTATION"?

The example of clean air politics regarding stationary sources has shown that the comparison of vertical and horizontal rationality in relation to the political structures corresponds, to a large extent, to the levels of national and regional or local politics. Broadly outlined legislation and procedures of program formulation are provided on the national level, which then gain significance in the local political processes in the sense of conditions, value limits, and restrictions on production. It is important to note that the specific meshing together of the vertical and horizontal rationalities makes up the characteristic features of the French political style. The very general French legislation functions as a prerequisite for the administration on-site to look for regional solutions. Moreover, just as the legislative process shows signs of horizontal connections, the process of implementation is also characterized by formal elements. Politics in a narrower sense, that is, legislation, does not stop on the national level but is continued in the context of subordinate political processes. Standard-setting procedures and thereby the concrete extent of pollution are regulated regionally and locally.

The debate on pluralism and corporatism outlined at the beginning leads to a similar conclusion. A clear classification according to one or the other model seems to be a problem. Pluralistic and corporatist decision making structures can be found on both the national and the regional and local levels. Although on both levels the strong state cannot be brought in as the sole explanation, the institutionally established and practiced decision making authority of the state still produces a lively etatism that not only is legitimated by the corresponding political institutions but is also firmly established in the heads of the actors. The state as the final authority in the integration of societal interests seems to be taken for granted by the actors of clean air protection. Etatism understood as a model of state-centralized political regulation is consequently completely out of the question for the formal, that is, institutional, French system. The question is, If and when the occasion should arise, why can structures be found in the political routine that do without an exhaustive supply of the arbitrary use of state decision making?

Along with the clear declarations for the belief in one or the other side of the debate, a theoretical approach is gaining significance that falls between the models. A theoretical possibility exists in the differentiation of the state–society relations according to sectors. In the area of research about corporatism, one speaks of "sectoral corporatism" (Lehmbruch 1984) or "mesocorporatism," which describes only the decision making structures of individual sectors or political arenas (cf. Cawson 1985). "The 'strong state' image of a France with a relatively unified bureaucratic executive which can form its own preferences and impose them even in the face of societal opposition remains useful in those policy areas that are close to the 'core' of governmental functions, especially taxation and basic infrastructure investment, but also other core functions such as the maintenance of public order and criminal justice, foreign relations and national defense" (Dunn 1995: 278). Accordingly, the specific type of relationship between the state and society changes depending on how close or distant the various sectors are perceived as being from these main functions of the state.

Keeler (1987) argues in a similar way. He states that the French political development is an "unbalanced or uneven nature of corporatization" that, according to the sector, displays four developmental stages: strong pluralism, structured pluralism, and strong and moderate corporatism. Corporatist political models result from three prerequisites. First of all, there has to be a governmental need for the support of organizations in the process of political regulation. In addition, the degree of structural agreement is important in regard to political goals and instruments. Finally, the capacity of an organization to mobilize and discipline its members plays a role. The stronger that these three conditions are in a political arena, the more probable it is that the political model will develop in the direction of corporatism. According to Keeler, various sectors took on a variably strong trend toward corporatization between 1958 and 1981 (Fifth Republic). Only the agricultural sector was classified by Keeler as fitting the criteria of strong corporatist decision making structures (Keller 1987).

A third possibility for the characterization of the French political style can be designated by the term "concertation" as defined by Atkinson and Coleman (1989) and Lehmbruch (1984). A prerequisite of this model is a strong, autonomous state that shares the responsibility of political decision making with only one strong interest group. According to Lehmbruch (1984), who describes the sector of employment politics in France as a model of "concertation without labor," one could describe the area of clean air politics as "concertation without environmental groups." Although officially more than one interest group participates in the planning process of clean air protection, only the interests of industry congruently continue to follow from the legislative process into the phase of implementation. Environmental interests are represented on a national level by the technicians of the Ministry of the Environment and not by the environmental organizations. "State officials must articulate objectives which are more encompassing than those of their private-sector partners and insist on standards that they alone set. . . . At the sectoral level, state officials seek an accommodation with business that not only meets the latter's need for freedom of action and economic support, but also is in step with a set of broader political objectives. Some of these will be established by the government of the day, but most will be negotiated over a period of time with business in the sector concerned" (Atkinson and Coleman 1989: 59).

The models are united, even if with some variety, regarding the dominant and active role of the French state and the expanded power of the executive in the context of political processes which began that the Fifth Republic. Its opposite is substantiated in the variously worded sociological approaches: "Whereas the theories of pluralism consider the system of interest representation also from a democratic theoretical perspective, the theories of corporatism argue on an analytically descriptive level about the functional representation of interests in regard to the aspects of political order and regulatory techniques" (Reutter 1991: 23).

These apparently opposing concepts are brought together again in France. It looks as if the division of the political system into two parts answers the question on the national level about the democratic understanding of the French society, and it answers the question about routine political regulatory business on the regional and local levels. It is difficult to decide if the national political style in the area of clean air protection should be strictly taken as a "structured pluralism" or classified as "concertation." In both cases the political process is characterized by relatively stable alliances between few actors, who can only, or primarily, come into being with an appropriate institutional background. The processes of structural approximation are also a result of the long-lasting relationship. The most important prerequisite for the arbitrariness of preferential or discriminatory treatment by the state, which is precarious from the viewpoint of the theory of democracy, is its autonomy. Only because of this autonomy is it possible to take into consideration the interests of industry or not to take into consideration the interests of the environmental protectionists, although both have sat on the same committee as representatives of their organizations. Wilsford calls this situation the "Symbolism of Consultation" (Wilsford 1988: 145f.).

It appears important that local politics function according to a political pattern with a shorter life and, therefore, that it can be more strongly disturbed. The need to regulate on-site is more directly and strongly oriented to local conditions. The electoral system suits these structures. In this way, the arbitrary use of power by the state is not quite removed, but it is indeed limited. An attempt to regain control of these dependencies for the benefit of cooperative political strategies is represented by the permanent offices. However, whether a wider scope for the representation of environmental interests will result from the respective interaction logic of the regional level is an empirical question that, at the moment, would probably be negatively answered, according to information from environmental organizations. In this respect, a study by Héritier characterizes the regional level as "very integrative and participatory" and in the end draws too optimistic a picture (cf. Héritier, Mingers, Knill, and Becka 1994: 147). Another question also remains to be empirically checked, that is, if the inclusion of societal interests, in this case environmental interests, in given political structures will actually lead to a more effective representation of these interests.

At any rate, at the moment, a change in the understanding of democracy, and, dependent on that, the representative political institutions appears to be imaginable only, if at all possible, when there are political crises. In comparison, change in the concrete regulatory policies seems to be less hopeless, since these policies are dependent on constantly changing political coalitions on-site. The mobilization of the public plays an important role for both. The sciences are also in great demand here. However, actively involved scientists and environmental protection groups are not the only ones who rarely pull in the same direction, but the sciences themselves, with the exception of the technical and engineering sciences, seem to be disorganized in regard to environmental problems.

The technical profession is the only element in the shaping of French politics that covers the entire political process from the definition of the problem to program formulation up to implementation. The consistent recruitment of administrative trainees from the elite schools increases the legitimacy of state centrality. There is no opening for other professions. In this respect, the technocrats are better organized and more closely united than the environmental protectionists. As a profession, technicians cover the gamut of the actor's level since they are at home in the administrative area as well as in industry. As a profession, they bridge temporary distances, for example, a change in government, that is otherwise connected with an exchange of actors. The technical profession, therefore, offers one point of convergence for the levels of the society and the organization regarding cultural patterns of interpretation.

Immergut (1992), using the politics of health as an example, showed that there is no interaction between the institutional structures and the implementation of policies because those who carry out political business have not created the institutional conditions they actually work in. This thesis can be at least confronted, so it seems, with the argument of the technical profession. A somewhat weaker and more actor-oriented institutional concept, in contrast, shows that the industrial organizations and the large enterprises do not plan and represent their preferences independently and removed from political institutions; rather, they demonstrate the possibility for the effective realization of interests by establishing and using the corresponding institutions.

In order to break through this technical dominance, many of those interviewed suggested, independently of each other, the establishment of a public discourse of all sciences related to environmental protection. The discourse should be transmitted to society through the medium of television in order to contribute to the development of the public's ability to make ecologically sound judgments (Interview Roqueplo).

For both Lascoumes and Roqueplo, the French policy process suffers from a lack of expert disputes, which means a fruitful competition not only between scientific positions within one science but rather between different sciences: "Scientific discourse always appears homogeneous; no one differentiates between the discourse of the chemists, the biologists, or the scientific ecology. . . . This is something typical of our immaturity" (Interview Lascoumes).

In this way, "science" always appears totally for or against the economy and either on one or the other side of a political issue, but not as a grouping of various perspectives and approaches, which just would be the expression of a horizontal (i.e., higher) rationality.

NOTES

1. France's rate of unemployment fluctuates between 11% and 12%, with a total population of 58,270,350 people (as per 1 January 1995). Estimates regarding those looking for employment come to 4 million.

2. In this context, it is quite important to point out that the Green Party began to participate in government with Lionel Jospin's assumption of office.

3. The Ministry of the Environment is a relatively small ministry, the weakness of which is expressed in a low budget and an equally meager staff: for the year 1994, the Ministry of the Environment had a budget of 1,653,210,692 French Francs (less than 1% of the total budget), of which 256,654,193 FF (15.5% of the entire budget of the Ministry of the Environment) was allotted to the administration responsible for clean air protection (Direction de la Prévention des Pollutions et des Risques). The maintenance of the ministry's affiliated agency ADEME and the research institute INERIS (Institut National de l'Environnement Industriel et des Risques) as well as the preparation of external studies and expert reports are all financed with these funds. The staff of the Service Environnement Industriel is made up of 65 employees, including secretaries; 10 of these employees are allotted to the Bureau de l'Atmosphère.

4. In the region Ile de France, the responsibilities in the area of industrial clean air protection are divided between the DRIRE (Direction Régionale de l'Industrie, de la Recherche et de l'Environnement, Departements of the Great Crown) and STIIC (Service Technique d'Inspection des Installations Classées-Paris and the three Departements of the Small Crown).

5. The majority of the complaints criticize irregularities in the context of the tests for environmental safety, and in 25% of the cases the authorization is then canceled (Interview Ministère de l'Environnement, Bureau du Contentieux, Carlier).

6. The offices (Secrétariat) have various divisions, such as air pollution, water pollution, industrial risks, or the transportation of dangerous materials, according to local necessities. "The S3PI commit themselves to developing the concertation and participation of the public, the transparency of administrative decisions, the information of the public" (DPPR 1994). Since then, eight such offices have been set up in areas covered by these problems.

7. A survey of 300 mayors seems to confirm this assumption: environmental interests ranked fifth behind that of unemployment, the struggle against "exclusion," education and training, and the economic development of enterprises. Moreover, only 10% of the mayors consider the struggle against air pollution to be especially important, whereas the garbage

problem is very popular with 71% (cf. *Libération* from 19 May 1995, "l'environnement ne passione pas le maires").

8. The stability and distinctness of the French network of actors in the field of clean air can be seen from the fact that the vast majority of people whom I interviewed knew each other and were able to qualify each other.

Chapter 5

Germany: Rule by Virtue of Knowledge

Carsten Stark

INTRODUCTION

In many comparative studies the German political style is described as "corporatist." Particularly from the American point of view, the reference to a political
style that is relatively free of conflict, strives for consensus, and is nevertheless
quite effective appears very appealing. Many of the practical disadvantages of a
liberal democratic idea seem to be circumvented by the German political style and
dissolved by communal ties and a consensus of values. But, of course, there are
two sides to every coin. Corporatism is certainly feasible. This feasibility, however, can exist only by giving up the liberal participating democratic idea and an
orientation toward the ideal of enlightened democracy. In the end, this form of
democracy is not based on participation and the pursuit of interests but rather on a
few experts' search for truth and the enlightenment of the public. I would like to
portray this form of democracy using the politics of ambient air quality protection
as an example. To do so, I first very briefly present the political instruments used
in Germany in this field. A short description of cooperative relationships in clean
air politics follows, which I designate with the term "permit-granting cartel."
Explanations of the legitimation of the permit-granting cartel come afterward. My
conviction is that a "rule by virtue of knowledge" or, to be precise, a "rule by
virtue of engineering knowledge" is the basis of legitimation for an institutionalized exclusion of the public in the political process, which, in terms of democratic
theory, can be designated as "democracy by enlightenment."

INSTRUMENTS OF REGULATION

In Germany attempts to deal with air pollution are primarily directed at the
source. Understood as prevention, these attempts primarily strive to reduce emissions. Ambient air quality standards exist for only a very few of the most frequently used harmful substances.[1] Emissions are regulated by permit-granting
procedures. Every citizen has a legally recoverable right to set up a facility that
emits harmful substances (the right to carry on a business), but he or she has to

maintain certain conditions that are checked in a formal procedure. At the end of this procedure the permit is then granted. The emission standards, which play a role in these procedures, are not, however, legally established; rather, they are, to a great extent, the object of negotiation. The one who runs the facility is obligated to keep up with the "state of technology"; thus, there are negotiations over what this "state" is in fact. To make these decisions about the state of technology easier for the authorities, a rule book, *Technical Guidelines to Clean Air* (TA-Luft), has been drafted, which, however, is only for internal use by the officials. It does not have a legal nature; thus, it does not give a legally recoverable right in court. Furthermore, the book is revised only every 10 years, so that it is never really at the newest state of technology itself. Therefore, the practice of clean air revolves around concretely establishing an up-to-date state of technology. This is where the real negotiations take place, and it is clear that these negotiations quickly become a purely technical matter since here it is primarily expertise that counts. The original law for clean air protection (Federal Ambient Air Quality Protection Law, the Bundesimmissionschutzgesetz [BimSchG]) is itself very general and simply refers to other rule books that do not have the same authority as a law.

To avoid leaving everything exclusively up to negotiation processes and to make up for the disadvantage of the frequently outdated TA-Luft, the standards of the private Association of German Engineers (Verband Deutscher Ingenieure [VDI]) are often used as a reference by governmental officials. This professional organization deals with the determination of the "state of technology" in its Commission on Clean Air Protection (Kommission Reinhaltung der Luft [KRDL]), which is financed by the state. The VDI can make this determination with its well over 1,000 members in much greater detail than a governmental office. The expression "state of technology" should not be confused with the state of technological possibilities. What is technically possible is never an issue. All governmental interventions, even those in the right to carry on a business, have to be appropriate according to the constitution (ban on excesses). That means that the negotiations over the state of technology also have to include this appropriateness both in the concrete permit-granting procedures as well as in the guideline decisions of the VDI or in the TA-Luft. Later on, I very precisely explain this central, special feature.

Negotiation processes oriented toward both technology and appropriateness are therefore the actual place of governmental intervention in regard to air pollution in Germany. The central instrument, the permit-granting procedure, is also strongly influenced by this orientation toward technology. The involvement of the public is planned for only in certain cases (in practice, for around 30% of the permit-granting procedures) and is also very time-limited. The determination of guidelines within the VDI occurs entirely without the involvement of the public, even without the awareness of the public.

NETWORKS OF ACTORS: THE PERMIT-GRANTING CARTEL

Described in this way, clean air politics in Germany is a classic case of corporatism (Jänicke and Weider 1997a). Both the legal formulation and the concrete, practical form of these politics result from an accommodation of interests between a few large organizations and the state. On the legislative level as well as on the level of the determination of legal terms effective for implementation, only a few actors play an important role in collaborating with governmental institutions. Although the term is not to be taken literally, I would like to call this circle of actors "the permit-granting cartel." What is meant by this term is that the parties that directly have something to do with the granting of a permit to industrial facilities are those that principally have a say in regard to German clean air protection. With this in mind, it is my opinion that a "cartel" exists on the level of drafting legislation as well as on the level of implementation, which, to a great extent, shuts out the interests of other actors. The state's part in this permit-granting cartel is made up of individual ministries in the federal and state government on the level of program formulation, and consists of individual permit-granting authorities on the level of implementation. The air polluters that belong to the permit-granting cartel include various industrial associations on the level of program formulation and the operators on the level of implementation. The public, citizens' action groups, and environmental organizations as well as political parties or Parliament play only a subordinate role in German clean air politics. These, as well as the courts, appear to the members of the permit-granting cartel as nothing more than significant disruptions of institutionalized relationships. The closer determination of undefined legal terms in the ambient air quality law takes place almost exclusively in this circle. Therefore, only in rare cases is the determination of the state of technology and the appropriateness of regulations carried out beyond the cooperation of the cartel members. However, the permit-granting cartel cannot simply be conceived of as a power clique that up until now was seen as successfully protecting itself against democratic efforts. On the contrary, we conceive of the permit-granting cartel as the organizational pattern of clean air politics. In other words, the permit-granting cartel is the organization of the legitimate policy network. Neither in its self-conception nor in the perception of the public is it a small community of interest groups that ignores the needs of the common good. Nevertheless, these interorganizational contacts within ambient air quality politics lead to a considerable difference between formal procedures and concrete negotiating patterns. Since program formulation is characterized by the fact that negotiating processes between ministries and industry, and interministerial agreements influence the concrete contents of a regulation far more than the *formal* procedures for participation, a similar structure is also found on the level of implementation. Here negotiations between those who run the facilities and the permit-granting officials, which take place *before* the actual permit-granting procedures, are decisive for their success and more or less guarantee the granting of a permit. The negotiations between entrepreneur and permit-granting officials do not run according to procedure, then, in spite of formal permit-granting procedures.

Thus, even the small number of procedures that allow for the formal participation of the public practically run without the public and, as a result, also without possible reference to procedural mistakes. Due to this difference between appearance and reality, the permit-granting cartel is cut off from the interests of, and the shaping of, opinion by environmental organizations, citizens' action groups, Parliament, political parties, the public, and the courts. Compromises are made within this permit-granting cartel, whose unquestioned position has to be seen as crucial for the success of the legal ambient air quality protection regulations. *This causal relationship comes about by the linkage of facility-related ambient air quality protection to undefined legal terms such as "the state of technology," and the "principle of appropriateness."* The German principle of cooperation, therefore, includes only actors who have something to contribute to these interest-laden interpretations of technology (Wolf 1988). For the permit-granting cartel, the danger of the undefined legal terms lies in the decisions made by the courts, which are not biased by interests. Therefore, none of the parties are interested in bringing disputed matters to court. What is more decisive, this does not happen in fact. In Germany approximately 1.5% to 3% of the applications for a permit are denied, and from these few cases, only about 3% end up in court again. Judicial objections by a third party are practically nonexistent, and if they do take place, then only in reference to a few large projects. The number of decisions made by the courts with regard to ambient air quality protection can be counted on one hand. Are the Germans, then, not especially aware of the environment? Or does perhaps everyone agree that everything possible has been done? Is there perhaps nothing to argue about? There really is, but the permit-granting cartel has been firmly established as the organizational model for legitimate politics in a political culture that is not one of disputes. German corporatism is fundamentally effective. Why?

INSTITUTIONAL RULES OF POLICY MAKING: RULE BY VIRTUE OF KNOWLEDGE

How is the permit-granting cartel legitimated as an organizational structure and legitimated in its interactive exclusion of external actors? Which *commonalities* exist in the system of clean air politics as predominant rules that allow for the actual basis of decisions not to be in a constant dilemma of legitimation by the intervention of an interested public?

An answer to these questions is found, in my opinion, in the legitimated behavioral pattern of *"rule by virtue of knowledge."* What is meant by that? Rule by virtue of knowledge is the *rationalized politics of being informed professionally.* This is based on legitimated political decision making "without politicians" (Schnabel 1979; Wolf 1988: 166). Knowledge does not necessarily correspond to reality here but is to be understood as a desirable and important basis of information for political decision making. Rule by virtue of knowledge means that political decision making processes are legitimated by selecting information for political decision making according to the criteria of scientific-technical "truth."

It is not the imposition by force nor the "neutral" exchange of different interests but rather the collection of various stockpiles of knowledge and their integration into a "correct" solution that is regarded as the means to rational decision making. Indeed, political decisions always represent a compromise of different interests; however, this compromise is not exclusively sought after. A consensus on the level of qualified specialists is also desired. Consensus does not mean, then, that one can live with a decision but that one is in agreement. This agreement is reached through the mutual reference to expertise. In this way, expertise dominates the political decision making process. Since expertise is divided up unevenly among the participating actors, the factualness of the discussion also legitimates the consensus within the previously described permit-granting cartel.

The ideology of the "objective" discussion, which seems to exclude the interests specific to the actors as much as possible, leads to a reduction of what is understood as a "political" process in decision making. It legitimates the informal negotiating processes between industry and the technocrats and finds its point of crystallization in technical standardization, which is seen as absolutely nonpolitical. In this way, political decision making is divided into two areas. In the large *informal* area, which I have described as decisive on the level of implementation as well as on the level of program formulation, relevant information is collected, and political consultation takes place. The other area includes the formal, legal representation of interests and needs to be seen as a less significant, ritualized pattern of behavior. Since only the latter area, which is rather unimportant in the practice of clean air protection, is seen as concretely political, and the former area is presented as a purely "objective"'discussion far away from particular interests, the permit-granting cartel is successful in representing its work as nonpolitical, which leads to an exclusion of formal political authorities such as the Parliament, political parties, environmental groups, and, above all, the public. This exclusion can, then, from the point of view of the permit-granting cartel, be considered legitimate because—due to its conception of itself—there are no *political* processes when other actors are not taken into account. Court decisions, the work of environmental organizations, and, not least of all, public opinion rather disturb, from this viewpoint, "objective" work since interests are presented in a non-"objective," nonscientific way. They disturb the ones involved in reaching a consensus and are, at best, seen as a mere stimulus for a renewed discussion of the issue. Therefore, they disrupt not only in a negative sense but also in a positive one. But they *themselves* never become a legitimate point of reference in decision making.

Politics is limited, in this respect, to disruptions of "objective" discussions by the media, the public, and politicians (and their wish to be reelected). Democracy is limited to the exclusion of non-"objective" opposition through enlightenment, because once the public has the "correct" knowledge about the "issue," it will no longer find any reason to disrupt the work of the permit-granting cartel.

In my opinion, this idea of rule by virtue of knowledge is based on (1) an integrated problem-solving approach, (2) a specific selection of relevant knowledge, (3) the linking of effectiveness with "objectivity" (German: *Sachlichkeit*), (4) the disqualification of justifiable interests of the public as non-"objective" and emotional, and (5) an understanding of democracy as enlightenment, not as the involvement of an interested public.

Integrated Problem Solving

German policy formulation is characterized by a special way of working on problems that I call the *integrated problem-solving approach*. The foundation of this approach is to gather up as much knowledge as possible that is found in society about a specific problem and to let this knowledge flow into legislation. In clean air politics, this approach is expressed in the hearing of interest groups, which include trade unions, employer associations, and industrial and environmental organizations, as well as experts such as judges, scientists, but also professional and trade associations. Here politics wants to introduce a law that has the broadest harmonization possible so as to ensure that the law will remain *long-lasting* in societal discussion. However, since different types of knowledge are connected to different interests, the integrated problem-solving approach can produce only *general*, cross-sectoral laws to which almost all of those involved will agree in their general form. The goals and contents of the federal ambient air quality protection law (BImSchG) are thus hardly ever the object of societal discussion. All of those interviewed by us think that the BImSchG is, in general, a good and, from an ecological point of view, sensible law. This also explains the fact that in the last 20 years the law has been amended only a few times and just in trivial points. Ultimately, this is the idea that is behind the principle of cooperation in environmental politics: the BImSchG remains general and thereby capable of achieving a consensus; the integrity of a law becomes its criterion of assessment.

This ideology of integration, however, is found not only on the level of legislation but also in the *intra*organizational work of the political actors. The actors make an effort to legitimate their specific interests with the totality of knowledge available to society. In the general struggle for political goals, the one will be armed best whose arguments have the broadest appeal. Thus, the Expert Council on Environmental Matters (Sachverständigenrat für Umweltfragen [SRU]) is composed of scientists from a great variety of special fields. In its discussions, there is an attempt to work toward a consensus in order to then present a widely agreed upon paper to the public. Minority opinions very rarely need to be considered here. Within industrial associations, too, such as the Federal Association of the German Industry (Bundesverband der Deutschen Industrie [BDI]), information about a great variety of sociopolitical areas is gathered, and one attempts to include this information in one's own position. Even if one is inclined to assume strategic behavior—why should one?—internal conflict also exists within an industrial association such as the BDI and is usually resolved by coming to a consensus through discussions.

The integrative approach is also found in political parties, parliamentary groups, and environmental associations and within the respective federal ministries themselves. Thus, within the Ministry for Economic Affairs, there is a department for environmental politics; this territory is not left to the Ministry of the Environment; rather, one tries to integrate political arguments about the environment into the internal definition of one's position. Similar structures are also found in the Ministry of the Environment or in the Ministry of Transport. One

anticipates the arguments of the others and more or less goes through the anticipated discussions internally in order to present an argument that is *as integrated
as possible* in the actual struggle of interests.

Within parliamentary groups there is also a variety of committees covering sociopolitical problems. These committees try to reach a compromise within the
internal discussions. These compromises are then able to survive in struggles
between the groups. The idea behind this is that the *better* (i.e., the *most integrated*) arguments generally become accepted in the end.

When using an integrated problem-solving approach, knowledge about the rationality of the other actors becomes especially important. One tries to acquire this
knowledge through the organization's internal anticipation of conflict. Consensus
in this context is a guarantee of integration since on this level an agreement
should be reached, and an integrated solution seems to be the best way to reach
this agreement. Since the most integrated solution is also considered to be the
best, knowledge that is produced by a consensus is the strongest weapon in the
actual political discussion.

The search for integrated knowledge, however, is not only understood as a
strategic operation of network actors. One is quite aware that integrated problem
solving is used as a strategy for exercising one's interests. Knowledge in this
context is always "interested knowledge," and, therefore, it cannot really be regarded as a basis for a consensus. The integrated problem-solving approach has
its highpoint, then, in the creation of an authority that is obligated to a purely
scientific search for the "genuine," the truly integrated solution that is apparently
free from particular interests. It is, therefore, no coincidence that such an authority was created in the form of the Expert Council on Environmental Matters. The
main task of this council is to provide the political decision makers with only
scientifically based suggestions for action. It is decisive that this authority was
created and maintained, although the suggestions for action that are produced
there are represented only rarely by the political authorities, too. Although the
interests of the participating actors are often infringed upon to a great extent, or
precisely because they are infringed upon so often to a great extent, the Expert
Council is given much more importance than similar institutions in other countries: it sets goals not only of an environmental and political nature but also based
on a consensus that hopefully will become the decisive factor in political regulations after many years of consensus making based on interest.

The Selection of Relevant Knowledge

As we will see, this describes the institutional rules of a level that is quickly
abandoned in the political discussions when it is no longer a question of general
goals in a law but of the *concrete regulations* as such. Concrete regulations are
not found in the ambient air quality protection law but in the numerous regulations and legal guidelines and, above all, in the technical standards. From the
point of view of the permit-granting cartel, it is no longer necessary to reach for a
consensus of the whole society where guidelines, not goals, are concerned. Here
just a legal agreement is necessary with the ones directly affected by the guide-

lines, that is, the one to whom a certain *order* is imposed sovereignly. Thus, it is also important here to determine *who is affected.* Trade unions, scientists, environmental associations, and so on are indeed *"participating* interest groups" that should be consulted in goal setting for the whole society, but they are not "directly affected actors." Therefore, their knowledge does not count in this context. Once again, it is knowledge that matters here; however, it is the knowledge about the situation and way of operating of those directly affected by the orders. Such information is regarded as indispensable if political authorities try to regulate in the areas of these nonpolitical interests. Therefore, in political decision making *cooperative* work is seen as very important. As the representative of public interests, the state has to arouse the conviction for environmental necessities in commerce and industry. First of all, then, a *consensus* with regard to the necessity of measures is to be reached. It is generally believed that without this consensus environmental regulations would hold no water because the state would be lacking the necessary knowledge for the regulation if commerce and industry refused to cooperate. Without the necessary knowledge, however, governmental regulations would not be successful; they would simply not be able to be implemented. Cooperation in decision making and consensus with regard to the necessity of regulations are, therefore, the basic requirements of governmental actions. The state, personified in negotiation partners from the bureaucracy, is understood here as the representative of the economy's societal environment; this idea fits excellently with the self-description of officials in the Ministry of the Environment seeing themselves as public servants.

The difference between the knowledge of those directly affected by pollution and that of those involved in the political process, because they are affected by official orders, describes, therefore, the basis of the relationship between industry and politics, which is represented by the ministerial bureaucracies. Since the ability to implement political measures and goals in the text of legal regulations is the issue on this level, no accommodation needs to occur with the other societal carriers of information. How are these others supposed to be able to contribute to the success of the legal regulations? Here success is more important than democratic legitimation. This is mainly also the case as, on the political side, parliamentary representatives and ministers can no longer be involved in the process of working out the details with commerce and industry. They are satisfied if their abstract goals are implemented, thus successful. Therefore, the more precise determination of the text of the legal regulations simply becomes the object of the "objective" discussion between the economy and the executive.

The work of the permit-granting authority is also seen in this way. Here the issue is not the voting on an executive decision, the permit, by the citizens who are affected by emissions but rather the voting on an administrative decision by the financially affected firms. Guided by the principle of appropriateness, the simplified view of "who is affected" runs through the determination of undefined legal terms and up to the implementation on-site.

The Differentiation of Political Spheres

Due to the limitation of the definition of legal regulations to a negotiation process between the economy and the ministerial bureaucracy, there is a differentiation of the political sphere into two different areas. In one area we find political goal setting and the production of a *general law*. In the other area, there is the apparently purely "objective" discussion over the *concrete contents* of the law. From the viewpoint of the permit-granting cartel, the latter area represents a rather nonpolitical field that covers an "objective" exchange of information between the economy and the executive. It is seen as nonpolitical because the only issue at hand for the executive is the *implementation* of political goals. As long as the implementation is not put off here, and the arguments based on the *expertise of those directly affected* (e.g., obtained by the federal office of the environment, the Umweltbundesamt [UBA]) can be countered with other arguments based on their own findings, then—it is argued—a one-sided imposition of interests on the part of the economy cannot result. Thus, the *integrity* of civil servants is what matters. On the one hand, civil servants do not make politics themselves. On the other hand, they have to protect the state from those who illegitimately politicize the issue (Interview Länderausschuß für Immissionschutz [LAI]). This bureaucratic conception of political work has, however, far-reaching effects. The actual contents of political regulations can be regarded only as oriented toward success, but not as democratically legitimate since the decisions affect the economy only in a financial sense, but in a broader sense affect all members of society. The closing of the "objective" sphere results, therefore, from a very limited definition of who is directly affected. This limitation ultimately leads to politics without politicians.

Where one sees himself or herself as not having sufficient expertise, the only option left is integration by cooperation in order to be able to carry out the goals of the law. Thus, one cooperates and thinks, nevertheless, that one is operating in a nonpolitical sphere. This structure is found in the federal office of the environment, for example. Although a multitude of talks with the associations and also with the VDI is an everyday occurrence, one holds the opinion here that "these political discussions come later; we only present the technical basis for these political discussions. But the political discussions take place in Bonn by listening to the interest groups involved" (Interview UBA).

This structure is even adopted by the VDI, which, to a great extent, is composed of representatives from the economy; however, the VDI also fulfills a more or less governmental function in that, by the creation of technical standards and the definition of appropriateness, it determines what all members of society have to accept in the form of technically produced risk. The VDI also sees its work as nonpolitical: "The VDI is not a stage for environmental associations, as these are very active *politically*. . . . one does not want to politicize this area, this technical-scientific discussion" (Interview VDI).

Legitimation is clearly made "objectively": actually the execution of legal regulations is a purely governmental task without any political meaning (LAI), but when the Executive lacks the necessary expertise, its staff can work "objectively" with other actors. Since this defines the VDI's legitimate working sphere, one is also completely blind to the fact that particular interests become noticeable in a very selective form through this cooperation. However, it is believed that the government receives help in discovering the truth in this way.

The accommodation of the ministerial bureaucracies and the economy, the standardization of regulations for the purpose of implementation, the determination of undefined legal terms, scientific advice on policy, and the setting of technical standards (i.e., the activities of the permit-granting cartel) are understood to ideally be *nonpolitical* events. Here ideally means that if everything is done properly (truly, correctly), then it is so. The actors who were interviewed by us were sure that not everything is done properly. Thus, the Federal Association for the Environment and the Protection of Nature (Bund für Umwelt und Naturschutz Deutschland [BUND]) complains that within the federal state committee for the protection of ambient air quality (LAI), there is a bias toward industrial interests, and governmental actors point to the too strong presence of industrial representatives within the VDI. Nevertheless, this critique means precisely the adhesion to the ideal picture: certainly it happens that people are engaged in politics in our nonpolitical sphere, but actually we should adhere to making an effort here toward a factual consensus. Actual politics (the struggle of interest groups) should, therefore, take place on another stage, such as in the hearing of interest groups concerned in the Parliament or in electoral campaigns. Thus, even where criticism comes up, and alternatives are suggested, our actors move within the described legitimated pattern of differentiated politics.

The "public sphere" of politics is described by the political actors as the legitimate sphere for the representation of interests to a very limited extent only. The fact that politics is also involved in the "objective"-scientific advice on policy by the representatives of interests is inconceivable from this viewpoint, even though this "objective" part of the ambient air quality protection plays a decisive role in political discussions.

Emotions and the Public

The described differentiation of the two political spheres in German clean air politics also determines the role that the public plays in this political context. In a political system where on-hand knowledge of associations and interests represented by them play the main role, the public can, at best, be understood simply as an organized civil society. Where there is no organization of the public, the public is seen as a diffuse grouping of personal interests that reacts with prejudice and "emotionally," so to speak, to political events. If or how the public is affected is a question of purely subjective problems (Interview BDI), a circumstance that does not live up to the politics of reaching a consensus based on "objectivity." This is one reason that the public plays practically no role in permit-granting procedures and is at most "aware" of hearings only on the level of program formulation. In standard-setting procedures, however, the public is completely excluded.

Under a rule by virtue of knowledge, the only ones who are in the position to have their interests heard are those who have extremely *rationalized* their collection of knowledge and information. Consequently, in the struggle of interest groups to make themselves heard, the only ones who can survive are those whose interests are *organized*. This is true even for experts and scientists, whose opinion can carry weight only, if they belong to an organization with a suitable *reputation*. It is especially true for the interests articulated in the public sphere. Within the permit-granting cartel, the battle over the correct solution to problems allows the public to have a place only in the form of civil societal organizations. On this level of "technical" questions, the public is practically equated with environmental organizations. *Therefore, environmental associations in Germany are seen not only as representatives of an ecological rationality but also, to a great extent, as the representatives of a public that is not involved in the decision making process.* The knowledge that the environmental associations collect through this function is then considered as much more important than the knowledge that the environmental associations have about the contents of the matter. "Objective" work is, in principle, not compatible with an emotional public. Here rationality and emotion oppose each other irreconcilably. From the point of view of the permit-granting cartel, therefore, the environmental associations are of no use. Because of their dual approach (representation of the public and representation of ecological rationality), environmental associations risk dividing themselves into two, whereby one of the sides, either the issue or the politics, has to suffer.

Here, too, a selection of relevant knowledge takes place. From the viewpoint of the permit-granting cartel, environmental associations can contribute knowledge only about the acceptance of regulations. Their knowledge about the technical problems is not interesting to the cartel; in fact, it disturbs the process of politics and the economy's coming to an accommodation on the feasibility of implementation. This cover-up takes place through the work of the environmental associations, so that in the end the environmental associations' fusing of technical work with the representation of fears articulated by the public disturbs the purely "objective" process of political formulation. Thus, it is no wonder that the environmental associations' claim to representation is not accepted. Their actions have not been legitimated in this sense. The public certainly has the right to organize in order to represent its interests. These organizations, however, are not allowed to have any influence on political work since they politicize a supposedly nonpolitical process in an illegitimate way. The public can introduce itself as a voting people. Above all, it can achieve what a representative of the state involved in environmental politics needs for his or her work: public pressure. This can help the matter or, rather, hinder it.

From an "objective" point of view, the public is not a participating actor; it is an actor that needs to be enlightened. Properly enlightened, the public would not represent its own particularistic interests but would serve as an instrument to achieve the "objectively" correct solution. From the point of view of "differentiated" politics, the public is simply allotted the formal-legitimate level. Due to its necessarily emotional irritability, the public has nothing to contribute to "objective" political work. Nevertheless, one can try to influence the formally legitimate area of politics for the benefit of one's own "objective'"political work. Here the public can disrupt but also be advantageous, just as "politics" can generally disrupt or promote technical work. The public is important where one can influence political processes by the creation of public pressure. This is achieved by the commitment of politicians and political parties to public opinion.

Public pressure becomes political pressure if the reelection of politicians is in the near future. In this sense, the public is seen only as an electorate, as the basis for legitimation, but cannot be allotted any role in the actual political process. The transparency of political decisions is attempted to be produced, therefore, by objectively informing the public rather than by creating an awareness for the participation of the public itself (Weber 1958: 518f.). *The reason for this is found in the semantics of truth of a rule by virtue of knowledge.* Under a rule by virtue of knowledge, democracy is understood to be an enlightenment of the public and not a participation of the public. This task of enlightenment is precisely the conception of working on and for democracy involved in the politics of clean air. Within a rule by virtue of knowledge, democracy can function and be superior to other systems of government only if the public has enough knowledge on which to base decisions in political elections. The voters are also working for the truth, not for their own interests. Voters are also obligated to use their knowledge for the common good. Understood in this way, democracy strives in the direction of a limit; it strives to keep politics close to nothing in that political discussions are attempted to be resolved by discovering the truth. To achieve this ideal, all of the political institutions are obligated to enlighten the public. Environmental associations, political parties, firms, and so on see their work for the public not as a promotion of their own interests but as a factual enlightenment so that responsible adult citizens themselves can form the correct opinion. Some environmental associations have specialized in this task of enlightenment and refrain entirely from political discussions. Governmental organizations, such as the federal office of the environment, also see one of their main duties as factual, nonbiased enlightenment.

THE ROLE OF THE PROFESSIONS: RULE BY VIRTUE OF ENGINEER'S KNOWLEDGE

The rules of a rule by virtue of knowledge that we have described are based on the idea of a nonbiased consensus, which can be achieved by objectifying an issue. This is the role, then, that expertise should play in political discussions. However, which "issue" is actually at stake in the political discussion is very important. In German environmental law the quality of the environment as such is not focused on, but technology is much more focused on, so that the latter also becomes the *pertinent point of reference.* The belief held is that the quality of the environment can be automatically improved through improved technology. This engineering-oriented belief forces rule by virtue of knowledge into particular contexts (Knoepfel and Weidner 1983: 105). The reliability of technical knowledge should compensate for the vagueness of the standardized basis for intervention. The more that legal regulations determine only the goals to be aspired to, due to the principle of integration and the resulting ability of the society to come to a consensus, the more important that the reliability of the knowledge and its ability to be assessed outside the law become. This also leads to an overriding presence of professional knowledge, in particular, knowledge in the areas of engineering and the natural sciences, in the administrative decision making process. The engineering profession is thereby given the most important role in clean air politics. Engineers decide whether a facility corresponds to the state of technology. This question is easily answered and objectified with the necessary expertise. This objective method occurs by way of technical regulations. Objectification is also sought after in the negotiations of the permit-granting officials with industry. The technical discussion of scientists and technicians shapes both the formulation of the text of the regulations, the TA-Luft, VDI guidelines, and implementation as well.

The differentiation of two political spheres in clean air politics described here is paralleled by the differentiation in professional discourse. *The apparently nonpolitical, impartial, "objective," and scientific work of the permit-granting cartel becomes qualified and specified by the engineers as agents of the technicist discourse.* The issue becomes the specialty. A very striking structural similarity exists between the mechanisms for closure of certain constellations of networks, institutionalized political understandings, and professional arrangements. By looking at clean air politics in this way, a clearer outline begins to appear: the rule by virtue of knowledge becomes the rule by virtue of engineer's knowledge. The noninstitutionalized participation of the public in political decisions (except in the cyclical elections) is grounded here in the devaluation of the relevance of primary experience (cf. Wolf 1988). Thus, it can be assumed that many of the institutional rules of clean air politics discussed by us have a parallel in the specific point of view of technicians and scientists, in their professional ethics, socialization, and a nonpolitical, professional group dynamic. Due to these reasons, not only does clean air politics appear to be shaped much more by the technical thematization of the issue than by the political discussion about the desired societal goal, but this technical discussion also appears to represent the door to the forum of the struggle of interests. This is a chance for interest-articulation, which the public administration has to face to the same extent as the environmental groups. A strong professionalization in the struggles of interests, which is oriented toward a technical discourse, can be found both in the public administration and in environmental groups. Bureaucracy becomes increasingly a technocracy. Environmental associations increasingly mutate into competitive firms well versed in technology that use technical discourse to integrate themselves into the system (cf. Rucht 1988: 290). In this way, the sought-after technical-scientific consensus also increasingly removes the environmental groups from the firsthand experiences of the citizens affected by the air quality and continues to increase the depoliticization of clean air politics.

The profession not only supports the differentiation of political spheres and the exclusion of prejudice from the permit-granting cartel but also provides the capacities for the integration of the different views: the struggle of interests is not fought with regard to goals to be reached but over technically oriented views of the matter. Here an evidently purely technical consensus seems to be much more possible than an obviously political consensus with regard to the determination of

goals. Beyond this *organized* representation of technical rationality there is, however, also an *informal* gathering of technical expertise that shapes clean air politics. Thus, it is also important to examine these informal contacts as the forum for
exchanging technological expertise. They characterize an unorganized area that
can be considered the basis of program formulation and implementation in ambient air quality protection. Ministries, permit-granting authorities, environmental
associations, and citizens' action groups are dependent on information to an ever
greater extent. This information is obtained from the described informal network
of technical professions (Christmann 1992). Beyond the organized advice on
policy by associations and organizations such as the Association of German Engineers or the state Committee on Ambient Air Quality Protection, these other in-
formation-dependent groups contribute to the further differentiation of political
spheres, to a rule by virtue of knowledge, and to the resulting exclusion, which is
considered legitimate, of the individual interests of those affected by the air quality.

Technology and the Law

The term "state of technology" is composed of two parts in the German ambient air quality protection law. One part is the determination of "what is technologically possible," and the other part, the determination of the "appropriateness
of the means." What is technologically possible is seen as an objective matter,
whereas appropriateness is mainly an issue of legally weighing the pros against
the cons. What is most important here is financial appropriateness.

The firm itself knows best about the financial situation of an industrial branch
or a firm on the market; however, the greatest amount of technical-productive
knowledge is also kept here. This knowledge must be exhausted for the determination of what is technologically possible. In determining the undefined legal
term of "state of technology," the industrial side has an important advantage of
knowledge over the state, a situation that in a rule by virtue of knowledge has
consequences since "that is why the official influence on business life in a capital-
istic age is very limited and very often state regulations derail in this area in unforeseen and unintentional ways or are made pointless by the *superior expertise of
those having an interest*" (Weber 1972: 673).

The principle of appropriateness protects those who have to implement the
standards from unjustified intervention in their rights, in this case, the right to
carry on a business. It is always in the interest of the industrial firms to strongly
protect their rights above all; they can always introduce the better arguments if a
change in their position in the market is anticipated due to an official or legal
intervention. In capitalism, the state has no chance of overtaking the entrepreneur
with free market economy arguments. In German clean air politics, the way out of
this situation is attempted in that the state dictates to the firms to at least provide
those technological means for the reduction of air pollution, the implementation
of which should not be inappropriate. The "state of technology," then, means only
that the best of the appropriate solutions is laid down. Which solution is chosen, is
a decision of the state! But where does the state get its information for this deci-

sion? Here there are at least two possibilities: the state itself can create organizations that concern themselves with these technological questions, or the state can have these questions answered by independent authorities. In Germany a mixture of both of these possibilities is practiced. On the one hand, the state created the UBA, which very comprehensively deals with technological questions. On the other hand, though, the state also transferred concrete tasks of technical standard-setting to private organizations such as the KRDL in the VDI, which are paid for these services. It is characteristic of the VDI as well as of the UBA to answer the questions about the "state of technology"; that is, it is asked about appropriateness *as well as* about what is technologically possible. Therefore, no authority in Germany solely determines the "state of technological possibilities" in order to make this information available for the negotiations between the state and industry about appropriateness. At least the ideas of business management have always formed an inseparable unit with the "state of technology," "which creates a task that is almost impossible to cope with for more than a few administrative judges, and that task is to differentiate between what is technologically possible and what is economically justifiable" (Mai 1994: 141).

Using the two parts of the idea of the "state of technology," one could ideally divide the work between two professions as a starting point. Whereas the technicians are responsible for the determination of what is technologically possible, it could be the task of lawyers to establish what is appropriateness. Since the latter can take place only based on the former, the technicians play a key role in this division of labor. Since in purely technically oriented organizations appropriate solutions are already searched for, there is no more need for specialized knowledge in the decision making process that would defend technical solutions with regard to legal claims from industrial firms affected by the law. This is especially understandable if one recalls that the most likely ones to take legal action, as a rule, are those who shape the concept of the "state of technology" on the technical side (permit-granting cartel). Thus, the legal profession in this division of labor increasingly fades into the mere business of a notary.

Engineers are educated in the natural sciences, but they differentiate themselves from the classic scientists through their practical orientation. Engineers are interested in the practical implementation of scientific discoveries; that is the difference in their professional identity. Because of this, they are constantly confronted with nonscientific, nontechnical influences on their work. The practical implementation of scientific discoveries always needs a balance of various viewpoints, which can appear only in practice. Thus, it is not surprising that engineers assume that they will find a feasible solution to technical problems in every situation. Their professional ethic has them look for the best solution, whereby the assessment of the solution not only is based on technical success but also depends on the course taken up in the search for a solution, on the methods used. Engineers are also mainly technicians in methods. They hardly see a technical problem to be solved as difficult. What is difficult, though, is to offer a practicable and effective solution to a technical problem. This leads to engineers, at least those who graduated from a technical school, considering financial, logistical, and per-

sonnel problems as important, too. In this sense, it is an intricate part of engineering behavior to always solve technical problems "in an appropriate way." It makes
no sense for a technician to exhaust all technical means "no matter how much it
costs" in order to solve a problem. In regard to technical clean air policy this
means that engineers always see themselves as responsible for the market-
economy side of the determination of the "state of technology." Whoever thinks
that one can use technicians only to determine the state of what is technologically
possible ignores the self-concept of the engineers.

It is decisive here that due to the self-concept of the engineers, the assessment
of appropriateness of a "state of technology" to be created becomes a technical
discussion about the "issue." Although statements about cost-benefit relationships
are made, this happens in a nonbiased way, according to the self-concept of the
engineers. Technicians can decide between conflicting interests "objectively,"
since there can only be *one* right solution. Special interests play a role in professional engineering discussions only insofar as they stand in the way of discovering
the truth and, consequently, in resolving conflicts between differing interests. This
leads to technicians' tending to base their work within organizations such as the
KRDL (i.e., their "authority to make judgments") on their "expertise" (Mai 1994:
182). In this way, there is a tendency to see the standard-setting work in the VDI
as a task of objective judgment and not as the result of a process of resolving conflicts between differing interests. *Engineers search for the objectively best solution in standard-setting work; due to the self-concept of the engineers, this can
never be a purely technical search. Someone who is not a technician sees something that appears to be a process of accommodating interests and is thereby
described as political; the technician views the same process as an identity-
forming component of his or her profession that is mainly "objective" and unbiased.*

The technical profession mainly plays a decisive role in German ambient air
quality protection through its organization in the KRDL of the VDI. The profession's power to define in regard to the determination of the "state of technology"
is important here. The technical profession does not merely consider the state of
what is technically possible but also considers the appropriateness of an intervention. This activity, which is carried out informally and comprehensively by engineers, is so widespread that within the KRDL standards are also made that have
little to do with the determination of the "state of technology" as such. It is also
the task of the KRDL to form a picture of the effects of ambient air quality and to
establish limits with regard to air quality. This is an activity that seems better
suited for doctors and biologists. However, the power of supposedly objective
scientific knowledge is great. That is principally because the effectiveness of the
standards is tied to this knowledge by the technical profession. As pointed out in
the previous section, the effectiveness of air pollution regulations is more important than the question of legitimacy. Due to their education and their profession,
engineers are the guarantee for this effectiveness. Effectiveness, not truth, is their
basic principle.

The state leaves it up to the technical profession and its self-concept to set technical standards for clean air policy and to determine the limits of harmful substances in the air. Even if the state does not take on the regulations produced by the VDI, there are still technicians in the UBA, the LAI, or the special governmental offices who do this job for the state. Even the committees, which pose a certain counterweight to the VDI, are mainly composed of technicians who share the orientation toward effectiveness of their profession. Thus, it is self-evident that in the UBA and the LAI technical solutions are also sought after that represent appropriateness. An organization that solely determines the state of what is technically possible consequently does not exist. *Clean air politics is legitimated by objectifying an issue that has, however, never been objectified anywhere in fact.*

Quite apart from the few and unimportant legal proceedings on the different levels, one sees that lawyers primarily play a role on the governmental side in clean air politics. Most of the areas of administration are monopolized by lawyers. This mainly has to do with the institutionalized closeness of jurisprudence with the state. Lawyers do not study at the German universities for an academic degree, but for a state degree. The content of lawyers' education and the prerequisites for their exams are consequently determined by the state, not by the universities. Not least of all, this helps the state to educate its senior civil servants itself. This tradition also leads to lawyers' having positions in the offices responsible for implementing clean air policy in the form of granting permits. Here, however, it is important to differentiate more precisely. In some states in Germany, the administration for technical matters (e.g., the office for the protection of ambient air quality or the office responsible for the enforcement of laws governing health and safety as well as conditions of work) can independently carry out simplified procedures for granting a permit, whereas procedures where the public is involved are permissible only following an agreement with the internal administration, as a rule, the governmental committee. While the administration for technical matters is primarily composed of technicians, they play only a minor role in the governmental committees. Here it is mainly lawyers who supervise the work of technical civil servants. In whatever way that the various responsibilities are divided up in the individual German states, they all have the purpose of supplementing the work of the technically well versed civil servants with the supervision and control of the legally trained civil servants. This is exactly what the people we interviewed from industry objected to.

Not only the arguments from those asking for a permit but also the general problems of legally regulating technical problems lead to the tendency of granting higher authority to purely technical administrations or to so-called offices for the protection of the environment. This involves a general reduction of formal, legal control and a strengthening of the informal technocratic discussions based on the law.

It can be assumed that the wish expressed by the firms asking for a permit, that the technical bodies responsible for clean air policy also be given the competence to make decisions, is related to the difficulties that result from a cooperation of technicians on the industrial side and lawyers on the governmental side. In contrast to technicians in the offices responsible for implementing clean air policy, a lawyer would never hold the opinion that a specific technical solution is the only possibility or that a specific "state of technology" or a specific limit to harmful substances is the only conceivable one. In comparison with that, the engineers have a hard time recognizing the political character of the technical standards. For lawyers it is not an unfamiliar idea that every technical solution could also be different, if another majority supported it. Technicians, in contrast, stress supposedly objective facts in their argumentation for or against a specific technical solution according to the idea that the search for "truth" has nothing to do with special interests, consensus is not always a compromise, and the "truth," therefore, cannot be found within a societal or political area of tension. These differences seem to allow technicians from the industry to negotiate with the specialist bodies in a much more promising way than with civil servants from the internal administration—lawyers, as a rule.

The general administration does not have a lot to oppose to the informal way, caused by technical discourse, in which the law is carried out. Certainly, lawyers can refer to formal procedures and sue for precise observation of regulations. However, in light of the strongly technically oriented system, the discussion about technology seems to many lawyers, whose practice includes the regulation of technical facts, to be like the fairy-tale "race between the rabbit and the hedgehog" (Mai 1994: 179). The question that arises here for many lawyers is if the law is in a position at all to regulate technological developments or if this should not entirely be the task of technical self-determination.

The law cannot be any kind of significant point of reference where the threshold for intervention by governmental regulation is determined by technology. The task of lawyers is increasingly reduced, therefore, to acting as a notary for "the record" (Bohne 1981: 57). This is where I see the decisive context in the division of labor between lawyers and technicians in clean air politics: Whereas the technicist discourse increases the capacity of the engineers to attain appropriate solutions and whereas the bulk of informal negotiations, which is understood as purely technical, makes politics' legality a technical matter, a reduction of legal consideration to the recording duties of a notary in a negotiating process that is not legally shaped is taking place at the same time. Just as the hearing of special interest groups involved in the procedure for drafting the law represents only the formal basis for legitimation of an already informally thought-out wording of a law, the legal discourse of clean air politics is reduced to the validation of purely technically oriented decisions. Therefore, one may also describe the totality of clean air politics as a struggle between professions, as a conflict between juridical reasoning and technical specialization, between intersubjective legal exegesis and the positivistic search for the "truth." This conflict seems to be resolved on all levels in the idea of a rule by virtue of engineering knowledge.

Technical Community

The identities and patterns of interpretation that are carried by the professions create significant, intersubjective obligations that are not always organized in the form of a professional community. They contribute to what we can call the informal community network. Next to the organized ways of cooperation, which take on a very significant role within clean air politics through the VDI as regards the profession of technicians, a rather informal relationship of mutual exchange of information exists without which German clean air politics would not be conceivable. Many actors have to rely on obtaining information about the state of things through ways other than the formal procedures for contact. This is decisive for the technical profession and the technical discourse. This mainly has to do with the complexity of the technical solutions to problems. Since these are always related to practice and since, thus, a multitude of contingencies has to be considered, technical knowledge cannot be produced in a laboratory. Once a technical solution is found, it cannot be easily applied to other problem situations. This circumstance promotes specialization within the technical profession. If one, then, is interested in the truly "objective" solution in the processes of considering the advantages and disadvantages of various solutions, it is necessary to have contact with the actual specialists in a specific area. Technicians from the ministries of the environment often maintain informal contacts with technicians from industry, attend professional seminars and informational events, or simply visit and tour facilities. In addition, organizations such as the VDI or the Chemical Industry Association (Verband der Chemischen Industrie [VCI]) organize events and invite all interested technicians. One meets in work groups organized by authorities or even by economic associations about a specific topic, not to reach a specific decision but just to form an opinion about a topic. One sees familiar faces and meets new people. Above all, one knows where to call and who has to be called if specific information is needed. These varied informal contacts are not just the expression of lobbying and the representation of interests, even if they are often pulled into this context. These contacts are both a completely undisturbed and, in a certain way, innocent interest of the engineers in information, that is, experience.

One belongs to this information-sharing community if one speaks the same language and feels obligated to common professional ethics. This includes that one has to show the others that one is an expert and is not pursuing any personal interests. One informs the others correctly, objectively. Even if the other knows that one belongs to an organization that may follow specific interests, he or she will assume that, due to common professional obligations to give only objective expertise, these specific interests are not of focal importance. Many of those interviewed are proud of their telephone record, which, they see as a qualitative guarantee of a network-producing objectivity. In this network, the membership to a certain organization does not count; merely the membership to the technical profession, to the team of experts, counts. The engineer seems to be an easy target for lobbyists, simply because he or she is blind to special interests. What seems important to me in this context is the common language. Engineers have a language that is free of all judgments outside of technical matters, whereas lawyers very conscientiously take into account economic, political, and social values in their language. Technical language favors the idea that those using this language are obtaining objective information. Apparently, special interests are not hidden in such a language but only appear to be possible in nontechnical matters. For this reason, many of those interviewed by us hold the opinion that they would immediately recognize an informant's attempt to convey his or her special interests. What they would see, in fact, however, is the nontechnical language. Engineers are blind to the fact that it is possible to convey interests in their objective, as it were, purified language. This is a theoretically untenable, yet very effective, position. How does this idea come about? It seems to me that one possibility may be education that takes place within the technical profession. In their education at a technical school, technicians mainly learn about the natural sciences. A positivistic understanding of science from a natural science point of view is also taught. Usually difficult to analyze, this understanding of science is taken on by technical professionals without realizing that, through the practical orientation of engineering and the accompanying maxim of effectiveness, variables that cannot be made objective are integrated into their reasoning. An industrial firm is not a laboratory; thus, positivistic truth cannot be searched for here. Nevertheless, a positivistic understanding of science within the technical profession leads right to this behavior. This attitude is also clearly underlined by the role attributed to other professions in clean air politics.

Medicine and Technology

In the eyes of the technical profession, there are two fatal, so to speak, accusations in regard to information offered. One accusation is that of representing special interests, and the other is the topic's lack of objectification. From the point of view of the technical profession, both of these accusations principally explain why other professions play only a very minimal role. Medicine especially does not appear to fit into the idea of an "objective" and truth-seeking science. According to the text of the ambient air quality protection law, a great significance could be given to medicine, human biology, or biology in order to protect people and animals, plants and objects from harm. One could think that the first step in the political accomplishment of this goal would include establishing what kind of air pollution can be harmful.

Ambient air quality levels draw up the limits as to what is harmful. Rationally speaking, there should be many ambient air quality levels because it is important. But then you quickly come to a limit: Who will tell you, what is harmful when and under which conditions? Only doctors can tell you that, and then only specialists . . . and if you ask them, you will notice that there is a great deal of uncertainty. And naturally there are no experiments on people in this area . . . that is all very difficult, the ambient air quality levels do not wear cement overshoes. . . . And you stand right against the wall, if you ask about cancer-causing substances, at what level does a substance become harmful? Doctors say that there is no limit. Any amount, even the smallest amount can cause cancer. (Interview Ministry of the Environment)

Through the standard of the "state of technology" set up by the engineers, the realization of goals prescribed by the law is more practicable and oriented to emission levels. Hence, the establishment of what is technologically possible serves as a basis for negotiation in the decision making process with regard to the ban on excesses in legal regulations. That the determination of the state of technological possibilities never takes place in fact but always includes the "appropriateness" of the means is not noticed here. This myth of objective technology legitimates the exclusion of medical facts from the legislation on clean air. A technological facility is either built, or it isn't; it is planned, or it has been realized somewhere else in the world. Apparently, there is nothing to quibble about. A person, however, gets sick with only a certain probability, and the factors that cause illness cannot be rigorously isolated. Whereas in engineering the practical implementation of scientific findings is in transition, the findings themselves are in transition in medicine. But how should one make sensible laws if the basic knowledge constantly changes and is constantly contestable anyway? The engineers' refusal of relativating scientific truth is accompanied by the lawyers' fear of the resulting legal uncertainty. With an emphasis on the harm that dangerous substances can cause, can't anyone living near a facility who suffers from lung cancer first sue the one who runs the facility and, second, sue the state as the one that agreed to the dangerous levels? Isn't it necessary to protect the state from such a flood of legal suits? One would inevitably have to ask all of these questions if the practice of clean air politics (i.e., the orientation to the "state of technology") had not been so successful.

THE CULTURE OF CLEAN AIR POLITICS

Not only clean air politics but the whole environmental field in Germany is shaped by an understanding of nature from both a scientific and anthropocentric point of view. The orientation to technology of the German ambient air quality protection law is firmly grounded here. The term "environment" makes this clear. Nature is not recognized as having its own importance, which would include the reason and right for its existence. On the contrary, it is conceived of as the environment of the society, as a medium for human existence. It is worthwhile to protect the environment due only to its relationship to people. Nature is the *environment* and always has a contextual relationship to society. Environmental legislation is "inexorably anthropocentric" (Meyer-Abich 1984: 54). This is clear in the ambient air quality protection law's orientation to the "state of technology" since in those cases in which none or only an insufficient type of technology for the protection of ambient air quality is available, the request for an official permit always has to be answered in favor of the ecology (cf. Übersohn 1990).

This understanding of nature is combined with a positivistic understanding of science. Because of this, anthropocentrically focused environmental relationships are always examined as causalities, as ascertainable cause–effect relationships, which have to be studied scientifically. This makes it clear why it is admitted that the environment has an influence on the life of *every* member of society, that is, that everyone is affected by environmental damage to some extent. Nevertheless, not everyone affected is considered to have the legitimacy to translate this into political demands. Every member of society can perceive the spoiling of his or her "life world" by environmental damage, but it is left up to the experts to discover only the inherent causalities and, in turn, make these revelations the basis for political intervention. Without a reference to scientific insinuations of causality, it is difficult to articulate one's interests. *Therefore, individual interest and the subjective perception of being affected by something are not the deciding factors for inclusion as a political actor; scientifically substantiated reputation and expertise are the deciding factors.* A culturally based reason for the institutional exclusion of the public from clean air politics can be seen here. The differentiation of clean air politics into two separate areas also has its foundation here. Whereas the public-formal area serves the articulation of fears with regard to harmful effects and, so to speak, represents the anthropocentric starting point for the political decision making race, the informal, supposedly nonpolitical area aids in the scientific analysis of these relationships of causality. However, since there is a chronological causal connection between the articulation of perceived harmful effects and political intervention, scientific reparation has to be understood to a much greater extent as scientifically sound prevention of damage to the environment under political regulation. From this viewpoint, nature is again controlled and manipulated for people's benefit through technological intervention. That clean air politics is carried on in this technological way of catching up, rather than as a sociopolitical process with foresight, is also proved by the exaggerated emphasis on the technical profession in comparison to lawyers but is not to be exclusively seen as the result of a positivistic understanding of science or even an anthropocentric understanding of nature. These understandings suggest a technical-manipulative relationship to nature, but they do not establish whether the relationship has a restorative or a preventive nature.

That there is so little space reserved for preventive clean air policy depends much more on a second level, where the technical profession's interests are strongly linked to economic rationalities. As shown before, rational-purposeful action corresponds exactly to technical-positivistic thinking. We can see a consequence of this relationship in that the principle of prevention is propagated in German ambient air quality protection laws and is established as an obligation of those running a facility but again is judged solely by the standard of the "state of technology." Mainly due to the technical profession's attitude, which has already been discussed, the "state of technology" should not be confused with the state of what is scientifically possible. Economic considerations receive much more weight than ecological or social ones. One can first talk about prevention in a nontechnical, but certainly scientific, way if there is no longer a legally grounded right to pollute the air, but rather, air pollution can be made to be dependent on a societal consensus that is decided in each individual case and not granted on principle. *The priority of the right to carry on a business over the protection of ambient air quality thus guarantees a restorative, technically oriented ambient air quality protection policy.* Ambient air quality protection legislation in the strictest sense is, therefore, not to be seen as a protection of the environment but merely as a technical limitation on damage. This structure allows it to appear more sensible, from the perspective of the state, both to cooperate with actors from industry and to fear jeopardizing its position by the articulation of interests by those "who are affected." This, however, usually leaves the societally legitimated, rational-scientific decision making horizon.

Covered by the technical profession and simplifying the communication between the state and the economy, the emission orientation of the German clean air protection law can also be seen as a further closure of the political decision making process to the special interests of those citizens who are affected by air pollution. Not only does the technicist discourse appear to these citizens as completely incomprehensible, but the nonpublic nature of the negotiating process closes the door to this nebulous sphere. At the same time, the emission orientation guarantees a definition of "who is affected" that neglects the interests of people who are, indeed, affected. The emission orientation turns the citizens affected by air pollution into spectators who do not have tickets to the game between the state and the business associations and firms that are affected by governmental regulations. An orientation to ambient air quality would not allow this definition of "who is affected" and would also put into question the work of the permit-granting cartel, but, on the other hand, faith in the government's principle of cooperation would be severely broken.

In my opinion, one can add the idealistic-consensual understanding of society that shapes the prevailing idea of clean air protection to the positivistic understanding of science and the anthropocentric understanding of nature. This can be demonstrated by an institutionally reinforced overestimation of discursive arrangements of experts (scientists) and the emphasis on a consensus necessary for the ascertainment of the truth. This is accompanied by a constant underestimation of the subjective-human side. Expert opinions, in this light, are the guarantors of the truth; their rationality is of a nature that is seen as *greater than society itself,* so to speak. This *idealistic* picture of scientific knowledge establishes, on the other side of the coin, the negative assessment of power and the politics of special interests (cf. Bergsdorf 1988: 18f.). Whoever recognizes the rationality of expertise and is convinced of the integrity of scientific knowledge can put his or her political involvement into getting an idea to be generally accepted. Therefore, environmental associations and citizens' action groups always fight more for the putting through of scientific knowledge than they do for individual needs, material interests, or the rights of participation in general.

The articulation of special interests always appears to be suspicious in this light, as it prevents a purely scientific and technical discourse. Those who have special interests try to obscure the truth as they argue; they sacrifice the right decision on the altar of the satisfaction of their own needs. Thus, no successfully socialized creature behaves in that way; at least no one publicly adheres to it. Not least of all the citizens affected by air pollution are attached to these ideas. As a rule, they do not see themselves as competent enough to intervene in the negotiations of the state with industry. From the citizens' point of view, one is satisfied with the political decisions made in clean air protection if the air is cleaner. The citizens do not feel that they are authorized to intervene; they even have to assume that a one-sided articulation of special interests would stand in the way of a right decision. If politics is thus legitimated, it needs one thing above all else: success.

The citizen of enlightened democracy recognizes the correctness of a political decision in success. For the citizen, it is also the effectiveness of politics, not the political process, that is the legitimating basis of a rule by virtue of knowledge. With this "acceptance of effectivity" the citizen takes his or her leave of the political decision making process. In a rule by virtue of knowledge, the positivistic understanding of nature has to lead inevitably into a positivistic understanding of politics, and this shuts citizens out and makes politics an objective science beyond special interests. From this standpoint, the state itself becomes a technician, a lab assistant who, through the provision of the right places and the framework for scientific and technical reasoning, makes possible the process of ascertaining the truth as a discourse of experts and fulfills the function of making this discourse rewarding for the common good.[2]

Considerations of human health, communal solidarity, or the quality of life as well as the right of nature itself are certainly discussed, but this discussion takes place only on the public level of politics, especially in the media. On the contrary, I would like to compare public-formal politics with ancient Chinese shadowboxing: it calms the soul (soul of the people) but does not hurt anyone. That these public discussions do not find their way into the arguments of the network agents is another proof of the powerful closure of the context that I call the "permit-granting cartel." Thus, there is a limit not only on the actors' institutionalized relationships but also *on the capability to reach these actors by reasoned arguments*. However, more than just different systems of speech are kept apart here. A limit on the possibilities of interpretation, whose permeability seems to exist on only one side, simultaneously reveals itself: technical values oriented toward effectiveness stick out in the political public much more than it is possible for the values of "life worlds" and solidarity, such as human health, to gain access to the real political process.[3] This seems to be based on the fact that the solution of technical problems does not depend on public discussion. Rather, public discussions are more likely to endanger the working of the system, within which political problems are depicted as purely technical. German clean air politics, therefore, demands a "depoliticization" of the mass of the population. To the extent to which the practical question of purpose is replaced by a technical question of defining a technical standard, the political public loses its functions (Habermas 1969).

The question is how this "depoliticization" of the masses is made convincing to the masses themselves. I think the answer is the increased acceptance of efficiency. The idea of a technically perfect solution to a problem with the priority of economic efficiency is no longer just a feature of the way engineers think; it has its place in the entire population. Technology and science are *also* a matter of ideology, whose power comes from not *only* being an ideology, like societal theories or dogmatic doctrines (Habermas 1969). Technology refers to an "objective" entity whose observation by way of the guiding positivistic understanding of science sees to it that the methods of technical intervention are also seen as objectively given. Such methods were always there in principle but had to be discovered or, rather, invented. This reference to objectivity involves the idea of an inherent legitimacy of progress producing practical constraints, which a politics based on the management of problems by restoration has to follow. Since this idea has been anchored in the societal mind, the reference to the important role of technology in German clean air politics, which was underlined in our interviews, can explain and legitimate why a process for the formulation of a democratic will regarding practical questions does not take place and has to be replaced by decisions by plebiscite about alternatives leading people in the formal political area.

POLITICAL REGULATION: EXPERT KNOWLEDGE AND THE PUBLIC ARTICULATION OF FEARS

In summary, one recognizes the connection between positivism, striving for a consensus, orientation of politics to results (acceptance of effectivity), and democracy: in a society that believes in scientific truth independent of position and special interests, a supposedly objective problem-solution can be produced only by a consensus, since compromises can never lead to the truth. The truth is binding for everybody, and it existed even before it was found. Compromises, on the other hand, are situational; they are always "shabby" compromises. Since, due alone to practical reasons, a consensus can never be a consensus of all citizens of a state, the consensus refers to representatives who themselves are legitimated not because they are mandated by the people but because of their obligation to objectivity through scientific reputation. It is the task of politics to find the objectively correct solution to a problem. The method used here is the discourse of experts, not the struggle of the representatives of special interests. If that's the way it is, there is no need for a participation of the ignorant masses, which would be downright detrimental to finding the truth. Here democracy can only mean that the masses represent that regulating element that has to be guided by enlightenment and propaganda to vote the "right" (true) way. However, decisions can be made only on a right solution. Therefore, the *result* of politics is crucial, not the *process*; one recognizes the empirical truth of the political regulation in the result. If the desired results are achieved, it makes no difference how they were generated. What is important is that one found the correct answer. Nevertheless, if one questions the procedure, he or she is seen as someone who is trying to deny an obvious success, which again would not be objective. Politics based on a consensus where there is a belief in a positivistic idea of truth robs democracy of its political topic. Here politics is reduced to nearly zero. The increased politicization of the public in environmental questions does not have to stand in opposition to this. On the contrary, we can explain the current political frustration by the growing contradiction between the measuring of politics by the standards of objectivity, on the one hand, and the recognized reality of struggles between interests in every stage of the political process, on the other hand, not only in the articulation of problems but also in the setting of standards. The historically grown idea of democracy by enlightened decision making no longer fits with the reality of the political business. Because a new, more realistic idea of democracy—taking into account that politics means conflict settlement always and in every stage of the process—has not been successfully established thus far in intellectual debates, dissatisfaction with democracy has grown. This political frustration has two features. There is, on the one hand, disappointment because it has become obvious that politics does not lead to objectively valid problem solutions. On the other hand, there is disappointment because the broader mobilization of citizens in matters of political decision making runs against the still-existing walls of scientific-technical rule. The technical experts are not used to compromising, nor are the citizens themselves. The result is that the claim to objectivity and the articulation of interests clash all the more. What is needed is a political process of many arenas, which are designed for a step-by-step compromising of interests and a step-by-step accommodation of technical reasoning with interest articulation. The idea of consensus democracy calls for reform by elements of a liberal and more pluralistic democracy of many arenas on many levels of political decision making. Thus, as opposed to what one would find in the United States, where not positivism but realism prevails, where a compromise is sought after but not a consensus, and where the procedure legitimates politics to a far greater extent than the result, democracy in Germany means enlightenment, not participation. Democracy is ideally a completely nonpolitical matter!

NOTES

1. In Germany there are air pollution regulations regarding facilities, regions, and products. Even though there are emission standards for over 100 substances, only about 10 are regulated by ambient air quality values (immissions). Clean air protection laws regarding products that forbid certain substances are almost of no significance. Based on these reasons, German clean air protection can be described best if it is thought of as the regulation of technical facilities.

2. This line of thought also has a long tradition in the formation of social theory in Germany. The most recent development is found in the unmistakably idealistic orientation of a theory of context control by Helmut Willke (1992a).

3. There actually appears to be an empirical confirmation of the colonization thesis by Habermas (1981). Whereas he tries to characterize the epitome of modern society with his thesis, I have, in my opinion, extrapolated a product that is specific to German political culture.

Chapter 6

The United States: Rule by Virtue of Competition

Claudia Jauß

INTRODUCTION

If one studies the political regulation of air pollution in the United States (i.e., the way the problem is handled, the chosen instruments and procedures, and the process of political decision making on the levels of program planning and implementation), a specific American dilemma stands out as the most obvious characteristic of the political culture, which is reflected in its regulatory practices. The dilemma has its roots in an understanding of democracy that considers the participation of individual citizens in political decisions to be ideal. According to this idea, every member of the political unit should be able to introduce his or her position and interests into the political process. The individual citizen is the final and decisive authority; his or her will is essential in reaching collectively binding decisions.[1]

The legitimacy of political decisions is measured, therefore, according to the extent to which the decisions comply with the will of the citizens. This highest principle of legitimation has caused the political decision making process in the United States to proceed in the name of the public and by including the public to an unusual extent. This, however, has consequences that negatively affect the problem-solving process. It overlooks that, in reality, not everyone can participate because he or she lacks the necessary resources to do so. Additionally, where an orientation to the public takes place, an efficient process is not always guaranteed. Where every individual has the possibility to participate, the process of reaching a decision becomes long and drawn out. Individual interests receive a high status, and their representatives are in the position to delay or block the decision making process. Decisions made on the program-planning level can also be put into question once again on the implementation level. The legitimacy of decision making processes is opposed to their efficiency.

This dilemma, which is illustrated in this chapter using the example of clean air politics, is, however, in no way absolute. It does not exist in the European countries studied in this book, since legitimacy there is not so much produced by an orientation toward the public but rather by informed actors working together on a supposedly objective matter. The way in which a problem such as air pollution is solved as well as the difficulties that arise are therefore quite dependent on cultural conditions and are different in each society. The development of these differences, the analysis of their problems, and a discussion of them in light of the considerations of democratic theories are the subjects of this chapter.

INSTRUMENTS OF REGULATION

The specific way in which the problem of air pollution is approached as well as the procedures that are selected for dealing with it not only form the substance of this study but also reflect cultural characteristics that are analyzed in more detail later on. American legislation regarding the regulation of air pollutants, the Clean Air Act, is characterized by ambitious goals, complexity, and rigorous measures that, however, are regularly evaded in practical implementation. The Clean Air Act attacks the problem of air pollution from two sides. The air quality of the whole country should be improved with the help of ambient air quality standards that primarily aim to protect human health and secondarily to protect the environment and other goods.

This protection of health and the environment can be reached only through concrete emission reductions at the individual emission sources. To this end, the Clean Air Act plans emission standards that, in most cases, lead to the installation of specific technologies at each source. Here the goal of protecting health and the environment obviously comes into conflict with the goal of economic growth and with individual entrepreneurial interests. These conflicts are dealt with by the introduction of economic incentives—a unique instrument that is not found as often in other countries.

A conspicuous feature of the Clean Air Act is its enormous complexity. It contains numerous individual regulations and individual sections for particular problems whose connection to each other can be understood only through closer study. This structure can be explained by how the law came into existence: measures were first decided upon and implemented, but they partially failed under practical conditions or needed to be adapted to them. In their new form, the measures were then taken into the next revision of the law or were used as a basis for further measures.

In spite of the inclusion of economic incentives, the implementation of clean air policy measures occurs, to a great extent, according to the principle of command and control: governmental authorities enact regulations that need to be followed by the affected industries. The state monitors the observance of the measures and penalizes noncompliance, should the case arise. Deadlines for the implementation of the standards should guarantee a quick actualization of the legal requirements. However, in view of the actual conditions on-site, these deadlines are regularly postponed.

Although the Environmental Protection Agency (EPA) defines and enforces the standards, the individual states are responsible for their concrete implementation. This institutionalizes the greatest possible control of state offices by the public. The standard-setting procedure as well as permit-granting procedures plan on the participation of the public. The EPA is obligated in the standard-setting procedure to make all the records used available to the public and to use only those records made public in the setting of standards so that anyone can check the decision. Failure to do this can result in decisions of the EPA being disputed in court, which also regularly happens.

Here we come up against the conflict between legitimacy and efficiency mentioned at the beginning. The standard-setting procedure has proven to be very lengthy. Contributing to this is the fact that the passage of a standard by the EPA is not the last word; rather, the whole procedure often has to be gone into again in subsequent legal proceedings. More recently, this problem has been dealt with by the use of a modified procedure. In regulatory negotiation (Reg-Neg), all interested groups sit down together and negotiate the content of the decision. All participants are subsequently obligated to abide by the result of the negotiations, to refrain from legal proceedings, and also to uphold the result upon a challenge by a third party. The dilemma manifests itself again in that these negotiations are again available to the public. How can these principles and structures of the American approach to regulation, which are made explicit here, now be explained?

The described way in which solutions to the problem of air pollution are chosen in the United States portrays well the political style in this country. This approach to problem solving can also be seen as the result of political processes. To what extent the political style is reflected in this approach is examined in this chapter as political structures and processes from four different, but related, points of view are analyzed in the field of clean air politics. This makes the political style explicit and explains the specific principles of regulation.

NETWORKS OF ACTORS: COMPETING FOR INFLUENCE

The first dimension is the structure of the networks of actors and the special relationships that can be made between the individual actors or groups of actors. What is more, one cannot speak of just one network in the United States; rather, many networks exist there.

On the level of drafting legislation, the Congress is the central actor. The drafting of legislation is characterized by negotiation processes between members of Congress or coalitions of individual members of Congress as well as by attempts on the part of numerous interest groups from industry and environmental movements to influence the way of thinking of the elected representatives in making the decisions. In this way contacts between industry and elected representatives exist in many respects. Representatives of industrial interests appear in the context of hearings before congressional committees. There are more informal relationships when industry makes its technical knowledge available to the representatives in Congress. Precisely in an area such as clean air politics, a great amount of detailed knowledge is necessary, and the individually elected representatives and their staff do not always have the resources to acquire this knowledge on their own. Consequently, they are dependent on external experts (Interview House of Representatives).

Given this situation, it is advantageous for the industrial lobbyists to influence and pressure the congressional representatives in their decisions. The lobbyists are all the more successful the more that they are in the position to mobilize potential voters from among the employees, customers, and those who are dependent on the industry. Furthermore, the influence of industry is dependent on how significant an industrial branch is for the economy of a particular state. If a firm is a significant employer among the constituency or if an industrial branch is especially important for the national economy, the representatives of these firms need to be listened to. Influence is normally exercised only on those congressional representatives who have a firm represented in their voting district. To strengthen their influence, individual industrial branches enter into coalitions even if such unions are more difficult in the area of the environment than, for example, when taxes are the issue (Interview Edison Electric Institute; Interview Chrysler).

The industrial representatives compete with the lobbyists of environmental groups for political influence and the mobilization of potential voters; the environmental groups, however, are dependent to a certain extent on the popularity of a topic. Only if a sufficient number of people in certain regions and at certain times attach sufficient importance to the subject of clean air protection is the exercise of political pressure by mobilization successful. The American public has a very positive attitude toward political measures for clean air protection. The environmental groups also make their technical knowledge available to congressional representatives (Interview Natural Resources Defense Council [NRDC], Driessen).

The executive branch of the government is also the object of lobbying attempts on the part of industry and environmental groups; however, the possibilities to influence a decision are minimal for both groups here because the members of the executive branch, except for the president, are not elected representatives and therefore, are less susceptible to political pressure by mobilization of the public. Here industry has better chances of access than environmental groups. They provide the members of the executive branch with technical information just as they do for congressional representatives (Interview Edison Electric Institute).

At the level of program planning, then, we find, on the one hand, a legislative competition between Congress and the president; on the other hand, a competition for the exertion of influence exists between industry and environmental groups. There is also competition within these groups so that they do not currently appear as uniform actors. Thus, a multitude of participating actors compete with each other. Much of the political process depends on who holds an important position in a particular decision, for example, who is the head of the relevant committee and who has access to this actor. Decisions under these conditions are the result of situation-based coalitions that can again fall apart for the next decision and form themselves anew. To a great extent, individual outputs depend on which of the competing factions hold a greater potential for power and more resources for exchange in a particular negotiation process.

In the standard-setting network, the EPA takes on the role of the central actor. On the one hand, it has a strong position of power in the network: its decisions are just as important for the individual states and for industry that have to implement the standards as they are for the environmental groups. On the other hand, its scope of action for negotiation is limited since it is bound by regulations that are sometimes very detailed, and beyond that, its activities are controlled by Congress (Interview EPA Office of Policy, Analysis and Review). Nevertheless, its scope of action for negotiation is still broad enough to make it an object of lobbying on the part of interest groups (Interview Edison Electric Institute; Interview NRDC, Driessen). In addition, there is a cooperative aspect deliberately set up by the EPA that dominates a large portion of network relationships and goes beyond the obligations of the EPA, which is to include comments of all of the interested parties in a standard-setting procedure.

Especially under the current agency director, Carol Browner, the understanding has been established that the practical experience of industry has tremendous significance for the drawing up of regulatory measures since better ideas and more expertise for the practical realization of clean air legislation possibly exist here. Therefore, intense exchanges of information take place, although the EPA had already asked industry for technical information earlier (Interview EPA Office of Policy, Planning, and Evaluation). Environmental groups can also introduce their technical knowledge into the network relationship. Since they are seen as the voice of the population concerned about the environment, the EPA is forced to include them in negotiations in the context of Reg-Neg and in other contexts. Although it seeks cooperation, the EPA can, in effect, always decide on appropriate measures itself. Industry and environmental groups regularly use the opportunity to take the EPA to court (Interview D.C. Circuit Court of Appeals; Interview Edison Electric Institute), so that an element of tension is always present in the relationship.

The competition between Congress and the executive branch also has an effect within the standard-setting network. On the one hand, Congress is responsible for the control and monitoring of the EPA's activities; on the other hand, the executive branch endeavors to bring its political objectives and ideas into the EPA. Additionally, it happens that the EPA voluntarily follows the executive orders of the president and submits to control by the Office of Management and Budget. Both currents of influence become critical if the president and Congress pursue opposing goals. In the relationship that the EPA has with Congress and as well as with the executive branch, there exists a hierarchic relationship.

Within the standard-setting network, a decisive role is taken by science since in this phase the assessment of health risks, natural science knowledge about the characteristics of certain susbstances, economic cost accounting, and technical know-how are significant. The scientists who are heard here occupy a variety of positions within institutions. The EPA employs its own experts on the Science Advisory Board (SAB) and the Clean Air Scientific Advisory Committee (CASAC). One of the most important tasks of these experts is to appoint external scientists from universities and other research establishments to hearings (Interview CASAC). Industry and environmental groups also employ scientists whose insights flow into various phases of the standard-setting procedure. As a closer discussion of institutional rules later on shows, the integration of science into the political decision making process is fairly politicized in comparison to that of other countries. Accordingly, scientists are integrated into a political process and influence political decisions with their opinions. It can be presumed that their research from time to time takes a direction that accommodates political interests. To what extent certain research results are demanded is not examined here.

The political dispute between the competing actors in no way comes to an end with the passage of a law. The establishment of the quasi-legal standards offers everyone who was not able to sufficiently introduce his or her position during the legislative process or did not even have access to the process a second chance to put through his or her interests. The EPA, then, stands in-between the legal guidelines, which are set by Congress and upheld often enough in court, the competition between Congress and the executive branch, and the lobbying attempts of the various interest groups. Since after the passage of a standard, a court appeal gives a third chance for interested parties to introduce positions that had not been considered, the standard-setting procedure becomes correspondingly long and drawn out.

In comparison to the phases of program planning and standard-setting, where we can speak of a relatively uniform network—even if this is not as stable as in other countries—on the level of implementation, there is a multitude of individual state and local networks. This is related to the fact that the procedure for granting permits for individual emission sources is principally carried out by the individual state agencies. The only national authority that is of significance in the implementation network is the EPA. In some cases it also acts as a direct permit-granting authority. It decides, among other matters, on the course of the permit-granting program of the individual states; that is, how the permit-granting procedure is run ultimately depends on the EPA and has to be approved of by the agency. When industry has to obtain the permit from the offices of the EPA in the individual regions, cooperation takes place. As Landy, Roberts, and Thomas (1994) have shown, it is necessary for the EPA to get involved in the positions of industry from time to time if a firm or an industrial branch occupies a significant position locally or in general for the national economy.

On the individual state level, the local permit offices are the point of contact for interest groups. It is typical that the authorities there, as shown in a study by Wood (1992), react more strongly to local conditions than the headquarters of the EPA when they make decisions for a specific region. Thus, they are more subject to lobbying attempts on the part of industry and environmental groups and to the general local economic and political situation. They also react more easily to public pressure.[2]

On the level of implementation, interested actors are offered a chance once again to introduce their interests. Thus, the political debate stretches out from program planning to individual cases of permit granting and brings about the situation where measures decided upon in Congress can be stopped at the various stations, delayed in their implementation, or, mainly on the level of implementation, newly interpreted. Particularly during implementation, measures often prove to be nonenforceable because they go against the actual local conditions. Thus, in the course of the history of the Clean Air Act, implementation deficits came up time and again, which then were often taken up in the revisions of the law. The complexity of the Clean Air Act is therefore attributed not only to the constantly changing coalition but also to the inclusion of practical experience in the legislative text.

Parallel to the described networks, there are relationships between industry and environmental groups—an unusual constellation, if one compares this with the other three countries. Whereas both, especially in the past, appeared as opponents, industry has realized that under certain circumstances it makes more sense to work together with the environmental groups, when possible (Interview Edison Electric Institute). Such cooperation saves industry time and expense and gives it predictable operating conditions because in negotiated compromises the probability of a disruptive intervention by an environmental group is less likely. Industry can also earn prestige by cooperating with environmental groups. On the other hand, the environmental groups are interested in working together with industry (Interview NRDC, Driessen). For them, cooperation with industry, under certain circumstances, means a quicker and less problematic tackling of environmental problems.

Cooperation between industry and environmental groups takes place in areas where there are common interests in spite of fundamentally divergent goals. Apart from that, an informal communication network exists between both interest groups (Interview Edison Electric Institute). What is most interesting is that such cooperation takes place at all. This leads to the conclusion that there are not as many ideological differences between both parties as is the case in Germany and France, for example, and that, therefore, a consensus exists that cooperation with an opponent is legitimate for the achievement of one's goals. We can record the fact that the political process in the United States is more adversarial and more strongly characterized by disputes than in European countries, although coalitions are possible, which would not be as conceivable in the other countries.

The network of American clean air politics is generally characterized by the involvement of a multitude of actors who compete with each other for influence in the formulation of collectively binding decisions. On the one hand, we have the actors of the political system who develop, plan, and implement bills and in no way form a single unit in the process. On the other hand, there are the representatives of interest groups who are forced to introduce their interests and positions in this process as completely as possible. The structure of the network is based not only on a political system of checks and balances where the individual constitutional bodies monitor each other but also on the first-past-the-post electoral system, which impels the congressional representatives to concentrate on the combination of interests in their respective constituency.

The network is relatively unstable and characterized by coalitions that form around a specific interest group or a specific topic. Both sides have advantages.

The political decision makers are often dependent on the information that the experts of the interest groups can give them, whereas, the interest groups obtain a chance to introduce their positions by access to the actors of the political system. Information is the life-breath of the legislative process in particular. The relationships of the actors, on the one hand, are characterized by the relative absence of obstacles that would prevent potential opponents from having contact with each other. In contrast to Germany and France, environmental groups and representatives of industry form coalitions in the United States, if there are common interests at stake. On the other hand, though, the network is characterized by a great deal of distrust and very adversarial relationships among the individual actors. Potential ideological differences are more easily set aside by concentrating on putting through respective particular interests.

INSTITUTIONAL RULES OF POLICY MAKING: INSTITUTIONALIZED PUBLIC INVOLVEMENT AND INFORMAL CONSULTATION

The political process can only partially be explained by the network relationships and the processes of exchange. They can only partially portray what constitutes the national style of regulation. To explain why the public has much more extensive opportunities to have a say in the standard-setting procedure than in the other countries studied, it is necessary to include further levels of explanation. Precisely the conflict that results from this public involvement, the lengthiness of the procedure, and the insecurity of the decisions require the consideration of further dimensions. Why is it that Reg-Neg, which is supposed to reduce the lengthiness of the procedure and the number of legal proceedings, again permits public involvement, which then partially cancels out the advantages of an informal procedure? To shed some light on this question, a few institutional rules are discussed that, to a great extent, guide the behavior of the actors in the network.

The catchphrase "institutionalized public involvement and informal consultation" most concisely describes these institutional rules. Public involvement is essentially the highest principle in the political decision making process. This principle is embodied in the Constitution and in numerous rules and regulations and seems to impose itself time and again in relation to other institutional rules. Through the first-past-the-post electoral system, which gives a special responsibility to the members of the legislative body in regard to their voters, politics for the public, in the interest of the public, is guaranteed; legal regulations enable the public to participate in political decision making. Expertise, which plays an important role in clean air politics since it is supposed to guarantee objectivity in decision making, is, to a certain extent, judged by the public.

However, we have seen that relationships between the actors in the network are, to an important extent, of an informal nature. The principle of public participation is undermined by these informal consultations. Whereas every citizen potentially has the chance to be informed about the political processes and to participate in the political decisions, only a selected few have access to the informal consultations. Who will participate is decided by specific criteria, for example, by the reputation of the actors. Public involvement and consultation are, therefore, in opposition to each other. This is alleviated only by the fact that the environmental groups are a part of the drawn-out decision making processes, assuming that one accepts the environmental groups as a representative of the public. There is the tendency, however, to legally establish the consultations and thereby make them more transparent for everyone.

Orientation toward the Public: Politics for the Public

Political behavior in the United States is oriented toward public opinion. This is true not only for politics in a narrow sense, where the political decision makers, especially those in the legislative branch, heed to the opinion of the voters, but also for the politics of firms, which have to justify themselves to the consumers. The elected representatives are directly responsible to their voters. Congressional representatives and state and local representatives are especially sensitive to pressure from this direction. Consequently, coalitions among industry have the purpose of mobilizing the public in order to put pressure on elected representatives (Interview Edison Electric Institute). Public opinion is so important for elected representatives that organizations with special interests use it to carry through their goals. But the orientation toward the public of American politicians not only is seen in the strategies of businesses but is also referred to by the politicians themselves (Interview Senate Committee on Environment and Public Works). Politics is there to carry out the will of the public (Interview House of Representatives). The priorities of the public determine the political agenda.

Congress is not the only part of the political system that orients its behavior to the public. The EPA does this as well (Interview EPA Office of Policy, Planing, and Evaluation). The EPA sees itself as an institution that serves the public. This institutional rule also applies to the actors in the economic system, namely, the businesses. They have to be able to justify their position to the public (Interview Edison Electric Institute). Public opinion is the final authority. It is crucial that the public is convinced of the credibility of an actor.

Thus, it can be concluded that an important institutional rule in the United States in the field of clean air politics is the orientation of the behavior of the actors toward the public. Politics is oriented toward the usually short-term, articulated needs of the public and attends to long-term problems less often, even though they are just as important. The question also comes up as to which public the actors orient their behavior. For political representatives, the public is equivalent to voters. Decisive, then, is not so much the opinion of the American public itself but the opinion of those factions of the public that are relevant to the respective individual political decision makers. Therefore, very particular interests, whose possible incompatibility can lead to a standstill in the activity of Congress, are, to a certain extent, represented in the political decision making process. Admittedly, the citizens of every constituency are represented by their elected officials, but the number of different interests that need to be considered in the political decision making process becomes very large.

Nevertheless, the public at least has its faction that is politically interested in the environment, represented not only among political actors, who are subject to many pressures, but also by environmental groups. These groups act without an explicit mandate from the public but nevertheless represent a faction of the population. The same is also true for industry. Representative of particular opinions, these interest groups act according to the idealized model that is characterized by the idea of the competition of opinions. Just as in the conclusion that emerged from the analysis of the political network, both sides certainly do not have equally good access to the political decision makers. Industry has a multitude of better resources and contacts and, thus, also more influence on the decision makers. Environmental opinion has to force its way through somewhere other than by direct access.

Involvement of the Public: Politics by the Public

The public has yet another significance. The public not only determines the behavior of actors but is also involved in many political decisions. This involvement of the public in decisions is a further institutional rule in the American political process, at least in the area of clean air politics. Everyone who is affected by a decision should have the opportunity to work on the decision and to express his or her opinions, and everyone should be taken into consideration. Fair and equal access to the decision making process is the ideal that one tries to realize.

This conception guides the legislative process as well as the standard-setting process and the implementation process and, to a certain extent, has been established in writing. In the legislative process, meetings are held by the respective committees with all of the interested groups to work on a bill (Interview Senate Committee on Environment and Public Works). In the standard-setting procedure, an involvement of the public is directly stipulated in various phases. In every phase of the standard-setting procedure, the EPA has to give a public account of its activities and put the basis of its decisions on file. Finally, in the implementation phase, the decisions of the respective officials in the permit-granting procedure are, as a rule, at least accessible to the public.

It is important not only that everyone who wants to say something is heard but that everyone also has to be fairly involved in the decision making process. Due to this right, however, the procedure becomes long and sometimes so drawn out that activities are delayed for a long time. This lengthiness of the procedure is one reason for the emergence of informal consultation. But here, too, the question again needs to be asked as to what extent the public is involved. Admittedly, every citizen is theoretically free to participate in hearings, but the environmental groups are the de facto representative of the public. Only in rare cases do individual citizens have the necessary time and the necessary financial resources to mobilize the expertise that is required for competent participation in the hearings. Thus, the environmental groups have the function of representing the faction of the public that is interested in regulations that protect the environment, even if the groups do not have any explicit instructions to do so. Actually, then, the involvement of the public as it should ideally occur is rarely possible. Here we have the familiar problem of the theory and practice of democracy.

Consultation

In spite of the involvement of the public in legislative and administrative decisions as part and parcel of the political process, the analysis of the network of American clean air politics shows that such decisions are also attributed to informal contacts. Here another institutional rule emerges, which will be designated with the term "consultation". In contrast to public involvement, consultation is not legally established. It can be understood, though, as opposing the idea of public involvement since it undermines the notion that the greatest possible number of affected people should directly have a say and that political decisions should be made as transparent as possible. Accordingly, contacts between the employees of the EPA and people representing others who are occupied with the standards, for example, are not permitted in advance of the implementation of public involvement.

Nevertheless, consultation is an institutional rule that no network actor can take away. Consultation is necessary due to very specific structural reasons (Interview House of Representatives). The political decision makers and their staff do not have the necessary time, personnel, and financial resources available to always fulfill their many and diverse responsibilities thoroughly and conscientiously. The Clean Air Act in particular is a very complicated law that even for experts is difficult to understand. These circumstances make consultation practically indispensable in helping to reduce the complexity of the matter for political decision makers. Accommodating to this need, interest groups from industry and environmental organizations try to assert their influence through lobbying. In addition, interest groups have an interest in receiving information about current events from the point of view of the political decision makers in order to adapt to the events and to be better able to plan their actions. Thus, consultation is also advantageous for interest groups.

Consultation emerges, though, out of the institutional rule of public involvement. Furthermore, it contributes to the reduction of disputes over a law or a standard later on. When previous arrangements with the most important interest groups have taken place, it is less likely that there will be subsequent difficulties in accepting and implementing the respective regulation (see Chapter 5 on Germany). Here is another reason that consultation is necessary. Thus, an informal network emerges, which was examined in the previous paragraphs. Consultation, then, serves the purpose of removing some of the detrimental consequences of involving the public. The prior hearing of interest groups reduces the lengthiness of the procedure since public discussion and possible legal proceedings at a later date are reduced. In addition, official hearings are shorter, if one is already essentially in agreement. The paralysis of the decision making process is easier to eliminate in informal talks, where the actors do not have to justify themselves to the media public in detail about their remarks, than in publicly settled disputes.

The principle of transparency and the involvement of all interested parties is, however, violated. The political decision makers do not consult with everyone; there are informal prerequisites for access. One important criteria is reputation (Interview Senate Committee on Environment and Public Works). Admittedly, there is always the possibility for groups that are not consulted to appear in official proceedings, but the advantage of having a share in the power to define the issue and membership in the informal circles are not available to these actors. The informal network has a certain exclusivity, although environmental groups also have access to it. In the meantime, there is, however, the tendency to legally establish these consultations that occur de facto. Here the idea of transparency of decisions and the accompaniment of democratic control by the public is again established. This is the case of Reg-Neg, whose negotiations are once again public. The previous informal contact between the EPA, on the one hand, and industry and environmental groups, on the other hand, will be more firmly institutionalized and made available to the public by making it part of the law.

One almost has the impression that the decision makers are at an impasse. Public involvement is the most important, highest principle of the political process, but it has disadvantages that, to a certain extent, are removed by informal consultation. This informal consultation, however, undermines the principle of public involvement and is therefore institutionalized; but, legalized, it is robbed of its informal nature and is thereby more transparent. It remains to be seen if this greater transparency will again result in more public involvement so that, as a result, decision making becomes a lengthier process again.

The problem of public involvement and consultation is closely related to yet another institutional rule. Public involvement in political and administrative decisions should satisfy the claim to a direct democratic process, but in addition it has, as is argued here, a monitoring function. It guarantees, at least to a certain point, that decisions of the political system of clean air politics are not made behind closed doors according to nontransparent criteria. Behind the concept of public involvement, then, is the idea that political decisions and the decision makers have to be monitored in their activities.

Expertise

Besides the already mentioned institutional rules in the political process in the field of clean air politics, expertise is of importance as well. Scientific expertise is meant here, which is important because of its perceived independence. In the United States, however, expertise is not as institutionalized as in Germany, and significance is not attached to it at every stage of the political process to the extent to which it is the case in Germany.

Since expertise plays quite a role in political decisions, those who want to carry through their interests have to introduce scientific expertise (Interview Senate Committee on Environment and Public Works). This is also true for administrative decisions (Interview EPA Office of Policy, Planning, and Evaluation). Obviously, expertise is used by decision makers to guide their decisions and to make it easier to justify a decision. The idea of supporting decisions with the greatest scientific precision possible contributes to the lengthiness of the standard-setting procedure.

This idea also implies that scientific expertise is utilized. If a regulation appears unreasonable to an interest group, the group often invokes scientific arguments. This leads to a situation where decision makers have to scientifically substantiate their decisions (Interview CASAC). Expertise is necessary in the political disputes about clean air protection because it represents objectivity. On the other hand, though, it is politicized and used arbitrarily by the competing actors as a means of gaining influence in a dispute. In addition, it is also obvious that expertise is a relevant criterion for decision making only as long as the interests of industry essentially remain untouched. If this is the case, then political pressure determines the decisions (Interview D.C. Circuit Court of Appeals). Scientific expertise is indeed relevant, but it does not take on the importance that it does in other countries in relation to other institutional rules.

Although actors use scientific results for their own purposes more so than in other countries, the importance of the scientific results comes from their presumed objectivity. In this context, it is interesting how the objectivity perceived as necessary nevertheless should be guaranteed there, where it appears to be indispensable: in the scientific work of the EPA. This happens by again falling back on the rule of public involvement in decisions and decision making processes.

The scientists of the EPA are those who first draw up the draft for a standard. However, their scientific expertise is not seen as objective enough. They have to show their work to a team of independent, external experts who review the work in public meetings. Most of the actors consider the scientific expertise of these experts as significant for political decisions because their expertise guarantees objectivity; that is, it is not tainted by special interests and gives credibility to the respective decisions (Interview CASAC).

Expertise is not accepted as objective per se, even though it is taken as an objective authority in competition among the interest groups. Even the external scientists have to prove their objectivity. Altogether, three mechanisms should guarantee objectivity. First of all, it is stipulated that a biased scientific and political composition of the committee is to be avoided. Therefore, the members are recruited from as many different disciplines and societal groups as possible (Interview CASAC).[3] Second, the experts of the advisory committee have to provide information about their finances (Interview Science Advisory Board). Third, what is most common is to allow the public to judge the independence of the experts (Interview Science Advisory Board). At least in this case, expertise is subordinate to public involvement and, to a certain extent, is dependent on it. Here, the priority of public involvement establishes itself again.

THE ROLE OF THE PROFESSIONS: PLURALISM AND COMPETITION

The third dimension to help understand the political style of regulation in the field of clean air politics is the way professional communities influence the political arena. These communities are an example of communal relationships in general, which are worthy of an explanation here. The focus on professional communities in an area such as clean air politics seems to be especially helpful since the solution of political problems relating to clean air protection appears, in many respects, to require professional expert authority. Legal expertise is necessary in the drafting of a bill, whereas knowledge in the areas of medicine, the hard sciences, and engineering is needed in the definition and implementation of concrete standards. For the time being, it can be assumed that these and other professions play a special role in the political arena. This role, according to the thesis set up here, goes beyond the provision of expertise and includes influencing the political arena through specific commonalities of the professions. Dominating professions introduce their definitions, their conceptions, and their ethics and can thus leave their mark on the political arena. To find out the precise role of professional communities, we need to ask which professions are represented in order to then look for indications that could give information about possible exertions of influence.

Second, the representation of professions in specific stages of the political process and the allocation of professions within the political arena (i.e., how work is divided up), can have specific consequences for the political arena. It is also important to know if given professions dominate, for example, given phases of the political process, if professions work together, or if there are difficulties in communicating among them. The professions can also exert influence by their uniformity or their complexity inside the political arena, by communicating with each other, or by isolating themselves from each other.

In regard to professional communities, those in the United States, in contrast to those in the three European countries, stand out in the diversification of the professions, especially in the standard-setting phase. Whereas lawyers dominate in the program-planning phase, and engineers and technicians in the implementation phase, a variety of professions is represented in the standard-setting phase. It is striking that economists have clearly played an increasing role in the political arena since around the end of the 1970s.

In both of the congressional committees responsible for clean air legislation, lawyers play a decisive role. This is due to the fact that when writing the text of a bill, it is necessary to be able to assess the consequences in which practical implementation of the written word can result (Interview House of Representatives).[4] In the House Committee on Energy and Commerce, approximately 95% of the committee members are lawyers (Interview House of Representatives, see also Senate Committee on Environment and Public Works). Interest groups also frequently dispatch lawyers as lobbyists to Washington who, due to their legal education, know how to talk to the decision makers there. The Natural Resources Defense Council (NRDC), for example, was explicitly founded as a group with an emphasis on legal work (Interview NRDC, Schprentz). Other professions, however, are represented less often in Congress. The minimal representation of technicians and engineers is problematic in this respect, since technical expertise is needed to assess political measures in the area of clean air protection. Engineers and natural scientists, then, acquire a special importance: they have relevant knowledge that they as employees of industry use to influence policy outputs (Interview American Institute of Chemical Engineers). Thus, during the debate over the Clean Air Act of 1990, for example, Congress was able to be convinced to include reformulated gasoline as a means of reducing the harmful chemical output of mobile sources in the bill instead of alternative fuels, as originally planned (Interview American Institute of Chemical Engineers).

In the standard-setting phase, however, a greater diversification of professions prevails. In the various divisions of the EPA, lawyers, doctors, natural scientists, social scientists, and economists are included in decisions, since a variety of expertise is considered necessary to accomplish the tasks of the agency (Interview Jim Democker, EPA Office of Policy, Analysis, and Review; Interview Carl Mazza, EPA Office of Air and Radiation; Interview Rona Birnbaum, EPA Acid Rain Division). The staff of the relevant scientific advisory committees, SAB and CASAC, who summon scientists in the course of the standard-setting procedure in order to once again independently review the decisions made by the EPA in a peer review process, are natural scientists, doctors, and engineers (U. S. Environmental Protection Agency, Science Advisory Board 1994: H-2–H-11; 11–13). Here there are exact regulations about the composition of the committees (Interview CASAC). For SAB, the following requirements must be fulfilled: "the SAB staff consists of 18 EPA employees: A Staff Director, an Assistant Staff Director, and the Director of the Committee Evaluation Staff; six scientists/engineers serving as Designated Federal Officers (DFOs), and nine support staff" (Interview CASAC: 10). The only exception is the head of the Environmental Economic Advisory Committee, who is an economist (Interview CASAC: 12). In recruiting experts, care is taken so that no single discipline dominates (Interview Randy Bond, CASAC), but here, too, natural scientists and engineers predominate as well as medical doctors. This appears to be logical: where standards are oriented toward the health of the population and have to be technically established, this expertise is exactly what is needed.

However, it is interesting that economists are clearly becoming more established in the political arena, which is demonstrated especially well by their representation on the standard-setting level. Not only the EPA itself but scientific advisory committees have also recently used the expertise of economists. Besides the inclusion of economists in daily decisions of the agency, an economic advisory committee was specially created in 1991. The Environmental Economic Advisory Committee has the responsibility "to assist and advise the Administrator and the Agency in analyzing the economic aspects of environmental decision making, and in analyzing the long-term environmental aspects of various approaches to valuing and/or discounting ecological resources and systems" (U. S. Environmental Protection Agency, Science Advisory Board 1994: 29).

Economic strategies are gaining ground. They have found their way into the political measures that regulate clean air protection and are then expressed one level lower in standard setting by the increased presence of economists. The most recent example is the introduction of tradable allowances for sulfur dioxide emissions, but its predecessors such as the Bubble Policy or the Netting Policy were also accommodations to business rationalities that broke through the dominating command and control approach. Another example of an economic strategy is the cost-benefit analysis, through the use of which the EPA has to take the resulting economic costs of its measures into account. In addition, business strategies and practices play an increasing role in the organization of the EPA itself where, for example, efforts are under way to streamline the bureaucracy and to staff positions with employees who have a knowledge of management (Interview EPA Office of Policy, Planning, and Evaluation, Atkinson; Interview CASAC).

The field of economics plays an increasing role in the political arena and puts the monopoly that natural scientists, technicians, and lawyers have in other countries into question in the United States. This (recent) inclusion of economic rationalities and the establishment of the economic profession in the political arena are, according to my thesis, a consequence of the minimal inclusion of industry, in relation to other countries, in regulatory decisions. In no other country does industry complain so much about the lack of cooperation of governmental officials and the minimal consideration of their arguments. However, more cooperation between governmental offices and industry takes place than these complaints would lead one to believe. Especially if a company or a branch of industry carries weight, it will be heard by decision makers, and concessions are often made in the implementation phase. However, legislation is set up more restrictively than in European countries. Orientation toward public opinion causes regulatory measures that make industry accountable for keeping the air clean to persistently remain intact. In times of recession or when a prevalence of pro-industry forces are in relevant decision making positions, the classic Emissions Trading Policy and the cost-benefit analysis were then devised to accommodate to industry. The allowance system for sulfur dioxide emissions was based on this idea.

In interest groups from industry and environmental organizations, there is a similar diversification of professions as on the level of standard setting. Except for lobbyists, who mostly have a legal background, interest groups are made up of natural scientists, social scientists, engineers, environmental planners, and economists (Interview David Branand, National Coal Association; Interview David Driessen, NRDC; Interview Robert Beck, Edison Electric Institute). It is interesting that the environmental protection groups—at least the big, nationally organized ones—do not question the expertise of the governmental level in that they do not, for example, use a stronger philosophical or pedagogical approach. The diversification of professions does not refer to these disciplines. A fundamental, ideological critique of the approach to clean air politics is as hard to find as a radical questioning of the current lifestyle. The relatively little fear of contact between industry and environmental groups is based on a more profound consensus with respect to the way of life and the basic measures that can be brought in to solve problems. Common ideas and the backgrounds of the professions that are involved in the political arena as well as the orientation toward the public contribute to this phenomenon, which does not allow any radical change in the current lifestyle to be considered as a means of environmental protection.

The level of implementation is again dominated by one profession, namely, the scientific-technical engineering profession. Whereas lawyers write the laws, technicians and engineers are occupied with the implementation of the previously formulated standards. Since on this level, technicians and engineers of the EPA have contact with technicians and engineers from industry, guidelines are derived from the self-conception of this profession.[5] "Their [engineers] training and experience led them to be concerned with fairness, practicality, and technical progressiveness. They wanted the rules to represent good engineering and they often saw their opposite numbers from the companies as professional colleagues as well as opponents" (Landy, Roberts, and Thomas 1994: 211; see also Interview Chrysler). In the implementation of standards, discussion between engineers, who are indeed on different sides but nevertheless speak and understand the same language, plays an important role in practical implementation. During concrete negotiating processes on-site, the intentions upon which the EPA headquarters based the specification of standards can be undermined. The implementation of the Clean Air Act can thus be made more difficult.

Due to their dominance in certain phases of the policy process, technicians and engineers as well as lawyers influence the political arena with their ethics. The frequent representation of lawyers is reflected in the especially adversarial atmosphere that prevails in spite of increasing cooperation and a readiness to discuss issues. They think in rather adversarial ways, in fair and unfair categories, and tend to bring a problem to court rather than solve it in negotiations. In the United States, therefore, legal proceedings occur frequently, whereas negotiated solutions and the willingness to compromise are rather rare in light of the possibility of insisting on the carrying through of one's own position (see Interview Chrysler). Similarly, the command and control approach dominates, which is based on the definition of the measures, which then have to be carried out and which are legally recoverable. In contrast to Great Britain, for example, where concrete measures are not legally established in individual cases, they are regularly negotiated between the actors involved. A similar type of thinking is found among technicians and engineers, who, as a rule, understand their task as scientists to be one of finding a perfect solution (see Interview Chrysler).

Clearly, economists also influence the political arena and bring about the inclusion of an element in the politics of clean air protection that is not as obviously felt in the European countries under study. In these countries, industry is involved in the political process in a completely different way, and, therefore, business rationalities themselves have more influence than in the United States, where a relatively hostile regulatory philosophy toward industry prevails, which only recently has been broken. This element, which cannot be found in the other three countries, is seen in the economic incentives that were developed at the end of the 1970s and now celebrate success with the allowance system for sulfur dioxide emissions. Cost-benefit analysis, another practice specific to America, also reflects the influence of economists.

The influence of the medical profession is given in that not only do emission standards need to be fulfilled, but there are also air quality standards of equal importance that are oriented toward the health of the population. This two-pronged approach to the political regulation of clean air protection is once again a sign of the representation of different professions, which are all relatively equal in the political arena. The way work is divided up between lawyers and technicians can be regarded, to a certain extent, as bringing communication problems with it that then cause problems in the implementation of the Clean Air Act. Someone with a knowledge of natural science who also understands the political language has the advantage of being able to influence legislative debates because he or she can bring the representatives of both sides together (Interview American Institute of Chemical Engineers).

However, it should be noted that in the United States communal ties do not necessarily exist due to common professional backgrounds; rather, they are the product of other common experiences or characteristics such as age, sex, congeniality, common heritage, interests, or schools (see Interview Chrysler). However, common ethics, which form the basis of these communities and have significance for the political arena through their influence, could not be identified.

THE CULTURE OF CLEAN AIR POLITICS

Up until now, networks, institutional rules, and professional communities were examined in order to arrive at an explanation of the American regulatory style in the field of clean air politics. This specific American style in comparison to the other countries implicitly concerns American (political) culture or the culture of the four countries in the study. The culture specific to the country is reflected in the regulatory style, which is also specific to the country. Therefore, the essential cultural features of American society that are pertinent to the political arena are reviewed later. These features are reflected in the structure of the network as well as in the institutional rules and in the representation of professions in the network. They shape the background of the network and determine the actions of the actors in the network, thereby influencing the political outputs of clean air politics.

The discussion about the problem of clean air protection and measures for its realization is taken as a starting point. The cultural patterns of the country will become clear in the concepts of nature and in the perception of the problem. At the end of this chapter, the connections between network, institutional rules, and professions are presented with the help of cultural patterns of interpretation, and the specific development of clean air politics in the United States is explained by the distinctive cultural features.

Concepts of Nature and Conflicting Goals

The discussion about the necessity and formulation of political measures of clean air protection in the United States proves to be a contest of interests represented by a value discussion in which certain groups of actors, most obviously industry and environmental groups, represent competing values. Admittedly, environmental groups point out economic problems, and representatives of industry also recognize the necessity of protecting human health; nevertheless, it can be formulated that health and intact nature, on the one hand, and economic growth and jobs, on the other hand, are values that fundamentally confront each other in the debate between both groups.

The public puts a high value on the protection of its health and critically judges governmental measures by this viewpoint (Interview Joyce Rechtschaffen, Senate Committee on Environment and Public Works). Accordingly, the protection of human health is an essential goal of the Clean Air Act, and this goal was also internalized by the employees of the EPA (see Interview CASAC). Corresponding to the significance of this goal, research results are oriented toward air pollutants and their effects on human health and are perceived by the public accordingly. Scientific results, which target the effects of air pollutants on human health, are presented at hearings concerning legal action for intensified measures of environmental protection (Interview Senate Committee on Environment and Public Works). Health is also an important value for representatives of industry as far as they, of course, have to breathe, too (Interview EPA Office of Planning, Policy, and Evaluation, Atkinson).

The frequent and uniform emphasis on the value of health in all of the groups of actors obscures the fact that there are conflicting goals regarding the development and necessity of political measures for clean air protection. These conflicts are demonstrated in the individual groups of actors, though they also run through the American public. Public opinion about given topics of clean air protection diverges according to economic and socioeconomic implications (Interview CASAC).

Thus, there is a discussion as to what extent a clean environment is in competition with economic efficiency. There is an increasing demand to weigh economic costs and benefits against environmental protection measures (Interview House of Representatives). The difficulties of standards oriented solely toward human health make themselves known (Interview House of Representatives.). This conflict between health protection and economic growth has also found its way into the activities of the EPA.

The discussion about concepts of nature and conflicting goals points to a few basic values of American society and American culture that also became clear in the networks, the institutional rules, and the professional communities. Expressed concretely, democracy, freedom, competition, and progress are the guidelines of American society. These values are also found in other societies and are studied here, therefore, in their specific American form.

Individual Freedom

A value of importance for American society that runs through, and influences, the field of clean air politics is individual freedom. The emphasis on individual freedom is an essential component of the American self-conception. This idea, which is rooted in the consciousness of many Americans and is often mentioned in politics, obviously conflicts with governmental regulatory measures that guide behavior in given ways. Accordingly, fundamental principles regarding the role of the state are regularly debated in political arenas that are especially relevant for the society, such as economic policy and social policy.

In the field of clean air politics there was such a discussion in the 1980s when the Reagan administration stood up for massive deregulation and made every effort to carry this through. The exercise of individual freedom was cited by the Reagan administration as important justification for its deregulatory program, in connection with which the clean air protection policies were also reformed—to the disadvantage of environmental protection. Whereas in the late 1960s and early 1970s there was a consensus that regulation by the state was necessary in this area due to the existence of external effects, there has been an argument since then over if and to what extent such intervention is justified or to what extent it is appropriate to use economic incentives. Since the Republicans achieved a majority in Congress in 1994, the debate over deregulation has again intensified.

Behind the deregulation discussion and next to the idea of competition is also the idea of the freedom of enterprises. In the context of economic arguments, a connection is made between individual freedom and the right of every entrepreneur to develop freely in competition with others and to be exposed to as little governmental regulatory measures as possible. Capitalism and personal freedom go hand in hand in this type of argumentation; they are inseparable. As a result of this debate, the Clean Air Act contains command and control measures as well as economic incentives that, in the context of regulation by the state, provide a certain scope of action. More recently, a similar change of direction by the regulatory officials to somewhat greater flexibility in the implementation of political measures for clean air protection can also be seen.

In a political system in which the opinion of the voters plays an essential role in political decisions and where, at the same time, the value of individual freedom is firmly anchored in the consciousness of these voters, measures will be found that affect the freedom of the individual voters to the least possible degree. This individual freedom is obviously important to most of the voters (Interview EPA Office of Policy, Planning, and Evaluation, Atkinson). This is more apparent in the area of mobile sources than in the area of stationary sources. Here, air pollution is admittedly contributed to by the automobile industry that produces the vehicles; however, it is essentially caused by the individual drivers who decide with their driving behavior if and how badly they will pollute the air. Finding measures here that would call every single car driver into account for his or her actions has not yet been successful in the United States (Interview Edison Electric Institute).

Here the importance of the voters' opinion and the voters' emphasis on individual freedom impose themselves in measures such as raising the price of gasoline or the expansion of the network of public transportation; they are rejected, and instead the automobile industry is obliged to cause a reduction of harmful chemical emissions through the installation of appropriate technology. This solution is extremely easy for, and thus popular among, the individual car drivers and voters because the responsibility can be completely handed over to the producers of automobiles.

Competition

The second characteristic principle of American society is the principle of competition. According to this principle, all individuals should be able to realize their goals in fair competition. Equal opportunity is therefore implied by the ideal. The principle of competition is especially evident in the economic rationalities of the Emissions Trading Policy, where an orientation away from regulation by the state and toward economic incentives has taken place. The interviewed staff person from the House of Representatives holds the opinion that this instrument could also be used on an international level and substantiates this as follows: "People understand money, people understand buying and selling things" (Interview House of Representatives). The idea of economic rationality is expressed here as an element that influences behavior.

This principle is reflected not only in outputs but also in the network, in institutional rules, and in professional communities. The network is made up of a multitude of interest groups from industry and environmental organizations that make every effort to represent their respective goals to the political decision makers and to introduce their goals into the decisions. In this network, the two big groups of industry on the one hand, and environmental organizations, on the other, compete not only with each other, but within these groups there is a lack of unity, and thus there is also a competition for access to the political decision makers. There are various networks on national and subnational levels whose members exchange information and consult with each other. It is crucial to gain access to this network if one wants to have a say in the political arena. It is especially desirable to be consulted, and the interest groups compete for the corresponding position in the network.

A multitude of competing actors who have access to the network and who represent their respective interests to the political decision makers has to be taken into account in the decisions. Each individual actor's resources play a role in gaining access to the network and in exerting influence. The individual regulations of the Clean Air Act also reflect the constellation of interests at the time of their resolution. In the political measures for clean air protection according to the Clean Air Act Amendment of 1990, for example, this is manifested in a tension between health protection and the maintenance of jobs. There is also a tension between health protection and the promotion of innovation, on the one hand, and economic viability and feasibility, on the other.

In the representation of professions in the network, we again find the principle of competition. First of all, it is interesting that economists and thereby economic thought have gained influence in the networks in the last few years. If one assumes that the majority of these economists are oriented to a free market economy, then ideas of competition will be spread even further by their presence in the political arena.

Progress

When talking about progress as a value and a principle of American society, then the specific American idea of progress is meant, which differs from the European version by a certain activism. It contains less theory and assumes that a problem first needs to be approached from a practical point of view. In the course of this practice, difficulties and disadvantages show up, which are removed in a

new attempt to solve the problem. In this way, the solution to a problem is constantly refined. That does not mean that theories do not play a role in the United
States, but practical experience is given more importance than in European societies. Once again we see the reflection of the famous pioneer spirit of Americans.

This trial-and-error way of operating also influences contact with science. A
theory or a thesis does not have to be 100% proven before one introduces it into
the scientific discussion. The theory is first presented, and modifications can be
worked out later. A temporality of scientific results is seen as legitimate, and one
is then more willing to accept such a temporality. Expertise is more easily doubted
than in Germany, for example, and, therefore, does not also have the significance
that it takes on in the German field of clean air politics. In addition, expertise,
where it is significant, has to be much more substantiated.

The specific American idea of progress has also made its mark on the Clean
Air Act as a whole. Its history is even a perfect example of the trial-and-error
approach. Passed relatively quickly in 1970 in the middle of a general environmental protection euphoria, great difficulties soon arose in its implementation.
Particular issues came up during the practical implementation, such as not keeping deadlines for the realization of ambient air quality standards; there was ex-
perimenting, for example, with elements of emissions trading, and in later ver-
sions of the law these practical experiences were adopted and established.
Regulations were made that were thought to be good and that through experience
proved to be impractical or not (Interview House of Representatives). The content
of the Clean Air Act is, therefore, a mixture of normative guidelines, theoretical
ideas, the current configuration of interests, and the consequences of practical
experience.

POLITICAL REGULATION: COMPETITIVE DEMOCRACY

The United States conceives of itself as a democratic country, and democracy
has a special tradition here. A sense of active participation in local politics and in
political decisions is more pronounced in the United States than in Europe. Although the representative democracy is established on a federal and state level,
there are still grassroots democratic ideas and elements according to which every
citizen should have the possibility to participate in political decisions. The idea of
the representation of the interests of individual citizens is also characterized differently here than in Europe, where these representatives are not as legally held
responsible as are the respective elected officials in the United States. Thus, the
fact that it is extremely common in the United States to turn directly to elected
representatives in writing with problems and complaints appears to be a specific
American characteristic to Europeans.

The sense of democracy and the involvement of citizens are also clearly institutionalized in the political arena of clean air protection. The democratic idea
runs through the political arena procedurally as well as in regard to contents in
that popular measures are often decided upon. The complexity of the problem of
air pollution requires consulting with many actors in the decision making process,
but public opinion always has to be taken into account, too. Thus, it happens that

the members of Congress primarily represent the interests of their constituents and are seldom subject to the constraints of political factions. The viewpoints of citizens, influenced by their own interests as well as by the media campaigns of environmental organizations and industry and, at the same time, reflected in the arguments of the interest groups and represented by these groups, find their way into the actions of political decision makers, who regularly ask for feedback from their voters. This and the necessity of taking particular interests into consideration at the same time lead to decisions that are frequently characterized by the conditions of the moment and afterward prove to be impractical and have to be again thought out and modified. In addition, it is also typical of the political culture in the United States to publicly resolve existing goal or value conflicts.

On the level of program planning, the orientation toward the public of the political decision makers leads to individual decisions that strongly reflect the respective trend of public opinion. The necessary consultation of different interest groups, which is needed for the exchange of information and for the interest groups themselves to be seen as important actors and as having the ability to mobilize potential voters, occurs but also requires taking the positions of industry into account. In light of implementation, the feasibility of measures, the arguments of industry, and its need for the consideration of business rationalities have to be included. The allowance system for sulfur dioxide emissions from electric power stations demonstrates a successful result of consultation. Developed by the Environmental Defense Fund,[6] it was supported by industry and found its way into the Clean Air Act Amendment of 1990.[7] In practice for a few years, it has continuously been positively assessed. Here the advantage of consultation becomes clear: The acceptance by the actors who have to implement it increases. It demonstrates how the value of a clean environment and human health as well as business efficiency and flexibility simultaneously find consideration in the decision.

The democratic idea of elected representatives of the people acting in the name of the people is found in their orientation toward the public. The population should be involved in political decisions as intensively as possible, and that is guaranteed by the corresponding involvement being procedurally established. Everyone who is affected by a decision should be able to express his or her opinion and be able to work on the decision. Everyone should be equitably involved in the decisions. Therefore, in the field of clean air politics during various stages of program planning and standard setting or implementation, public involvement is planned. For the most part, however, the individual citizens are represented by interest groups—even though they have no formal basis of legitimation.

The democratic idea is also found in the institutional rule of monitoring. Already established in the political system in the principle of checks and balances, the idea is also found in the field of clean air politics. Public involvement itself as well as the courts fulfill this monitoring function. For the network, the idea of monitoring means that many governmental actors are involved that mutually monitor each other, whose positions for political decisions have to be considered, and that all serve as contacts for interest groups. The establishment of the idea of monitoring governmental decisions in constitutional reality often appears in the form of the possibility of using legal proceedings.

The dominating institutional rule of public involvement with its idea of monitoring and transparency at the roots of this rule and its consequence of taking many different points of view and interests into account sharply influences the regulations in the legislation of clean air protection and their implementation. This rule is established at numerous stages of the political process. The negative consequences of this legitimation of political decisions by the orientation toward the public are reflected in the implementation of clean air politics and reveal the specific American dilemma between legitimacy and efficiency. By listening to all the points of view and by the constraint of having to justify every decision to the public, standard setting turns out to be a lengthy process that, as a rule, does not stay within the legally established time frames. Under these conditions, informal talks are illegitimate and have to be avoided, but then the advantages that these talks have in regard to the efficiency of the procedure are omitted. Problems in implementation are the result. After a standard is passed, it is not rare for it to be challenged once again, this time in court. Here it is shown how much the idea of the involvement of every citizen in political decisions, the right of everyone to introduce his or her interests into the political process is also established in the constitutional reality. The other countries studied here do not have the problems in implementation to the extent that is found in the United States because from the beginning intensive talks between those regulating and those regulated take place and the interests of industry have a stronger influence on the regulatory process. But then a large part of the public is excluded from the decision making process.

NOTES

1. Since the debate on the Constitution of 1789, there has been a fundamental discussion about the way in which the will of the people should ideally be manifested. On the one hand, direct democracy is seen as the only real form of democratic government. This is seen mainly on the local level, where the assembly of citizens is still common today. On the other hand, there is the principle of representation, which is especially established on the federal level. According to that principle, the people, who themselves are divided into different interest groups, elect their representatives, who are in a better position than the people to reach political decisions regarding the common good. For more about this discussion, see Mewes (1990: 28 – 32).

2. For concrete cases of permit granting from the 1970s and 1980s, see Wood (1989: 71 – 89).

3. For the precise composition of the Science Advisory Board, see EPA, Interview Science Advisory Board: "About 55% of them [the experts] come from academics, from the university, about 15% from industry, another 10% from independent consulting operations, about 4% from the environmental community, and then there are independent research organizations that exist in the country as well, and they represent about 10%."

4. Such representation, however, is not absolutely necessary. It is quite conceivable that professionals other than lawyers could be involved in the legislative decision making process and could deal with nonlegal aspects of collectively binding decisions. In this way, later problems of implementation could be anticipated.

5. For an example, see Landy, Roberts, and Thomas (1994: 204–237).

6. "Those market-based programmes: the Environmental Defense Fund was basically the inventor of that, and we've supported their effort," Interview Edison Electric Institute. See also Interview House of Representatives: "Acid rain was a good example where the environmental groups took the position which I thought was remarkable for them, that one ton of SO_2 anywhere in the country was equivalent. So they supported the emission trading system."

7. However, there were some difficulties, since there were considerable differences between the individual states, especially between the midwest states, where the mining of high-sulfur coal is an important economic factor, and the East Coast states, where, due to the prevailing wind direction of the Northern Hemisphere, the sulfur dioxide of the coal burned in the West leads to too much acidity in the soil and lakes.

Chapter 7

Cultures of Democracy: Historical Formation and Contemporary Challenges

Richard Münch

INTRODUCTION

Our case studies and their comparison led us to the elaboration of specific ideal types of politics characterized by specific features and causal effects. In terms of democracy we may describe them as "representative democracy," "etatistic-republican democracy," "consensus democracy," and "pluralist competitive democracy." Finally, these democracy types should be unfolded further by way of linking exemplary contributions to the political philosophies of the countries under review to the results of our case studies and their comparison. In doing so, we pursue the question as to how far and in what form the types of democracy may handle conflicts and are able to form society politically while maintaining their social integration, and how much they are able to form the future on the basis of a consensus.

UNITED KINGDOM: REPRESENTATIVE DEMOCRACY

Preliminary Remarks

The negotiations in the British compromise network take the shape of informal consultations in a variety of overlapping forums. Dealing with conflicts refers to the claim of a fair share in the framework of an established tradition of mutually respected rights and interests. The formation of a synthesis results from the inclusion of the particular into evolved traditions of societal practice. Strong and lively associations of the civil society form the corresponding framework. The compromise network is embedded in the extended context of professionalism, of institutional rules and political culture. Professionalism is oriented toward practice and operates according to the principle of practicality. The institutional rules require fairness, reciprocity, mutual respect, appropriateness, accommodation, and the recognition of authorities steeped in tradition. Political culture is characterized by the idea of a representative democracy anchored in civil society. We may refer the ideal type of the compromise network, which is most marked in Great Britain, to these structural elements (Diagram 7.1).

Diagram 7.1
The British Compromise Network in the Context of Professions, Institutional Rules, and Political Culture

Specification   Opening

		Conflict as claim to a fair share in the framework of tradition	Arenas of informal consultation
Professions		Compromise Network	
Practical Professionalism Practicality		Strong associations of civil society	Synthesis by embedding the particular into the tradition of societal practice
Institutional Rules		Political Culture	
Fairness Mutual Respect Respect for traditional authority		Representative Democracy rooted in Civil Society	

Closure   Generalization

Policy Networks: Forecourts of Informal Consultation

In England more than in any other country politics remains firmly anchored in civil society. This is also underlined by the structure of the policy networks and the character of the process of the harmonization of interests taking place within these networks (Vogel 1983, 1986). The political center is surrounded by a range of forecourts to politics graduated according to their proximity to the center and their related influence, where experiences are gathered, interests are harmonized, and policy suggestions are thought out and worked out. Due to the forecourts' multiple grading and interconnection, a maximum of possible interests can be included in the policy process, and yet the inner core will be protected against too fast, unbalanced initiatives that would increase conflicts. Policy initiatives have to get through the interlinked forecourts, thus experiencing a substantial polishing before they can gain political relevance in the center. On the one hand, this provides a chance of inclusion to the various interest groups, and, on the other, they have to adjust to the arrangement of interests to the same degree as they advance to the core of the policy process from the outside. In this way, all sorts of radicalism of ideas and recklessness of interests will be polished so much that the different parties can reach a compromise.

Side by side with the process of polishing of ideas and interests is the informal consultation as the predominant form of cooperation between the authorities and the government, on the one hand, and the interest groups, on the other. An informal consultation takes place between persons who usually know each other well, and it takes place in an atmosphere of mutual trust and the openness of articulating freely one's own position, while at the same time respecting in principle the positions of others as being at least worthy of discussion. The informal consultation does not inch into the limelight, as this would disturb the confidential cooperation. The public's mobilization by an interest group in negotiation appears as a breach of confidence that makes open cooperation difficult further on. The public's mobilization might expose negotiation partners inappropriately to the public so that agreements may undermine the reputation of one or both parties. The pressure exerted by the public narrows the scope of what can be negotiated, since a position articulated in public can no longer be abandoned without one's losing face. This applies both to the process of program formulation during the consultation between the ministerial bureaucracy and the interest groups and to the process of implementation of laws in agreements between the controlling authorities and the companies. As a rule, the informal agreement creates results accepted by both parties so that there is rarely a reason for legal action and the resulting intervention of the courts (O'Riordan 1979: 239; Vogel 1986: 92–97; Knill 1995: 110–112).

Due to the executive's dominance in program formulation, the networks have been grouped around this focus; yet they feature manifold gradings toward the outside and are strongly branched so that they may absorb a relatively fragmented articulation of interests without focusing them in representative big associations. In this way a struggle of everybody against everybody cannot occur. The wide opening and grading of the forecourts and the polishing of interests in informal consultation with a far-reaching elimination of public controversies are a means to counteract the struggle of everybody against everybody (Vogel 1983: 102–103; 1986: 83; Knill 1995: 25). The political style of informal consultation, which is kept away from the public, has traditionally settled in England and is formally legitimated up until today by the Official Secrets Act of 1889, which involves the secrecy of official data (Burmeister 1990: 215; Shils 1956). The reason for this can be found in the Parliament's supremacy whose debates exclusively represent the public, while the administration's task is nothing but carrying out the Parliament's decisions in strict neutrality. Apart from the parliamentary debates, no other centers of politics are accepted. The admission of the public to such secondary centers would bring about an undesired fragmentation of political power. In Parliament, politics should be made before the public's very eyes, whereas a consultation free from the obligations of public representation should be possible to harmonize the interests, when it comes to the preparation and implementation of the laws.

One aspect of the Westminster Parliament's supremacy is that the regional bodies and communities do not possess any individual political rights but may act exclusively on the basis of revocable single permissions attributed by the Parliament. Citizens' interests should be protected by the representative Parliament once and not several times by various bodies, since this might easily involve insoluble contradictions and conflicts of power (King 1993: 217).

Institutional Rules of Policy Making: The Politics of Practicality

The *informal* institutional rules—informal as the whole negotiations themselves—guiding the policy process are responsible for the polishing of the different standpoints. The rule of *reciprocity* is at the forefront: the actors in the political process do not regard themselves so much as opponents wishing to implement their standpoint over the other party, but rather as partners dependent on a confidential cooperation. They are aware that they will do harm to themselves in the end when they do not respect the other party and let it get its rights, too. Mutual confidence is considered a great good that will not be put at risk by reckless actions. The negotiations' informal character, hidden from the public, generally unites people who know each other well and work together in the long run. A personal mutual confidence may evolve in this context, and the persons involved appreciate this good so that they undertake great efforts to maintain this confidence. Consequently, the policy process is supported more by persons that respect and trust each other than by formal rules that lay down the rights to a say exactly (Richardson, Gustafsson, and Grant 1991).

The informal process of political negotiations depends to a high degree on persons and the influence they carry due to their reputation. Political initiatives, therefore, depend on winning very influential personalities for their purposes so as to gain access to a forum of policy formation. They have to be handed on by such influential personalities so as to get through the chain of forums from the outside to the inside. Consequently, the language of influence dominates, which requires a high degree of investments in personal relationships of the actors in the political process. Influence is a means of communication with a slow effect. The building up of influence needs a lot of time. It is only in long-term, solid, and confidential relationships that influence may grow just to remain available as a permanent resource that will not vanish quickly. Its maintenance depends on the further care of personal relationships. This long-term character of the building up and maintenance of influence, in turn, requires political initiatives to get through the chain of forums slowly when advancing to the center of politics. They will succeed in doing so only when they submit themselves to the further informal rules. The participants in the negotiations expect mutual readiness to approach the other party and not to cling unwaveringly to their standpoint to allow for accommodation.

The measures proposed and taken in the end should suffice to the criterion of *appropriateness*, that is, respect the rights and interests of those concerned. An intervention in such rights and interests and the costs arising from that should be in an appropriate relationship with the effect attained thereby.

What is deemed appropriate is concretized further by the rule of *practicality*. Regulatory measures must be tested in practice and fit into an existing practice. It is not theoretical reason that counts but practical success and the practicability under conditions of a given practice. Whether or not a measure is suitable can be proven only in practice. Therefore, the legislation leaves a relatively wide scope for concrete negotiations during implementation. The former prerequisite (i.e., that the protection of humans, animals, and the environment should be made with the "best practicable means") complies precisely with this criterion of practicality. This includes the control of the air quality by measuring the whole of existing emissions instead of controlling emissions at each source. It is not the respect of technical standards at all cost that matters, but the measures' practical conse-quences regarding the factual air quality but also regarding the technical and financial possibilities of a company. Replacing the "best practicable means" with the "best available technique not entailing excessive costs" (BATNEEC) and with the "best practicable environmental option" (BPEO) does not automatically in-volve a radical turning away from the practice of the "best practicable means." It rather concerns the adjustment of the European Union's (EU) clean air guideline, which has been geared to the direct control of emissions with the latest technical means under the influence of Germany, to the previous British practice. It is not the best available technique that is applied, but the one that does not create exces-sive costs (i.e., that is appropriate and complies with the sideline conditions) (Weidner 1987; Royal Commission 1988; Knill 1995: 208–230).

Inclusion of Expert Knowledge: Incremental Improvement of Politics by Growing Empirical Evidence

The relationship between politics and scientific advice fits precisely into the picture described of the British policy process thus far. Graded and interlinked forecourts form a sort of filter that scientific research results have to go through before attaining political relevance. New results have to adapt to the wealth of experiences of the scientific common sense in order to attract attention (Knoepfel and Weidner 1985: 24; Weidner 1987: 116). Epidemiological research over a longer period of time is more significant than unique experimental results, espe-cially when gained in animal experiments and when their transmission to humans can be doubted. This is proven by the differing reactions in the United States and the U.K. to research unveiling a carcinogenic effect of the pesticide Aldrin/Dieldrin and the medicine estrogen. In the United States Aldrin/Dieldrin was canceled from the list of admitted chemicals in September 1974 by the Envi-ronment Protection Agency, while estrogen may be sold only with warning on the instruction leaflet since 1977 upon intervention of the Food and Drugs Agency. In Great Britain, however, scientists challenged the American research results, since they are not based on long-term epidemiological studies. Moreover, the positive effects of estrogen on women after their menopause were emphasized (Gillespie, Eva, and Johnston 1979; McCrea and Markle 1984). Political measures will be taken only when absolutely reliable research results are sufficiently backed by experience and when the negative aspects of a practice undoubtedly overrule its positive sides. The late reaction to the epidemic cattle disease BSE and the evidence of a possible transmission to humans precisely fits into the framework of this hesitant regulation style.

Results differing from the standard and idiosyncratically working researchers are provisionally cast aside so that they will not disturb and can be referred to and/or called back should the situation have changed. They are not eliminated once and for all but are left within the horizon of experiences, even so in a marginal position. They are tolerated and perhaps even respected but are regarded as not relevant and applicable. Controversies are not carried out until one side is eliminated completely, but only to the point where preeminence becomes evident. Those in the weaker position remain on stock for later consideration. In scientific research, this style of dealing with controversies was demonstrated by the example of C. B. Barkla, Nobel Prize winner in physics from Edinburgh. Barkla developed a theory on X-ray emission, the so-called J-phenomenon, which was not able to make its way in the scientific community. Nevertheless, despite all contrary evidence Barkla stuck to his theory for a long time. This did not hinder the community of physicists, however, from promoting the careers of Barkla's pupils eagerly and considering Barkla himself a still serious colleague of relevance to their professional work, such as his job as an examiner at the London Kings College (Wynne 1976, 1979; Aretz 1990: 225–232).

The recently promoted, more extensive inclusion of doctors and biologists when compared to other countries and the correspondingly lower dominance of physicists, chemists and engineers do not mean a complete turnaway from the classical dominance of the latter, but receive their legitimation from the traditional practice of orientation toward the quality of the environment and its effect on humans, animals, and plants instead of a fixation on isolated emission values (Boehmer-Christiansen and Skea 1991: 15–16). However, this also underlines the preference given to practice when compared to theoretically and analytically established findings. In practice, everything is in connection with every other thing, and the knowledge used has to be consequently varied. Moreover, these findings have to make their proof themselves in practice and must be linked with one another. The orientation to practice requires a comprehensive interdisciplinarity. The emphasis on an integrated protection of the environment is fully in line with this strategy (Weale 1996). The environment is not protected by an isolated application of individual knowledge and techniques but by cooperation in practice, where the most differing findings and techniques are combined into an integral set. Therefore, it is essential for the experts involved to understand each other. They must look beyond the boundaries of their area and be able to impart their knowledge in a language understandable to everybody and free from technical terms. In this way, the different expert knowledge remains linked to a common sense that is reproduced and developed further in common conversations. When filling commissions, attention is paid to the fact that the members not only are firmly anchored in their specialist field but have done cross-sectoral work before; as a rule, they are members not only of a single specialist organization but of various expert and nonexpert groups (Boehmer-Christiansen and Weidner 1995: 120–125). The variety of their organizational inclusion should guarantee that they can participate in the integration of completely different prospects and standpoints. When integrating the different standpoints, a compromise acceptable for all parties must be found. In order to reach such a compromise, all parties must show a basic understanding for the others' positions and be prepared to cut back in their own standpoints. In the framework of this compromise culture, the trusting cooperation and the respect for informal rules of proceeding are more important than the unlimited realization of one's own standpoint (Eckstein 1961: 30–31).

Ideas of Legitimation: The Political Philosophy of Representative Democracy

So far, we have worked out the structural pattern of policy networks, institutional rules, and the inclusion of expert knowledge. All three levels of the policy process are in a relationship of homology with each other. Finally, they find their correspondence and legitimation in the historically evolved political philosophy of the representative democracy.

England's political culture does not know the concept of a state facing society as an independent unit, as this was emphasized especially in German political philosophy (Nettl 1968: 562; Badie and Birnbaum 1983: 121–124). The representation of society by *its own* government replaces the contrast between state and society. At the same time, the tradition is maintained symbolically that this is the government of Her Majesty the Queen. The queen, for instance, reads out the prime minister's governmental program to the Parliament. On the one hand, this symbolic act attributes the dignity of Her Majesty the Queen to the government, and, on the other, its taking place in Parliament clearly points out where the actual rulers are to be found: among the representatives of the people. The monarchy combines both the nation's history and unity, while the Parliament mirrors the current constellation of the situation of power and interests. The Crown and its government are not *above* society but *inside* society, which is represented by the Parliament, just as the Crown was regarded as part of the community of its environment in traditional corporate society (Dyson 1980: 39; Rose and Kavanagh 1976). The government does not protrude from society in order to form the executive power of an independent state but remains attached to society (Grimm 1991: 123–124). The government is an organ instituted by society whose task is to cope with emerging conflicts, to preserve the inner and outer peace, to protect the lives, property, and freedom of its citizens. In this respect John Locke justifies the stepping away of the people from the natural state to form a political community in his contract theory. Its purpose is to preserve the lives, property, and freedom of its members. The term of political community alone shows that politics is not differentiated into a state but forms a unity together with society (Locke [1690] 1963, vol. 2, Chapters 7–9).

The citizens united in a political society are not transformed into citizens of a state (as is the case with Rousseau) who subordinate their particular interests to the public will. Rather, they remain citizens who have joined together exclusively for the purpose to protect their individual interests against attacks from inside or outside. Their association is rooted in the convergence of the interest in their own lives, their own properties, and their own liberties. From their association in a political society, they institute a government whose task is to realize the purpose of the political society. In order to tie the executive power firmly to the citizens' interests, a legislative body is instituted above it in the form of a representative body, which has the task of transforming societal interests into laws. The "consent of the governed" is produced in Parliament, which is binding for the government. The executive is entrusted with carrying out the laws. Moreover, it has to have the federate power to represent the polity toward the outside and to protect it, along- side the prerogative power to act in the interest of the polity at short notice should this become necessary. The judicature is typically not set apart by Locke, although the construction of a political society by the social contract expressly establishes the rule of the law to which the government (executive) is subject, too. The legis- lative body is itself the central place for the law's rule, and it joins both legislative and judicature. Up to the present day the Parliament is therefore not only the highest legislative body but also the highest judicial one, just as Locke put it. This is justified by the fact that in the Parliament the people judges itself in the form of its representatives and consequently does not acknowledge any authority above the people (Locke [1690] 1963: vol. 2. Chapters 11–13). Different from the United States, the transformation of Locke's model of a political society did not involve a formally worked out concept of checks and balances. Instead, the British form of a representative democracy has gradually evolved over the centuries, with Locke's model serving, at best, as an interpretation aid used to understand the historically effective ideas of politics' purpose and the relationship between politics and soci- ety as well as the delimitation of the thinking on democracy prevailing in England as opposed to the ways of thinking that have developed in other cultural tradi- tions.

The idea of a representative democracy has been realized, above all, in the concentration of political power on the part of the legislative and the clear pre- eminence of the House of Commons over the House of Lords. After the Glorious Revolution in 1688, the House of Commons proved to be the winner in the clash with monarchy, which strove toward absolutism in line with the models to be found on the European continent at that time. The Parliament's supremacy be- came the counterpart of the absolutism on the European continent (Laski 1938; Butt 1969). The House of Commons was the representative organ of the landown- ers and affluent citizens. Their victory over the Crown was not considered a sub- version of traditional conditions but rather a reinstitution of the old law according to which the estates possessed the privilege of essential liberties and self- government where the king was not allowed to interfere. The Magna Carta of

1215, which was won hard by the barons, is the first written testimony of this limitation of royal power with respect to society. The Petition of Rights of 1628, the Habeas Corpus Act of 1679, and, last but not least, the Bill of Rights of 1689 confirmed the validity of this tradition of an autonomous society in the struggle against the absolutism of the seventeenth century and decisively withdrew the legitimacy from any governmental power independent of society. With the transfer to the House of Commons, the governmental power returned to society after it had to be left to royal absolutism provisionally. The concentration of political power in the House of Commons also involves preeminence over both the executive and judicative. The executive is but the Parliament's governing committee. It covers the front rows of the governing majority and, backed by its majority, faces the minority opposition, which is spearheaded by the potential future government, the opposition's shadow cabinet. Judicative depends on legislature in that Parliament considers itself at the same time the country's highest court, the High Court of Parliament. In fact, the law lords of the House of Lords exercise the highest judicial power in the country. However, the Parliament's power is limited again by both executive and judicative. With the increase of governmental activity, the executive's administrative staff has grown far beyond that of the legislature so that, meanwhile, ministry committees bear the main load of work when working out legislative initiatives. It is true that the government is still considered the Parliament's governing committee, and it depends on the support of the parliamentary majority, yet the weight has shifted to such a degree that, above all, a government headed by a powerful prime minister leads its parliamentary majority to the direction it aims at (Bagehot 1963; Jones 1965; Mackintosh 1977; Foley 1993).

This development was assisted by the majority vote system and the resulting clear allocation of governmental power to a single majority party as well as the corresponding emergence of a two-party system in Parliament, for parties other than the two big counterplayers—in modern times, these are Labour and the Tories—are hardly ever able to win a seat in Parliament. Therefore, Parliament is characterized by the permanent debates between a relatively uniform governing party led by the prime minister and a relatively uniform opposition party headed by its chairman. Both parties are guided mainly in parliamentary discussion so that the parliamentary faction occupies a leading role for the party as a whole. This is evidence of the fact that representative democracy as a representation of society in governmental action will become a reality only when it is complemented by the government's guiding responsibility toward society. It is not astonishing, therefore, that the British form of democracy in particular is characterized by a very marked leading role of the elite over the masses. The deference to this leadership manifested by the mass of the population complies with the elite's claim to leadership (Kavanagh 1971; Jessop 1974: 30–48, 124–143; Moore 1976).

The restriction of parliamentary power by the judicative results from the tradition of the common law. In the seventeenth century, Edward Coke laid down the independence of the courts in his interpretation of the common law in an argument with King James I that was formative for the further development (Little

1969: 167–217). The common law is the law arising, in practice, from judicial dispensation of justice and is continued by the latter. When the Parliament is considered a high court, this means that the laws passed by the Parliament as positive law must not trespass traditional law; they may, at best, develop it and adjust it to the current requirements but not reverse it. Therefore, the courts usually interpret parliamentary laws in the light of the handed-down law and, in doing so, ensure that the legal development proceeds gradually and that the essential parts of traditional law—above all civil rights and liberties—are not violated (Stein 1964; Street 1973).

The Parliament becomes a representative organ reflecting all societal interests, which are harmonized in the framework of public policy due to free discussion. Much earlier than the parliaments on the European continent, the British Parliament emancipated from being a mere representation of estate interests toward developing into the entire society's central reflexive organ. Regarding the question as to how independent the Parliament should be of the electors' interests, opinions diverge widely. Whereas conservative spirits such as Edmund Burke stress independence, liberals like John Stuart Mill strive toward a stronger liaison between the Parliament and the electors with both, however, representing moderate positions that are not opposed diametrically. According to Burke, too, the MPs will be able to determine the common good only if they share common interests, sympathy, feelings and wishes with their constituency (Burke (1775) 1897: 9, 19, 48 and footnotes).

After John Locke, John Stuart Mill, above all, characterized the liberal understanding of the democratic representative government. In his *Considerations on Representative Government* he wanted to see all societal interests represented in Parliament. Like Tocqueville, Mill feared the destruction of freedom through the tyranny of a democratic majority (Mill 1977: 81–83, 156, 176–178, 217–218, 460, 558; Tocqueville 1945, vol. 1: Chapter 15). From an ideal point of view, the representative government is the best form of government as it remains rooted in society and includes the citizens in its governing action: "There is no difficulty in showing that the ideally best form of government is that in which the sovereignty, or supreme controlling power in the last resort, is vested in the entire aggregate of the community; every citizen not only having a voice in the exercise of that ultimate sovereignty, but being, at least occasionally, called on to take an actual part in the government, by the personal discharge of some public function, local or general." (Mill 1977: 403–404). It is the government's task to promote all societal interests. Nevertheless, it is not its task to realize any interest, but it should rather make sure that the citizens will unfold the best side of their character and learn to separate appropriate interests from inappropriate ones. A free society can exist only when the citizens acquire a feeling for what is right or wrong. It is therefore the government's foremost task to promote the development of this feeling by including the citizens in the responsibility for the common good, by teaching them about what is right or wrong. In order to guarantee the government's orientation to the common good, a differentiated voting system depending on the degree of education was deemed necessary to him (Mill 1977: 324–325, 353–357).

The government has an educational task to allow for a free societal life in the future that can do with little control on the government's part. Only in this framework is the idea of a laissez faire, which is represented by Mill himself, feasible (Mill 1977: 305, 322, 348, 393, 411–412, 417–418, 467–469, 535–536).

The liberal society requires a network of mutual respect and support and moral feelings toward each other. Both David Hume and Adam Smith recognized this fact as early as in the eighteenth century (Hume [1748/1751] 1962: 183–232; Smith [1759] 1966). Both complemented the idea of a free society serving the promotion of the benefit for all with the idea of a society where the citizens are associated by moral feelings of sympathy and compassion. This position is the intellectual counterpart to the emergence of a civil society with a lively associational life, which has turned out so characteristic for the British way into modernity. Only against this backdrop of experiences can the optimism of utilitarianism and liberalism in the nineteenth century be understood.

When Bentham's utilitarianism declares the greatest degree of happiness of the greatest number of people to be the basic moral principle, it is understood tacitly that the citizens have so much compassion for each other that they do not want to realize their individual happiness at the expense of the others (Bentham [1789] 1970). Herbert Spencer's conviction that the government can be ousted to the background more and more in an industrial society with a fully developed division of labor and market liberties has to suppose that a person's moral character grows simultaneously with the liberties. As far as this does not happen on its own, the government should interfere for a certain time trying to educate people to being good, morally sensitive citizens (Spencer [1897–1906] 1975).

This connection of individual liberties with the development of the citizens' moral character remained intact in the further development of liberalism. Succeeding Mill, Thomas Hill Green carried on this idea (Green [1883] 1929; [1886] 1986). Whereas Mill entrusted the government with the positive task of the citizens' moral education to lead a conscious, responsible, and free life, Green was mainly interested in the government's removing all obstacles that hinder the citizens' moral learning process. The government is to enable the citizens to act responsibly within society and for society. Paternalism would actually prevent people from becoming responsible, conscious citizens who commit themselves to the common good. It is important to create the necessary preconditions to help all people join in this learning process:

> The true ground of objection to "paternal government" is not that it violates the "laissez faire" principle and conceives that its office is to make people good, to promote morality, but that it rests on a misconception of morality. The real function of government being to maintain conditions of life in which morality shall be possible, and morality consisting in the disinterested performance of self-imposed duties, "paternal government" does its best to make it impossible by narrowing the room for the self-imposition of duties and, for the play of disinterested motives. (Green [1886] 1986: § 18)

It became clearer and clearer toward the end of the nineteenth century that the morally integrated society cannot develop on the way of individual learning processes alone, not even when the government removes all obstacles. Consequently, the New Liberalism recalls the government's more active role (Richter [1964] 1983: 267–291). In a publication that appeared in 1911, Leonard T. Hobhouse described the New Liberalism in a formative way (Hobhouse [1911] 1964). He requires the government to carry out social reforms, thus ensuring a fair distribution of burdens and rewards depending on the functions taken over in the production process marked by the division of labor and, in this way, limit excessive wealth and avoid poverty. Only in this framework stipulated by the government can citizens unfold their moral character and take part in the production of the common good in the interest of everybody. Society can develop only with the cooperation of the citizens, and this cooperation must be promoted by the government's providing the necessary motivation for the citizens to cooperate. This motivation can be expected only from citizens' being able to count on society's support themselves (Hobhouse [1911] 1964: 69, 76–81, 98–106).

What the New Liberalism recognized as an obstacle to developing the cooperation of free citizens (i.e., the insufficient inclusion of the mass of the population, the working class in particular, in sharing in politics, economy, and society) has been made the focus of their politics by the labour movement, headed by the Labour Party and the trade unions. The fair sharing in societal life, affluence, and political decision making has always been the main topic of all opposition movements in Britain, starting with the Radical Party in the 1860s right through to the Labour Party's politics in the twentieth century, passing by the more radical Chartist movement in the 1830s and 1840s, the moderate trade union movement since the 1850s, and the Fabian Society in the 1880s (Wolfe 1975). Their way has always included the extension of civic associations so as to create a complement to the exclusive character of the associations of the privileged classes and thus open up access to civil society to the disadvantaged classes. The foundation of associations alone allowed the opposition movements to help the underprivileged gain a better sharing in society. On the other hand, radical attempts of a societal subversion failed. The inclusion of the formerly excluded required rather an access to society's existing institutions than their basic transformation. As politics is bound into civil society, the abolition of disadvantages is, first and foremost, done by innovations of the civil society, which means the creation of associations and the representative participation of the associations' leaders in the management of politics, economy, and society. Inclusion is done through the extension of the elite with the representatives of the new associations who, in turn, form the links with the mass of the population. This version of inclusion may be called a representative co-optation of new leadership elites into the group of the established elite. It is the characteristic feature of the British way of a gradual inclusion of ever wider groups of the population into the sharing in politics, economy, and society, since the way into modernity was taken in the seventeenth century.

The main feature of societal change, which was brought about, above all, by the Labour governments and the politics of the trade unions after World War II, was mirrored by the formation of a typically British civic corporatism. Its particular feature is the direct cooperation of companies and trade unions on a company level, with the government showing as much reservation as possible. It is not state laws but informal arrangements turning into common law and that form the framework for cooperation (Clegg 1976; Ashford 1981: 136–166). The system of closed shops (i.e., companies that are firmly tied to a trade union with negotiations taking place predominantly on a company level) has become the characteristic feature of this civic corporatism. Consequently, the latter's delegalization by the Thatcher government in 1990 must be interpreted as a breakup of civic corporatism and the return to the principles of classic liberalism (Bellamy 1992: 10).

Margaret Thatcher was interested in reviving the faith in the moral quality of individual self-responsibility and the inherent moral responsibility for one another and for the whole of a liberal society, in the sense of the classic liberalism, just as it was formulated by Samuel Smiles, the "high priest" of the Victorian character formation, in his writing *Self-Help* (1859) (Bellamy 1992: 10): "If the nation is only an aggregate of individual conditions . . . then it follows that the highest patriotism and philanthropy consists, not so much in altering laws and modifying institutions, as in helping and stimulating men to elevate and improve themselves by their own free and individual action" (Smiles [1859] 1925: 3). The titles of Smiles' writings paradigmatically mirror the marriage of liberalism and Victorian morality. Alongside his publication *Self-Help*, other typical writings such as *Character* (1871), *Thrift* (1875), and *Duty* (1880) can be found. They praise the inventors, discoverers, researchers, and entrepreneurs whose moral exemplariness has been the foundation of Great Britain's greatness (Smiles [1859] 1925: 3).

In the nineteenth century, liberalism and Victorian morality complemented each other just as, in the eighteenth century, Adam Smith saw the unfurling of the market embedded into a network of mutual moral feelings (Briggs 1954; Perkin 1969; Collini 1979, 1985; Fielden 1968–69; Bellamy 1990; 1992: 9–57). Margaret Thatcher's linkage of neoliberalism with her bourgeois-marked moral rigorism is a resurrection of this tradition 100 years after it seemed to have come to an end (Warpshot and Brock 1983; Jenkins 1987; Ewing and Gearty 1990).

Problems of Conflict Settlement: The Inertia of Established Practices

Negotiations are determined in the British policy making process by the law of inertia. This means that an existing practice will be changed slowly and gradually, new things must fit into the existing practice and must be worked on to this end, and no comprehensive changes are made but only smaller repair works. Regulations must respect the rights and interests of those concerned and must not go beyond the generally accepted limits of appropriateness. The good side of this established compromise culture is the trusting cooperation, the protection against unforeseen changes, and the respect of the evolved arrangement of rights and interests. The negative aspect is shown by politics' weakness in regulation when basic reforms are required as a result of a changed situation. The model does not offer any means for this. Therefore, a need of reforms has accumulated in Great Britain over several decades after World War II after the country lost its colonies, which were the basis of its affluence, and after it was ousted from its leading position on the world market by the rising European and non-European competition.

This need of reforms could not be coped with by the governments at first. This situation was frequently described as the "English disease" (Ashford 1981).

Margaret Thatcher cut that Gordian knot when she came to government in 1979. To do so, she was forced to leave the existing framework of political culture, violate the institutional rules, and make use of her majority power to an extent that had not been seen in decades before. The control of the government's power by the network of informal consultations was done away with. Informal negotiations and compromising were replaced with open confrontation and the intransigent application of the political power available. Slowly moving influence was pushed to the background by the fast and direct application of political power. This applies, above all, to Thatcher's fight against the trade unions, whose power was broken, and to the measures she took to privatize state-run companies and deregulate the employment market and various industrial fields. In this process, the way was prepared for a more liberal unfolding of the market forces by way of political power (Wapshot and Brock 1983; Kavanagh 1987; Jenkins 1987; Ewing and Gearty 1990). On the one hand, regulations of the market were abolished, but, on the other, further existing regulations—especially as regards the protection of the environment—were transformed from an informal consultation practice to an interplay of an arm's-length setting of standards determined by law and company self-control. Both measures were designed to cut the administrative expense of time and staff and to save costs. The cost-benefit analysis developed into a comprehensive regulation concept that guides not only regulatory measures in terms of their contents but also the process itself. The effectiveness of measures should be linked with a maximum of efficiency, that is, cause the lowest possible amount of costs. The change of the controlling style away from informal consultation toward fixed official stipulations whose respect is to be guaranteed by the companies themselves with random samples taking place selectively only was suggested by the EU's emission-oriented and standardized guidelines beyond the will to save costs and Thatcher's distrust of informal consultations. The EU guideline has standardized admission processes even more and now also includes the obligatory information of the public (Knill 1995: 161–234).

The frequently discussed question is whether Margaret Thatcher has completed a revolution and, in doing so, has not only given green light to the market but also turned the country's political culture upside down. We can certainly say that due to its inertia the established political culture of compromising would not have brought about such basic changes by itself as Margaret Thatcher ensured in fact. These fundamental changes were possible only as a result of a breakout from the corset of political compromising. In a larger sense, this fact of a successful breakup of the previously valid rules of the game and the, at least temporary, implementation of a new game (i.e., the display of majority power to an extent that was unthinkable before) could be called a revolution. The rules of the game were not adjusted to new situations, but they were simply canceled. With this, it was demonstrated openly that the government's scope of power, which is limited only by conventions and not by a written constitution, can be used beyond the tacitly acknowledged boundaries under unusual circumstances. This unusual situation arose since, over the decades, the conventional restriction of the scope of power reduced the government's political capacity of action to a minimum, more than in any other modern Western country.

By no means, however, has Margaret Thatcher succeeded completely in reforming British society. Her reform plans partly met with substantial resistance and could, therefore, not be realized as planned. The practices of informal consultation were revived where they should be removed. This applies, for instance, to the practice of the permission procedures, as was proven by our case study. There was a return to informal consultations in the run-up to the formal procedures, simply because the companies were unable to fill in the permission forms for the establishment of plants without the help of the inspectorates. It is to be expected that the culture of informal consultation, which grew over the centuries, will not disappear completely after one and a half decades of tough struggles against it. It will most probably recover, lead politics back onto calmer ground, and make the decision processes slower again.

As far as the contents of politics is concerned, the New Labour government will certainly not set the clocks back to 1979 but rather look for careful amendments to the too far-reaching measures undertaken by the conservative governments of Margaret Thatcher and her successor, John Major. Regarding the political contents, Margaret Thatcher's policy may, moreover, be interpreted as a return to Locke's original concept of a political society and the union of liberalism and Victorian morals. This political society elects a government that merely protects its members' rights to life, freedom, and property. It is to leave that scope to society that it needs for the realization of individual rights and offer it that degree of protection which safeguards against interventions into these rights both from inside and outside. According to Margaret Thatcher's ideas, which definitely mirrored the opinion of a majority of people, the British society moved too far away from these ideas of a society of free individuals, thus entering into the bonds of a domination of corporations. The civil society of free associations developed into a corporate society unable to carry out reforms. Yet the newly gained liberties involved distortions in the societal structure, which, in turn, can be considered the basic reasons for the victory of Tony Blair and his New Labour Party in the 1997 elections. The new areas of poverty, crime, and the decline of public sectors and institutions require a politics that succeeds in directing the market forces into socially acceptable tracks without suffocating them. It is a balancing act that has to safeguard the newly gained liberties and, at the same time, revive those elements of a culture of a fair share and trusting agreement of measures that were damaged and removed by Margaret Thatcher (Krönig 1997a, 1997b).

Concluding Remarks

Let us finally gear our analysis of the political compromising model prevailing in the United Kingdom to its ability to handle conflicts in such a way that, on the one hand, this ensures social integration and, on the other hand, helps to cope with the big questions of the formation of the future, that is, that the future will be coped with on a consensual basis. The following answer can be found to this question: conflicts are frequently polished, dampened, and guided into the tracks of pragmatically manageable questions by the network of civic political associations and their frequently overlapping memberships as well as by the system of interlinked forecourts to politics so that, as a rule, they do not attain the level of basic discussions. Therefore, politics was more and more entangled in the traps of civil society and has thus been hindered from implementing basic reforms. The recovery of its capacity to form the future was possible only by a coup at the expense of the loss of the evolved consensus. The prerequisite to this coup was a pairing of the jammed-up pressure of sufferance and Margaret Thatcher's iron will to implement her plans and her ability to legitimate the neoliberal reform program with the help of the country's cultural tradition. The production of social integration is the central and still unsolved task of the new Labour government. It is possible that the civic bonds will contract so much that a new attempt at liberation will be required one day.

Briefly, the primary force of policy making is the mostly informal rules of consultation and decision making. They oblige new social movements to respect the spectrum of the established experience and practice in order to be included, so that innovations have to be appropriate and supported by experience; conflict settlement is normally effective within the boundaries of the tradition; only the government's use of power in extraordinary situations of crisis allows for conflict settlement outside these boundaries. Consensus is normally carried on in stepwise, evolutionary adaptation to new situations.

FRANCE: ETATIST REPUBLICAN DEMOCRACY

Preliminary Remarks

In the French conflict network the negotiations of the policy process appear in the form of circles of selective concertation under a state-administrative leadership. Conflicts are held as a struggle for victory or defeat. The formation of synthesis is made by the administrative-elitist definition of public interest. The civic associations exist as parasites of the state. The further embedding of the conflict network into the context of professions, institutional rules, and political culture is as follows: there is an elitist-technicist professionalism geared toward technical rationality. The institutional rules emphasize both hierarchy and technocracy. The political culture is characterized by an etatistically reversed republicanism (Diagram 7.2).

Policy Networks: Centers of Concertation

A main feature of the policy network prevailing in France, which has changed only little, is the strong concentration on few influential actors on the side of the state-administrative elite, the sectoral differentiation at the expense of a far-reaching coordination, and the selective concertation with privileged representatives, especially those from the industry, whereas the remaining groups are extremely fragmented and have a wide gap between themselves and the center. The ministries cooperate closely with selected associations from a branch of business, which are therefore ready to cooperate, whereas the others remain generally excluded from the negotiations.

Diagram 7.2
The French Conflict Network in the Context of Professions, Institutional Rules, and Political Culture

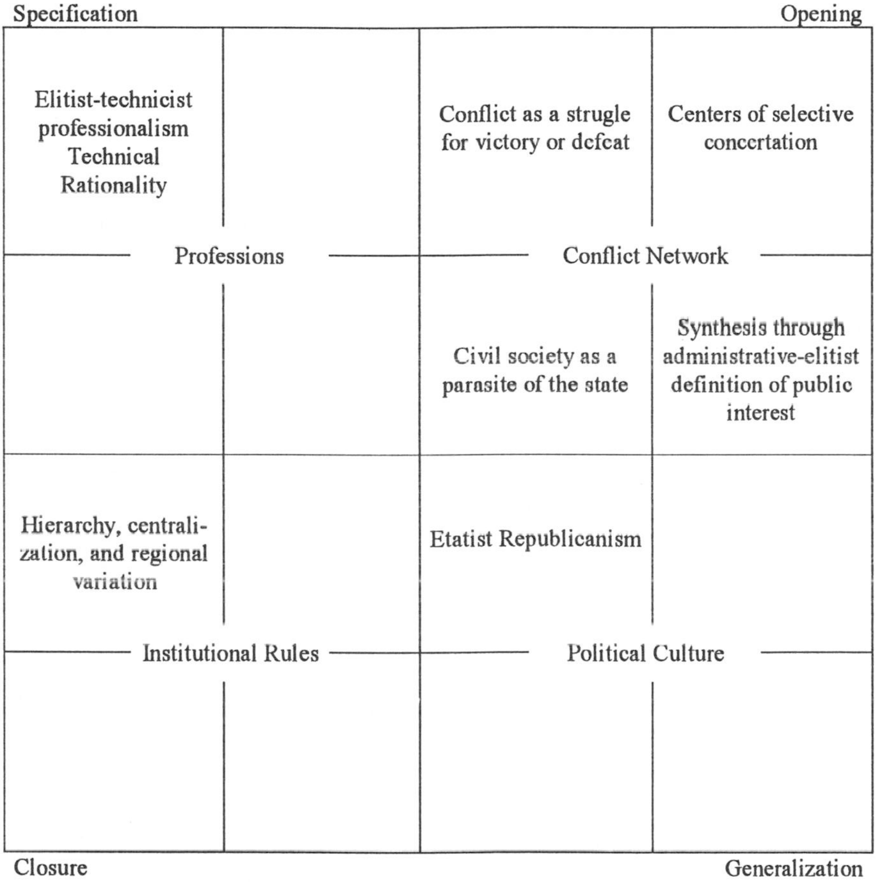

Specification   Opening

Elitist-technicist professionalism Technical Rationality	Conflict as a strugle for victory or defeat	Centers of selective concertation
— Professions —	— Conflict Network —	
	Civil society as a parasite of the state	Synthesis through administrative-elitist definition of public interest
Hierarchy, centralization, and regional variation	Etatist Republicanism	
— Institutional Rules —	— Political Culture —	

Closure   Generalization

The struggle for the privilege of having access to the state power dominates the activities of associations, groups, and clubs. Even Tocqueville described this struggle of societal groups for the period of the ancien régime (Tocqueville [1856] 1966). The associations depend on the minimum privilege of recognition and annual financial subsidies by the state just to secure their existence. The same goes for environmental groups. They need the state's agreement to receive at least some bread crumbs. In this way, civil society is made a parasite of the state. Society does not live on its own, but rather on multiply graded and more or less generous privileges of the state. This also creates a dependence of the state on its para-

sites. It needs their assistance in forming society. Since, as a rule, privileges become a sort of common law, it is extremely difficult for the state to change the
privileges granted over a long period of time. A study on notaries, for instance,
reveals how this profession has succeeded in defending its privilege of sealing
contracts on behalf of the state with a firm quota of the jobs available against all
attempts for reforms, the last ones being made by Mitterand's left-wing government (Suleiman 1987). Another example is the attempt of the first woman minister of the agriculture of the socialist government in 1981 not to cooperate with the
privileged farmers' organization but with other groups. Her attempt failed, as
other organizations did not have the necessary potential of influence among the
farmers (Stevens 1992: 275). On the one hand, the state has to take the privileged
groups into account, but, on the other, selective concertation means that the followers of the less privileged groups revolt against state measures. Spontaneous
protest actions that flare up over and again are a specific feature of French politics. The language of power is ruling here. The struggle for access to state power
characterizes the situation. The most recent attempts to make the circle of groups
admitted to concertation as large and representative as possible diverge from the
previous practice of selective concertation. It is hard to estimate today whether
this is just a nine-day wonder or the beginning of a new style of politics. Even in a
bigger concert, the game continues with the old means, that is, reaching for the
privileged seats in the first row in a move to have better access to state power. The
old game for power is not over; it is only played under new conditions.

Institutional Rules of Policy Making: Hierarchy, Centralization, and Regional Variation

Both the formulation and implementation of policies are made hierarchically,
that is, under the state's obvious leadership. The active integration of societal
groups, right through to the parties, into the process of policy formulation and
implementation is replaced with the frequently only strategic reference to an
imaginary public interest that the elite determines in representation of the people.
The wide consensus formation by including all the groups concerned and interested is regarded as an obstacle to the *rational* finding of a decision (Ammon
[1989] 1994: 136–158). The administrative centralism can look back on a long
history in France whose result is obvious when looking at the concentration of the
economic, political, and cultural events in the Parisian basin, the corresponding
underdevelopment of the periphery regions, and the star-shaped extension of all
traffic ways with the Parisian center as their starting point (Ammon [1989] 1994:
136–158). Yet it would not be true to state that the periphery is dead and that all
life is concentrated in the center. It is rather the permanent struggle for central
power versus the periphery's own rights that has determined the country's development up until today (Bourjol 1969; Grémion and Worms 1968). Administrative
centralization starts in the ancien régime with the deprivation of power from the
aristocracy's local bearers of power. They became dependent courtiers of the king
in Versailles. The climax of this development was the breaking up of the parliaments in 1771. Everywhere the royal directors and their subdelegates took over

the legal supervision of local bodies. Certainly, it was possible from time to time to undermine this supervision or enforce an agreement, yet the center and the periphery were generally forced to enter into a relationship of mutual distrust, of power and counterpower that made their cooperation and integration very difficult.

As Tocqueville demonstrated in his classic work on the ancien régime and the Revolution, the country's administrative centralization was carried on by the Revolution. It was merely given a different political regime (Tocqueville [1856] 1966). The country was subdivided on the drawing board into *départements* of about the same size, contrary to all evolved regional communities. This subdivision was based on the criterion that the representative of the state's central power, the prefect, should be in a position to reach his *département's* frontiers in a day's ride. The Chaptal Act of 17 December 1800 deprived the local institutions fully of their power. The district councils were appointed by the prefect from the notables on-site. Ever since that climax of the centralization wave there have been approaches to decentralization, though with very modest results.

A decisive change occurred with the left-wing government's Decentralization Act of 2 March 1982, which was complemented by the Act of 6 February 1992. Since that time, the 36,000 communities encompassing frequently fewer than 1,000 inhabitants have been given greater authorization to make decisions, as have the *départements' Conseil généraux* and the *Conseils régionaux*, which unite several *départements*. The subprefects in the communities and the prefects in the bigger cities, *départements*, and regions have to control only whether the locally made decisions are in line with the laws in force (Mendras and Cole 1991: 122–142; Graziani 1985; Müller-Brandeck-Bocquet 1990; Kukawa 1993). The power in negotiations between the center and the periphery has shifted slightly toward the periphery. At the same time it is shown that local mandate holders can achieve even more as they succeed in attaining a piece of departmental, regional, and central state power by accumulating posts beyond that of a mayor (Kukawa 1993: 21–22). This underlines that, more than in any comparable country, the whole societal life in France is a struggle for power and, to be more precise, a struggle for an access to the decisive positions that are predominantly on a state level. Those who want to advance local developments, introduce a new philosophy, art or literature, scientific findings, or collections of a museum have to possess the power of access to central institutions: institutes, academies, journals, publishing houses (Latour 1984; Bourdieu 1984, 1992; Baier 1988: 125–140). An interesting example from the history of science is the struggle between the corpuscular theory and the wave theory of light between 1815 and 1822. Fresnel, representing the wave theory and being an unknown provincial engineer, was able to defend his position against the supporters of the corpuscular theory only, when he succeeded, with the help of François Arago, to gain a foothold in the central Parisian research institutions. He was assisted by the fact that, in the end, Arago made his way against his main adversary, Jean-Baptiste Biot, in the struggle for the most powerful positions in the scientific community (Frankel 1976; Aretz 1990: 182–209).

Even after the decentralization that started in 1982, the decisive policy networks are still comparatively strongly centralized. However, the frequently abstract formulation of the laws leaves much scope for negotiating their implementation on-site. In the past, this covered, above all, an arrangement between the
industry and the prefect in charge; in the meantime, however, it involves a wider
group of actors—at least formally—due to the extended formal participation
rights of the citizens and the required making public of authorization proceedings
(Worms 1966; Grémion and Worms 1968; Bourjol 1969; Grémion 1976; Graziani
1985; Müller-Brandeck-Bocquet 1990; Kukawka 1993). Due to the tradition of
the centralized etatism it must be expected, however, that the extended formal
participation rights are satisfied materially to a limited extent only in the long
run. Even though the network moves some way from a closed to a more open
pattern, from an exclusive to a more inclusive pattern, and from a centralized to a
more decentralized pattern, especially in policy implementation, it is nevertheless
still miles away from the policy networks in the United States whose pattern in
this context is developed much further, not least of all because it is firmly rooted
in the cultural tradition of the country.

With decentralization, however, the periphery gained a piece of power from
the center that can be used to block the center's policies. In doing so, the periphery may profit from the abstract character of most laws. As it usually takes years
until the laws are concretized and made applicable by decrees—including set
arrêtés and even more specific *circulaires*—by the administration's specialist
departments and since in this way the original political vigor vanishes, and the
laws are submitted to the retaining of proven patterns of action, which is so typical for the administration, the laws frequently do not reach the periphery in the
way that they were conceived by the center. This leaves a traditional scope to the
periphery for acting according to its own management, occasionally even against
the center. The center's claim to dominance is faced with an obstinate periphery
living its own traditional life far away from the center. The prefect always had to
come to terms with the notables, as he depended on their cooperation irrespective
of his formal competence and the formally lower competence of the local and
regional bodies. Consequently, the opposite of the French state's centralism is the
variety of landscapes, towns, and communities, which has never disappeared.
Likewise, society's fragmentation forms the counterpart to state unity. It is true
that the state penetrates society, the regions, towns, and communities, yet only at
the surface and without fully reaching out to the depth of their structures (Braudel
1986). The rule via abstract laws and their administrative application via decrees,
arrêtés, and *circulaires* does not enter into the hearts and concrete lifestyles.
Therefore, regions, towns, suburbs, communities, and societal groups live their
own lives, remaining moderate on a calm ground yet possibly yielding resistance
against the state's dominance from time to time. Consequently, one may often
observe with a certain astonishment how helpless a state that insists on its inner
and outer sovereignty becomes when facing the regularly arising protest actions
and blockades of interest groups and the acts of violence of young people in the
suburbs who lack perspectives (Kepel 1987, 1994; Dubet and Lapeyronnie 1994).

State centralism and societal variety but also disunity and societal decline are two sides of one and the same medal, since the centralism is unable to unite the state and the society. Certainly, the new way of decentralization offers new chances of self-responsibility to the periphery yet is unable to solve the old problem of an *integration* of center and periphery materially. Therefore, the new rights are used by the periphery much more to better unfold their traditional resistance against the center. In this context, the old problem of a lacking mediation between state and society by well-developed civil associations is coming up, which are not simply understood as a protective zone against the state's desire for power but rather as an active part maintaining more than just particular interests and ready to make their contribution to the functioning of the whole system.

Inclusion of Expert Knowledge: The Technical Elite

The elite of engineers and scientists trained at the Ecole des Mines, Ecole des Ponts et Chaussées, and the Ecole Polytechnique and organized in the Grands Corps (such as the Corps des Mines, Corps de Ponts et Chaussées) represents a way of thinking that transforms knowledge into a legitimate claim to lead society to its own benefit. Up until today, the technicoadministrative elite has embodied an understanding of dominance by virtue of expert knowledge that was shown up by Saint-Simon and his followers, Enfantin and Bazard, in a certainly exaggerated and therefore societally not feasible way but that was nevertheless striking and informative; in a changed manner, it was also demonstrated by Auguste Comte (Saint-Simon 1865–1878, vol. 42; Saint-Simon 1924; Ramm 1956; Salomon-Delatour 1962). It covers the passage from governing persons, to the administration of objects in a "perfect hierarchy." This is how Wolfgang Schluchter summarizes his analysis of Saint-Simonism (Schluchter 1972: 20–33). We take up Schluchter's analysis in a culture-specific interpretation in the following considerations.

Saint-Simon and the Saint-Simonists believed that the permanently progressing development of knowledge will free people from distress, misery, and shortage and will therefore make the struggle for the distribution of scarce resources superfluous. Therefore, no repressive rule will be required to stabilize exploitation and suppress revolts against the bad conditions. The state's monopoly on violence and application of power to secure the existing order may be replaced with society being headed by the experts of aesthetics, knowledge, and production management. The artists, scientists, and industrialists form the managing elite that does not use power but its better knowledge and the complementary agreement based on insight to assist workers, craftsmen, and farmers in their activities, which are ultimately beneficial for everybody. By virtue of their aesthetic sense, the artists may provide models for a satisfying life, the scientists supply the necessary knowledge to realize this satisfied life, and the industrialists educate the workers in the production of the means required for it. The artists replace the priests, and the scientists take the place of politicians; in this way, knowledge is substituted for power. The industrialists occupy the position of the capitalists; their actions are not geared toward exploiting the workers but toward instructing them to work for the benefit of the whole society. Capitalism's class rule and class antagonism dissolve in a perfectly harmonized hierarchy where the rulers and their subordinates do not face each other as antagonists but where an elite that is responsible for the whole will assist the lower ranks in the production of societal affluence for the benefit of all (Ramm 1956: 41–51).

Since the existing order of property does not assign the ranks optimally according to knowledge and capacities but to origin and inherited or not inherited—and therefore lacking—capital, it should be abolished and transformed into an order where everyone reaches exactly the place where he or she can best unfold his or her abilities for his or her own advantage and the benefit of all. Everyone should be employed in line with his or her abilities and be paid in accordance with his or her achievements. Consequently, there will not be a perfectly equal allocation of payments but an unequal payment depending on the achievements made, which will, on the one hand, do justice to the person in question's individual contribution to the whole and, on the other, produce the greatest benefit for the lowest ranks, as they profit from the corresponding increase in the overall performance as everybody else does, though to a lower extent. The functional hierarchy is a meritocracy, an order that allocates one's rank in line with the performance produced for the whole. It is a rational performance order depending on maximum knowledge and planned organization. It must be secured to this end that everybody will occupy the right position for himself or herself and for the whole with the best being attributed the top positions. According to the Saint-Simonists, the order of property and the bequeathing of accumulated riches to following generations are the greatest obstacle to this order, since inherited advantages may be used to obtain better positions (Salomon-Delatour 1962: 104–111).

In a parable, Saint-Simon demonstrated that the loss of the inherited aristocracy might certainly make the French sad but could be easily coped with, while the loss of scientists, technicians, industrialists, and the whole working population would have to bring them to despair, as this would rob them of the basis of their existence (Ramm 1956: 27–28). Nevertheless, the Saint-Simonists were unable to bring about a change in this respect. Until today, French society has been characterized by a marked inequality in the distribution of riches based on birth within a certain class and/or group when compared to other highly developed countries. Origin determines the future as in no other developed Western society. The country boasts a very clearly differentiated class and group structure that in no way complies with the idea of a meritocratic allocation of ranks depending on performance. However, the central organization of the educational system right through to the elite colleges is expected to help this idea to become a reality. The all-encompassing examination system, which foresees an exam for even the smallest educational unit and the system of Concours (i.e, admission to the elite colleges by way of strict competitive admission tests, which can be passed only after having attended the corresponding preparatory classes) is to help everyone to reach his or her position in society that best suits his or her abilities, while the best should be brought to the top. All empirical research shows, however, that reality is still far away from that idea, since the inherited economic, social, and cultural capital in Bourdieu's sense still has the most decisive influence on the fact where the individual people will ultimately end up in the marked system of rankings, what preparatory classes they attend, and what exams they pass (Bourdieu, 1982: 193–209, 378–99; 1986; 1981; Prost 1992).

Meritocracy is still a fiction, whereas technocracy is an even more lively reality. Technocracy is the rule of the scientific-technical elite, which is at the top of society and is able to recognize, thanks to its knowledge, what is in the public interest of the entire society and from what every individual will ultimately benefit most. The struggle of interests for the implementation of specific interests by way of power is replaced by an instruction of society by the elite of knowledge. The comprehensive development and application of the scientific-technical knowledge not only extends the scope of possible actions but generally realizes the good life in the end. People's dominance over humankind is replaced by the common, methodical rule over nature for the benefit of all people. Technical progress overcomes shortage and, with it, the struggle for essential resources. It makes politics superfluous and replaces it with the transformation of knowledge and technology into an increasing standard of life by an expert administration of the whole life (Salomon-Delatour 1962: 82–93).

The administration is not the government's executive body; rather, it replaces the government when it comes to the methodical organization of societal progress. In the framework of such thinking, governing can be understood only as the setting of partial targets on the long way of progress. Therefore, governing means planning, which, in turn, requires scientific-technical expertise, that is, the preeminence of scientists and technicians. Seen from this point of view, the government as the translation of a democratic formation of a majority on the basis of the articulation of interests from the bottom to the top—from the individuals, interest groups, parties, and the public right through to Parliament—appears as an immature, transitional solution, a crisis that is unable to provide society with enough knowledge to gain the appropriate insight into what is necessary to reach the common goal of the permanent improvement of the conditions of life. Negotiations between the state and the interest groups, and parliamentary and governmental discussions therefore have to be enlightened by the knowledge of the technicoadministrative elite in a move to overcome the particular standpoints so as to bring public interest to the fore. Consequently, the technicoadministrative elite is attributed the decisive role to steer the political process toward the realization of the public interest. Negotiations in the policy process should therefore not be seen as a "bargaining" but rather as a concertation under the auspices of the technicoadministrative elite. As soon as the technicoadministrative elite can play this role uncontestedly, society will find itself in well-arranged conditions; if this is not the case, it will go through a stage of crisis where interests conflict immediately, where pure egoism, and struggles for power are ruling, and where the law of the stronger and the oppression of the weak by the strong prevail over a generally acknowledged dogma that is useful for everybody.

All in all, the Saint-Simonists see historic development as a cyclical sequence of organic epochs of societal integration –that is, characterized by a strong religious faith—and epochs of egoism and disintegration without any common faith. At the same time, they place this cyclical sequence of organic and critical epochs into the framework of an evolutionary development from small, right through to ever bigger social units, of a growing internal and external pacification by the legal order of the social conditions, of an increasing removal of oppression and exploitation by the formation of an order for the benefit of the whole and of each individual, guided by the progress of knowledge, which leads toward a growing scientification of all areas of life. At the end of this development is the organic order of a functional hierarchy, where all antagonisms dissolve in a complete meritocracy. The epoch guided by science does not mean the end of religion, but rather its perfect realization, since only the comprehensive, scientific discovery of nature's laws makes it possible to allow people to be relieved from distress, misery, and fear and lead a free and fulfilled life (Salomon-Delatour 1962: 36–37, 57–58, 76–81, 103–111).

To play the role of the great savior of humankind, science must be rooted in as deep a faith of people as the religions of former epochs of human history. It also requires its cathedrals and its catechism to make its knowledge enjoy the appropriate respect and thus be able to spearhead society's progress. Different from Auguste Comte ([1852] 1970), who has science—although with an almost religious character—take the place of religion and metaphysics, Saint-Simon and the Saint-Simonists integrate science into the development of religions toward the highest level of monotheism, which is embodied by Christianity. In the laws discovered by the scientists, in the unity of the unveiled world order both the existence and the providence of God, who reigns the world, are revealed. Science does not replace religion but represents the highest level for humans to discover God's acts in the world: "If one assumes a religious though raised standpoint, which no-one has reached before, then science will show itself—far away from retaining this character of atheism which is considered its typical feature—as an expression of the capacity given to humans to recognize gradually and progressively the laws with which God reigns the world, or in brief: the *Plan of Providence*" (Salomon-Delatour 1962: 225). Christianity is the religion in whose framework science is supported by the faith in God. In believing in a plan of God, the scientists can devote themselves to the task of unveiling this plan in the universe's laws (Salomon-Delatour 1962: 224–225, 259, 281–289).

To allow the principles of science to guide the practice of societal action, a comprehensive and in-depth education of humans is indispensable. Education ensures a sharing of humans in scientific knowledge so that the methodical organization of progress by the elite of knowledge can more and more be based on humans' insight, thus making the application of constraints superfluous (Salomon-Delatour 1962: 172–174). Since shortages are removed more and more so that the struggle for life resources is no longer necessary and since people's insight into what is necessary for the benefit of all is growing, increasingly less political constraint is required. Politics dissolves in the interplay of art, science, and industry in the framework of a perfecting of the moral order of a world community that makes itself seen in the universalism of Christianity. The artists should mediate the ability for universal liking as the basis of the growing world community, the scientists are to unveil God's plan that leads humankind toward this goal, and the industrialists should ensure the methodical organization of production, making people free from distress and misery (Salomon-Delatour 1962: 94–102, 157–159, 172, 206–207, 257–259).

Ideas of Legitimation: The Political Philosophy of Republican Democracy

The homologous structural pattern of policy networks, institutional rules, and inclusion of expert knowledge that we have worked out so far finds its correspondence and legitimation in the historically evolved political philosophy of the republican democracy, whose first representative is Jean-Jacques Rousseau.

From Rousseau's republican point of view, the practicing of private liberties—such as the unfolding of freedom on the market—implies that the strong will supersede the weak and that only the successful ones will be able to enjoy liberties, whereas all others will have to bear distress, misery, and oppression (Rousseau [1754] 1964a). In the end, however, everyone suffers from the disordered realization of private autonomy. Expressed in terms of modern political economy, the negative, external effects of individual rational action make life difficult for us and wreck the enjoyment of private liberties. Contrary to Locke's liberal contract theory, according to Rousseau, the problem is not simply solved by private people's appointing a government that, acting as their representative, guarantees the maintenance of their private liberties. For Rousseau, the order of liberty requires a shift of individual activities from the private to the political sphere. Private persons have to become citizens and, in this role, practice their political autonomy by self-legislation. The citizens will be able to observe their rights without suffering mutual damage only when they find out together what complies with their general will contrary to the private persons' wealth of individual interests (Rousseau [1762] 1964b: vol. 1, Chapter 6; vol. 2, Chapter 3). This means that the realization of individual rights assumes a lively and comprehensive democratic legislation. The democratic practice must create the substantial preconditions for practicing individual rights. There will be no realization of subjective rights without the public will's legislation. This fact favors a comprehensive activity of the state, which, however, the citizens have to control themselves in order to prevent the state from getting independent of society. At the same time, the citizen's precedence over the private person is bound to overcome group particularism. In the framework of such a "strong democracy," it is possible for the citizens to develop a commonly shared concept of good life inside which individual liberties can be arranged in a way that grants a fair share to everybody. As far as the public will is concerned, both the good and the just are regarded as identical.

It was clear for Rousseau that this idea of a republican democracy could be realized only within a clearly visible city-state, such as his hometown of Geneva. Yet the French Revolution in 1789—and most extremely the Jacobins—started to realize Rousseau's idea in the large territorial state of France. They wanted the particularism of the old estates to be overcome by the one and indivisible nation. A nation was to be understood as the union of all citizens into a willful community. This was expressed most strikingly later on by Ernest Renan in his frequently quoted lecture given at the Sorbonne in 1882 (Renan 1947). The nation's unity is at the basis of the republic, and it is the state's task to satisfy the nation's will. But where is the nation's will given its expression? The Parliament as a representative organ is the stage for group particularism rather than the place for the public will to form. Instead, the administrative elite, which mostly received a technical training at the Grandes Ecoles and is organized in the Grands Corps, has always claimed to represent the public will against the particular interests of societal classes, strata, and groups. Consequently, especially under a markedly technocratic-administrative rule, the idea of a republican democracy was realized in a completely different manner than intended by Rousseau originally. The state embodies the public interest toward society's group particularism. At the head of the Fifth Republic the president represents the nation's general interest; the technocratic-administrative elite realizes the public will in the everyday business of policy formulation and implementation on his behalf. They are doing so by referring to the elitist competence of scientists and technicians from the central state institutions for research and technological development. Cooperation with the societal groups is made in the form of a concertation under a state-administrative guidance; in this process, selected representatives, especially from industry, are included who themselves form part of the elite, in particular as they have been generally trained at the Grandes Ecoles and have frequently come from the state administration to occupy leading positions in the private and state-run industry, a fact that is called pantouflage (Suleiman 1974, 1978; Bourdieu 1989).

The administrative elite's pillars are the Grandes Ecoles and the Grands Corps. The Grandes Ecoles educate the elite's offspring. Having attended a renowned lycée and then a two-year preparatory class, these promising young people are admitted to a Grande Ecole after having passed an admission test in the form of a competition; this school is specialized in educating the elite for state, administration, and economy. As far as their ranking is concerned, the universities are below the Grandes Ecoles, with the Sorbonne in Paris surpassing traditionally the universities in the province. Contrary to the Grandes Ecoles, the universities have to educate the growing mass of students over various levels of examinations. Those who succeed in overcoming the hurdle of the admission test to a Grande Ecole have, all at once, become junior members of the elite. This is, not least of all, mirrored by a salary that will definitely guarantee their living.

The breeding of an elite is an institution inherited from the old absolutist state, which was carried on by the Revolution, by Napoleon, and by all later regimes. The Ecole nationale des ponts et chaussées, the Ecole des mines de Paris, and the Ecole de Mézières were founded by the ancien régime. Their task was to educate highly qualified engineers for both the armed forces and the state administration. In 1794, at the time of the Revolution, the Ecole normale supérieure was created. In 1811 Napoleon restructured it as a place of education for lycée teachers. It has become the central school of the intellectual elite. For the scientific-technical elite, Napoleon established the Ecole polytechnique. At the same time, the universities were broken up and subdivided into educational units according to departments, and they were directly put under the control of the Ministry of Education. The universities were said to have served as an instrument of the church's authority on education at the time of the ancien régime. They were not reestablished before the end of the nineteenth century (1897), without, however, ever reaching the same ranking as the Grandes Ecoles. The need to educate the nation's elite was instead met by the foundation of further Grandes Ecoles. At the beginnings of the Third Republic, the Ecole libre des sciences politiques was created as a private institution that was taken over by the state after 1945, transformed into the Institut d'études politiques, and complemented with 11 institutes in the province. After World War II, the Ecole nationale d'administration (ENA) was established. It has become the place of education for the absolute leadership of state, administration, and economy and has ousted the Institut d'études politiques to the level of a preschool preparing for admission to the ENA.

The Grands Corps are the elite's central associations. The most important ones are the Corps Conseil d'Etat, Inspection de Finances, Ponts et Chaussées, and Mines. Appointment to leading positions in administration goes via the Grands Corps. They form the center of control. The best graduates of a year at one of the Grandes Ecoles will be admitted to a Grands Corps and remain members of it for the rest of their lives, even if they move to a post in the economy (*pantouflage*). Those who go to a different administrational department, to politics or economy—which happens more and more often—are considered provisionally delegated and, therefore, remain affiliated to their Corps, tied to the latter's spirit, and serve its penetration into other areas of society. This creates a dense network of the elite uniting administration, politics, and economy under the leadership of the Grands Corps. This elitist network is the French state's heart of power. It was from here that the transformation of a society that was still considerably marked by agriculture in 1945 into a highly industrialized one was driven on within the shortest possible lapse of time. The characteristic feature of this development was the close cooperation of state leaders, administrative elite, and big industry. On the one hand, it involved the exemplary steep rise of big technologies—nuclear energy, Ariane, TGV, Concorde, and telecommunication—but, on the other, split up the economy into a high-tech big industry and a backward small industry. In the interest of the state's sovereignty, the big industry was extended at the expense of the small and medium-sized businesses and against occasional resistance from the Green movement. Nuclear energy is the most prominent example of this development. In a cooperation between the Ministry of Industry, the state-run nuclear department, the state-owned electricity company, and the monopoly manufacturer, Framatome, the country was extensively covered by nuclear plants as a response to the oil crises in the 1970s and to achieve its complete independence of energy. In doing so, competing manufacturers were removed, as were the local protests of the antinuclear movement. Locally split resistance was unable to object to the centrally controlled implementation of nuclear energy. The prime minister made the program a top-priority matter of public interest (*utilité publique*). Only written objections could be filed against the plants' commissioning by citizens living in the immediate neighborhood of a planned nuclear plant; moreover, these could refer only to the location and possible effects on the environment. Since it was only the note of approval that decided upon safety standards, they were consequently not the topic of public discussions and objections. Such objections are a lost cause anyway in proceedings of the French administrative courts when state interests are concerned, as no independent administrative courts exist. The Conseil d'Etat is the highest administrative organ and the highest administrative court at the same time. This structural context explains why the construction of a nuclear plant took three years less in France in the 1980s than in the Federal Republic of Germany and even five years less than in the United States (Kiersch and von Oppeln 1983).

The hardly controlled interlacing of political leadership, administration, and economy makes itself felt in the fact that uninhibited abuse of power and the intermingling of office bearers in dubious monetary transactions are hardly ever proclaimed as a scandal with far-reaching consequences. Compared to other countries, they are not exploited both journalistically and politically and pursued by the courts and frequently do not involve any consequences such as resignations. This shows that there is no effective power to counteract the center of political leadership, administration, and economy that might publicize scandals and enforce political corrections. Parties, associations, the media, and the courts have too weak a position to do so, and/or their existence depends too much on the center of power. The affairs of the 1980s, for instance, which mostly petered out without any result, mirror this picture of a hardly controlled center of power: in 1983, for example, the publicized financial transactions of President Giscard d'Estaign and ELF-AQUITAINE president Albin Chaladon during the 1970s; in 1985, the blowup of a Greenpeace boat operating against French nuclear tests; in 1986 the affair of two Irishmen maintaining links with the Irish Republican Army who were ordered by President Mitterand's secret antiterror group to install explosive devices in a flat in the Parisian suburb of Vincennes; in 1986/1987, the Carrefour affair, concerning dubious financial operations of the minister for cooperation with the former colonies; in 1987 the violation of the arms embargo against Iran by the firm Luchaire; in 1989 the insider transactions regarding the takeover of the privatized bank group Société Générale and the state-owned company Péchiney American Can. These were affairs that did not develop into scandals entailing far-reaching political consequences (Bornstein 1994).

Problems of Conflict Settlement: Technical Rule without Roots in Society

For our research of the policy process in France, this look back on Saint-Simon's doctrine—just because it is so exaggerated—offers an interesting access to an understanding of the latent structures of thinking that form the cultural basis for the fact that the technicoadministrative elite claims supremacy in the determination of public interest, leads negotiations with interest groups of its choice selectively and sectorally, not as a bargaining but as a concertation process, and refuses an opening of the policy process to a wider range of groups and to the public or at least undermines it as much as possible. In doing so, it ties down the interest groups even more to their particular standpoints and makes them the parasites of the state unable to assume any responsibility going beyond their own scope (Suleiman 1987: 318–322). The parties remain stuck in ideological struggles, as they do not have to bear responsibility for the whole. The Parliament is merely a place where these struggles are fought out, not a place where workable solutions for the outstanding problems are worked on, as the responsibility for these is claimed by the technicoscientific administration. Government is unable to base itself on a *political* consensus worked out by the Parliament and the parties but needs the technicoadministrative elite in order to make the "public interest" valid beyond the struggle of parties and interests. Consequently, "public interest" floats in the air, far above the morass of a completely different reality of the struggle of interests, the politics of power, the exclusion and oppression of the weaker by the stronger. The "concerted" solutions, designed on the drawing board, do not combine with society so that its fragmentation continues again and again. Instead of the general agreement with the measures taken in the "public interest," these are supported selectively by privileged, parasitic interest groups; moreover, they are implemented by central state power. At the same time decisions are diluted, weakened, and avoided by the subordinate bodies in the periphery, and over and again, open resistance is displayed by protest actions flaring up at short notice or lasting for a longer time that mobilize smaller groups or masses and sometimes even include the exertion of violence. In these actions, society, which is only insufficiently bound into the policy process, strikes back against a state that is dominated by its technicoadministrative elite. On the one hand, this state attaches great importance to its internal and external sovereignty but, on the other, is frequently plagued by sudden feelings of weakness and can display its strength only at the expense of its parasitic utilization by privileged groups (Crozier 1963, 1970).

More than one and a half centuries after the Saint-Simonists, the problems are still recognizable in France that result from the dominance of a technicoadministrative elite claiming to represent public interest but unable to ground this public interest on a wide societal basis and applying it only loosely to a fragmented society. In his work on the technological society, Jacques Ellul described the perversion of the Saint-Simonist doctrine into a technocracy that dominates society (Ellul 1964). Here, too, we can give Schluchter's analysis a culture-specific interpretation (Schluchter 1972: 186–193). Ellul characterizes modern technology by six central features: *automatism* in the application of available technology; *self-extension* of technique by technique, since any technical invention allows for new discoveries and applications; *monism* in the sense of a lack of alternatives—there is no way toward the future beyond ever more perfected technique; the indispensable *linking* of individual techniques into a coherent overall complex; *technical universalism* in the sense of global validity and distribution; and *autonomy* of technique in the sense of its development and justification from itself (Ellul 1964: 79–147).

According to Ellul, technology is embedded in specific cultures in a traditional society. It is a means to attain the ends that are determined as legitimate by culture and is always restricted by the culturally prevailing ideas of good life. Culture determines and forms technology, not vice versa (Ellul 1964: 64–77). In modernity, however, this relationship reverses more and more to the opposite. "Technique itself, *ipso facto* and without indulgence or possible discussion, selects among the means to be employed. The human being is no longer in any sense the agent of choice" (Ellul 1964: 80). Technique determines culture and is even becoming culture itself. Technique penetrates more and more deeply into all spheres of life. Production technique, organizational technique, and human technique complement each other in this dominance over life (Ellul 1964: 22). The traditional life worlds, which reproduce themselves in the form of more or less tacit agreements on the continuation and renewal of concepts of good life and fair order, are replaced by technical civilization geared toward a permanent increase of the technical possibilities to dominate human life. Means are no longer searched for to attain given ends, but the steady extension of technical means causes a permanent search for possibilities for their use. The technical means create the needs that they have to satisfy. The ever closer association of scientific research, technical development, and mass production involves a circle of acceleration of the whole process (Ellul 1964: 85–94).

The intensification of technical progress and the production of needs with their subsequent satisfaction develop into an end in itself. The good life can be considered only a permanent increase in the unfolding and meeting of needs, while the fair order is an opening of this program of growth to everybody, that is, ultimately to all people on earth. With this, however, people will lose any chance to continue and renew any concepts of good life and fair order out of tradition, which are contrary to this momentum. People will completely lose control of what is good and bad, fair and unfair; this will be left to a natural development process where people may interfere to accelerate or decelerate it but are unable to change it basically. What is technically feasible will make its way under the terms of an unlimited, open competition on the market and will integrate moral thinking itself. Every new technique that determines our way of life will legitimate itself by referring to the fact that it implies a benefit for all, whose content can be determined concretely only by this new technique. Technique and its permanent further development become themselves the determinant of the content of a ubiquitous moral utilitarianism. This process can be observed in all technical inventions; the most recent example is genetic engineering. After initial protests have waned, the coalition of discoverers, inventors, producers, and consumers brings about the gradual removal of taboos and the spreading of the technique and the inherent way of life in the interest of a general "increase in benefit." Ellul already dealt with the prediction of scientists, claiming that in 2000, the breeding of genetically well-equipped people will be possible by in vitro fertilization (Ellul 1964: 432–433).

If we carry on Ellul's approach in the way described, we will gain an understanding of what today—more than 30 years after the publication of his book on the technological society—is understood by a technocratic rule that does without any doctrines, ideologies, and politics and leaves our well-being to a process that seems to run according to purely factual points of view to "increase the benefit" for all of us (Ellul 1964: 280–284). It is a technocracy where it is less the technocrats that rule over people than a scientific-technical-industrial momentum that dominates both technocrats and all other people alike. In a technocracy, the state will disappear inside the technical development process that drives itself forward. The ideas of the good and the just dissolve in a ubiquitous utilitarianism that regards the maximization of the production and satisfaction of needs as the realization of the good and the just no matter what technique, what needs, and what inherent way of life it concerns.

There is no doubt that the state is more than ever before prone to this momentum of the interplay of technical rationalism and moral utilitarianism under the terms of global communication, capital, goods, and service flows. Nevertheless, even in times of a greater national-state sovereignty the French state, in particular, spearheaded this movement, which ends up in the transfer of the state's sovereignty to the scientific-technical-industrial process. The preeminence of the technicoadministrative elite in the policy process is the driving force behind this development. Ambitious political projects carried out in the interest of external national state sovereignty and the internal extension of a technical infrastructure—nuclear power, steel production, TGV, Concorde, telecommunication—have become the automatism and the spearheads of the scientific-technical-industrial rationalization (Ammon [1989] 1994; Neumann and Uterwedde 1986; Cohen 1992). The fact that these are projects of the state, the administrative elite, and big industry, which are little anchored in society otherwise, involves the strange dualism of a fully rationalized big industry and a traditional small industry. Here, too, the low entanglement of state and society becomes obvious (Adam 1982).

The state's hiding behind the facade of technical rationalism, which has long been observed in France, undermined the intellectuals' confidence in politics' democratic formability. This can be seen in particular in Michel Foucault's political theory. His comprehensive genealogy of power describes in great detail how the state's power develops away from open repression toward ever more subtle forms of a power that is completely rationalized by science and whose repressive character is no longer visible in the end. People's liberation from this power, however, is a chimera. The facade of science conceals a power that dominates people right into their most inner core in an invisible way so that they are unable to get free from it in the traditional way, as it cannot produce anything but a further increase in the rationalized power that dominates them. Ultimately, it is rationality itself that assimilates people and deprives them of every chance to escape its control. Referring to the history of punishment, sexuality, and insanity in Western culture, Foucault describes the process of rationalization and sublimation of power by the scientification of knowledge. Research by scientific means leaves no retreat to the offender, the sexual deviant, the insane from the eyes of the scientific control organs (Foucault 1969, 1975).

People's domination is perfected and inescapable to the extent to which those who are observed accept science's rational discourse. Foucault points out that discourse itself is power's most subtle tool. The rules of discourse control what can be talked about. Bans and the differentiation between reason and insanity, truth and falsity control the central themes. Comments, author, and the disciplinary organization of knowledge serve as internal control factors. Rituals, discourse groups, and doctrines decide on the admission to a discourse. Since any discourse necessarily works with such rules of control, the discourse is ultimately the most subtle form of the exertion of power on people. Completely contrary to Jürgen Habermas' discourse theory, it therefore offers no escape from the clutches of power into a world that is free from domination (Foucault 1971; Habermas 1985).

Habermas' discourse theory, which is based on Kant's optimism of reason and his idea of enlightenment, regarding the dissolution of power must remain strange to Foucault. His starting point is not Kant's understanding of a reason that unfolds itself in discursive processes but, rather, Descartes' understanding of a rationality that frees itself from all traditional tutelage but at the same time has an ever firmer and farther-reaching grip on the world. Those who are educated in Descartes' thinking are unable to get away from an ultimately instrumental access of rationality to the world. Descartes' first rule in his work *Discours de la méthode* puts the clarity of the immediately reasonable thought, which is free from any traditional book knowledge, at the beginning of every use of reason. Starting there, analytical breaking down, logical deduction and the completeness of the objects conceived are to open up the whole world (Descartes [1637] 1963a: 586–587). The positive sciences realize this idea of a reason that opens up the world by the discovery of nature's laws (Descartes [1637] 1963a: 613–632; 1963b: 80–84, 158–204). Science enables people to dominate nature for their sake, to free them from distress, grief, and disease and prolong life. The rationality of a science based on Descartes is therefore an aid for people to dominate nature instrumentally but offers no protection against the instrumental access of science to people themselves. It is true that science makes people the masters of nature, yet not without its becoming the master of humankind at the same time. Foucault drew this conclusion from Cartesian reasoning in particular astuteness and conciseness. Therefore, people's way toward liberation does not lead along reasonable discourse but only along the understanding of the vicious circle of domination through discursive liberation and along subversion. The circle of power can ultimately be broken only by power and not by knowledge, since knowledge has become our time's power. However, such a logically consistent position invites the reproach that it is not possible to break the circle just as it remains tied to power itself and cannot attain a concept of reasonable understanding that might break the limits of instrumental reason, which is trapped in the bonds of power.

What we can excellently recognize in the light of Foucault's perfectly explained understanding of power based on instrumental rationality is the status that sheer protest enjoys in French politics as a form of democratic participation. As knowledge and power have joined forces to an impregnable bastion under the rule of the technicoadministrative elite, every attempt at discursive settlement of conflicts seems to be doomed to fail. It will either gain access to power and will then be submitted to its logic or bounce off its walls. Under such conditions, protest appears as the best strategy. It is a form of political action that, by itself, overcomes the state's definition of the rules of the game, a life form beyond the state's power; it does not run the risk of being corrupted by negotiations and allows to express one's accumulated rage regardless of the rules of courtesy and negotiation diplomacy (Kiersch and von Oppeln 1983; Keck 1993; Brickman, Jasanoff, and Ilgen 1985: 61, 84, 101–102, 233–238, 252–254, 305–306; Knoepfel and Weidner 1980: 93–96; Knoepfel and Weidner 1985). In their basic criticism of the state's power, the intellectuals in France can look back upon an incomparable tradition that stretches from the *philosophers* of the prerevolutionary Enlightenment right through to Sartre and *Les Temps Modernes* and the intellectuals of our present time from Foucault to Baudrillard. The state's critics in the Dreyfus affair at the end of the nineteenth century—headed by Émile Zola and his article "*J'accuse*" in *L'Aurore*—were insulted as "intellectuals" by the conservative supporters of the state's action against Dreyfus. This was the birth of a peculiar name for the writers and philosophers who try to exert a critical influence on public opinion (Zola 1898; Bering 1978; Debray 1981).

Different than in England, Enlightenment in France had to struggle against suppression and prosecution by state and church. Consequently, the intellectuals' position became even more radical. When they were able to exercise state power at the time of the Jacobin rule (1793–1794), they unfolded a regime of terror. During the Dreyfus affair, the intellectuals required the Third Republic's commitment to citizen and human rights; during the national-socialist occupation they formed the backbone of resistance. However, they were not integrated into the state's reconstruction after World War II. Therefore, they decided on a general criticism of power, especially by referring to Marxism. Sartre pursued the project of a linkage of existentialism and Marxism, whereas the poststructuralists and postmodernists from Foucault to Baudrillard continued the Marxist project of fundamental criticism in a different way (Sartre 1964; Foucault 1969; Baudrillard 1981). In May 1968 the intellectuals' great day seemed to have come, yet it did not develop into more than just a brief affair with a wider group of the population. The consequence was great disillusionment, a turning away from Marxism, a breakup into individual groups from the extreme Left, to the New Right of the New Philosophers, from an escape into new subjectivism, to the commercialization of philosophy as an easily digestible talk-show (Glucksmann 1977; Lévy 1977).

If we take Foucault's theory of the unity of knowledge and power as the most concise expression of intellectual thinking with regard to power, then protest seems to achieve not only greater success but also more legitimacy when compared to the participation in negotiations and mere public discussions. The political process falls apart in the dualism of an administration of the public interest by a technicoadministrative elite that is above society and the articulation of society's interest groups channeled toward a parasitic existence or sheer protest. Under such conditions, politics' weakness of regulation shows itself by the fact that measures are taken with reference to public interest that provoke storms of protest, since they do not meet any understanding. Since the technicoadministrative elite has become a haven of public interest but maintains only "concerting" selective links with the privileged societal groups, the political measures that is has worked out lack societal roots and, therefore, support by society. The Parliament has been degraded to the level of a forecourt of politics and can therefore be merely a place of ideological exhibition fights. It does not invite the formation of consensus having an influence on public discourse and tying the societal groups into the common responsibility for public welfare. The public discourse provides mainly ideological debates that cannot build a bridge to politics suited to solve problems. The Parliament's weakness, the ideologization of public debates, the transfer of the power of decision to administration, the technicoadministrative definition of public interest on the drawing board, and the selective and parasitic entangling of state administration and privileged interest groups rob politics of that power of regulation that it needs to cope with societal problems. It is easy to see, therefore, that under such conditions politics' arena is transferred to the street over and again (Kimmel 1991).

A rising number of critics point at the technicoadministrative elite and put the blame for the misery of French politics on its position of power. Consequently, it should be deprived of power to some extent. First of all, this concerns a reform of the elite schools and the access to the leading positions of administration (Schmitt 1991). The elite schools should no longer recruit their students mainly among the children of their former graduates, but among wider groups of the population, and the administration should no longer search its top officials in the elite schools only. Even if these well-meaning reform attempts will have a chance at all in view of the power of self-recruiting of educational capital, they will not go far enough. The position of power of the administrative elite can, in the long run, be restricted appropriately only when, first of all, the Parliament is given more power and replaces the administration as the center of the formation of consensus and, second, when the inclusion of interest groups into the policy process breaks sectoral boundaries, overcomes the barrier of selectivity, and is put on a wider foundation. The members of the technicoadministrative elite do not owe their position of power simply to a usurpation of power made by themselves, but especially to the weakness of the other power holders, above all, the Parliament and the civil society. Since the state is confronted with strong societal groups that, however, remain fragmented so that there is no prepolitical civic overcoming of interest contrasts, the interlacing of state and societal groups assumes only selective parasitic forms (Suleiman 1987: 299–330). Consequently, no formation of consensus will be possible from civil society and its entanglement with the state. The Parliament is unable to bridge the gap between the ideological positions and the particular interests and can therefore make no contribution to a workable formation of consensus. What remains in the end is the interplay between the president, who is far away from all political warfare, and his government, which frequently avoids the Parliament, and the administration. The administration remains the dominant force when it comes to the concrete elaboration of political measures. A breaking of the vicious circle of the detached administration of the public interest by the technicoadministrative elite, on the one hand, and, on the other hand, the parasitic exploitation of the state by privileged interest groups and the continually flaring protest actions of those who either want to reject interventions into their privileges or belong to those who are systematically disadvantaged and excluded is therefore not yet to be seen.

Concluding Remarks

Can we, finally, target our analysis of the etatistic policy model, which is prevailing in France, to the question in what way and to what extent conflicts can be settled in such a form that, on the one hand, social integration remains guaranteed and, on the other, the big challenges of the future can be coped with and the future can be formed on a consensual basis? This question can be answered in the following way: conflicts are coped with by state-administrative power in the sense of public interest, which is, however, defined by the administrative elite in a merely technical manner in a selective concertation with privileged interest groups that have become parasites of the state. The one-sided and selective definition of public interest and the lacking inclusion of all societal groups involve eruptions of street protests at regular intervals, which are then taken up by the parties, trade unions, and intellectuals and transformed into basic conflicts. Only if it is possible to extend these protests into a comprehensive crisis of the state can drastic reforms be carried out that, so far, however, always flew back into the old system.

The primary force of policy making is the center of power in the government, the administrative and technical elite. It allows conflict settlement in a form that gives preference to the sovereignty of the state. Innovation is limited to the goals of the government and lacks openness for the broader variety of societal experimentation. Inclusion of new social movements is hindered by the established structure of power and concertation with privileged organizations. Consensus formation takes place under the guidance of government and top administration and is counteracted by the passing by, protest, and rebellion of those groups that feel to be not included. The differentiation between central administration and regional variation, vertical and horizontal rationality helps the regions, local communities, and groups live with the traditionally established centralism.

GERMANY: CONSENSUS DEMOCRACY BY RULE OF LAW

Preliminary Remarks

In the German synthesis network, the negotiations of the policy process are predominantly conducted in committees of competent experts. Conflicts are carried out as a struggle for the coordination of subjective rights by objective law. A synthesis is formed by subsumption of the particular to the general in general laws. The neocorporatist cooperation between the state and the big organizations forms the framework for this. The network is embedded into the following context of professions, institutional rules, and political culture: an objectivist professionalism is oriented to the "state of the art." The institutional rules focus on objectivity and expert competence. The political culture is characterized by the idea of a consensus democracy and the idea of a state guided by the rule of the law (*Rechtsstaat*) (Diagram 7.3).

Diagram 7.3
The German Synthesis Network in the Context of Professions, Institutional Rules, and Political Culture

Specification   Opening

		Conflict as a struggle for the coordination of subjective rights by objective law	Committees of expert knowledge
Professions		Synthesis Network	
	Objective Professionalism State of Technology	Neocorporatist cooperation of state and large associations	Synthesis through subsumption of the particular to general laws
Institutional Rules		Political Culture	
	Technicality and expert knowledge		Consensus democracy established by the rule of the law

Closure   Generalization

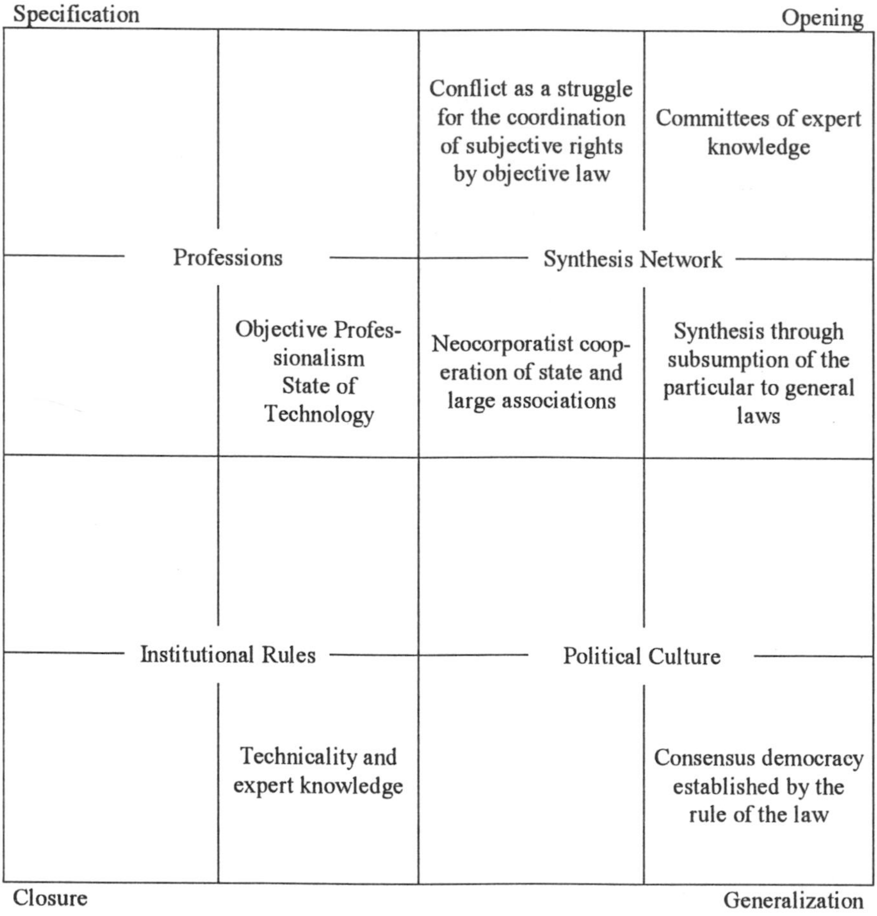

Policy Networks: Expert Committees

The policy network in Germany was characterized essentially by the cooperation of state, large associations, and science; this is usually referred to as neocorporatism. During program formulation, a neocorporatist policy network supports the search for synthesis by general law. Interests are focused by the big organizations and introduced into the process of program formulation in a relatively integrated form. There is a close cooperation between the state, especially the ministerial bureaucracy, and the big organizations. The network between these two poles is relatively centralized and closed so that it is hard for newly formed organizations and social movements to penetrate this cartel-like closed network. They can achieve this goal only by introducing additional expertise. From the program formulation right through to the implementation, the policy process is determined by the technical discourse of the experts, which differs in a strange way from the public discourse that is pushed toward emotionality. There is an almost unbridgeable gap between these two pillars. The public's stronger articulation through the media ensures that heavy atmospheric waves pile up that cannot easily be calmed down with an "enlightenment" on the part of the experts, as this was the case at times of politics' more reduced penetration by the media. So far, the policy process was dominated by the language of truth. This language, however, helps less and less when it comes to creating an understanding beyond the expert commissions toward the wide public. But this is precisely the claim arising from politics' increased penetration by the media. The consequence of the widening gap between technical discourse and emotionalized public is that the old model of consensus democracy does not work any longer. The frequently conjured up capacity for the solution of problems and force of society's formation of the German consensus model are about to be paralyzed. Debates held during the 1990s concerning Germany as an industrial location have made the consensus model itself the target of criticism and put the blame for the so-called reform jam on it. Obviously, nobody is satisfied with this model anymore, not even those big organizations that have so far benefited from their membership in the authorization cartel. The model of the consensus democracy has entered into a legitimation crisis (Scharpf 1991; Decker 1994).

Institutional Rules of Policy Making: Application of Generally Valid Law

Kant's legal and political doctrine results in a republican constitution that gives priority to a morally guided liberal state under the rule of law as against a democracy that makes people of flesh and blood take part in the political decision making processes. In this sense in Germany the idea of a state under the rule of law gained a much firmer foothold than the idea of democracy—starting with the General Prussian Land Law (Scheuner 1956; Kunig 1986; Schmidt-Assmann 1987; Böckenförde 1991: 143–169). The liberal state under the rule of law will safeguard individual liberties by general law worked out by experts as fiduciary representatives of the citizens. The more that the citizens themselves have a say by participation rights beyond the election of the representative organs, the more that the factual elaboration of laws and their application are put at risk. A comparison of the administrative court control of administrative decisions shows precisely how the idea of a state under the rule of law as it developed in Germany differs from the Anglo-Saxon rule of law. In the United States the legal control of administrative decisions exclusively covers the fairness of the process, but in no way the contents of the decisions (Scharpf 1970: 14–38). The reason for this is

simply that many administrative decisions are taken by the regulation authorities
that do not "apply" a detailed law but carry out a Congress order given by way of
an outline of a law and, in doing so, give concrete contents to the law only by
including those who are interested. Consequently, there will be no separate taking
of evidence as regards the contents. The situation is completely different in Germany, where the legislator wants to settle a matter comprehensively in a law.
Where general terms are required for this—such as the application of the "state of
the art"—the concretization by expert organs is regarded as a merely technical
problem and is not left to an open discussion between different interests. Consequently, the control of administrative decisions by the administrative courts does
not refer to the more or less fair consideration of all the relevant interests or to the
conformity to rules of the legal process only, but also to the correctness of the
decisions with regard to their contents in line with the legal situation. In doing so,
the administrative court assumes that the law has an objective meaning, and,
therefore, the administration court has to establish whether or not an administrative decision complies with the law's objective meaning. The objective meaning
can be concluded from the wording and must be differentiated from the legislator's contingent motives. When talking about the legislator's intention, this is
made only in the objective sense as it should read in view of the law's wording. It
is assumed here that the rights of the citizens have been allocated their appropriate place in the law itself and are adjusted to each other so that they will be with-
drawn from the arbitrariness of situational negotiations (Scharpf 1970: 38–52).

The wider the scope for negotiations—for example, for admission processes—
the greater the difficulties that the usual sense of justice has to face. It may be
acceptable when cooperation with the organizers of plants takes place in the admission process. If, however, this cooperation is to include third parties, too, the
terrain of legal practice is abandoned, and one will move toward an open struggle
for power for which the ruling sense of justice offers neither rules nor foundations
for its authorization. These are the deeper reasons that our research in Germany
revealed that as far as clean air is concerned, the threads of power are united in
the hands of an admission cartel that tries to keep new interest groups away from
the inner core of the decision making processes. The rule is exercised by virtue of
knowledge. Those who do not possess this knowledge will necessarily not articulate rational motives but only irrational emotions and fears and can, therefore, not
be taken for serious. This rather requires a comprehensive enlightenment of those
who don't know about the situation as it is presented from an expert point of view.
As we discovered, this results in a strange disparity between the expert bodies that
back objectivity and the public discussion that is guided by emotions. So far, the
environmental groups have been unable to bridge this disparity. When they want
to be included, they have to accept the principle of objectivity. If they do not want
to be taken by it, they will remain in the offside of an irrational production of fear.
In the implementation of laws, the idea of a state under the rule of law and the
objectivist understanding of science do not allow for a wide participation beyond
those who are directly concerned by a regulation. In this phase, above all, there is
no understanding for the concretizing of laws by means of an extensive harmoni-

zation of interests, as this is done in the United States. It is possible to have general legal terms put in concrete form only by expert bodies. In this political culture, the participation of the public in this stage of the policy process is defined more as an event of enlightenment of those who know for those who don't know than a chance for the harmonization of interests. Interests are referred to program formulation. This is the place where as many different perspectives and interests as possible are taken into account so as to transform the variety of interests into a synthesis in the form of a general law (Dahrendorf 1971: 151–231).

Inclusion of Expert Knowledge: The Rule of Experts

The expert knowledge applied is to add objectivity to the process by forming a synthesis of the different points of view. This understanding of objectivity is rooted deeply in the history of philosophy and science. Science's target is to overcome the contradiction between opposing positions by the fact that they are "abolished" dialectically in a more general synthesis. One example from the history of science is the synthesis of the precritical Kant to settle the struggle between the Newtonians and the Leibnizians on the origins of the world. From the Newtonians' point of view, the world was created by God of his own free will and could have looked different as well. According to the Leibnizians, however, God made the world in line with rational principles that could not have looked different. Kant's synthesis was that the world in its laws evolved from a chaos of gaseous fog and that the order resulting from this chaos can be explained only by the plan of a God. This means that in the origins of the world, in the chaos, a *will* of God can be discerned from which the world developed *according to its laws* (Iltis 1973; Aretz 1990: 232–252).

The objectivist understanding of science, which is geared toward a synthesis, marks the policy process ruled by experts. The focusing of expertise in representative commissions of the German Research Association, the German Standardization Institute and the Association of German Engineers leaves hardly any scope for pluralism and competition. The policy process aims at a synthesis in order to find an integrated solution to the problems. A synthesis does not create a compromise between the particular interests but offers a comprehensive frame to realize them even more extensively in a new quality. Legally seen, this performance is brought about by general legal terms—such as the term "state of the art"—that are then put in concrete forms by the experts in line with the development of knowledge. However, due to the high degree of generalization, the laws take a great distance to concrete reality. The gap between law and reality can be bridged only during the implementation of the laws. As a matter of fact, this makes a field political that normally does not have a political but rather an administrative and objective-legal character according to the prevailing understanding of the relationship between democracy and state under the rule of law. Therefore, action groups that file their requests in this stage of the administrative process are quickly pushed toward emotionality and frequently even toward the illegitimacy of civil disobedience right through to violent resistance.

Ideas of Legitimation: The Political Philosophy of Consensus Democracy by Rule of Law

Policy networks, institutional rules, and the inclusion of expert knowledge correspond with each other; that is, they have entered a relationship of homology. The structural pattern supported by these three components finds its correspondence and legitimation in the historically evolved political philosophy of the consensus democracy established under the rule of law. The first formulation of this philosophy was introduced by Immanuel Kant.

The idea of a consensus democracy is expressed in the striving for taking into account all the relevant aspects and interests in the program formulation and for merging them in a generally formulated law that harmonizes the most different aspects and interests and their exposition. The law is formulated in general terms and is concretized during implementation by expert commissions such as the Clean Air Commission (Kommission zur Reinhaltung der Luft, KRDL). Finally, it is applied by the authorities after uniform regulations have been established with those concerned. The laws are to display a high internal and external level of integration; that is, internally, they should unite a maximum variety of interests, and, externally, they should be consistent with other relevant law. They should guarantee a long-term, predictable order of the social relations between freely acting individuals. The order of individual liberties is a result of the general law, that is, above all, a task of formulating the wording of the law that requires particular juridical expertise. The participation of those concerned is once again made through know-how of the experts whose perspectives have to flow into legal work. In this sense, democracy as political participation in the working out of laws is interpreted to be as wide as possible a mobilization of expertise. Even the environmental groups have to fit into this model by trying to add expertise or by being considered "experts" for the population's fears. On the other hand, the public, which is created by the media, appears highly emotionalized and is therefore unsuitable as a source of "proper" solutions to problems. It rather requires "enlightenment" by the experts' knowledge.

The historical roots of this specific kind of consensus democracy can be traced back to the first sovereignty doctrines of the enlightened absolutism by Pufendorf, Thomasius, and Christian Wolff. According to their doctrines, the prince's sovereignty guarantees the freedom of the individuals. Only under his legislation do the liberties of the individuals enter into a well-arranged system that prevents them from colliding. The prince gets his sovereignty from the contract of the citizens to hand over to the prince the role of safguarding their natural liberties. The prince is committed to this, and as long as he meets his obligation, the citizens will have no right to a further control of the prince's rule. Such a restriction of the prince's sovereignty would make legislation a matter of the struggle for power of particular interests and would do harm to the protection of a system of well-arranged liberties. Thomasius and Wolff allocate not only the legal protection of the individual liberties to the prince but also the citizens' moral guidance to use their liberties properly. That the prince will fill in this part appropriately is especially guaranteed by the juridical expertise of his legal experts who are responsible for the elaboration of the legal system of well-arranged liberties (Pufendorf [1667] 1922; Thomasius [1710] 1971; Wolff [1736] 1975).

There is no doubt that Kant's legal and political doctrine has had the most lasting impact on Germany's legal and political thinking. This doctrine also emphasizes fully the ordering of individual liberties by general law. In his practical philosophy, Kant points out that a moral order cannot result from the sum of individual interests, as these contrast strongly and can change at any time. The main feature of a moral order, however, is its binding validity for everybody at any time. A moral order may obtain this binding validity only for rational grounds to which everyone has to agree of his or her own free will as far as he or she is guided by reason only. In this sense, the standard of validity of a moral order is the universalizing principle of the categorical imperative. Moral principles may make a claim to validity only when they can be made general law. Here, fulfillment of one's duty and liberty will merge. By adopting only those maxims of their own will to which anyone guided by reason would have to agree, people will at the same time attain the highest level of moral autonomy. Freedom and obedience to the universally valid moral law are then two sides of one and the same medal.

From a formal point of view, Kant's legal and political doctrine follows the same argumentation lines. Whereas the moral law brings people's inner freedom into a valid order, the law set by the state has the task to harmonize people's outer liberties. Yet again, this order cannot simply be established as a sum of the individuals' particular interests. It is not even possible from these interests—as Hobbes did it paradigmatically—to declare people's contractual agreement to join in a political community and put their action under generally valid laws. As people's determination to freedom cannot be realized in the natural state due to the conflicts that will inevitably arise in a limited space, people can be guided only by reason and not by interests to enter into a legal-civil state (Kant [1793] 1964: 144). This contract is not historical fact but an idea born out of reason, which serves as the yardstick of human coexistence (Kant [1793] 1964: 153). The state, which exists for rational grounds as stipulated in the contract, has the task of harmonizing the unfolding of people's outer liberties by general legislation: "Law is also the epitome of the conditions under which the arbitrariness of one and the arbitrariness of the other are joined together according to a general law of freedom" (Kant [1797] 1956: 337).

A general law must bring the unfolding of particular interests in the exertion of outer liberties into an order that prevents them from colliding and makes them compatible with each other. This order of outer liberties cannot result from a sum of articulated interests, as they are tagged along unavoidably with what has to be overcome: their collision. A different quality of the formulation of laws is required. As in his justification of the moral principle (Kant [1788] 1956: 125–155), Kant refers once again to a principle of generalization, which, in this case, relates to the law. Only those laws may raise a claim to validity that every legal being has to accept as a reasonable citizen (Kant [1797] 1956: 432–434; [1793] 1964: 150–153, 154–156). It is not the citizen as an interested party who is demanded here, but rather the reasonable citizen able to recognize the integrative force of general laws. In this way, Kant arrives at a democracy principle that merely represents a different formulation of the legality principle of the harmonization of outer liberties according to a general law and corresponds to the moral principle formally. Whereas the moral principle links the validity of moral rules to the agreement of every reasonable *person*, the democracy principle requires the agreement of every reasonable *citizen*. In this way, Kant arrives at a strange understanding of democracy. Democracy means the self-legislation of reasonable citizens. They will follow only laws that they have established themselves. In this way, in his legal and political doctrine Kant harmonizes freedom and submission to the law, as he did in his moral philosophy. While it is the realization of the inner freedom in the moral law, on the one hand, it is now the realization of the outer liberties in the general law. In this way, the citizens' freedom and the obedience of the subjects merge into one unity (Kant [1793] 1964: 145–153; [1797] 1956: 432).

Consequently, the citizens' consensus is the criterion for the validity of the law, more precisely, not that of the citizens as material beings with specific needs or as members of a stratum with particular interests, but rather as reasonable beings. Ideally, the citizens have to get rid of the particularism of their sensorial nature and group adherence in order to recognize the general validity of laws at all. In doing so, the democracy principle is adjusted to the legality principle in a way that it will lose any empirical content. Basically, this kind of democracy can perfectly do without democrats of flesh and blood. It is not the factual agreement that counts but rather the capability to agree of citizens guided by reason. Though, in Kant's eyes, the republic would be the ideally best form of government to meet his criterion of reasoned consent, this yardstick may also be applied by a monarch with regard to the laws, possibly with the help of legal experts and/or expert commissions in general (Kant [1797] 1956: 431–437). This representative application of the democracy principle by experts may, however, involve even a reversal of the situation. If this happens, the democracy principle will not determine the legality principle, but the latter defines the fulfillment of the democracy principle. In this case, the merit to be agreed to is not the criterion for a law's validity, but the harmonization of liberties in a general law as established by the experts will form the criterion for the merit of a certain law to be agreed to.

Due to their lead in knowledge, the experts explain to the citizens which laws are worthy of their agreement and which ones aren't. This reversal of the conditions between the legal and the democratic principle results in a strange change of Kant's idea of enlightenment (Kant [1784] 1964). Normally, according to Kant, it concerns the liberation of people from their self-induced immaturity. Not all people, however, are in a position to achieve this themselves in the same way. For the citizens' comprehensive enlightenment the public use of reason by an audience is required. In this public use of reason, citizens who are able to think independently can guide the others to approve of the independent use of reason in its exemplary use. The enlightened scholars, in particular, can help the not enlightened, immature people who are still stuck in their sensorial nature and interests to arrive at a reason that helps them gain inner freedom and a competent participation in public life. It is only consequent that Kant left no room for legitimate civil disobedience or even resistance in the light of this idea of a republic based on the strict use of reason (Kant [1793] 1964: 156; [1797] 1956: 439–443). Instead of order, both will entail the anarchy of the natural state where the law of violence rules instead of the law of reason. An order of reason cannot be established by way of violence, but only by reason. When an empirically set order does not comply with the standards of reason, it will not be led back on the way to reason by some irrational violence, but exclusively by the public use of reason in public discussion. An order of reason can be produced by words only, but not by violence.

Problems of Conflict Settlement: The Conflict between Objective Constraints and Democratic Dispute Settlement

But what other solutions can be found at all to the consensus democracy's legitimation crisis? When looking for solutions, we will, above all, arrive at approaches that themselves are too closely linked to the model of the consensus democracy. This applies especially to the attempt to regain legitimacy by means of an improved welfare output and also to the attempt to develop the consensus-democratic model consequently into a deliberative democracy.

Democracy by Output?

Seamlessly fitted into the model of a consensus democracy managed by experts is the idea to measure democracy with the yardsticks of the welfare output of politics and to improve this welfare output, in contrast to its capacity to admit and process a maximum input by participation. This idea is promoted, for instance, by Fritz Scharpf in view of the limitations of political participation resulting from the substantial transfer of politics onto the European level (Scharpf 1997). In order to meet this output criterion, politics must necessarily be guided by experts who are in a position to demonstrate the standards that allow a maximum state of welfare to be attained. "Pareto Optimum" and "Nash Balance" are the reference points of such a democracy of experts. The Pareto Optimum has been reached when an improvement for some members of society requires the same level of compensations for the others to avoid that their situation will be worse than before. The problem about this approach is the fact that, as a rule, neither the direct nor the indirect consequences resulting from a certain measure for those concerned, can be explicitly determined. From one party's point of view they may appear different than from another one's and, usually, both views are supported by experts. Therefore, in most cases no generally accepted calculation of the Pareto optimum will be achieved.Consequently, there is no way open to bypass the legitimation of policies by integrative cooperative political practice. Legitimation cannot be attained through objective technical knowledge, but exclusively through a practice that knows how to join technical knowledge, interests, and publicly articulated concern in such a way that—in each individual case and in all phases of the policy process, from program formulation through to program implementation—a cooperation will be produced where consented legitimacy goes hand in hand with the consideration of interests, concerns, and technical knowledge. This cannot be designed on the drawing board but only in a practical way, depending on each individual case, by the trial-and-error method. There is no doubt that political practice in America lives up to these requirements better than the consensus-democratic policy model.

Democracy by Deliberation?

The consensus democracy's legitimation crisis requires a renewal of the relationship between democracy and the rule of law. Jürgen Habermas' model of a deliberative democracy aims at this development. It takes up Kant's legal and political theory and tries to repair its democracy deficit with the help of discourse theory (Habermas 1992: 109–165). In line with Habermas' model of a deliberative democracy, the rule of law requires a better foundation in the form of a comprehensive understanding of a deliberative formulation of politics. By practicing their political autonomy through a varied inclusion of public discourses into the policy process, the citizens are to learn collectively to place their particular perspectives and interests into a generally workable frame that ensures a maximum scope to unfold their private autonomy and that is fair to everybody and accepted by everybody (Habermas 1992: 217–226, 435–467). In the light of the results revealed by our survey, this might be regarded as a plea for bridging the gap between merely technical expert discourses and the emotionalized public discourse. Since it is not the harmonization of interests that matters but the agreement on factually correct and fair solutions to problems, such a renewal of consensus democracy would be the result of a new objectivity in the sense of the original idea of the harmonization of the plurality of interests in a general legal frame instead of their direct situational accommodation as in the American model of a liberal democracy.

Of course, Habermas is well aware of the fact that there are interest conflicts that cannot be solved by agreements and therefore require a situational accommodation (Habermas 1992: 222–223). Yet his plea for a stronger deliberative foundation of politics attributes the leading edge to the model of consensus democracy and understands the liberal model, at best, as an addition introduced into the framework of consensus democracy. Consequently, Habermas remains attached to the consensus-democratic model, which separates the production of "communicative power" from the application of "administrative power" in governmental and administrative actions by forming a consensus in public discourse. The "communicative power," which is produced in public discourse, is transferred into "administrative power" by the Parliament's legislation; it must not have much scope for negotiations left, since otherwise the influence of particular interests without any obligation for a public justification may easily circumvent a consensus produced by communication. Consequently, according to the model drawn up by Kant, the law must bring all interests onto a level of reconciliation within legislative wording due to its binding validity and integrative power and must exclude as far as possible incalculable follow-up negotiations. For Habermas, democracy and the legal state join into a unity dictated by the principle of universalization in the same way as this was shown by Kant before. The conversion of the principle of universalization to discursive procedures does not change the logic of this model basically. Being a regulative idea, the discourse justifies a democracy without democrats from flesh and blood. In his efforts to bring the democracy's consensus model to today's level, Habermas gets trapped in the snares of a democracy that is dominated by the principles of the legal state. He remains tied to a legal-objectivistic tradition of thinking that has long been overtaken by reality.

The deliberative democracy model is far away from all realities of political practice and in no way lives up to the negotiations in all stages of the policy process that are indispensable and take place in fact. Above all, it overestimates the scope available for the formation of a consensus by communication and the necessary objectification of the decision making process. On the other hand, it underestimates the need for procedures of the fair accommodation of interests. The American model of a pluralist competition democracy, in contrast, shows how negotiation and participation of the public can be tied to one another in all stages of the policy process. In this way, both functions—the public justification and the accommodation of interests—may be satisfied in a more realistic way than if they were distributed to different spheres. It is then easier to link objectification, accommodation of interests, and the public articulation of concerns instead of making them irreconcilable opponents. Their linkage produces a practically effective legitimacy, whereas their separation makes the gap between objectification, interests, and the public articulation of concerns unbridgeable and thus leads toward a legitimation crisis straightaway. Consequently, Habermas' recipe is not suitable to solve the legitimation crisis of consensus democracy. It even supports the continuation of this crisis and strengthens it further.

The question arises as to whether Habermas' model of consensus democracy can, in fact, repair the deficiencies of the old model or whether it will have to face the same problems. In any case it also tries to overcome political problems by discourse—even so this has been extended with the perspectives of new social movements. It looks for the agreement on the general, especially for solutions to problems in terms of justice, which are therefore worthy of agreement. Like Kant, he clearly prefers the just over the good (Habermas 1996: 320–325). The good is banned into the sphere of the particular life forms of nations, groups, and private persons. In this way, the problems of the accommodation of interests, compromising, and the determination of the common good are pushed to the margin. It is precisely here where Habermas' model of a deliberative democracy meets its weak points. It constructs an ideal type of the rule of law's democratic foundation that is so far away from real disputes that it works as an ideal model but offers little more than hope for the language's rationally motivating power in the reality of political conflicts. The model remains attached to the language of truth and, despite the conversion to a more comprehensive communicative term of truth, is entangled in the same problems as the old model of consensus democracy. A workable improvement can be achieved only when it is possible to link Habermas' consensus model at equal terms with elements borrowed from republicanism, liberalism, and representative democracy. In view of the grown plurality of interests, more scope for a direct harmonization is required. To avoid excessive competition and ensure a peaceful coexistence despite different lifestyles, civic cooperation and a compromise culture are required such as we experienced it in England prior to Margaret Thatcher's neoliberal reforms—and obviously in a too marked version, as those reforms demonstrated. Since the maximum unfolding of interests and the maximum realization of rights will blast the boundaries of a culturally, socially, and ecologically workable life, allowing for cultural consensus, social integration, and ecological balance, there is also a need for a common elaboration of concepts of a good life in the framework of a republican understanding of democracy. Since, the larger the political units, this cannot be produced according to the model of Rousseau's assembly democracy, it is the Parliaments where this common determination of the good life should be made. Contrary to the existing trend, part of politics would have to be returned to the Parliaments (Schulze-Fielitz and Gößwein 1991). As, in a global context of life, this can no longer be reserved to national Parliaments alone, these questions must be dealt with increasingly by the representative organs below and above their levels, that is, in communities, the European Parliament, the United Nations, and other global institutions such as the World Trade Organiszation. In the context of such a multilevel model of democracy, consensus democracy will find its place, especially in the critical reflection of established particular traditions. Consensus democracy cannot replace the other models of democracy and cannot subsume them. Rather, it has to enter into a partnership imparting equal rights to all concerned.

Politics as Administration according to Objective Constraints?

In "consensus democracy," politics is trapped in a web between the triangle of technical discourse, neocorporatism, and emotional public. It seems to have lost any capability to form the future. In the 1950s and 1960s, Arnold Gehlen and Helmut Schelsky presented theoretical analyses of the scientific-technical civilization aiming at a deeper understanding of this deprivation of the power of politics (Gehlen 1956, 1957; Schelsky 1959, 1965; cf. Schluchter 1972: 193–235). Describing a seemingly inevitable development, they also provide the legitimate foundations for a lasting farewell to politics. According to these analyses, its inability to form the future is not due to a mistake or a provisional weakness; it is not a limited crisis that has to be coped with but rather an inevitable, permanent state of politics in the scientific-technical civilization.

Other than Saint-Simon and the Saint-Simonists, Gehlen and Schelsky do not see the rule in the scientific-technical civilization legitimately in the hands of the elite of knowledge but inevitably anchored in factual laws that escape from any decision and free political regulation. In late modernity no elite of experts rules over those who don't know; it is rather the case that factual laws work practically on their own and against any attempt of intervention. The experts may merely discover these factual laws and bring them to the point but cannot form them themselves. Consequently, their actions can no longer be described as "rule" but at best as the administration of a development process that is determined by laws that are inaccessible to political control. Different from Ellul or Foucault, who turn Saint-Simon's heritage into a criticism of the sublimation of power hidden in the process of scientific-technical rationalization, Gehlen and Schelsky consider this an inevitable development that, realistically, does not allow a normative statement at all.

According to Gehlen's anthropology, man is a world-open, constantly needy creature with little instinct and excessive drive. To develop his own personality and guarantee a predictable relationship with his fellow men, man requires secondary external control beyond the reduced control by instinct that sets him free of the uncertainties in his relationship toward himself and others. The institutions of societal life meet this function. They relieve man from his struggle for existence (Gehlen 1955; 1957: 17–19). Therefore, man has to externalize, to estrange from himself in the institutions to get back to himself and build up a safe existence. In this process, the institutions not only serve the satisfaction of needs but also man's realization as a moral being. They unite instrumental and creative action in a synthesis (Gehlen 1957: 116).

This unity is, however, dissolved in the technicoscientific civilization. It is replaced by the complementary relationship between technical progress and the increase in consumption and enjoyment. The union of science, technique, and industry builds up superstructures that have emancipated themselves from their guiding images rooted in the Enlightenment and carry themselves according to their own laws; moreover, they drive themselves forward toward ever greater technical perfection. The further existence of the institutions no longer depends on their fulfilling an ideal mission but on their making their performances more and more perfect according to their own laws. Technical progress becomes an end in itself and no longer needs to be justified by guiding images of the good life. It practically becomes the good life itself, as it forms the foundation for an unlimited unfolding of needs (Gehlen 1957: 57–61; 1963: 253–256).

The institutions and individual actions no longer require the brackets of a binding morality. The superstructures of economy, technique, and industry rather cause an increase in affluence, allowing for a maximum satisfaction of people's needs and making the coping with conflicts through a common morality superfluous (Gehlen 1957: 11–12, 40, 49, 54–57). Morality becomes a matter of one's personal lifestyle. Together with morality, however, politics becomes superfluous, too. It no longer needs to decide on the formation of the future. All it can do is maintain the scientific-technical and industrial development process as the foundation of the increasing affluence and maximum satisfaction of needs. The relationship between the means and the ends turns round insofar as it is no longer the common ideas of a good life that determine the ends and then the means needed for their realization, but the technical means that produce the ends and needs required for their mass distribution via industrial production and that are, of course, strongly supported by an ever more comprehensive promotional machinery: "The system is not only based on the pre-condition of the right to an affluent life, it tends toward making the opposite, that is, the right to the relinquishment of an affluent life, impossible by producing and automating the consumers' needs itself" (Gehlen 1957: 80; see also 1956: 14). The process of the formation of institutions, which allowed for the development of the freely acting subject, ends in the complementary relationship between scientific-technical-industrial development

dynamism and idle subjectivism. Aesthetics replaces morality as the outer frame
of human action, whereas consumption becomes the exclusive contents of human
efforts (Gehlen 1957: 44–47, 57–61, 78–81). This loss of the moral and political
control of societal development cannot be stopped by a return to the institutions,
since these have long been scientificated and thus become a part of the scientific-
technical and industrial superstructure. These are, it is true, subject to permanent
reflection, which can, however, be geared only toward technical perfection. The
question of "what ought to be done" dissolves into nothingness under being submitted to permanent reflection (Gehlen 1957: 23–28).

What is to be done becomes a matter of will and of individual preferences.
Science cannot help. It cannot supply a synthesis of a global view and, in no case,
a synthesis of a normative quality. It has rather long dissolved in a number of
individual sections that are all making their particular contribution to improving
the technical dominance over the world. The question as to whether this results in
a meaningful totality escapes from scientific answers. Under these conditions, the
complementary development of technical progress and maximum unfolding of
needs is only possible though extremely precarious form of societal existence.

For Arnold Gehlen, the late modernity's scientific-technical civilization certainly undergoes a necessary process, yet it leads this process, which was once
started by the Enlightenment, toward a tragic end contrary to the Enlightenment's
original intentions: the dialectics of the Enlightenment. Helmut Schelsky arrives
at a very similar description of the scientific-technical civilization yet replaces
tragedy with the cool analysis of a process that escapes from any normative statement as it makes its way anyway irrespective of what we want. According to
Schelsky, technique in the scientific-technical civilization is no longer merely an
instrument for the realization of given targets but part of a superstructure where
science, technique, and industry combine into a self-reproducing system whose
end in itself is the increase in the technical disposal of the world. In this way, the
scientific-technical civilization makes technique more than just an instrument to
rule the world; rather, it becomes a societal matter of fact, the world as such
(Schelsky 1965: 456–460).

There is no more choice for us to live outside a world that is fully controlled by
science and technique. Science and technique are not merely tools to form the
world according to our ideas. They have absorbed all moral concepts and are our
world themselves. The distinction between subject and object, cognition and application, theory and practice dissolves in the one scientific-technical world. In
this world, there are increasingly more possibilities for action, but at the same
time it is increasingly less possible to say what we ought to do. The binding character of standards is washed away by the stream of cognition and the technical
increase in the possibilities of action. In individual cases, means may still be referred to ends, but the whole of societal development can no longer be coped with
so easily (Schelsky 1965: 450). In the process of the permanent extension of cognition, factual laws offer a supporting pillar for the attempt to control society.
Neither morality nor democracy can direct this process, as they do not live up to
science's reflexive level. Moral judgments and democratic decisions have to sub-

mit to the permanent questioning by scientific reflection and will not be the rock in the ocean of the process of cognition. They rather drift apart into their smallest components in this ocean (Schelsky 1965: 456–460).

In Schelsky's eyes, the well-known attempts to explain the whole thing by way of the classic theory of society are not up-to-date; "class rule," "industrial rule," and "managerial rule" are categories that describe the structures of an epoch gone by but miss by far the radically changed structure of society in the scientific-technical civilization (Schelsky 1965: 456–457; see also 26–29, 384–385). Rule is no longer identifiable as a web of positions but vanishes in a process of the enforcement of factual laws that is tangible with regard to neither the position nor the person involved. The experts do not exercise any control either, as they do not take decisions that could also be taken otherwise; instead, they merely establish factual laws from which none of us can escape. Therefore, democracy has long ceased to be the program for us to pin our hopes on. Being a counterpart to the authoritarian rule, it is—like that—tied to the old concept of ruling via decision making competence. When the possibilities for taking decisions disappear, it is unable to survive. Although its outer appearance may remain unchanged, it is hollowed out from inside and secretly replaced by the technical state:

> The technical argument makes its way unideologically. It therefore is effective below each ideology and eliminates the decision making level which was formerly borne by the ideologies. All this can be summarized by the thesis that in this development the phenomenon of the direct rule of man over man dissolves practically from inside both in a social and a political sense; therefore, old forms of rule may remain empty shells. The change of democracy into a "technical state" requires no revolution in a social or political sense, no constitutional amendment, no ideological conversion. It merely requires the increasing use of all kinds of scientific techniques and the technical state will be created inside the old shell. (Schelsky 1965: 460)

What can, at best, accompany the enforcement of factual laws is the permanent reflection on what is going on. Its institutionalization informs us about the events into which we are entangled as a result of our action. Yet it is unable to provide us with yardsticks that help us to assess the normative contents of the events. The normative has been completely absorbed by the factual (Schelsky 1965: 471; see also 250–275).

According to Schelsky's analysis, politics can no longer be considered the center of societal control. It is nothing else but a part of a differentiated superstructure developing according to factual laws. The loss of this center merely leaves us the permanent reflection on the events that happen irrespective of what we want. With this description of a scientific-technical civilization, Schelsky established an approach in the 1950s and 1960s that has been carried on by Niklas Luhmann since the end of the 1960s in extreme radicalism and consequence: the differentiation of society into a complex of autopoietically operating subsystems is nothing else but a superstructure unfolding according to factual laws and without a controlling center. The obsolete explanatory patterns of a past epoch, which can no longer grasp the new reality, according to Schelsky, are put into the arsenal of outdated, old European thinking by Luhmann. Schelsky's verdict on the vanity of all normativeness, the failing of every attempt to classify societal events in normative terms, which only allows for institutionalized permanent reflection, returns in Luhmann's systemic perspective. It regards society's self-observation within society as the only acceptable form to refer to society and its development. It appears logical that the society as a communicative context necessarily has to develop into a world society that can hardly be considered controllable from a center, even from an empirical point of view (Luhmann 1981, 1984, 1986, 1997).

In Luhmann's eyes and confirming Gehlen's and Schelsky's viewpoints, politics has long lost the power to control society. It is reduced to retaining politics' contingency. Since there are no better arguments to defend one's position vis-à-vis competing alternatives, each position becomes as arbitrary as any other when submitted permanently to alternative views so that, by the basic opening of the decision making process, politics may merely ensure that sufficient motives remain available for taking part in the game further. When defeats can at any time be reversed into victories, no radical conclusions that may threaten the system will be drawn from a defeat. Politics' only realistic maxim is to keep the boat afloat and avoid basic discords. Politics' incapability of regulating society is not a structural deficiency and cannot be ascribed to the lacking character of the politicians, but it is the reverse side of the only possible form of politics. This result matches exactly the consequences drawn from the analyses presented by Gehlen and Schelsky (Luhmann 1981, 1986).

In the analyses introduced by Gehlen, Schelsky, and Luhmann, the consequences of a political culture are revealed where rule by virtue of knowledge is enhanced to a subjectless process of the unfolding of superstructures. The political struggle for the future merely appears as an insignificant symbolic process that accompanies the inevitable events with more or less ado but cannot influence them. Politics becomes an event geared exclusively toward retaining a sufficient number of motives for the further participation in the game. If it is to be more, public excitement, lamenting about the bad conditions, emotionality without any consequences or "communication of fear" will be the results (Luhmann 1986: 237–248), but no workable contribution to the formation of politics, since "practical constraints," "factual laws," "inner laws," and the "autopoiesis of societal subsystems" escape from normative control anyway. Public discussion's tendency toward emotions is the complementary counterpart of politics that is reduced to maintaining a good mood by the rule of factual laws. With the ever-deeper penetration of the media into this leaderless politics, the chances multiply that the calm grounds of an "unmotivated" acceptance of the events—which results from people confiding in basic contingence and the consequent reversability of the events—develop into a raging stream that brings fears from the depth to the surface. The production of emotions to raise print-runs and viewing rates is faced helplessly by a politics that is merely geared toward maintaining contingency.

The unchained emotions will contribute to put the neocorporatist arrangement of state and big organizations under cross-fire. That arrangement gave the proper structural support to the interplay of factual constraint and maintenance of contingency. It ensured a relatively stable situation of interests and gave an orientation to politics that was hidden by both the hint to factual constraints and the reference to the system's openness. Essentially, this concerns the pact described by Gehlen between the technical progress and the unbounding of individual desires according to the program of increasing affluence (Gross 1994). Morality, ethics, and politics were replaced by the machinery of the unlimited maximization of a technical domination over the world, affluence, and the individual satisfaction of needs. This imprisoning of politics by the triangle of factual constraints, neocorporatism, and emotionalized public is definitely of a universal importance and can, to a certain extent, be observed in all highly developed societies. Our case studies show that it is most apparent in the framework of the structural arrangement of political networks, institutional rules, professional groups, and political culture prevailing in Germany. Here where we discover the literature that reflects and legitimates this reality.

Nevertheless, the previously described model of consensus democracy has stumbled into a deep crisis since the student movement at the end of the 1970s and was therefore prone to the winds of change. The consensus has broken up. Ever since, talks have gone about a "rediscovery" of politics. Did this actually result in a structural change going beyond mere rhetoric? Our case study seems to prove much more that the "invention of politics" is nothing more than rhetoric (Beck 1993), as it obviously remains stuck in the structures of the old model; that is, it is widely pushed toward emotionality and communication of fear and has been unable so far to bridge the gap between technical discourse and neocorporatist rule, on the one hand, and the emotionalized public, on the other. Urged by the changed situation that is forced upon politics by the pluralization of interests, the medialization of the public, the Europeanization and globalization of problems, and decision making competences, the weaknesses of the historically evolved structures of networks, institutional rules, professional groups, and political culture stand out blatantly. Whether politics will be entangled even stronger in its own structural constraints or will be able to find a way out is a question that cannot be answered so far.

Politics Dominated by Bureaucratic Spirit

A return to Max Weber shows how far the structural problems of the policy model elaborated in our clean air study on Germany go back (Weber 1971: 245–291, 306–443, 505–560). In Weber's eyes, a rule of bureaucracy and the related bureaucratic mentality developed in the empire, since the Parliament possessed too little rights to exercise control. At the same time, politics was dominated onesidedly by a declining stratum, the Prussian landowners and their particular interests. The bourgeoisie was therefore hindered in unfolding its responsibility for society, while the working class was not sufficiently mature to take over this role (Weber 1971: 545–560). Consequently, Weber predicted the danger for the young Weimar Republic following the empire, that it would be torn between the extremes of bureaucratic rule, the particularism of interests, and the demagogy heated by the media (Weber 1971: 245–291, 320–350). He considered a "leaderless democracy" in this sense doomed to fail. In its place he developed a concept of democracy whose structures allow for a political leadership that is marked by an ethics of responsibility overlooking the whole. Politicians acting in an ethically responsible way argue in favor of a matter full of passion, perceptiveness and willingness to compromise; they take over full political responsibility for their decisions and present their plans to the public with full account of their consequences. Their ethics of responsibility differs from an ethics of conviction in that the good end does not justify all means and itself requires being weighed against other ends. They distinguish themselves from mere political realists in that they do not consider the acquisition and maintenance of power an end in itself but rather a means for the political formation of society according to their convictions. They want to gain the public's support for these convictions but always insert them into the context of the daily demands and the web of consequences and side effects (Weber 1971: 545–560).

To allow a democracy to develop with a political leadership guided by an ethics of responsibility, a special structural arrangement is required. The rule of bureaucracy must be restricted by a strong Parliament. Being a Parliament for speeches and work, it serves the selection of leading personalities trained in commission work, compromising, and the search for public support for their own standpoints. A strong political leadership with a strong ethics of responsibility should recruit the public's support for coping with the big political tasks and thus prevent politics from falling prey to the interplay of particular interests and bureaucratic rule as was the case in the empire.

Weber's analysis of the structural weaknesses of a politics dominated by bureaucratic spirit, particular interests, and demagogy has lost nothing of its topical character. It can easily be applied to the current model of politics whose structural weakness is rooted in the interplay of technical discourse, neocorporatism, and emotional public. Rule by virtue of knowledge is an extended form of bureaucratic rule; neocorporatism means the rule of particular interests; and the emotionalized public includes the extension of demagogy in the excesses of our time's media industry. According to Max Weber, the answer to current politics' structural weaknesses should be found in a restrengthening of Parliament, which was deprived of its power by different sides: first, by the expert commissions; second by pre- and postparliamentary negotiation democracy of the neocorporatist and, more recently, also pluralistic style, that is, by a short-term interest politics to the detriment of the responsibility for the whole and for future generations; third, by a public where the production of moods ousts the responsible advocacy for a cause; fourth, by the transfer of politics to the executive in the wake of its Europeanization; and fifth by the ousting of the political by the economical in the wake of globalization. Therefore, the chances are rather bad for a strengthening of national Parliaments in the political process. They would have to make their way against forces that will increase in effect in the future rather than decrease. This also means that a thoroughgoing healing of politics' structural weaknesses according to Weber's advice can most probably not be anticipated.

Concluding Remarks

What conclusions can we draw from our analysis of the synthesis model prevailing in German politics with regard to the question as to how far and in what form it is able to process conflicts in such a way that social integration will be safeguarded, the big questions of the future can be coped with, and a formation of the future is possible on a consensual basis? We may give the following reply to this question. On the one hand, more than in the other countries, politics aims at an objectification of conflicts by using scientific-technical expertise and involves the neocorporatist integration of the big organizations into legislation. On the other hand, the public is regarded as a sphere of the articulation of fears that have to be proven as being unfounded with the help of a more or less open information policy, that is, by enlightenment. Politics is split in two separate areas: technical policy making and the emotionalized public.

In the past, this model of coping with conflicts and regulating society politically worked rather well insofar as the expert knowledge could present itself coherently, the big associations involved were able to speak on behalf of the entire society, the program of the increase in affluence mitigated conflicts, and the public was represented by the oligopoly of national daily and weekly newspapers and the monopoly of the broadcasting corporations under public law. In the meantime, however, all these conflict-reducing factors have lost in significance so that the demands to coping with conflicts and forming the future have increased. Ecological conflicts were at the beginning of this process and are followed by the discussion on Germany as a location of economic investment and prosperity that proves the dwindling strength to cope with conflicts and to form the future. It can be assumed, therefore, that the negative sides of the synthesis model will come to the fore more than before under the new societal conditions. These make themselves seen in the desperate holding on to the objectification of conflicts by way of scientific expertise, although the coherence of the scientific knowledge does not exist anymore, and the public is made uncertain rather than reassured by the "enlightenment" due to the contrasting expert reports. The "factual constraints" are turned into politics without there being an awareness for the processes required to cope with the new conflicts. The neocorporatist structures block changes, and the program of affluence is questioned ecologically and loses its social-integrative strength in the new world economy, while the new, fully commercialized media scene seizes every straw that might form the topic of a story to heat up emotions.

The old synthesis model has lost its foundation; the conflicts sharpen, increase in numbers, and become more varied so that they cannot be coped with according to the old patterns. In this way, politics gets trapped in a muddled situation where it can neither sufficiently process conflicts nor retain social integration or form the future. Since the foundations of the old model have eroded so much, the way toward the future appears extremely uncertain. Among the four countries surveyed, Germany seems to be the one that has to give up most of its previous policy model on its way into the future. As this is a painful, lengthy process, the country will, in the long run, have to live with the dilemma that reality departs more and more from the ideal model of politics but that no workable new model has been found so far for the new reality. The deeper emotionalization of the public will go side by side with the further scientification of politics, the cooperation of state and big organizations will no longer ensure the integration of society and produce new zones of marginalization, and the affluence consensus will become fragile and will have to give way to conflicts on ecological balance and the social distribution of economic growth.

Briefly, the primary force of policy making is knowledge generated and applied by professional experts and the rule of law. This means that consensus formation is oriented to the formulation and application of general law, based on the knowledge of experts. Therefore, innovations result primarily from the generation of generalizable knowledge and less from the broader, stepwise experimentation with new elements of problem solution. The inclusion of new social movements is difficult because they do not conform to the requirements of expert knowledge. Conflict settlement takes place in terms of subsuming particular interests under the roof of general laws. The result is that conflicts are settled in theory at the cost of real negotiations between different interests.

UNITED STATES: PLURALIST COMPETITION DEMOCRACY

Preliminary Remarks

In the United States' competition network, negotiations usually take the form of a marathon of the accommodation of interests in a wealth of arenas. Conflicts are carried out as a bargaining for even the smallest advantages. A synthesis is formed by the continually renewed marking of the scope of interests in the framework of the pluralism of civic organizations. The further context of the network is as follows. The pluralistic professionalism is geared toward empirical evidence and practical efficiency. The institutional rules underline equal opportunities and the public. The political culture is distinguished by the idea of a pluralistic competition democracy (Diagram 7.4). In the United States the model of a pluralistic competition democracy has most extensively been realized in an empirical way. One should have a close look at it when one expects a promising democratization of the future to result from the opening of political decision making processes to a direct participation beyond the mere act of election (cf. Schmalz-Bruns 1995: 233–269).

Policy Networks: Arenas of Competition

The American policy networks are distinguished by great openness, inclusiveness, decentralization, and fragmentation and, out of all comparable networks, are most similar to the pattern of market exchange under tough competition. In this political culture of open competition, lobbyism is attributed a significance that is greater than in any other country. The Congress has officially recorded 5,000 lobbyists. All in all, the number of lobbyists active in Washington is estimated at approximately 40,000 (Bowles 1993: 207). Their number and importance are so high as all stages of the policy process offer so many entrances for explicitly permitted intervention and as neither the parties nor the interest organizations focus the different interests to a workable volume. Lobbyists do not simply represent interests. Their offices are major sources of influence for the policy process. They establish contacts between the interested parties and the politicians and are actively involved in the production of coalitions to implement certain measures.

Diagram 7.4
The American Competition Network in the Context of Professions, Institutional Rules, and Political Culture

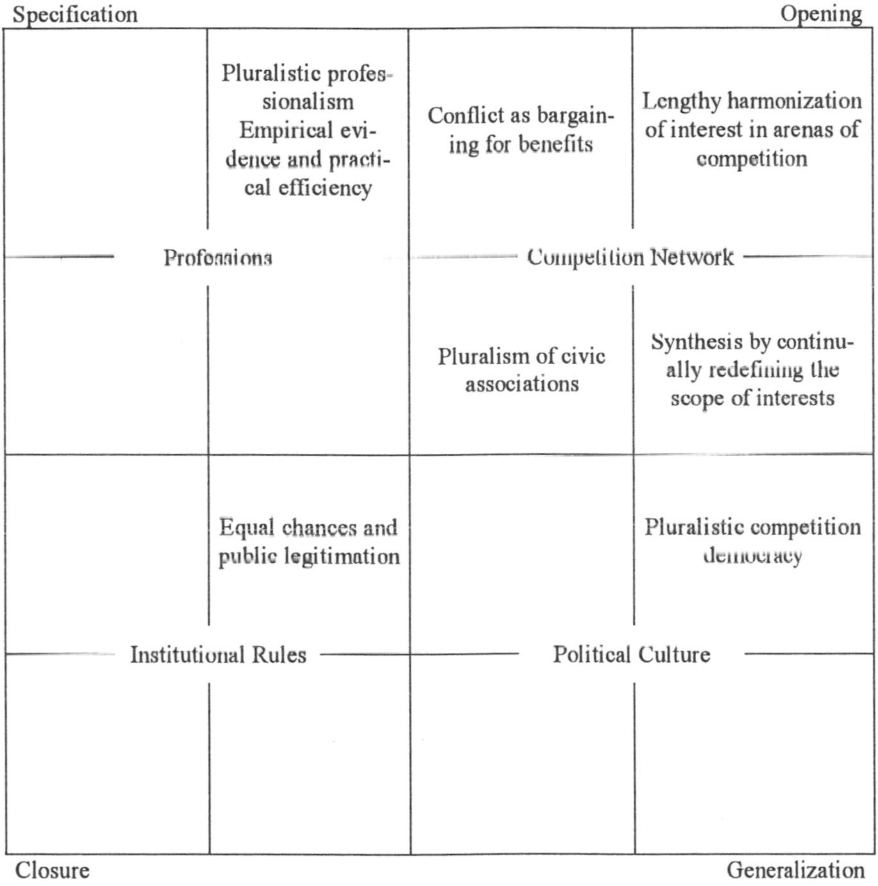

Specification   Opening

	Pluralistic professionalism Empirical evidence and practical efficiency	Conflict as bargaining for benefits	Lengthy harmonization of interest in arenas of competition
Professions		Competition Network	
		Pluralism of civic associations	Synthesis by continually redefining the scope of interests
	Equal chances and public legitimation		Pluralistic competition democracy
Institutional Rules		Political Culture	

Closure   Generalization

In the open network of American politics they act as decisive links between the society and the state. The more that they have become professional, the more that they have developed into decisive actors. They can be successful only to such an extent as they prove trustworthy vis-à-vis their clients (the interested parties) and the politicians (senators, members of the House of Representatives, ministers, and administration people). They will succeed in doing so only when they consolidate the justification of the interests presented in a sustained way and can refer to true information and successful partnerships. The representation of interests by lobbyism has developed into an industry whose success is measured by the fact to what extent interests are supplied and converted into the formation of policies. The sector's growth mirrors the increased variety of the articulated and supplied interests. The lobby has become a central turntable of politics. It can be recognized as a logical development of the model of a liberal democracy under the terms of the direct professional representation of a maximum number of rights and interests. Just as the administrative elite has become the trustee of the public will in France, professional lobbyism has developed into a sort of fiduciary of the idea of a liberal democracy in the United States that is not concerned with the compulsive imposition of a public will but rather with the maximum unfolding of a pluralism of individual interests (Berry 1984; Petracca 1992).

The work of the lobby makes as many interests as possible flow into the policy process, which are mediated with one another from program formulation through to program implementation and the settling of conflicts at the courts so that all those concerned attain a maximum satisfaction of their interests. Those who want to persist here require influence. This influence, however, is not a result of central solidarity or loyalty but of proven and expected achievements for a clientele of interested parties, for mandate holders in the Congress, and for civil servants in administration and the regulation authorities. This concerns a communication medium that must be handled with the utmost care and whose availability and value can be subject to considerable variations due to the fast sequence of political developments. The policy process as a whole is little predictable. Due to the changing situations and new information it may constantly take surprising new ways. The policy programs are hardly coherent due to the variety of interests involved and, as a rule, set only a frame. Consequently, a wealth of interests will still influence the programs' concrete presentation in implementation and legal proceedings. Influence is the language of the network. Yet it requires a lot of time and money to gather information and scientific evidence and introduce them into the policy process and to foster relationships and mediate partnerships. Therefore, money is an important secondary currency. The tremendous expenditure in gathering, processing, and distributing information and scientific evidence consumes ever higher amounts of money (Ricci 1993: 166–171; Sabato 1984; Goodwin 1988; Sorauf 1988).

The protagonists of political competition are in an armament race regarding the foundation of their positions and the satisfaction of their clientele. Both the senators and members of the House of Representatives need an ever greater staff. Particularly influential senators employ up to 70 people (Bowles 1993: 132). Consequently, the lobbyists' offices are extended more and more to keep abreast in the big game of the professional mediation of interests. From this we may conclude that only interests with a solid financial background have a chance to make themselves heard. This does not mean necessarily, however, that this covers the interests of big industry only. Since the 1970s, public interest groups have recorded an upsurge and have succeeded with the help of entrepreneurial initiative to recruit a large number of affiliates and, with their fees, build up a strong representation of nonindustrial interests—from civil rights right through to consumer and environmental protection. A famous example is Ralph Nader, a lawyer who succeeded in creating a veritable empire of public interest organizations (Berry 1977; McFarland 1976, 1984; Schlozman and Tierney 1986; Rothenberg 1992; Ingram, Colnic, and Mann 1995). Nevertheless, it cannot be deduced from the extension of the scope of active interest groups that all rights and interests will be taken into consideration at equal shares. In the race for the best positions in the political process, those rights and interests will be left behind that are unable to articulate themselves in a sufficiently professional manner and thus become serious partners in the negotiation process.

Institutional Rules of Policy Making: The Race for Political Success

Since the only thing that the citizens have in common is the general interest in the unfolding of their private liberties, the only thing to which the political process must be geared is the promotion of private liberties and the settling of individual conflicts arising thereby. It is therefore a typical feature of the American legislation that the Congress supplies only a frame, which will then be filled by special regulation agencies such as the Environmental Protection Agency (EPA). In line with the system of checks and balances, the regulation agencies form, on the one hand, part of the administration of the president, who also appoints the top executives, yet, on the other hand, they are under the direct control of the Congress. The ministry in charge, the Congress commission, and the regulation agency share the power, and the weights shift from the Congress commission to the agency from program formulation through to the implementation, with the ministry in charge assuming an intermediary function.

The number of efficiently represented rights and interests varies between the different political fields. Wherever a specific branch of industry is being regulated, a so-called iron triangle has emerged that is formed by the regulation agency in charge, the corresponding subcommission in Congress, and the representatives of the regulated branch of industry. The latter may exercise a strong influence on regulation. The number of those who are actively interested has multiplied, and, above all, a number of public interest groups have joined the race to participate in the policy process. This applies, in particular, to the regulation field covered by the EPA. This sector is not dominated by a specific interest group and stands out due to particularly tough struggles in which the industry, environmental groups, and science take part (Rosenbaum 1995). The entire policy process is a very complex matter—not only as far as the implementation itself is concerned but also as regards the program formulation—that requires the accommodation of a wide variety of rights and interests. In this process many more actors are involved than in any other country. This means that, right from the start, legislation is not aimed at discovering the public will, the public welfare, or the common good, but rather a framework that takes into account as many rights and interests as possible. This frame is filled under the guidance of the regulation agency in charge whose task is to allow all the relevant rights and interests to come up by including their representatives into the decision making process. Both as regards the program formulation and its implementation, the complete inclusion of the public—which, again, is more comprehensive than anywhere else—has the function to provide a chance to interested parties that have not been included from the beginning to register their rights and interests. This concerns less the filtering out of a public opinion that represents the common good, but rather the extension of the scope of individual interests that have been taken into account.

By concretizing this frame, the regulation agency by no means puts an end to the race for the consideration of rights and interests. With the actors involved being fully conscious of it, this is just an intermediate stage of a never-ending race. In its further course, it is up to the courts to support the rights of the interested parties that are eager to institute legal proceedings (McSpadden 1995). Once again we may establish that nowhere else in the world are so many legal proceedings taken as in the United States. This is the case because, in the sense of the tradition of the case law, the courts have the task to concretize laws in practice even in the application of positively set law due to the latter's guideline character. As the whole is understood as an endless process of accommodating rights and interests, the laws do not have to take their definite form, which is coherent in itself, from the very beginning and do not have to regulate any detail. It is sufficient to mark a few boundary posts and to set the stone rolling, insufficient and fragmentary as this may be. The actors involved are fully aware of this beginning's inadequate character. They consider the initial version a draft that has to be worked on in the further process right through to court practice and back from there again, when the law is revised to obtain an ever more subtle harmonization of rights and interests (Meier 1985: 9–36).

Inclusion of Expert Knowledge: Competition for Scientific Evidence

In this process, science plays a significant role, though less a role of an objective institution that terminates the struggle of interests by recognizing what is generally valid—as this is the case in Germany, above all—but rather that of a weapon used by those involved in a debate to consolidate their argumentation. Inevitably, lawyers also assume a special position in the struggle for rights and interests; this applies both to program formulation and implementation (Jasanoff 1995). The scientists, on the other hand, are more requested to serve those who are struggling. This is proved by their pluralistic structure, which can be observed here as in no other country. The competition for acceptance on an open market characterizes science as nowhere else. A thoroughly investigated example from the history of science that underlines this process is the competition between the Charm model and the Colour model to explain the so-called J-psi particle in high-energy physics. In the open competition, the Charm model ascertained itself step by step due to continuous improvements and the gathering of minor partial successes by providing explanatory tools for a variety of researchers in different fields. It was less a revolution at one blow but rather the painstaking gathering of credits (Pickering 1990; Aretz 1990: 151–182).

There is no uniform line in science but a varied, differentiated scene: scientists from universities, public research centers, state-run institutions, industrial research centers, think tanks, and public interest research institutes dispute about the proper evidence. A person who asserts something has to confirm it with scientific evidence. But as so many different interests are sharply and publicly presented, science appears more as a means to support the struggle of those involved than an objective authority above all parties. Of course, experts have to prove their credibility in the struggle of the parties to underline that their results are confirmed beyond party limits by a variety of different sources (McCrea and Markle 1984; Gillespie, Eva, and Johnston 1979; Brickman, Jasanoff, and Ilgen 1985: 174–180, 187–217; Meier 1985).

Due to the necessity to consolidate political positions with scientific evidence, it is not by accident that scientific research centers do policy-relevant research much more comprehensively than in other countries and introduce their results permanently into the political process. The so-called think tanks occupy a prominent position here (Ricci 1993). Their number has grown tremendously. While 32 think tanks were established in Washington between 1910 and 1969, 56 were added between 1970 and 1989 (Ricci 1993: 281; footnote 76). They live on political job research and carry out enormous marketing expenditure to find political customers for their research work. In this way, politics and science join forces so that a phenomenon similar to the contact between science and economy arises. The policy programs' product cycles shorten. New research results require ever faster responses of the actors from a policy field. This acceleration of the proliferation of new research results has not necessarily to be answered with ever-new laws. Instead, the laws' guideline character allows for permanent selective amendments in the implementation of laws whether it is via the regulation agencies or the courts.

In this context, the special importance of efficiency makes itself felt, too. The successful professionalization of economics has ensured that economists and their way of thinking exercise a substantial influence on policy programs, more than in other countries. Since the economists show an extraordinary confidence in the markets, they make sure that ever more market-shaped proposals to solve the problems are introduced into the policy process. This includes deregulation proposals for markets that were regulated so far (aviation and telecommunication, for instance) or the issue of marketable certificates for the permission to emit harmful substances but also the relinquishing of regular infringements on production—such as by the determination of safety standards—in favor of the manufacturer's comprehensive product liability. The safety of the consumers should be safeguarded less by state control of the product's qualities but by the manufacturer's liability for damages resulting from the use of a product. Therefore, consumers are inundated with instruction leaflets when buying a product that warn against all imaginable risks when the product is not used properly. The manufacturers, in turn, try to protect themselves against claims for compensation attaining, as a rule, millions of dollars. This is underlined, for instance, with the example of a McDonald's customer who burned a thigh with hot coffee. In the United States, extremely active consumer protection organizations and consumer-friendly courts replace the state's regular control. This is regarded as a more efficient form of consumer protection. This is especially the case as the policy process is marked by the economists more than in other countries. Moreover, the still-dominant lawyers are trained not in the legal consolidation of the formulation of laws but, instead, in the representation of their clients' rights and interests, in working out the wording not of laws but of contracts (Meier 1985: 77–118).

This particular feature of the policy formation fits seamlessly into the idea of liberal democracy where the main problem is to place the rights and interests of the private citizens at the top of the hierarchy of values. The citizens should not be hindered by unnecessary regulating infringements of the state on society when unfolding their civil rights and liberties but should merely be allowed to ask for the state's protection when they suffer harm through the use of these liberties by other private citizens or the measures taken by state authorities. Louis Hartz got to the heart of this idea of a liberal democracy in a paradigmatic way in his classic study on *The Liberal Tradition in America* (Hartz 1955). It is only logical that the courts have to bear the major part of the burden of this protection of individual rights. Their prominent position forms the counterpart to the state's restraint from regulating infringements on society and the complementary dominance of market-shaped relationships (McSpadden 1995). Science is involved in the corresponding discussions more than anywhere else, since the opponents try to prove or reject causalities minutely by scientific means (Jasanoff 1990, 1995). In this way, a growing mutual outbidding of scientific evidence takes place. Those who are unable to produce a sufficient amount of scientific evidence will fail in their struggles. In this sense, the opponents believe in science as an authority independent of the parties, though only if expert reports cannot be shaken by counterreports. This can, however, be considered only a provisional cease-fire, which will end immediately when new evidence sheds a different light on the matter in question.

The struggle for rights forms the frame where science is set off. Therefore, the leadership is not in the hands of the scientists. The lawyers are the masters of the process that underlines expressly the thesis of a "judicial democracy." The entire political culture is marked by the model of court action. Its complementary counterpart—market exchange—interferes directly in the holding of political and legal quarrels. The settling of conflicts is not regarded as a struggle for everything or nothing but as a negotiation for more or less, where all those concerned may leave as winners. In the program formulation stage it is necessary to take into account the rights and interests of as many actors as possible. Therefore, a guideline law is aimed at, as a rule, that offers a chance to being taken into consideration in the implementation to as many rights and interests as possible. In addition, it is not unusual for the actors to establish coalitions based on mutual benefits. The actors promise their support in matters where they do not have a fixed opinion when they receive, in turn, the others' support for their own position in a matter that they consider important. Political practice implies the permanent search for potential partners in political *business*, especially as practice is only little determined by central party constraints or other group loyalties. Politics is considered a market exchange under competitive conditions where it is important to win as many partners as possible for one's own cause by offering them one's support in other matters. In this way, all may hope to benefit from the exchange (Kraft 1995). The same practice characterizes the implementation of laws as not simply a detailed and precisely formulated law is applied but rather a guideline law is concretized step by step and developed further in negotiations with the regulation authorities. Here, too, partners have to be found in exchange for one's own support.

Even litigation involves an extent of negotiations that is unthinkable in other legal cultures. In civil and even criminal law proceedings, negotiations are led outside the court hearings: in civil law proceedings this is done to reach a settlement and, in criminal law proceedings, to reduce the sentence in exchange for a confession on a few, usually less important counts. In civil law, as a rule, the party threatened by high claims for compensation offers a confession of limited guilt for correspondingly lower compensation in order to avert the risk of a defeat. In the case of a settlement, the plaintiff will draw a lower, though, safe benefit; the defendant has to pay a compensation, which is, however, lower than if his or her unlimited guilt was established. In criminal law, the prosecution may offer to cancel one or another count when a confession is made on other points; this proposal may also be filed by the representative of the defendant. In this bargaining process, the strict differentiation between right and wrong is replaced by the scoring of benefits when deciding on right or wrong depending on the quality and quantity assessed for the culpable action. A zero-sum game is converted into a winning game for both parties (McSpadden 1995; Schumann 1977; Maynard 1984).

Ideas of Legitimation: The Political Philosophy of Pluralist Competition Democracy

The structural pattern of homologous policy networks, institutional rules, and forms of inclusion of expert knowledge displayed so far finds its correspondence and legitimation in the historically evolved political philosophy of the pluralistic competition democracy, which was conceived at the time of the foundation of the Union in the *Federalist Papers*. Based on John Locke's draft of a polity with a liberal constitution, the founding fathers of the American Constitution attached great importance to protecting, above all, the citizens' civil rights and liberties (Locke [1690] 1963). The protection of these rights is the state's foremost duty. This also implies that the rights of the individual must be protected against inadmissible infringements by the state. Therefore, the constitution is to prevent any type of concentration of power right from the start. Executive, legislature, and judicature should not only be separate powers but control each other. The subdivision of powers between the federation, the individual states, and the communities is to serve the same purpose. On the federal level, the subdivision of the Congress into the Senate and the House of Representatives is to ensure a division of powers within the legislature. No permanent majority rule should come into existence. This effort for a varied control of state power has extensively been documented in the *Federalist Papers*. In this imagination of a liberal democracy described by the founders of the Constitution, the state is necessary to channel the development of the citizens' individual liberties properly and to prevent them from hindering each other. Yet, its power must be distributed between authorities that control each other so that it will not destroy the citizens' individual liberties (Hartz 1955; Dahl 1967; Wood 1969; McDonald 1985; Ellis 1993). The authors of the *Federalist Papers*, Alexander Hamilton, John Jay, and James Madison, were led by a distinctive republican spirit. However, in their view, the republic does not exist in its own right. It is dedicated to safeguard the individual rights and liberties of the people. Whereas Hamilton tended to give the state more power to maintain social life, it was particularly Madison who was concerned about the balancing out of state powers in order to rule out any form of domination at the expense of the people's individual rights and liberties. This is why we characterize the model of democracy designed by the founding fathers of the United States first of all as a liberal democracy rather than a republican one, although there are, in fact, also some elements of republicanism, as we will see later on.

This concept of a liberal democracy is diametrically opposite to Rousseau's model of a republican democracy. Seen from a liberal viewpoint, Rousseau's public will seems to be the ideological padding of the state's totalitarian rule over the individual. When the individuals are to unfold freely, they will ultimately attain as many different concepts of a good life as correspond to their number. The pluralism of moral concepts and lifestyles is therefore the inevitable reality of a free society. In the liberal's eyes, this pluralism can be transformed into a uniform public will only by way of force and oppression. A liberal democracy can, consequently, be nothing more than a formal process to deal with conflicts that arise when private liberties are unfolded (Guéhenno 1994: 41–45). This can only rarely be achieved by legislation in advance, but as a rule only after the actual conflict has emerged, that is, in a court action. This is why in the American realization of the idea of a liberal democracy, the courts have gained a greater weight than in any other country. We may even talk of a "judicial democracy" here. "I am not aware that any nation of the globe has hitherto organized a judicial power in the same manner as the Americans," established Tocqueville (Tocqueville 1945, vol. 1: 98; cf. Bowles 1993: 166–205).

Problems of Conflict Settlement: Steady Change with Unknown Result

The negotiation marathon usually produces the marginal groups of those who don't have the appropriate means to influence the political process. As the entire politics is geared toward the articulation of rights and interests and their most direct harmonization between their protagonists—from program formulation and implementation to the legal settlement of litigation—the weak will hardly make themselves heard without being given a voice. This shows one limit to the realization of the liberal democracy model by the professionally organized representation of interests. The other limit is the relinquishment of any attempt to oppose to the pluralism of individual interests the idea of a public welfare, a public interest, a common good, or a commonly defined good life beyond the mere harmonization process. What extent of common ground is possible in the framework of liberal democracy is reflected by the common interest in a maximum, mutually harmless unfolding of interests. Linked with this is the idea of justice saying that a societal order will only and exclusively be considered just when it offers all its citizens the maximum scope to unfold their rights and interests. This need not forcibly involve the same result for all, but the chances must be distributed equally. When unequal results are produced, those who come out worse must still attain a far better result than in any other order.

The Liberal Idea of Democracy

John Rawls most strikingly pointed out the idea of justice in liberal democracy (Rawls 1971; 1993). According to Rawls, rationally calculating people in a hypothetical original state and under the veil of ignorance would agree on two basic principles of justice:

1. Everybody should have the same basic liberties at his or her disposal;

2. Inequality can be justified only insofar as it will offer an advantage to those who come off worse, too, and as everybody has the same chance right from the start to assume any position in the unequal system.

It is decisive to note that the individuals in the original state do not know their future positions but, from the point of view of a possible future *individual* benefit, decide on a basic order that offers the same chances to everybody and admits inequality insofar as everybody will benefit from it. People decide in their quality as monads and see cooperation with others from the point of view of the individual maximization of benefits. Their expected individual benefit is the motive for their agreeing upon the basic order. Basically, they are not able to transcend the horizon of their individual interests by socialization and to arrive at a determination of the public welfare beyond the sum of individual interests. Seen from Rawls' liberalism, such a determination of the public welfare by socialization must basically appear as an arbitrary constraint exercised on the individual, a limitation of his or her individual liberties. From this point of view, liberty can be understood only as private autonomy. Consequently, political autonomy is a fiction that manages to make collective constraint appear as freedom.

In a pluralistic society, everyone will develop his or her own ideas of a good life which cannot be reduced to a homogeneous concept without an arbitrary constraint. Without this arbitrary constraint, it is possible to reach an order that leaves a scope to any idea of a good life only as long as these ideas do not hinder each other and as long as no inequalities are created that do not offer an advantage to those who come off worse, too. Rationally calculating individuals will be in a position to agree upon such an order without any constraint. They will regard this order as just insofar as it offers equal chances to everybody and provides greater advantages than any other order. In this sense, there can only be a common justice, but no common good.

Rawls' argumentation cannot be challenged when one accepts his concept of the human being as a rationally calculating, benefit-maximizing individual who regards company with others exclusively from the viewpoint of individual advantages. It must not be taken into account, however, that people can unfold their personality only in company with others, as Michael Sandel correctly argued against Rawls' thesis (Sandel 1982). The theories of the development of personality presented by Durkheim, Simmel, Freud, and Mead right through to Parsons, Piaget, and Kohlberg show that everybody develops his or her own personality in the course of his or her growing into ever farther reaching communities, extends his or her empathy and moral consciousness, and thus becomes definitely more capable of looking at the world from the angle of an ever more comprehensive "we." This allows the individuals to transcend their individual interests, qualify them, and put them into the context of a common order (Joas 1997). In the same degree as the individuals take this route, they will be able to agree upon more than just the ideal scope for the unfolding of their individual interests. When they socialize and cooperate, take a common viewpoint, they can also arrive at concepts of a *good* coexistence, which go beyond the mere definition of scopes for the individual maximization of benefits.

In a common societal order not only abstract justice is realized but also the concrete good. The decisive prerequisite for this is humankind's socialization and a political leadership to society that does not stop at organizing a race by fair rules of the game but is able to address people in their role as citizens in public deliberation so as to motivate them to create their conditions of life together according to the concepts of a common good life (Weber 1971: 245–291, 320–350, 545–560). On this way, it is also possible to exercise political autonomy in a pluralistic society, and private autonomy can be included into the concept of a common good life. Anyway, there is no abstract private autonomy in society. It can unfold only in life-worlds containing more than just abstract standards of justice. Therefore, the political formation of society must inevitably be more than just a competition of interests under the terms of equal opportunities. It requires the conscious further development of the existing life-world with its latent concept of a good life and a just order under new societal conditions. When it loses sight of this task, it will leave the life-world to a natural process of change beyond any human control.

It is true that Rawls' theory of justice is not suited to justify ghettos in the cities, but we can hardly extract more than programs of affirmative action. Over the approximately 30 years of their existence, these programs have changed nothing in the reality of the exclusion of marginal groups, as they themselves produce winners and losers according to the logic of competition. It is here that Rawls' theory could be used to plead for compensation payments of the welfare state to those who definitely came off badly; however, the limit of these payments should be exactly at a point beyond which the motivation for self-support gets lost. How wide or narrow this point is set is a matter of interpretation and is subject to political developments.

Communitarian and Republican Ideas of Democracy

What is less permitted by the model of a liberal democracy as it is prevailing in the United States is the orientation of the political process to the discovery of a commonly supported good life, since the everyday political process is geared toward the maximum unfolding of rights and interests and their accommodation. "When power is in countless independent hands, all dependent on public opinion, each hand responds to the constituencies to which it is attuned" (Wilson 1997: 83). This is how James Q. Wilson describes the political process in America just to show how difficult it is to orient political decisions toward standards of the common good and against active interests and existing moods. The Senate and the House of Representatives include, first and foremost, a number of committees and subcommittees whose negotiations are aimed at mediating interests. On the other hand, the plenary sessions are considerably less significant as regards both their volume and importance (Bowles 1993: 135; Smith and Deering 1984). Therefore, the Congress is not a place to define a common good life. This place cannot be discovered at the courts either, not even at the Supreme Court. Their task is to see that no single individual is hindered in exercising his or her rights. They make sure that a maximum number of people can take part in the race for the greatest possible unfolding of rights and interests and that this race will be carried out according to fair rules. Yet, it is outside their competence to develop concepts of a good life that are binding for everybody. The president comes closest to this role due to his or her responsibility for his or her electors. Especially via the media, he or she can exercise a considerable influence on the public formation of opinion. Therefore, as a rule, strong presidents initiated a fundamental restructuring of society and the corresponding sideline programs. These include Lincoln's policy to abolish slavery, F. D. Roosevelt's New Deal; Kennedy's civil rights policy, and—however we may assess it—Reagan's neoconservative "revolution." Outside such unusual historical situations, the president is himself or herself but a player in the political game who may succeed from time to time to introduce one or another of his or her ideas into the policy process and make it a success. In political everyday business it is liberalism and, in unusual historical situations, it is republicanism—this is how Bruce Ackerman takes up these two contrasting democracy concepts (in analogy to Thomas Kuhn's theory of scientific revolutions) and places them in a sequence of stages of political development just to point out that in the American political reality, both concepts of democracy have been linked systematically (Ackerman 1984, 1991; Kuhn 1962). In this interpretation, republicanism is useful to a limited extent only, namely, in decisive stages of change, whereas in the stage of political normality, only the liberal concept can do justice to the pluralism of interests and concepts of life. In historical stages of radical change, the citizens have to reach an agreement on basic questions on how they want to live together in the future. In such situations, it is up to the president to formulate public opinion precisely, shape it decisively from the top, and convert it into concrete measures. Ackerman takes three prominent examples to underline the capability of American democracy to leave the level of the private individual's normal politics to enter the level of the citizen and to pave the way basically for the further common life: the epoch of the creation of the Constitution by the Federalists; the epoch of the Reconstruction by the Republicans after the Civil War;

and the epoch of the New Deal of the Democrats under the leadership of F. D. Roosevelt (Ackerman 1991).

The protagonists of communitarianism—including a strong republicanism—cannot be satisfied with this moderate union of republicanism and liberalism. In their eyes, the political reality has drifted much too much toward liberalism. That's why politics dissolved in the struggle of egoist interests and does not possess any more formative power at all. According to the communitarians, elements of the orientation to public welfare, to republicanism, and to political association with the goal of ensuring a common formation of a commonly shared good life and a just society for all were pushed to the background. In their best-seller *Habits of the Heart*, Robert Bellah and his coauthors reminded of the fact that the foundation of the first colonies in New England was, to a substantial extent, the work of the associated settlers who established the tradition of a common regulation of public affairs (Bellah et al. 1985; Tocqueville 1945; Miller 1954, 1956; Ellis 1993: 8–12). When approaching the New World in 1630, John Winthrop urged his crew on board the *Arbella* to lead a life in community: "We must be knit together in this work as one man, we must entertain each other in brotherly affection, we must be willing to abridge ourselves of our superfluities for the supply of others' necessities, . . . we must delight in each other, make others' conditions our own, rejoice together, labor and suffer together, always having before our eyes . . . our community as members of the same body" (Winthrop 1963: 198). In John Winthrop's Massachusetts theocracy, however, only religiously qualified male adults were admitted to the formation of common public affairs. Thomas Hooker and Roger Williams were not prepared to accept this rule of a religious elite and founded the new colonies, Connecticut and Rhode Island, in the immediate neighborhood. They established a tradition free from all religious ties and extended to all male adults that covered the common regulation of public affairs. Here in New England, we find the roots of living communal democracy as a common matter of associated citizens that is unique in the world. On the other hand, in his play on a witch-hunt in Salem, Arthur Miller strikingly pointed out the other side of a strong communal democracy, namely, suppression, exclusion, or prosecution of nonconformism (Miller [1953] 1968).

Bellah and his coauthors also remember the second source of republican tradition created by the founding fathers of the American Constitution in 1789. They were influenced not only by John Locke but also by James Harrington. Whereas in Locke's eyes, the citizens join in a political community only to protect their lives, their property, and their freedom, Harrington promotes Aristotle's understanding of politics as a common public matter of virtuous citizens. According to Harrington, a flourishing democratic polity must be ruled by a strong, politically active elite (Harrington 1955). This republican element in the tradition of the American Constitution was pointed out in particular by John Pocock (Pocock 1975: 506–552; 1981; see also Adams 1973; Kahn 1989).

The republicanism as it was presented by James Madison in the *Federalist Papers* is miles away from Rousseau's model of a closed, homogeneous city republic. In the famous "Federalist No. 10," Madison deals with the question as to how the domination of the state by the "factionalism" of the interest groups and the establishment of a rule of the majority over the minority can be avoided (Madison [1787/1788] 1961). He considers the federal republic the most suitable form of government for this. In a federal republic, two main conditions prevent the domination of politics by the "factionalism" of interest groups and the majority: the representative government and a suitable number of electors per representative—neither too many nor too few. In this way, the representatives will, on the one hand, remain in touch with the electors but, on the other, have to integrate a greater number of different interests of their electors into a coherent policy. The representatives can develop a responsibility for the whole, for the common good of the polity without, however, losing their sense for the interests of the individual electors.

In Madison's eyes, Rousseau's city republic means the death of individual liberties. These are much better accommodated in a greater federal state. Yet, in such a federal state only a representative government that is responsible to the whole and that remains tied to the pluralism of the electors' interests through the MPs can find a balanced relationship between the public welfare and the individual liberties. Consequently, Madison does not aim at republicanism as such but at a balanced relationship between republican and liberal elements. In his eyes, the federal republic is better suited for this than a direct participation democracy, as this either falls apart in the factionalism of the interest groups or develops into a rule of the majority over the minority. At the same time, this supplies an argument in favor of a federal state and against a mere confederation of sovereign individual states. Due to the clearer distribution of interests, the latter would tend toward a majority rule:

> The smaller the society, the fewer probably will be the distinct parties and interests composing it, the fewer the distinct parties and interests, the more frequently will a majority be found of the same party; and the smaller the number of individuals composing a majority, and the smaller the compass within which they are placed, the more easily will they concert and execute their plans of oppression. Extend the sphere and you take in a greater variety of parties and interests; you make it less probable that a majority of the whole will have a common motive to invade the rights of other citizens; or if such a common motive exists, it will be more difficult for all who feel it to discover their own strength and to act in unison with each other. (Madison [1787/1788] 1961: 83)

In the political philosophy of our century, John Dewey developed a concept of a participative democracy rooted in pragmatism, which regards the political process as a common learning where the individual prospects are geared toward common goals. Public reflection plays a major role here where the societal collective makes sure of the common wants. By renewing community life with all its possibilities of including the individual into common matters and by including the public across all political affairs, a counterweight should be created to the tendencies toward society's anonymization in the big cities, the falling apart of society into an individualism that lacks in ties, toward commercialization and the rule of experts over the lay-people. It may be seen as the attempt to transport the republican tradition into mass society (Dewey 1927).

In the more recent constitutional discussions, it was, above all, Frank Michelman who reminded of the republican tradition (Michelman 1986, 1988, 1989). Jürgen Habermas took up this debate in his search for the appropriate linkage of legal state and democracy (Habermas 1992: 324–348). From this debate and its critical reception by Habermas we may gain further insights into the tight relationship between liberalism and republicanism in American democracy.

Michelman points out that the political process must be interpreted not only as a harmonization of private interests but also as a process in whose course the citizens try to discover the common good by common deliberation (Michelman 1989: 450–452). Therefore, it must be the task of the courts and, above all, of the Supreme Court to examine how far the political process meets the requirements of a comprehensive deliberation and integration of all opinions—also those that were lacking before—during legislation to ask for amendments, if necessary (Michelman 1988: 1529–1532). This role of the Supreme Court (i.e., to guarantee a permanent reduction in the distance between the republican ideal and the reality of a dominant interest politics) was underlined, in particular, by Cass R. Sunstein. He refers to examples of judicial control by the Supreme Court, where laws were considered unconstitutional due to a discriminating classification under the argument of a lacking reasonable analysis. Based on these examples, Sunstein argues that the Supreme Court assesses laws according to a reasonable analysis in a deliberative process and makes sure in this way that interest politics fits into a republican-minded legislation process. He establishes that the Supreme Court applies this criterion far more often to administrative acts than to the Congress' legislation, since otherwise the Court will become a player in the political game. In this case it might be suspected of taking a particular standpoint just as do all other political authorities and actors (Sunstein 1990: 163–192; 1985: 58–59).

If the Supreme Court is to act as a fiduciary of republicanism, it would have to carry out this task actively toward legislature. Here, however, the precarious construction of a republicanism that is administered by the Supreme Court in a fiduciary way becomes evident. This is expressly pointed out by Jürgen Habermas in his critical discussion of this constitutional debate from the point of view of a discourse-theoretically founded theory of deliberative democracy (Habermas 1992: 340–348). In Habermas' eyes, republicanism must assume life-worlds to be homogeneous to an extent that does not exist in modern pluralistic societies. Therefore, liberalism is not only an expression of a bad reality that has to be changed and approached to the ideal of republicanism but also an expression of a state of emancipation of a relatively narrowly defined community of citizens from the constraints of a tradition that is accepted uncritically. Modern pluralism's potential of liberties cannot be guided into well-arranged tracks by republicanism without any unfounded constraint. The same applies to communitarianism. It joins republicanism in the subordination of interest politics to the determination of the common good by the united citizens. In line with Rousseau's theory, republicanism conceives the union of citizens as a new quality of association; according to

Madison, representative government is seen as a corrective to interest politics, because it is obliged to the whole. Both consider it an overcoming of the particularism of life-world traditions of the societal groups. On the other hand, communitarianism expressly follows on these value-forming traditions in the prepolitical space (family, neighborhood, communities) and wants to include these into a comprehensive political process that builds up a community where it is important to elaborate an intergroupal common good from the existing, though particular, traditions (Sandel 1982; MacIntyre 1987; Taylor 1988).

Both the republican and the communitarian strategy to overcome liberalism's negative sides are doomed to fail in the light of the modern reality of the pluralism of interests and concepts of life and in view of the inherent return to a no longer justifiable extent of collective constraint imposed on the individual, if we follow Habermas' theory. Yet, Habermas is far from supporting liberalism and leaving politics completely to the process-regulated accommodation of interests. He sees a solution to the problem in the completion of liberal interest policy with frame-building deliberative politics on a discourse-ethical foundation (Habermas 1992: 435–467). He believes that communication by language per se covers a sufficient amount of integration potential to make the pluralism of interests and concepts of life fit into a workable order. For this, the citizens' inclusion in life-world traditions, firmly established communities, and clearly demarcated spaces is no longer an indispensable prerequisite. All that is needed is to give sufficient room to communication in the political process so that social movements can make the peripheral voices heard in the center of political deliberation. It is true, however, that under these conditions only a type of a just order can be reached where all concepts of life will get their right provided that they can be integrated into a commonly justifiable and correspondingly acceptable order. All stronger requirements of the common good must give way to the universally just and can make a claim to further existence only insofar as they can be integrated into a generally just order as particular concepts of life of particular communities, for example, nations. The just is given clear priority over the good. With this, Habermas attributes a burden of integration to the purely linguistic communication that can easily make it collapse when it comes to the concrete formation of common human life beyond the determination of abstract standards of justice. Discourse ethics and the deliberative democracy model can replace neither liberalism nor republicanism nor communitarianism but merely complement them. Without a countercontrol by republican and communitarian elements, discourse ethics and liberalism may even join forces and ensure that the expansive realization of rights and the maximization of satisfying interests act together in a global consumer society. The question as to how it can be prevented that democracy falls victim to unfiltered interest politics can therefore not be answered only with a reference to the integrative power of linguistic communication in a multilevel process of public discourse from family, school, and job to community, media public, and the Parliament, that is, in a deliberative democracy.

Language's feeble power of integration brings us straight back to the discussion about the republican elements in the tradition of the American Constitution.

When we come back to James Madison's republicanism, which is "more realistic" when compared to that of Rousseau, and when we confront it with our research of the American policy process, we will, even from this point of view, discover a strong discrepancy between theory and reality. The representatives in Congress can less and less play the role of incorporating interest politics into the responsibility for the whole and the search for the common good. Instead, Congress, with the dominant role of the committees and subcommittees and the relatively weak role of the plenum, has become a field of ever more intensively promoted interest politics. The weight of the negotiations was transferred from the plenum to the subcommittees and from there to the lobby. This field of program formulation is furthermore complemented with the fields of implementation and legal disputes that are dominated by interest politics more than in any other country. The Supreme Court is unable to become a republican authority either that assists in the search for the common good. Its primary task is the protection of individual rights against all inadmissible infringements of either private or state parties. According to the principle "equal rights for all," it helps to realize conditions of life that involve an improvement of the chances for all to practice their rights in fact. Moreover, all courts have to decide on conflicts where rights confront each other so that it becomes clear which right is given priority in which situation. In all cases, however, the realization of rights is in the focus, not the conception of a common good. In the tradition of the common law, legal decision is, moreover, fixed to justice in individual cases and implies a high degree of negotiations on the extent of guilt and punishment, culpable action and compensation to the mutual benefit of the litigants. This means that the principle of the individual maximization of benefits has become an integral part of legal practice and is therefore hardly embedded in comprehensive conceptions of the common good in this practice. Nevertheless, the courts take decisions on the appropriate or inappropriate use of rights by the individuals and their appropriate or inappropriate limitation. This leaves the door open for considerations on what a good life looks like where rights fit into a workable order. By taking such decisions, the courts exercise a practice of everyday definition of a common good life and do not merely determine legal or illegal action. Of course, in doing so they move on shaky ground and act between the blind reproduction of evolved traditions and their uncertain renewal under changed conditions. Yet this complies exactly with the courts' position in the framework of the common-law tradition. They do not simply apply traditional and fixed law but continue a legal tradition. The legal tradition contains ideas of the good life; therefore, the courts do not only take legal decisions but also reproduce and renew a concept of good life. But as the renewal of the law is so controversial and brings the interest groups into the arena, it is hard for the courts to meet this task differently than an arbitration court controlling the fair carrying out of interest conflicts and ensuring the maximum consideration of all interests. Therefore, little scope is left for the definition of the common good (Jacob 1965; Rüschemeyer 1973).

The weighting between the republican and liberal elements in American politics has shifted considerably toward liberalism. The political process covers an endless chain of the unfolding of a maximum number of interests. At the same time, justice presents itself as the maximum extension of the scope for the practising of rights and realization of interests for all. The question as to whether the sum of this maximization of rights and interests will, ultimately, result in a good life can hardly be asked today, as in all political authorities and in all stages of the policy process the maximization of rights and interests prevails.

Is it possible at all to shift the weights some part toward a renewal of republicanism without exercising unjustified constraints? This could, if at all, be done only in the sense of Madison's republicanism. The legal process would have to mirror the usually unconscious continuation of ideas of a good life and make them aware to all those concerned and to the public. As a rule, individual courts will be overtaxed with this task. The Supreme Court could best carry out this job. To make coping with this task easier, it would require the assistance of a scientific service dedicated to exactly this job: find out by way of projection what type of common life will result from the decisions taken in individual cases for an anticipated practice of action. The more obvious that the dependence of the good life on decisions is, the less that it can be left to an uncritical legal practice, and the faster we will meet the limits of coping with the problem by legal practice, since the political character of the matter comes to the fore. This means that political procedures are required. First of all, it's the Congress' turn. A strengthening of the plenum when compared to committees and subcommittees would shift the weight slightly toward Madison's republicanism. This can certainly be no more than a marginal transfer of weights, since it is not possible to forgo the mediation of interests in committees and subcommittees due to the poor prepolitical concentration of interests.

Big decisions about the future life in responsibility for the common good can, however, be taken only by a powerful president in cooperation with the public that he or she has impregnated with his or her conviction in extraordinary historical situations and be converted into political programs (Greenstein 1990; Neustadt 1990). The post of the American president is particularly suited for this task. It is, however, but one out of several powerful authorities in the system of checks and balances. Without the support of the Congress, which acts independently even when the president's party has the majority of votes in both houses, the president will achieve nothing. This was experienced recently by Bill Clinton, whose ambitious plans were cut down by the Congress, especially in environmental policy, where he worked together with his vice president, Al Gore, and who is worried about the future of the ecological balance in his book and in health care, where his wife and adviser, Hillary Clinton, is active. The investigations on Clinton's various affairs, which were strategically exploited by his opponents, headed by an ambitious special investigator and lawyers lusting for money and publicity, the spectacle staged by the media, and the petering out of his initiatives in both environmental and health policy against the barrier of interests clearly demonstrate how politics is threatened to vanish in the Bermuda triangle of the production of pseudopolitical events by the media to entertain the public, legal action at any cost, and interest politics to the bitter end.

Concluding Remarks

Let us finally target our analysis of pluralist competition democracy as it is prevailing in the United States to the question as to how far and in what form it is capable to process conflicts so that social integration will be retained yet the big questions of the future can be coped with, that is, that a consensually supported formation of the future is possible. We can give the following answer to this question: conflicts are split up into innumerable single struggles, where even the tiniest advantages are being fought for from the first initiatives in Congress through to court action. The political process has a tremendous capacity to absorb conflicts, far more than in any other country. This includes, however, that by far the largest number of conflicts peters out somewhere in the ocean of endless negotiations and therefore does not succeed in reaching the goal of being passed as a law. But even then the conflict parties won't get peace, as they always have to expect that in the subsequent implementation process and by way of legal proceedings, the opponent will gather advantages. Since nothing has been decided for sure, the conflict parties will always remain motivated to take part in the game further on, although they cannot gain but minimum benefits. All in all, they act in the awareness that they can constantly draw advantages from certain parts of the policy process. They see themselves as actors in a winning game for all with a growing sum of benefits, not as actors in a zero-sum game, where they risk their necks. In this system of innumerable single struggles, however, the big questions of the formation of the future will easily perish. They can hardly be envisaged. Having been asked once, it easily happens that they are crushed by the machinery operating for the accomplishment of individual interests. Only in unusual historical situations can a president—having the required fortune—win the public for the implementation of comprehensive reform programs and reject particular interests with its support.

Briefly, the primary force of policy making is the broad and finely differentiated network of actors. Access to that network is open for everey new articulation of problems and is therefore favorable to innovations. Conflict settlement is very competitive; it is an endless process of competing for the slightest advantages. There is a broad inclusion of new social movements on the basis of their competitiveness, because there is no once-and-for-all settled structure of power. Consensus formation takes place as competition in a trial-and-error procedure of the permanent piecemeal improvements of always imperfect policy programs.

CONCLUSION

What should ideally be the democracy of the future? Systematically assessed, all of the democracy models surveyed offer their advantages, dangers, and disadvantages, their special problems and dilemmas. Signs for the future, however, point toward the American model of a liberal and pluralist competition democracy (Münch 1998: 363–414). This is also supported by the change in the sideline conditions of future politics, which were listed at the beginning of this chapter: (1) the scientification of politics with a simultaneous politicization of science; (2) the medialization of politics; (3) the professionally organized pluralism of interests; (4) the multiplication of forums for negotiation; (5) the transfer of political competences onto the level of the European Union and the accompanying multiplication of levels for political negotiations and the strengthening of negotiation democracy when compared to parliamentary democracy; and (6) the globalization and consequent deterritorialization and opening of all political spaces of action.

Our analysis of the American competition democracy has demonstrated that this democracy model—like all other models—involves specific structural weaknesses resulting from the concentration of political events on this extreme type of democracy while at the same time structural elements from all other democracy elements exist at the margin. Therefore, a well-balanced development toward the future of a liberal and pluralist competition democracy should carefully see to the maintenance and/or extension of the structural elements borrowed from the other democracy models in a move to institutionalize counterweights to balance the excesses of competition democracy. This is what we may wish, yet reality will be characterized, on the one hand, by the trend toward competition democracy and, on the other, by the multiplication of the structural weaknesses of the other democracy models in their countries of origin under the changed sideline conditions of global modernity.

A reasonable way toward the future can build on the evolved structures and aim at their productive transformation only while taking into consideration one's own structural weaknesses and their removal by borrowing structural elements from the alternative democracies. Seen systematically, the four democracy models taken together supply the structural elements for a balanced democracy. Since, however, democracy cannot be designed on the drawing board, each country necessarily has to conceive its way toward the future as a development of institutions starting logically from its own evolved structures and maintaining its core there. It is no problem to learn from the other countries when taking this way. If, however, this is done without prior examination of the consequences on one's own institutional and cultural frame of reference and without paying attention to the specific problems and dilemmas of the structural elements borrowed from the others, the undesired consequences will no surprise.

Structural elements of democracy can bear their usual fruit only in tailor-made institutional and cultural surroundings. Transposed to other institutional and cultural contexts, they will quickly die without the preparation and cultivation of institutional and cultural surroundings adjusted to their needs. Otherwise, they may affect their surroundings so much that nothing will work anymore. In either case, if we change our historically evolved institutions and cultures to stay "competitive" without knowing enough about the consequences of our work, we shall face a period full of great surprises.

Interviews

UNITED KINGDOM

- A major automobile association
- A major chemical company
- Acid Rain Review Group
- Air Quality Division DoE
- Association of Metropolitan Authorities
- Automobile Association (AA)
- Former employees of the Petroleum Industry Association
- Environmental Protection and Industry Division DoE
- Green Party
- Greenpeace
- Imperial College for Science and Technology
- Institute for European Environmental Policy
- Institution of Environmental Health Officers (IEHO)
- London Borough of Greenwich
- London Boroughs Association
- MP Liberal Democrats
- National Environment Technology Centre
- National Power PLC
- Pollution Policy Division (PPD) HMIP
- Public Policy Division DoT
- Regulatory Systems Division (RSD) HMIP
- Society of Motor Manufacturers and Traders
- Transport 2000
- Transport Research Laboratory DoT
- U.K. Centre for Economic and Environmental Development
- Vauxhall PLC

FRANCE

- ADEME, Service de Recherche Scientifique Impact et Milieux, Elichegaray
- Agence de l'Environnement et de la Maîtrise de l'Energie, Direction de l'Action Régionale et Internationale (ADEME), Herz
- Association de la Prévention de la Pollution Atmosphérique (APPA), Sommer
- Association Française des Ingénieurs et Techniciens de l'Environnement (AFITE), Faugeron
- Association Française pour la Normalisation (AFNOR), Combes
- Bulle Bleue, Ray
- Centre International de Recherche sur l'Environnement et le Développement (CIRED), Hourcade and Cros
- Centre Interprofessionel Technique d'Etudes de la Pollution Atmosphérique (CITEPA), Bouscaren and Legonie
- Chambre de Commerce et d'Industrie de Paris (CCIP), Vaudois
- Conseil Régional d'Ile de France, Direction de l'Environnement et de la Culture, Bonis
- Laboratoire Central de la Préfecture de Police (LCPP), Service des Pollutions, Alary
- Les Amis de la Terre, Boucher
- Les Verts, Dufour
- Libération, Service Politique and Editor Environment, Crié
- Lascoumes, sociologist (sociology of law)
- Roqueplo, sociologist and polytechnician
- Ministère de l'Environnement, Bureau de l'Atmosphère et de l'Energie, Chambon
- Ministère de l'Environnement, Bureau de l'Atmosphère et de l'Energie, Foray
- Ministère de l'Environnement, Bureau du Contentieux, Carlier
- Ministère de l'Industrie et du Commerce Extérieur, Direction Régionale de l'Industrie, de la Recherche et de l'Environnement (DRIRE), Ile de France, Zacklad and Spittler
- Préfecture de Police, Service Technique d'Interdépartementale d'Inspection des Installations Classées (STIIC), Du Fou De Kerdaniel
- SHELL-CHIMIE, Service Environnement, Dubreuil
- Surveillance de la Qualité de l'Air en Ile de France (AIRPARIF), Lameloise
- TOTAL, Raffinage Distribution, Service Environnement, Ceruette
- -Ministère de l'Industrie et du Commerce Extérieur, Secrétariat Général des DRIREs, Roche

GERMANY

- Allgemeiner Deutscher Automobilclub (ADAC), Franke (Environmental Politics)
- Bund für Umwelt und Naturschutz Deutschland (BUND), Kühling

- Bund für Umwelt und Naturschutz Deutschland (BUND), Schuschke
- Bundesumweltministerium (BMU)
- Bundesumweltministerium, ehem. Ministerialdirigent Feldhaus
- Bundesverband Bürgerinitiativen Umweltschutz (BBU), Schott
- Bundesverband der Deutschen Industrie (BDI), Sander (Dept. for Environmental Politics)
- Bundesverkehrsministerium
- Bundeswirtschaftsministerium (Dept. for Environmental Politics)
- Bündnis 90/Die Grünen, District Party Group Bamberg
- Bürgerinitiative Bitterfeld, Peter
- Bürgerinitiative Bitterfeld, Schreier
- Christlich Demokratische Union (CDU), Parliamentary Party Group, Kahl (Member of the Committee on Environment)
- Christlich Demokratische Union (CDU), Regional Parliament Group Sachsen, Franke (Chairman of the Committee on Environment)
- Christlich-Soziale Union, Spokesman Environment, County Council Bamberg
- Deutscher Landkreistag
- Gesellschaft für rationale Verkehrspolitik (GRV)
- Greenpeace Deutschland, Smidt
- Hoechst AG, , Immissionschutzbeauftragter, Wortmann
- Industrie und Handelskammer (IHK), Zeiger (Expert on Environment)
- Länderausschuß für Immissionschutz (LAI), Pütz (Chairman of LAI, Ministry of the Environment NRW)
- Müllverbrennungsanlagenbetreiber, Technical Director
- Müllverbrennungsanlagenbetreiber, Administrational Director
- Opel AG, Immissionschutzbeauftragter, Kinzel
  Partei des Demokratischen Sozialismus (PDS), Regional Party Group Sachsen-Anhalt, Lüderitz (Chairman of the Committee on Environment)
- Raffinerie Leuna, Glanz (Person in Charge of Air Pollution Control)
- Sachverständigenrat für Umweltfragen (Management)
- Sozialdemokratische Partei Deutschlands (SPD), Parliamentary Party Group Schütz (Member of the Committee on Environment)
- Sozialdemokratische Partei Deutschlands (SPD), District Pary Group, Bamberg
- Staatliches Amt für Umweltschutz Dessau, Freihube
- Staatliches Amt für Umweltschutz Dessau, Hein
- Staatliches Amt für Umweltschutz Dessau, Maiwald
- Staatliches Amt für Umweltschutz Halle, Rieger (Head of Department on Air Pollution Control)
- Technischer Überwachungsverein (TÜV) Hannover-Sachsen-Anhalt, Güter
- Umweltbundesamt (UBA)
- Umweltministerium Sachsen-Anhalt, Dörfel
- Umweltministerkonferenz (UMK), Hertling (Ministry of the Environment SA)

- Umweltministerkonferenz (UMK), Hein (Ministry of the Environment NRW)
- Verband der Chemischen Industrie (VCI), Lenz (Head of Department on Air Pollution Control)
- Verband der Chemischen Industrie Ost (VCI), Uhlig
- Verband der Deutschen Automobilindustrie (VDA), Wöhrl (Head of Department on Environmental Politics)
- Verband Deutscher Ingenieure (VDI), Expert on Questions of KRdL

UNITED STATES

- American Institute of Chemical Engineers
- American Iron and Steel Institute
- American Lung Association (2 Interviews)
- American Petroleum Institute
- California EPA Air Resources Board (2 Interviews)
- Center for Clean Air Policy
- Chrysler Corp.
- Council on Environmental Quality
- D.C. Circuit Court of Appeals
- E PA Science Advisory Board
- Edison Electric Institute
- EPA Acid Rain Division
- EPA Air Program
- EPA Clean Air Compliance Analysis Council
- EPA Clean Air Scientific Advisory Committee
- EPA Office of Mobile Sources
- EPA Office of Planning, Policy, and Evaluation/ Air Policy Division (2 Interviews)
- EPA Office of Policy, Analysis, and Review
- General Motors
- House of Representatives
- INFORM
- National Coal Association
- Natural Resources Defense Council (2 Interviews)
- Resources for the Future
- Senate Committee on Environment and Public Works
- South Coast Air Quality Management District
- Senate Committee on Environment and Public Works
- South Coast Air Quality Management District

Bibliography

Abbott, Andrew. *The System of Profession. An Essay on the Division of Expert Labor.* Chicago: University of Chicago Press. 1988.

Ackerman, Bruce. "The Storrs Lectures: Discovering the Constitution." *Yale Law Review.* 93. 1984, pp. 1013–1072.

Ackerman, Bruce. *We the People.* Vol. 1: *Foundations.* Cambridge: Harvard University Press. 1991.

Adam, Gérard. "Les petites entreprises: un monde contrasté." In: Reynaud, Jean-Daniel and Grafmeyer, Yves. *Français, qui êtes-vous?* Paris: Documentation Française. 1982, pp. 181–189.

Adams, Willi Paul. *Republikanische Verfassung und bürgerliche Freiheit. Die Verfassungen und politischen Ideen der amerikanischen Revolution.* Neuwied: Luchterhand. 1973.

Ammon, Günther. *Der französische Wirtschaftsstil.* 2nd ed. München: Eberhard. (1989) 1994.

Andrews, Richard N. L. "United States." In: Jänicke, Martin, and Weidner, Helmut (eds.). *National Environmental Policies. A Comparative Study of Capacity-Building.* Berlin: Springer. 1997, pp. 25–44.

Aretz, Hans-Jürgen. *Zwischen Kritik und Dogma. Der wissenschaftliche Diskurs.* Wiesbaden: Deutscher Universitätsverlag. 1990.

Ashford, Douglas E. *Policy and Politics in Britain. The Limits of Consensus.* Oxford: Blackwell. 1981.

Atkinson, Michael M., and Coleman, William D. "Strong States and Weak States: Sectoral Policy Networks in Advanced Capitalist Economies." *British Journal of Political Science.* 19. 1989, pp. 47–67.

Badie, Bertrand, and Birnbaum, Pierre. *The Sociology of the State.* Chicago: University of Chicago Press. 1983.

Bagehot, Walter. *The English Constitution. Introduction by Richard Crossman.* London: Oxford University Press. 1963.

Baier, Lothar. *Firma Frankreich. Eine Betriebsbesichtigung.* Berlin: Wagenbach. 1988.

Baudrillard, Jean. *Simulacres et simulation.* Paris: Galilée. 1981.

Beck, Ulrich. *Die Erfindung des Politischen.* Frankfurt a.M.: Suhrkamp. 1993. (English translation: *The Reinvention of Politics.* Oxford: Polity Press. 1996.)

Becquart-Leclercq, Jeanne. "Kommunalpolitik in Frankreich. Die Dezentralisation und ihre Folgen." In: Wehling, Hans-Georg (ed.). *Frankreich. Eine politische Landeskunde.* Stuttgart u.a.: Kohlhammer. 1989, pp. 187–220.

Bellah, Robert N., Madsen, Richard, Sullivan, William M., Swidler, Ann, and Tipton, Steven M. *Habits of the Heart. Individualism and Commitment in American Life.* Berkeley: University of California Press. 1985.

Bellamy, Richard. *Liberalism and Modern Society.* Cambridge: Polity Press. 1992.

Bellamy, Richard (ed). *Victorian Liberalism: Nineteenth Century Political Thought and Practice.* London: Routledge. 1990.

Bentham, Jeremy. *An Introduction to the Principles of Morals and Legislation.* Ed. Burns, J. H., and Hart, H.L.A. London: Attslone Press. (1789) 1970.

Benz, Arthur. "Commentary on O'Toole and Scharpf: The Network Concept as a Theoretical Approach." In: Scharpf, Fritz W. (ed.). *Games in Hierarchies and Networks. Analytical and Empirical Approaches to the Study of Governance Institutions.* Frankfurt a.M.: Campus. 1993, pp. 167–175.

Bergsdorf, Wolfgang. *Über die Macht der Kultur. Kommunikation als Gebot der Politik.* Stuttgart: DVA. 1988.

Bering, Dietz. *Die Intellektuellen. Geschichte eines Schimpfwortes.* Stuttgart: Klett-Cotta. 1978.

Berry, Jeffrey M. *Lobbying for the People: The Political Behavior of Public Interest Groups.* Princeton: Princeton University Press. 1977.

Berry, Jeffrey M. *The Interest Group Society.* Boston: Little, Brown. 1984.

Böckenförde, Ernst W. *Recht, Staat, Freiheit.* Frankfurt a.M.: Suhrkamp. 1991.

Boehmer-Christiansen, Sonja, and Skea, John. *Acid Politics: Environmental and Energy Politics in Britain and Germany.* London: Belhaven Press. 1991.

Boehmer-Christiansen, Sonja, and Weidner, Helmut. *The Politics of Reducing Vehicle Emissions in Britain and Germany.* London: Pinter, 1995.

Bohne, Eberhard. *Der informale Rechtsstaat. Eine empirische Untersuchung zum Gesetzesvollzug unter besonderer Berücksichtigung des Immissionsschutzes.* Berlin: Dunker and Humblot. 1981.

Borgards, Cornelia. "Länderbericht Frankreich." In: Münch, Richard, et al. *Zweiter Arbeitsbericht des Projekts "Die gesellschaftliche Kontrolle technisch produzierter Gefahren. Eine vergleichende Studie zu Kontrollverfahren in Deutschland, USA, Frankreich und England auf der Basis von vier theoretischen Modellen."* Düsseldorf: unpublished report for the Deutsche Forschungsgemeinschaft. 1996, pp. 337–411.

Bornstein, Stephen E. "The Politics of Scandal." In: Hall, Peter A., Hayward, Jack, and Machin, Howard (eds.). *Developments in French Politics.* Houndsmills, Basingstoke, and London: Macmillan. 1994, pp. 269–281.

Bourdieu, Pierre. *Esquisse d'une théorie de la pratique, précédé de trois études d'ethnologie kabyle*. Genève: Droz. 1972. (English translation: *Outline of a Theory of Practice*. Cambridge: Cambridge University Press. 1997.)

Bourdieu, Pierre. "La réprésentation politique. Eléments pour une théorie du champs politique." *Actes de la recherche en sciences sociales*. 36/37. 1981, pp. 2–24.

Bourdieu, Pierre. *La distinction. Critique social du jugement*. Paris: Minuit. 1982. (English translation: *Distinction. A Social Critique of the Judgement of Taste*. Cambridge: Harvard University Press. 1984.)

Bourdieu, Pierre. *Homo academicus*. Paris: Minuit. 1984.

Bourdieu, Pierre. "Three Forms of Capital." In: Richardson, John G. (ed.). *Handbook of Theory and Research for the Sociology of Education*. Westport, Conn.: Greenwood Press. 1986, pp. 241–258.

Bourdieu, Pierre. *La noblesse d'état: grandes écoles et esprit de corps*. Paris: Minuit. 1989. (English translation: *State Nobility. Elite Schools in the Field of Power*. Stanford, CA: Stanford University Press. 1998.)

Bourdieu, Pierre. *Les règles de l'art*. Paris: Edition du Seuil. 1992. (English translation: *Rules of Art*. Oxford: Polity Press. 1996.)

Bourjol, Maurice. *Les institutions régionales de 1789 à nos jours*. Paris: Berger-Levrault. 1969.

Bowles, Nigel. *The Government and Politics of the United States*. Houndsmills, Basingstoke, and London: Macmillan. 1993.

Braudel, Fernand. *L'identité de la France. Espace et histoire*. Paris. 1986. (English translation: *Identity of France*. London: HarperCollins. 1991.)

Brickman, Ronald, Jasanoff, Sheila, and Ilgen, Thomas. *Controlling Chemicals. The Politics of Regulation in Europe and the United States*. Ithaca, N.Y., and London: Cornell University Press. 1985.

Briggs, Asa. *Victorian People*. London: Odham Press. 1954.

Brulle, Robert J. "Environmental Discourse and Social Movement Organizations: A Historical and Rhetorical Perspective on the Development of U.S. Environmental Organizations." *Sociological Inquiry*. 66/1. 1996, pp. 58–83.

Bryner, Gary C. *Bureaucratic Discretion. Law and Policy in Federal Regulatory Agencies*. New York: Pergamon Press. 1987.

Budge, Ian, and McKay, D. *The Changing British Political System. Into the 1990s*. Essex: Longman. 1989.

Burke, Edmund. *Burke's Speech on Conciliation with America*. Ed. H. Lamont. Boston: Ginn. (1775) 1897.

Burmeister, Joachim H. "Akteneinsicht in Großbritannien." In: Winter, Gerd (ed.). *Öffentlichkeit von Umweltinformation. Europäische und nordamerikanische Rechte und Erfahrungen*. Baden-Baden: Nomos. 1990, pp. 211–248.

Butt, Ronald. *The Power of Parliament*. 2nd ed. London: Constable. 1969.

Cawson, Alan (ed.). *Organized Interests and the State: Studies in Meso-Corporatism*. London: Sage. 1985.

Centre Interprofessionnel Technique d'Etudes de la Pollution Atmosphérique

(CITEPA). *Études documentaires n° 113*. 1994.

Christmann, Gabriela B. "Über die 'Institutionalisierung' und 'Verwissenschaftlichung' des ökologischen Protests auf lokaler Ebene." *ZfU*. 4and92. 1992, pp. 454–480.

Clegg, Hugh. *The System of Industrial Relations in Britain*. 3rd ed. Oxford: Blackwell. 1976.

Cohen, Elie. "Formation, modèles d'action et performance de l'elite industrielle: l'example des dirigeants issus du corps des Mines." *Sociologie du Travail*. 4. 1988, pp. 587–614.

Cohen, Elie. *Le colbertisme "high-tech"*. Paris: Hachette. 1992.

Collini, Stefan. *Liberalism and Sociology: L. T. Hobhouse and Political Argument in England 1880–1914*. Cambridge: Cambridge University Press. 1979.

Collini, Stefan. *The Idea of 'Character' in Victorian Political Thought*. 5th ed. London: Transactions of the Royal Historical Society. 1985.

Collins, Randall. "Changing conceptions in the sociology of the professions." In: Torstendahl, Rolf, and Burrage, Michael (eds.). *The Formation of Professions. Knowledge, State and Strategy*. London: Sage. 1990, pp. 11–23.

Comte, Auguste. "Catéchisme positiviste ou sommaire exposition de la religion universelle, en onze entretiens systématiques, entre une femme et un prêtre de l'humanité." Paris: L'Auteur. 1852. In: *Œuvres d'Auguste Comte*. Vol. 11. Paris: Anthropos. 1970.

Cook, Karen. S., and Whitmeyer, J. M. "Two Approaches to Social Structure: Exchange Theory and Network Analysis." *Annual Review of Sociology*. 18. 1992, pp. 109–127.

Cooper, C. David, and Alley, F. C. *Air Pollution Control. A Design Approach*. 2nd ed. Prospect Hights, Ill.: Waveland Press. 1994.

Cooper, Philipp J. "Toward the Hybrid State: The Case of Environmental Management in a Deregulated and Reengineered State." *International Review of Administrative Sciences*. 61. 1995, pp. 185–200.

Costain, W. Douglas, and Lester, James P. "The Evolution of Environmentalism." In: Lester, James P. (ed.). *Environmental Politics and Policy. Theories and Evidence*. Durham, N.C., and London: Duke University Press. 1995, pp. 15–38.

Crozier, Michel. *Le phénomène bureaucratique*. Paris: Edition du Seuil. 1963. (English translation: *The Bureaucratic Phenomenon*. Chicago: Chicago University Press. 1967.)

Crozier, Michel. *La société bloquée*. Paris: Edition du Seuil. 1970. (English translation: *The Stalled Society*. New York: Viking Press. 1973.)

Daele, Wolfgang van den. *Zum Forschungsprogramm der Abteilung "Normbildung und Umwelt"*. Berlin: Wissenschaftszentrum Berlin, working paper FS II 91–301. 1991.

Dahl, Robert A. *Pluralist Democracy in the United States. Conflict and Consent*. Chicago: Rand-McNally. 1967.

Dahrendorf, Ralf. *Gesellschaft und Demokratie in Deutschland*. München: Deutscher Taschenbuch Verlag. 1971. (English translation: *Society and Democ-*

racy in Germany. Westport, Conn.: Greenwood. 1980.)

Debray, Régis. *Voltaire verhaftet man nicht. Die Intellektuellen und die Macht in Frankreich.* Köln-Lövenich: Hohenheim. 1981.

Decker, Frank. *Umweltschutz und Staatsversagen. Eine materielle Regierbar-keitsanalyse.* Opladen: Leske + Budrich. 1994.

Department of the Environment. *Integrated Pollution Control and Local Author-ity's Air Pollution Controls.* Public Access to Information. London. 1989.

Department of the Environment. *Integrated Pollution Control. A Practical Guide.* London. 1994.

Department of the Environment. *Air Quality—Meeting the Challenge.* London. 1995.

Descartes, René. "Discours de la méthode." In: Descartes, René. *Œuvres philosophiques.* Vol. 1. Paris: Garnier. (1637) 1963a, pp. 567–650.

Devall, Bill. "Deep Ecology and Radical Environmentalism." In: Dunla, Riley E., and Mertig, Angela G. (eds.). *American Environmentalism. The U.S. Envi-ronmental Movement 1970–1990.* New York: Taylor. 1992, pp. 51–61.

Dewey, John. *The Public and Its Problems.* London: Allen and Unwin. 1927.

Direction de la Prévention des Pollutions et des Risques (DPPR). *Rapport d'activité.* Paris. 1994.

Douglas, Mary, and Wildavsky, Aaron. *Risk and Culture: An Essay on the Selec-tion of Technological and Environmental Dangers.* Berkeley: University of California Press. 1982.

Dubet, François, and Lapeyronnie, Didier. *Im Aus der Vorstädte. Der Zerfall der demokratischen Gesellschaft.* Stuttgart: Klett-Cotta. 1994.

Duhamel, Olivier. *Le pouvoir politique en France, la Ve République, vertus et limites.* Paris: Edition de Seuil. 1993.

Dunlap, Riley E. "Public Opinion and Environmental Policy." In: Lester, James P. (ed.). *Environmental Politics and Policy. Theories and Evidence.* Durham, N.C., and London: Duke University Press. 1995, pp. 63–114.

Dunn, James. "The French Highway Lobby. A Case Study in State-Society Rela-tions and Policy Making." *Comparative Politics.* 27/3. 1995, pp. 275–295.

Dyson, Kenneth. *The State in Western Europe. A Study of an Idea and Institution.* Oxford: Martin Robertson. 1980.

Eckstein, Harry. *A Theory of Stable Democracy.* Princeton: Center of Interna-tional Studies. 1961.

Edelman, Murray. *Politics as Symbolic Action.* New York: Academic Press. 1971.

Eder, Klaus. "The Rise of Counter-Culture Movements against Modernity: Nature as a New Field of Class Struggle." *Theory, Culture and Society.* 7. 1990, pp. 21–47.

Eder, Klaus. *The New Politics of Class. Social movements and Cultural Dynamics in Advanced Societies.* London: Sage. 1993.

Ellis, Richard J. *American Political Cultures.* New York: Oxford University Press. 1993.

Ellul, Jacques. *The Technological Society.* New York: Vintage. 1964.

ENDS (Environmental Data Services), and Allott, Keith. *Integrated Pollution*

Control—The First Three Years. London: Environmental Data Services. 1994.

Ewing, Keith D., and Gearty, Conor A. *Freedom under Thatcher.* Oxford: Oxford University Press. 1990.

Fielden, K. "1968–69, Samuel Smiles and Self-Help." *Victorian Studies.* 12, pp. 155–172.

Foley, Michael. *The Rise of British Presidency.* Manchester: Manchester University Press. 1993.

Foucault, Michel. *L'archéologie du savoir.* Paris: Gallimard. 1969.

Foucault, Michel. *L'ordre du discours.* Paris: Gallimard. 1971.

Foucault, Michel. *Surveiller et punir. La naissance de la prison.* Paris: Gallimard. 1975.

Foucault, Michel. *Politics, Philosophy, Culture. Interviews and Other Writings 1977–1984.* London: Routledge. 1988.

Frankel, E. "Corpuscular Optics and the Wave Theory of Light: The Science and Politics of a Revolution in Physics." *Social Studies of Science.* 6. 1976, pp. 141–184.

Frankel, Maurice. *The Social Audit Pollution Handbook.* London: Macmillan. 1978.

Geertz, Clifford. *The Interpretation of Cultures.* New York: Basic Books. 1973.

Gehlen, Arnold. *Der Mensch. Seine Natur und seine Stellung in der Welt.* 5th ed. Bonn: Athenäum. 1955.

Gehlen, Arnold. *Urmensch und Spätkultur. Philosophische Ergebnisse und Aussagen.* Bonn: Athenäum. 1956.

Gehlen, Arnold. *Die Seele im technischen Zeitalter.* Hamburg: Rohwolt. 1957.

Gehlen, Arnold. *Studien zur Anthropologie und Soziologie.* Neuwied-Berlin: Luchterhand. 1963.

Giddens, Anthony. *The Constitution of Society: Outline of the Theory of Structuration.* Cambridge: Polity Press. 1984.

Gillespie, Brendan, Eva, Dave, and Johnston, Ron. "Carcinogenic Risk Assessment in the United States and Great Britain. The Case of Aldrin/Dieldrin." *Social Studies of Science.* 9. 1979, pp. 265–301.

Glucksmann, André. *Les maîtres penseurs.* Paris: Grasset. 1977.

Göhler, Gerhard. "Politische Institutionen und ihr Kontext. Begriffliche und konzeptionelle Überlegungen zur Theorie politischer Institutionen." In: Göhler, Gerhard (ed). *Die Eigenart der Institutionen. Zum Profil politischer Institutionentheorie.* Baden-Baden: Nomos. 1994, pp. 19–46.

Goodwin, R. Kenneth. *One Billion Dollars of Influence: The Direct Marketing of Politics.* Chatam, N.J.: Chatam House. 1988.

Graziani, Paul. *Le nouveau pouvoir: essai sur la décentralisation.* Paris: A. Michel. 1985.

Green, Thomas Hill. *Prolegomena to Ethics.* Oxford: Clarendon. (1883) 1929.

Green, Thomas Hill. *Lectures on the Principles of Political Obligation and Other Writings.* Cambridge: Cambridge University Press. (1886) 1986.

Greenstein, Fred I. (ed.). *Leadership in the Modern Presidency.* Cambridge: Harvard University Press. 1990.

Grémion, Catherine, and Muller, Pierre. "De nouvelles elites locales?" *Esprit.* 1990, pp. 38–47.

Grémion, Pierre. *Le pouvoir périphérique. Bureaucrats et notables dans le système politique français.* Paris: Edition du Seuil. 1976.

Grémion, Pierre, and Worms, Jean-Pierre. *Les institutions régionales et la société locale.* Paris: Edition du Seuil. 1968.

Grimm, Dieter. "The Modern State: Continental Traditions." In: Kaufmann, Franz-Xaver (ed.). *The Public Sector—Challenge for Coordination and Learning.* Berlin: de Gruyter. 1991, pp. 117–139.

Gross, Peter. *Die Multioptionsgesellschaft.* Frankfurt a.M.: Suhrkamp. 1994.

Große, Ernst Ulrich, and Lüger, Heinz-Helmut. *Frankreich verstehen. Eine Einführung mit Vergleichen zu Deutschland.* Darmstadt: Wissenschaftliche Buchgesellschaft. 1993.

Grove-White, Robin. "Großbritannien (Politisches System und Umweltverbände)." In: Hey, Christian, and Brendle, Uwe (eds.) *Umweltverbände und EG.* Opladen: Westdeutscher Verlag. 1994, pp. 171–214.

Guéhenno, Jean-Marie. *Das Ende der Demokratie.* München and Zürich: Artemis and Winkler. 1994.

Habermas, Jürgen. *Technik und Wissenschaft als Ideologie.* Frankfurt a.M.: Suhrkamp. 1969.

Habermas, Jürgen. *Theorie des kommunikativen Handelns.* Frankfurt a.M.: Suhrkamp. 1981. (English translation: *Theory of Communicative Action.* Oxford: Polity Press. 1980.)

Habermas, Jürgen. *Der philosophische Diskurs der Moderne.* Frankfurt a.M.: Suhrkamp. 1985. (English translation: *Philosophical Discourse of Modernity.* Oxford: Polity Press. 1990.)

Habermas, Jürgen. *Faktizität und Geltung. Beiträge zur Diskurstheorie des Rechts und des demokratischen Rechtsstaats.* Frankfurt a.M.: Suhrkamp. 1992. (English translation: *Between Facts and Norms. Contributions to a Discourse Theory of Law and Democracy.* Cambridge: MIT Press. 1996.)

Habermas, Jürgen. *Die Einbeziehung des Anderen.* Frankfurt a.M.: Suhrkamp. 1996. (English translation: *The Inclusion of the Other.* Cambridge: MIT Press. 1998.)

Hanf, Kenneth, and Scharpf, Fritz W. (eds.). *Interorganizational Policy Making. Limits to Coordination and Central Control.* London: Sage. 1978.

Hanf, Kenneth, and Toonen, Theo A. J. (eds.). *Policy Implementation in Federal and Unitary Systems. Questions of Analysis and Design.* Dordrecht: Martinus Nijhoff. 1985.

Harrington, James. *The Political Writings.* New York: Liberal Arts Press. 1955.

Harrison, Richard D. "Who Do We Think We Are?" In: *Conservation News* No. 3–4, Winter 1977/78, pp. 2–13.

Hartz, Louis. *The Liberal Tradition in America.* New York: Harcourt, Brace, and World. 1955.

Haskell, Thomas L. (ed.). *The Authority of Experts. Studies in History and Theory.* Bloomington: Indiana University Press. 1984.

Heidenreich, Martin. "Verallgemeinerungsprobleme in der international vergleichenden Organisationsforschung." In: Heidenreich, Martin, and Schmidt, Gert (eds.). *International vergleichende Organisationsforschung. Fragestellungen, Methoden und Ergebnisse ausgewählter Untersuchungen.* Opladen: Westdeutscher Verlag. 1991, pp. 52–82.

Héritier, Adrienne. "Regulative Politik in der Europäischen Gemeinschaft: Die Verflechtung nationalstaatlicher Rationlitäten in der Luftreinhaltepolitik–Ein Vergleich zwischen Großbritannien und der Bundesrepublik Deutschland." In: Seibel, Wolfgang, and Benz, Arthur (eds.). *Regierungssystem und Verwaltungspolitik. Beiträge zu Ehren von Thomas Ellwein.* Opladen: Westdeutscher Verlag. 1993, pp. 52–82.

Héritier, Adrienne. "Umweltregulierung im Wandel. Regulierungsvielfalt und Möglichkeiten der Instrumentenwahl in der Europäischen Union." In: Hiller, Petra, and Krücken, Georg (eds.). *Risiko und Regulierung. Soziologische Beiträge zu Technikkontrolle und präventiver Umweltpolitik.* Frankfurt a. M.: Suhrkamp. 1997, pp. 176–94.

Héritier, Adrienne, Knill, Christopher, and Mingers, Susanne. *Ringing the Changes in Europe. Regulatory Competition and the Transformation of the State. Britain, France, Germany.* Berlin: de Gruyter. 1996.

Héritier, Adrienne, Mingers, Susanne, Knill, Christoph, and Becka, Martina. *Staatlichkeit in Europa: Ein regulativer Wettbewerb. Deutschland, Großbritannien und Frankreich in der Europäischen Union.* Opladen: Leske und Budrich. 1994.

Hobhouse, Leonard T. *Liberalism.* London: Williams and Norgate. (1911) 1964.

Holznagel, Bernd. *Konfliktlösung durch Verhandlungen.* Baden-Baden: Nomos. 1990.

Hume, David. *Enquiries concerning the Human Understanding and concerning the Principles of Morals.* Ed. L.A. Selby-Bigge. Oxford: Clarendon. (1748/1751) 1962.

Iltis, C. "The Leibnizian-Newtonian Debates: Natural Philosophy and Social Psychology." *The British Journal for the History of Science* . 6/24. 1973, pp. 343–377.

Immergut, Elen M. *Health politics : interests and institutions in Western Europe.* Cambridge: Cambridge University Press. 1992.

Ingram, Helen M., Colnic, David H., and Mann, Dean E. "Interest Groups and Environmental Policy." In: Lester, James P. (ed.). *Environmental Politics and Policy. Theories and Evidence.* Durham, N.C., and London: Duke University Press. 1995, pp. 115–145.

Jacob, Herbert. *Justice in America. Courts, Lawyers, and the Judicial Process.* Boston: Little, Brown. 1965.

Jänicke, Martin. "Erfolgsbedingungen von Umweltpolitik im internationalen Vergleich." *Zeitschrift für Umweltpolitik.* No.3. 1990, pp. 213–232.

Jänicke, Martin, and Weidner, Helmut. "Germany." In: Jänicke, Martin, and Weidner, Helmut (eds.). *National Environmental Policies. A Comparative Study of Capacity-Building.* Berlin: Springer. 1997a, pp. 133–156.

Jänicke, Martin, and Weidner, Helmut. "Summary: Global Environmental Policy Learning." In: Jänicke, Martin, and Weidner, Helmut (eds.). *National Environmental Policies. A Comparative Study of Capacity-Building*. Berlin: Springer. 1997b, pp. 299–313.

Jänicke, Martin, and Weidner, Helmut (eds.). *Successful Environmental Policy. A Critical Evaluation of 24 Cases*. Berlin: Edition Sigma. 1995.

Jänicke, Martin, and Weidner, Helmut (eds.). *National Environmental Policies. A Comparative Study of Capacity-Building*. Berlin: Springer. 1997.

Jasanoff, Sheila. "Contested Boundaries in Policy-Relevant Science." *Social Studies of Science*. 17. 1987, pp. 195–230.

Jasanoff, Sheila. *The Fifth Branch. Science Advisers as Policymakers*. Cambridge: Harvard University Press. 1990.

Jasanoff, Sheila. *Science at the Bar. Law, Science, and Technology in America*. Cambridge: Harvard University Press. 1995.

Jauß, Claudia. "Länderbericht USA." In: Münch, Richard et al. *Zweiter Arbeitsbericht des Projekts "Die gesellschaftliche Kontrolle technisch produzierter Gefahren. Eine vergleichende Studie zu Kontrollverfahren in Deutschland, USA, Frankreich und England auf der Basis von vier theoretischen Modellen*." Düsseldorf: unpublished report for the Deutsche Forschungsgemeinschaft. 1996, pp. 253–336.

Jenkins, Peter. *Mrs. Thatcher's Revolution. The Ending of the Socialist Era*. Cambridge: Harvard University Press. 1987.

Jessop, Bob. *Traditionalism, Conservatism and British Political Culture*. London: Allen and Unwin. 1974.

Joas, Hans. *Die Entstehung der Werte*. Frankfurt a.M.: Suhrkamp. 1997.

Johnson, Terry. "Expertise and the State." In: Gane, M., and Johnson, T. (eds.). *Foucault's New Domains*. London: Routledge. 1993, pp. 139–152.

Jones, G. W. "The Prime Minister's Power." *Parliamentary Affairs*. 18. 1965, pp. 167–185.

Judge, David. "Parliament and Industry: Bridging the Gap." *Parliamentary Affairs*. 45/1. 1992, pp. 51–65.

Kahn, Paul W. "Reason and Will in the Origins of American Constitutionalism." *Yale Law Journal*. 98. 1989, pp. 449–517.

Kant, Immanuel. "Beantwortung der Frage: Was ist Aufklärung?" In: Kant, Immanuel. *Werke in sechs Bänden*. Vol. 6. Ed. Wilhelm Weischedel. Frankfurt a.M.: Insel Verlag. (1784) 1964, pp. 53–61.

Kant, Immanuel. "Kritik der praktischen Vernunft." In: Kant, Immanuel. *Werke in sechs Bänden*. Vol. 4, Ed. Wilhelm Weischedel. Frankfurt a.M.: Insel Verlag. (1788) 1956, pp. 103–302.

Kant, Immanuel. "Über den Gemeinspruch: Das mag in der Theorie richtig sein, taugt aber nicht für die Praxis." In: Kant, Immanuel. *Werke in sechs Bänden*. Vol. 6 Ed. Wilhelm Weischedel. Frankfurt a.M.: Insel Verlag. (1793) 1964, pp. 125-172.

Kant, Immanuel. "Die Metaphysik der Sitten." In: Kant, Immanuel. *Werke in sechs Bänden*. Vol. 4 Ed. Wilhelm Weischedel. Frankfurt a.M.: Insel Verlag.

(1797) 1956, pp. 303-643.

Kavanagh, Dennis. "The Referential English: A Comparative Critique." *Government and Opposition*. 6. 1971, pp. 333–360.

Kavanagh, Dennis. *Thatcherism and British Politics. The End of Consensus?* Oxford: Oxford University Press. 1987.

Keck, Otto. *Information, Macht und gesellschaftliche Rationalität*. Baden-Baden: Nomos. 1993.

Keeler, John T. S. *The Politics of Neocorporatism in France. Farmers, the State, and Agricultural Policy-Making in the Fifth Republic*. New York, and Oxford: Oxford University Press. 1987.

Kempf, Udo. "Frankreichs Regierungssystem, Präsident-Regierung-Parlament." In: Wehling, Hans-Georg (ed.). *Frankreich. Eine politische Landeskunde*. Stuttgart u.a.: Kohlhammer. 1989, pp. 105–139.

Kepel, Gilles. *Les banlieues de l'Islam*. Paris: Edition du Seuil. 1987.

Kepel, Gilles. *A l'ouest d'Allah*. Paris: Edition du Seuil. 1994.

Kessler, Marie-Christine. *Les Grands Corps de l'État*. Paris: Presses de la Fondation National des Sciences Politiques. 1986.

Kiersch, Gerhard, and von Oppeln, Sabine. *Kernenergiekonflikt in Frankreich und Deutschland*. Berlin: Wiss. Autoren-Verlag. 1983.

Kimmel, Adolf. "Innenpolitische Entwicklungen und Probleme in Frankreich." *Aus Politik und Zeitgeschichte*. 47–48. 1991, pp. 3–15.

King, Desmond. "Government Beyond Whitehall." In: Dunleavy, Patrick, Gamble, Andrew, Holliday, Ian, and Peele, Gilian (eds.). *Developments in British Politics*. London: Macmillan. 1993.

Kistenmacher, Hans, Marcou, Gérard, and Clev, Hans-Günther. *Raumordnung und raumbezogene Politik in Frankreich und Deutschland*. Hannover and Paris: ARL. 1994.

Knill, Christoph. *Staatlichkeit im Wandel. Großbritannien im Spannungsfeld innenpolitischer Reformen und europäischer Integration*. Wiesbaden: Deutscher Universitätsverlag. 1995.

Knoepfel, Peter, and Weidner, Helmut. "Normbildung und Implementation: Interessenberücksichtigungsmuster in Programmstrukturen von Luftreinhaltepolitiken." In: Mayntz, Renate (ed.). *Implementation politischer Programme*. Königstein/Ts.: Anton Hain. 1980, pp. 82–104.

Knoepfel, Peter, and Weidner, Helmut. "Die Durchsetzbarkeit planerischer Ziele auf dem Gebiet der Luftreinhaltung aus der Sicht der Politikwissenschaft. Ergebnisse einer internationalen Vergleichsuntersuchung." *ZfU*. 1983, pp. 87ff.

Knoepfel, Peter, and Weidner, Helmut. *Luftreinhaltepolitik (stationäre Quellen) im internationalen Vergleich*. Vol. 4: *Frankreich*. Berlin: Edition Sigma. 1985.

Kraft, Michael E. "Congress and Environmental Policy." In: Lester, James P. (ed.). *Environmental Politics and Policy. Theories and Evidence*. Durham, N.Y. and London: Duke University Press. 1995, pp. 168–205.

Kraft, Michael E. *Environmental Policy and Politics. Toward the Twenty-First Century*. New York: HarperCollins College. 1996.

Kraft, Michael E., and Vig, Norman J. "Environmental Policy from the 1970s to the 1990s: Continuity and Change." In: Vig, Norman J., and Kraft, Michael E. (eds.). *Environmental Policy in the 1990s. Toward a New Agenda*. Washington, D.C.: Congressional Quarterly Press. 1994, pp. 3–29.

Krönig, Jürgen. "Der neue Zuchtmeister." *DIE ZEIT*. 11. July 1997a, p. 4.

Krönig, Jürgen. "Schwindelgefühle in Swinging Britain. Die Tories haben das Land modernisiert, Labour verspricht eine neue Moral." *DIE ZEIT*. 18. April 1997b, pp. 9–10.

Kuhn, Thomas S. *The Structure of Scientific Revolutions*. Chicago: University of Chicago Press. 1962.

Kukawka, Pierre. "Dezentralisierung in Frankreich: Bilanz und Perspektiven." *Aus Politik und Zeitgeschichte*. 32. 1993, pp. 17–23.

Kunig, Philip. *Das Rechtsstaatsprinzip*. Tübingen: Mohr Siebeck. 1986.

Kurth, Markus. "Länderbericht Großbritannien." In: Münch, Richard, et al. *Zweiter Arbeitsbericht des Projekts "Die gesellschaftliche Kontrolle technisch produzierter Gefahren. Eine vergleichende Studie zu Kontrollverfahren in Deutschland, USA, Frankreich und England auf der Basis von vier theoretischen Modellen"* Düsseldorf: unpublished report for the Deutsche Forschungsgemeinschaft. 1996, pp. 413–551.

Kwa, Chunglin. "Representation of Nature Mediating between Technology and Science Policy. The Case of the International Biological Programme." *Social Studies of Science*, 17. 1987, pp. 413–442.

Lahusen, Christian. *The Rhetoric of Moral Protest. Public Campaigns, Celebrity Endorsement and Political Mobilization*. Berlin, and New York: Walter de Gruyter. 1996.

Lahusen, Christian. "The good government. Cooperative Environmental Regulation in a Comparative Perspective." *European Environment*. 10/6. 2000 (in press).

Lahusen, Christian, and Jauß, Claudia. *Lobbying als Beruf. Interessengruppen in der Europäischen Union*. Baden-Baden: Nomos Verlagsgesellschaft. 2000.

Landy, Marc K., Roberts, Marc J., and Thomas, Stephen R. *The Environmental Protection Agency. Asking the Wrong Questions. From Nixon to Clinton*. New York, and Oxford: Oxford University Press. 1994.

Larson, Magali S. "The Production of Expertise and the Constitution of Expert Power." In: Haskell, Thomas L. (ed.). *The Authority of Experts. Studies in History and Theory*. Bloomington: Indiana University Press. 1984, pp. 28–80.

Larson, Magali S. "In the Matter of Experts and Professionals, or How Impossible It Is to Leave Nothing Unsaid." In: Torstendahl, Rolf, and Burrage, Michael (eds.). *The Formation of Professions. Knowledge, State and Strategy*. London: Sage. 1990, pp. 24–50.

Lascoumes, Pierre. *L'Éco-pouvoir, Environnement et Politiques*. Paris: La Découverte. 1994.

Lascoumes, Pierre, et al. *L'Environnement entre Nature et Politique, un Patchwork mal Cousu. Les Images de l'Environnement et de ses Politiques dans la Presse*, CNRS. Paris. 1993.

Laski, Harold. *Parliamentary Government in England.* London: Allen and Unwin. 1938.

Latour, Bruno. *Les microbes: guerre et paix suivies d'irréductions.* Paris: Métailié. 1984.

Laumann, Edward O., and Knoke, David. "Policy Networks of the Organizational State: Collective Action in the National Energy and Health Domains." In: Perrucci, Robert, and Potter, Harry R. (eds.). *Networks of Power. Organizational Actors at the National, Corporate, and Community Levels.* New York: Aldine de Gruyter. 1989, pp. 17–55.

Lehmbruch, Gerhard. *Proporzdemokratie. Politisches System und politische Kultur in der Schweiz und in Österreich.* Tübingen: Mohr Siebeck. 1967.

Lehmbruch, Gerhard. "Concertation and the Structure of Corporatist Networks." In: Goldthorpe, John H. (ed.). *Order and Conflict in Contemporary Capitalism.* Oxford: Clarendon Press. 1984, pp. 60-80.

Lehmbruch, Gerhard, and Schmitter, Philippe (eds.). *Patterns of Corporatist Policy making.* London: Sage. 1982.

Lester, James P. (ed.). *Environmental Politics and Policy. Theories and Evidence.* Durham, N.Y., and London: Duke University Press. 1995a.

Lester, James P. "Federalism and State Environmental Policy." In: Lester, James P. (ed.). *Environmental Politics and Policy. Theories and Evidence.* Durham, N.Y. ,and London: Duke University Press. 1995b, pp. 39–60.

Lévy, Bernard-Henri. *La barbarie à visage humain.* Paris: Grasset. 1977.

Lijphart, Arend. *The Politics of Accommodation—Pluralism and Democracy in the Netherlands.* Berkeley: University of California Press. 1968.

Lipnack, Jessica, and Stamps, Jeffrey. *Networking: The First Report and Directory.* New York: Dolphin Books. 1991.

Little, David. *Religion, Order, and Law. A Study in Prerevolutionary England.* Oxford: Basil Blackwell. 1969.

Locke, John. *Two Treatises on Government. The Works.* Vol. 5. Aalen: Scientia. (1690) 1963.

Lowe, Philip, and Ward, Stephen. *British Environmental Policy and Europe. Politics and Policy in Transition.* London: Routledge. 1998.

Luhmann, Niklas. *Politische Theorie im Wohlfahrtsstaat.* München-Wien: Günther Olzog Verlag. 1981. (English translation: *Political Theory in the Welfare State.* Berlin: de Gruyter. 1990.)

Luhmann, Niklas. *Soziale Systeme. Grundriß einer allgemeinen Theorie.* Frankfurt a.M.: Suhrkamp. 1984. (English translation: *Social Systems.* Cambridge: Stanford University Press. 1989.)

Luhmann, Niklas. *Ökologische Kommunikation.* Opladen: Westdeutscher Verlag. 1986. (English translation: *Ecological Communication.* Cambridge: Polity Press. 1989.)

Luhmann, Niklas. *Politische Steuerung: Ein Diskussionsbeitrag.* Politische Vierteljahresschrift 30. 1989, pp. 4–9.

Luhmann, Niklas. *Die Gesellschaft der Gesellschaft.* 2 vols. Frankfurt a.M.: Suhrkamp. 1997.

MacIntyre, Alasdaire. *Der Verlust der Tugend. Zur moralischen Krise der Gegenwart.* Frankfurt a.M. and New York: Campus. 1987.

Mackintosh, John. *The British Cabinet.* London: Methuen. 1977.

Madison, James. "Federalist No. 10." In: Hamilton, Alexander, Madison, James, and Jay, John. *The Federalist Papers.* Ed. C. Rossiter. New York: Mentor. (1787/1788) 1961, pp. 77–84.

Mai, Manfred. *Die technologische Provokation. Beiträge zur Technikbewertung in Politik und Wirtschaft.* Berlin: Edition Sigma. 1994.

Majone, Giandomenico. "Science and Trans-Science in Standard Setting." *Science, Technology and Human Values.* 9/1. 1984, pp. 15–22.

Majone, Giandomenico (ed.). *Regulating Europe.* London: Routledge, 1996a.

Majone, Giandomenico. "Regulatory Legitimacy". In: Majone, Giandomenico (ed.). *Regulating Europe.* London: Routledge, 1996b, pp. 284–301.

March, James G., and Olsen, Johan P. *Rediscovering Institutions. The Organizational Basis of Politics.* London: Free Press. 1989.

Marsh, I. "Interest Groups and Policy making: A New Role for Select Committees?" *Parliamentary Affairs.* 1986, pp. 469–489.

Martinot-Hoffmann, Vincent "Frankreichs Parteiensystem nach den Parlamentswahlen." *Aus Politik und Zeitgeschichte.* 32. 1993, pp. 10–16.

Maynard, Douglas N. *Inside Plea Bargaining. The Language of Negotiation.* New York: Plenum. 1984.

Mayntz, Renate. "Networks, Issues, and Games: Multiorganizational Interactions in the Restructuring of a National Research System." In: Scharpf, Fritz W. (ed.). *Games in Hierarchies and Networks. Analytical and Empirical Approaches to the Study of Governance Institutions.* Frankfurt a.M.: Campus, 1993, pp. 189–210.

McCormick, John. *British Politics and the Environment.* London: Earthscan. 1991

McCrea, Frances B., and Markle, Gerald E. "The Extrogen Replacement Controversy in the U.S.A. and U.K.: Different Answers to the Same Question?" *Social Studies of Science.* 14. 1984, pp. 1–26.

McDonald, Forrest. *Novus Ordo Seclorum: The Intellectual Origins of the Constitution.* Lawrence: University Press of Kansas. 1985.

McFarland, Andrew W. *Public Interest Lobbies.* Washington, D.C.: American Enterprise Institute. 1976.

McFarland, Andrew W. *Common Cause: Lobbying in the Public Interest.* Chatam, N.J.: Chatam House. 1984.

McSpadden, Lettie. "The Courts and Environmental Policy." In: Lester, James P. (ed.). *Environmental Politics and Policy. Theories and Evidence.* Durham, N.Y., and London: Duke University Press. 1995, pp. 242–274.

Meier, Kenneth J. *Regulation. Politics, Bureaucracy and Economics.* New York: St. Martin's Press. 1985.

Mendras, Henri, and Cole, Alistaire. *Social Change in Modern France.* Cambridge: Cambridge University Press. 1991.(French original: La *Seconde Révolution française.* Paris: Gallimard. 1988.)

Mény, Yves. "La république des fiefs." *Pouvoir*. 60. 1992.

Mény, Yves. *Politique comparée. Les démocraties: Allemagne, États-Unis, France, Grande-Bretagne, Italie*. 4th edition. Paris: Montchrestien. 1993.

Messner, Frank. "Kontinuität und Wandel in der Umweltpolitik der USA am Beispiel der Gesetzgebung zur Luftreinhalt." *Zeitschrift für angewandte Umweltforschung*. 6/1. 1993, pp. 67–80.

Mewes, Horst. *Einführung in das politische System der USA*. Heidelberg: C. F. Müller Juristischer Verlag. 1990.

Meyer-Abich, Klaus M. *Wege zum Frieden mit der Natur. Praktische Naturphilosophie für die Umweltpolitik*. München u.a.: Hanser. 1984.

Michelman, Frank I. "The Supreme Court 1985 Term, Foreword." *Harvard Law Review*. 100. 1986, pp. 4–77.

Michelman, Frank I. "Law's Republic." *The Yale Law Journal*. 97. 1988, pp. 1493–1537.

Michelman, Frank I. "Conceptions of Democracy in American Constitutional Argument: Voting Rights." *Florida Law Review*. 41. 1989, pp. 443–490.

Mill, John Stuart. *Essays on Politics and Society. Collected Works*. Vols. 18, 19. London: Routledge and Kegan Paul. 1977.

Miller, Arthur. *The Crucible. A Play in Four Acts*. Harmondsworth: Penguin Books. (1953) 1968.

Miller, Perry. *The New England Mind. From Colony to Province*. Cambridge: Harvard University Press. 1954.

Miller, Perry. *Errand into the Wilderness*. Cambridge: Harvard University Press. 1956.

Mitchel, James. "Britain: Privatisation as Myth?" In: Richardson, Jeremy J. (ed.). *Privatisation and Deregulation in Canada and Britain*. Aldershot: Dartmouth. 1990, pp. 14–37.

Moore, David C. *The Politics of Deference*. Hassocks: Harvester. 1976.

Moore, Gwen, and Whitt, J. Allen (eds.). *The Political Consequences of Networks*. Greenwich: Jai Press. 1992.

Müller-Brandeck-Bocquet, Gisela. "Dezentralisierung in Frankreich—Ein innenpolitischer Neuanfang." *Die Verwaltung*. 23. 1990, pp. 49–82.

Münch, Richard. *Theorie des Handelns*. Frankfurt a.M.: Suhrkamp. (1982) 1988. (English translation: *Theory of Action. Towards a New Synthesis Going beyond Parsons*. London: Routledge. 1987.)

Münch, Richard. "Autopoiesis by Definition." *Cardozo Law Review*. 13/5. 1992, pp. 1463–1471.

Münch, Richard. *Die Kultur der Moderne*. 2 vols. Frankfurt a.M.: Suhrkamp. (1986) 1993a.

Münch, Richard. *Das Projekt Europa. Zwischen Nationalstaat, regionaler Autonomie und Weltgesellschaft*. Frankfurt a.M.: Suhrkamp. 1993b.

Münch, Richard. "Politik und Nichtpolitik. Politische Steuerung als schöpferischer Prozeß." *Kölner Zeitschrift für Soziologie und Sozialpsychologie*. 46. 1994, pp. 381–405.

Münch, Richard. *Dynamik der Kommunikationsgesellschaft*. Frankfurt a.M.:

Suhrkamp. 1995.

Münch, Richard. *Risikopolitik*. Frankfurt a. M.: Suhrkamp. 1996.

Münch, Richard. *Globale Dynamik, lokale Lebenswelten. Der schwierige Weg in die Weltgesellschaft*. Frankfurt a.M.: Suhrkamp. 1998.

Murley, Loveday (ed.). *Clean Air around the World. National Approaches to Air Pollution Control*. Berlin: Springer. 1995.

Murphy, Raymond. *Social Closure. The Theory of Monopolization and Exclusion*. Oxford: Clarendon Press. 1988.

Nash, Roderick. "Rounding Out the American Revolution. Ethical Extension and the New Environmentalism." In: Dunlap, Riley E., and Mertig, Angela G. (eds.). *American Environmentalism. The U.S. Environmental Movement 1970–1990*. New York: Taylor and Francis. 1992, pp. 242–255.

Nettl, John P. "The State as a Conceptual Variable." *World Politics*. No. 7. 1968, pp. 559–592.

Neumann, Wolfgang, and Uterwedde, Henrik. *Industriepolitik. Ein deutsch-französischer Vergleich*. Opladen: Leske + Budrich. 1986.

Neustadt, Richard E. *Presidential Power and the Modern Presidents*. New York: Free Press. 1990.

Oeyen, Else (ed.). *Comparative Methodology. Theory and Practice in International Social Research*. London: Sage. 1990.

Offe, Claus. *Disorganized Capitalism. Contemporary Transformations of Work and Politics*. Cambridge: MIT Press. 1985.

O'Leary, Rosemary. "The Progressive Ratcheting of Environmental Laws: Impact on Public Management." *Policy Studies Review*. 12/3–4. 1993, pp. 118–136.

O'Riordan, Timothy. "The Role of Environmental Quality Objectives in the Politics of Pollution Control." In: O'Riordan, Timothy, and D'Arge, Ralph (eds.). *Progress in Resource Management and Environmental Planning*. Vol. 1. Chichester: John Wiley. 1979, pp. 221–258.

O'Riordan, Timothy, and Cameron, James (eds.). *Interpreting the Precautionary Principle*. London: Earthscan. 1994.

O'Riordan, Timothy, and Weale, Albert. "Administrative Reorganization and Policy Change: The Case of Her Majesty's Inspectorate of Pollution." *Public Administration*. 67. Autumn 1989, pp. 277–294.

Ostrom, Elmar. "Institutionelle Arrangements und das Dilemma der Allmende." In: Glagow, Manfred, Willke, Helmut, and Wiesenthal, Helmut (eds.). *Gesellschaftliche Steuerungsrationalität und partikulare Handlungsstrategien*. Pfaffenweiler: Centaurus-Verlagsgesellschaft. 1989, pp. 199–234.

O'Toole, Lawrence J. "Multiorganizational Policy Implementation: Some Limitations and Possibilities for Rational-Choice Contributions." In: Scharpf, Fritz W. (ed.). *Games in Hierarchies and Networks. Analytical and Empirical Approaches to the Study of Governance Institutions*. Frankfurt a.M.: Campus. 1993, pp. 27–64.

Parsons, Talcott. *Politics and Social Structure*. New York: Free Press. 1969.

Parsons, Talcott. *The System of Modern Societies*. Englewood Cliffs, N.J.: Prentice-Hall. 1971.

Perry, Allen H. *Environmental Hazards in the British Isles.* London: Allen and Unwin. 1981.

Petracca, Mark P. *The Politics of Interest: Interest Groups Transform.* Boulder, Colo.: Westview Press. 1992.

Pickering, Andrew. "The Role of Interests in High-Energy Physics: The Choice between Charm and Colour." In: Knorr, K. D., Krohn, R. and Whiteley, R. (eds.). *The Social Process of Scientific Investigation. Sociology of the Sciences: A Yearbook 4.* Dordrecht u. a.: Reidel. 1990, pp. 107–138.

Pizzorno, Alesandro. "On Rationality and Democratic Choice." In: Birnbaum, Pierre, and Leca, Jean (eds.). *Individualism. Theories and Methods.* Oxford: Clarendon Press. 1990, pp. 295–331.

Pizzorno, Alesandro. *Le radici della politica assoluta.* Milano: Feltrinelli. 1993.

Pocock, John G. A. *The Machiavellian Moment. Florentine Political Thought and the Atlantic Republican Tradition.* Princeton, N.J.: Princeton University Press. 1975.

Pocock, John G. A. "Virtues, Rights, and Manners." *Political Theory.* 9. 1981, pp. 353–368.

Prost, Antoine. *Education. Société et politiques. Une histoire de l'enseignement en France, de 1945 à nos jours.* Paris: Edition du Seuil. 1992.

Pufendorf, Samuel von. *Über die Verfassung des deutschen Reiches.* Ed. H. Breßlau. Berlin: Reimar Hobbing. (1667) 1922.

Ragin, Charles I. (ed.). "Issues and Alternatives in Comparative Social Research." *International Journal of Comparative Sociology.* 32/1–2. 1991, pp. .

Ramm, Thilo (ed.). *Der Frühsozialismus. Ausgewählte Quellentexte.* Stuttgart: Kröner. 1956.

Rawls, John. *A Theory of Justice.* Cambridge: Harvard University Press. 1971.

Rawls, John. *Political Liberalism.* New York: Columbia University Press. 1993.

Rehbinder, Eckard. *Das Vorsorgeprinzip im internationalen Vergleich.* Düsseldorf: Werner-Verlag. 1991.

Renan, Ernest. "Qu'est-ce qu'une nation? Conférence faite en Sorbonne le 11 Mars 1882." In: Ernest Renan. *Œuvres complètes.* Vol. 1. Paris: Calman-Levy. 1947, pp. 887–906.

Renn, Ortwin. "Style of Using Scientific Expertise. A Comparative Framework." *Science and Public Policy.* 22/3. 1995, pp. 147–156.

Rest, Alfred. *Luftverschmutzung und Haftung in Europa. Anspruchsmöglichkeiten auf nationaler, internationaler und völkerrechtlicher Ebene.* Kehl: N. P. Engel Verlag. 1986.

Reutter, Werner. *Korporatismustheorien. Kritik, Vergleich, Perspektiven.* Frankfurt a.M.: Peter Lang. 1991.

Ricci, David M. *The Transformation of American Politics. The New Washington and the Rise of Think Tanks.* New Haven, Conn., and London: Yale University Press. 1993.

Richardson, Jeremy. *Government and Groups in Britain: Changing Styles.* Strathclyde Paper on Government and Politics No. 69, University of Strathclyde. Glasgow. 1990.

Richardson, Jeremy, Gustafsson, Gunnel, and Jordan, Grant. "The Concept of Policy Style". In: Richardson, Jeremy (ed.). *Policy Styles in Western Europe*. London: Allen and Unwin. 1991, pp. 1–16.

Richardson, Jeremy, and Jordan, Grant. "Policy Communities. The British and European Policy Style." *Policy Studies Journal*. 11/4. 1983, pp. 603–615.

Richter, Melvin. *The Politics of Conscience. T. H. Green and His Age*. Lanham, Md.: University Press of America. (1964) 1983.

Rootes, Christopher A. *The Green Challenge: The Development of Green Parties in Europe*. London: Routledge. 1995.

Rose, Richard, and Kavanagh, Dennis. "The Monarchy in Political Culture." *Comparative Politics*. No. 7. 1976, pp. 548–576.

Rosenbaum, Walter A. "The Bureaucracy and Environmental Policy." In: Lester, James P. (ed.). *Environmental Politics and Policy. Theories and Evidence*. Durham, N.Y., and London: Duke University Press. 1995, pp. 206–241.

Rossi, Hugh. "Parliamentary Select Committees." In: Macrory, Richard (ed.). *Environmental Challenges—The Institutional Dimension*. London: International U.K. 1990, pp. 29–34.

Rothenberg, Lawrence S. *Linking Citizens to Government: Interest Group Politics at Common Cause*. New York: Cambridge University Press. 1992.

Rothgang, Heinz. *Die Friedens- und Umweltbewegung in Großbritannien*. Wiesbaden: Deutscher Universitätsverlag. 1990.

Rousseau, Jean-Jacques. "Discours sur l'origine et les fondements de l'inégalité." In: Rousseau, Jean-Jacques. *Œuvres complètes* Vol. 3. Ed. B. Gagnebin and M. Raymond. Paris: Gallimard. (1754) 1964a, pp. 109–237.

Rousseau, Jean-Jacques. "Du contrat social ou principes du droit politique." In: Rousseau, Jean-Jacques. *Œuvres complètes*. Vol. 3. Ed. B. Gagnebin and M. Raymond. Paris: Gallimard. (1762) 1964b, pp. 347–470.

Royal Commission on Environmental Pollution. *The First Report*. Cmnd. 4585. London: HMSO. 1971.

Royal Commission on Environmental Pollution. *Fourth Report. Pollution Control: Progress and Problems*. Cmnd. 5780. London: HMSO. 1974.

Royal Commission on Environmental Pollution. *5th Report. Air Pollution Control. An Integrated Approach*. London. 1976.

Royal Commission on Environmental Pollution. *10th Report. Tackling Pollution—Experience and Prospects*. London. 1984.

Royal Commission on Environmental Pollution. *12th Report. Best Practicable Environmental Option*. London. 1988.

Royal Commission on Environmental Pollution. *18th Report. Transport and the Environment*. London. 1994.

Rucht, Dieter. "Gegenöffentlichkeit und Gegenexperten: Zur Institutionalisierung des Widerspruches in Politik und Recht." *Zeitschrift für Rechtssoziologie*. 9. 1988, pp. 290–305.

Rüschemeyer, Dietrich. *Lawyers and Their Society. A Comparative Study of the Legal Profession in Germany and in the United States*. Cambridge: Harvard University Press. 1973.

Rüschemeyer, Dietrich. "Comparing Legal Professions Cross-Nationally: From a Professions-Centered to a State-Centered Approach. Law and Social Inquiry." *The Journal of the American Bar Foundation.* No. 3. 1986, pp. 415–446.

Rüschemeyer, Dietrich. "Different Methods—Contradictory Results? Research on Development and Democracy." *International Journal of Comparative Sociology.* 32/1–2. 1991, pp. 9–38.

Sabatier, Paul A., and Hanf, Kenneth. "Strategic Interaction, Learning and Policy Evolution: A Synthetic Model." In: Hanf, Kenneth, and Toonen, Theo A. J. (eds.). *Policy Implementation in Federal and Unitary Systems. Questions of Analysis and Design.* Dordrecht: Martinus Nighoff. 1985, pp. 301–333.

Sabato, Larry J. *PAC Power: Inside the World of Political Action Committees.* New York: Norton. 1984.

Saint-Simon, Claude-Henri de. "Doctrine de Saint-Simon. Deuxième année." In: Saint-Simon, Claude-Henri de. *Œuvres de Saint-Simon et d'Enfantin.* Vol. 42. Paris: E. Dentu. 1865–1878, pp. 149–432.

Saint-Simon, Claude-Henri de. *Doctrine de Saint-Simon. Première année.* Ed. C. Bougléand and E. Halévy. Paris: Mr. Rivière. 1924.

Salomon-Delatour, Gottfried (ed.). *Die Lehre Saint-Simons.* Neuwied: Luchterhand. 1962.

Sandel, Michael. *Liberalism and the Limits of Justice.* Cambridge, Mass.: Cambridge University Press. 1982.

Sartre, Jean-Paul. *Marxismus und Existenzialismus. Versuch einer Methodik.* Reinbek bei Hamburg: Rowohlt. 1964.

Scharpf, Fritz W. *Die politischen Kosten des Rechtsstaats.* Tübingen: Mohr Siebeck. 1970.

Scharpf, Fritz W. "Politische Steuerung und Politische Institutionen." *Politische Vierteljahresschrift.* 30/1. 1989, pp. 10–21.

Scharpf, Fritz W. "Die Handlungsfähigkeit des Staates am Ende des zwanzigsten Jahrhunderts." In: *Politische Vierteljahresschrift.* 32. 1991, pp. 621–634.

Scharpf, Fritz W. "Einführung: Zur Theorie von Verhandlungssystemen." In: Benz, Arthur., Scharpf, Fritz W., and Zintl, Reinhard (eds.). *Horizontale Politikverflechtung. Zur Theorie von Verhandlungssystemen.* Frankfurt a.M.: Campus. 1992a, pp. 11–27.

Scharpf, Fritz W. "Koordination durch Verhandlungssysteme: Analytische Konzepte und institutionelle Lösungen." In: Benz, Arthur., Scharpf, Fritz W., and Zintl, Reinhard (eds.). *Horizontale Politikverflechtung. Zur Theorie von Verhandlungssystemen.* Frankfurt a.M.: Campus. 1992b, pp. 51–96.

Scharpf, Fritz W. "Coordination in Hierarchies and Networks." In: Scharpf, Fritz W. (ed.). *Games in Hierarchies and Networks. Analytical and Empirical Approaches to the Study of Governance Institutions.* Frankfurt a.M.: Campus. 1993a, pp. 125–165.

Scharpf, Fritz W. (ed.). *Games in Hierarchies and Networks. Analytical and Empirical Approaches to the Study of Governance Institutions.* Frankfurt a.M.: Campus. 1993b.

Scharpf, Fritz W. "Games in Hierarchies and Networks: Introduction." In:

Scharpf, Fritz W. (ed.). *Games in Hierarchies and Networks. Analytical and Empirical Approaches to the Study of Governance Institutions.* Frankfurt a.M.: Campus. 1993c, pp. 7–23.

Scharpf, Fritz W. "Positive und negative Koordination in Verhandlungssystemen." *Politische Vierteljahresschrift. Sonderband 24.* 1993d, pp. 57–83.

Scharpf, Fritz W. "Demokratische Politik in der internationalisierten Ökonomie." *Working Paper 97/9.* Köln: Max-Planck-Institut für Gesellschaftsforschung. 1997.

Schelsky, Helmut. *Ortsbestimmung der deutschen Soziologie.* Düsseldorf: Diederichs. 1959.

Schelsky, Helmut. *Auf der Suche nach Wirklichkeit. Gesammelte Aufsätze.* Düsseldorf: Diederichs. 1965.

Scheuner, Ulrich. "Begriff und Entwicklung des Rechtsstaats." In: Dombois, H., and Wilkens, E. (eds.). *Macht und Recht. Beiträge zur Lutherischen Staatslehre der Gegenwart.* Berlin: Luthersches Verlagshaus. 1956, pp. 76–88.

Schlozman, Kay, and Tierney, John. *Organized Interests and American Democracy.* New York: Harper and Row. 1986.

Schluchter, Wolfgang *Aspekte bürokratischer Herrschaft.* München. List. 1972.

Schmalz-Bruns, Rainer. *Reflexive Demokratie.* Baden-Baden: Nomos. 1995.

Schmidt-Assmann, Eberhard. "Der Rechtsstaat." In: Isensee, J., and Kirchhoff, P. (eds.). *Handbuch des Staatsrechts.* Vol. 1. Heidelberg: Müller. 1987, pp. 987–1043.

Schmitt, Karl. "Die politischen Eliten der V. Republik: Beharrung und Wandel." *Aus Politik und Zeitgeschichte.* 47–48. 1991, pp. 26–36.

Schnabel, Fritz. "Politik ohne Politiker." In: Wollmann, H. (ed.). *Politik im Dickicht der Bürokratie. Leviathan Sonderheft 3.* Opladen: Westdeutscher Verlag. 1979, pp. 49–70.

Schulze-Fielitz, Helmuth, and Goßwein, Christoph. "Bundesgesetzgebung als Prozeß." In: *Aus Politik und Zeitgeschichte.* 36–37. 1991, pp. 18–26.

Schumann, Karl F. *Der Handel mit Gerechtigkeit.* Frankfurt a.M.: Suhrkamp. 1977.

Shils, Edward A. *The Torment of Secrecy.* Glencoe, Ill.: Free Press. 1956.

Short, John Rennie. *Imagined Country. Society, Culture and Environment.* London: Routledge. 1991.

Simmel, Georg. "Der Begriff und die Tragödie der Kultur." In: Simmel, Georg. *Hauptprobleme der Philosophie/Philosophische Kultur. Gesammelte Essays.* Frankfurt a.M.: Suhrkamp. 1996, pp. 385–416.

Smiles, Samuel. *Self-Help, with Illustrations of Conduct and Perseverance.* London: Routledge. [1859] 1925.

Smith, Adam. *The Theory of Moral Sentiments.* New York: Bohn. (1759) 1966.

Smith, Martin, Marsh, David, and Richards, David. "Central Government Departments and the Policy Process." *Public Administration.* 71. 1993, pp. 567–594.

Smith, Steven S., and Deering, Christopher J. "Committees in Congress." *Congressional Quarterly.* 1984, pp. 125–165.

Sorauf, Frank. *Money in American Elections.* Boston: Scott, Foresman. 1988.

Spencer, Herbert. *The Principles of Sociology.* Vols. 1–3. Westport, Conn.: Greenwood Press. (1897–1906) 1975.

Stark, Carsten. "Länderbericht Bundesrepublik Deutschland." In: Münch, Richard, et al. *Zweiter Arbeitsbericht des Projekts "Die gesellschaftliche Kontrolle technisch produzierter Gefahren. Eine vergleichende Studie zu Kontrollverfahren in Deutschland, USA, Frankreich und England auf der Basis von vier theoretischen Modellen."* Düsseldorf: unpublished report for the Deutsche Forschungsgemeinschaft. 1996, pp. 133–252.

Stein, Ekkehart. *Der Mensch in der pluralistischen Demokratie. Die Freiheitsrechte in Großbritannien.* Frankfurt: Europäische Verlagsanstalt. 1964.

Stevens, Anne. *The Government and Politics of France.* Houndsmills, Basingstoke, and London: Macmillan. 1992.

Strauss, Anselm, and Glaser, Barney. *The Discovery of Grounded Theory. Strategies of Qualitative Research.* Chicago: Aldine. 1967.

Streeck, Wolfgang, and Schmitter, Philippe C. (eds.). *Private Interest Government. Beyond Market and State.* London: Sage. 1985.

Street, Harry. *Freedom, the Individual and the Law.* Harmondsworth: Penguin. 1973.

Suleiman, Ezra N. *Power and Bureaucracy in France. The Administrative Elite.* Princeton: Princeton University Press. 1974.

Suleiman, Ezra N. *Elites in French Society. The Politics of Survival.* Princeton: Princeton University Press. 1978.

Suleiman, Ezra N. *Private Power and Centralization in France. The Notaires and the State.* Princeton, N.J.: Princeton University Press. 1987.

Sunstein, Cass R. "Interest Groups in American Public Law." *Stanford Law Review.* 38. 1985. pp. 29–87.

Sunstein, Cass R. *After the Rights Revolution. Reconceiving the Regulatory State.* Cambridge: Harvard University Press. 1990.

Swidler, Ann. "Inequality and American Culture. The Persistence of Voluntarism." In: *American Behavioral Scientist.* 35/4–5. 1992, pp. 606–629.

Switzer, Jacqueline Vaughn, and Bryner, Gary. *Environmental Politics. Domestic and Global Dimensions.* Boston: Bedorf and St. Martin's. 1998.

Taylor, Charles. *Negative Freiheit? Zur Kritik des neuzeitlichen Individualismus.* Frankfurt a.M.: Suhrkamp. 1988.

Teubner, Günter, and Willke, Helmut. "Kontext und Autonomie: Gesellschaftliche Selbststeuerung durch reflexives Recht." *Zeitschrift für Rechtssoziologie.* 1. 1984, pp. 4–35.

Thomasius, Christian. *Kurzer Entwurf der politischen Klugheit, sich selbst und andern in allen menschlichen esellschaften wohl zu raten und zu einer gescheiten Conduite zu gelangen.* Frankfurt a.M.: Athenäum. (1710) 1971.

Thompson, Grahame, Frances, Jennifer, Levacic, Rosalind, and Mitchell, Jeremy (eds.). *Markets, Hierarchies and Networks. The Coordination of Social Life.* London: Sage. 1991.

Tocqueville, Alexis de. *Democracy in America.* 2 vols. New York: Alfred A.

Knopf. 1945. (French original: *De la démocratie en Amérique*. Paris: Gallimard, 1951.)

Tocqueville, Alexis de. *The Ancient Regime and the French Revolution*. London: Fontana. 1966. (French original: *L'Ancien Régime et la Révolution*. Paris: Michel Levy freres. 1856.)

Toonen, Theo A. J. "Implementation Research and Institutional Design: The Quest for Structure." In: Hanf, Kenneth, and Toonen, Theo A. J. (eds.). *Policy Implementation in Federal and Unitary Systems. Questions of Analysis and Design*. Dordrecht: Martinus Nighoff. 1985, pp. 335–354.

Übersohn, Gerhard. *Effektive Umweltpolitik. Folgerungen aus der Implementations- und Evaluationsforschung*. Frankfurt a.M.: P. Lang. 1990.

U.S. Environmental Protection Agency, Science Advisory Board. *Science Advisory Board FY 1994 Annual Staff Report. The Year of Reinvention*. Washington, D.C., EPA-SAB-95-001. 1994.

Vobruba, Georg. "Wirtschaftsverbände und Gemeinwohl." In: Mayntz, Renate (ed.). *Verbände zwischen Mitgliederinteressen und Gemeinwohl*. Gütersloh: Verlag Bertelsmann Stiftung, 1992, pp. 80–121.

Vogel, David. "Cooperative Regulation. Environmental Protection in Britain." *Public Interest*. 72. 1983, pp. 88–106.

Vogel, David. *National Styles of Regulation. Environmental Policy in Great Britain and the United States*. Ithaca, N.Y.: Cornell University Press. 1986.

Vogel, David. *Kindred Strangers : The Uneasy Relationship between Politics and Business in America*. Princeton: Princeton University Press, 1996.

Waarden, Frans van. "Über die Beständigkeit nationaler Politikstile und Politiknetzwerke." In: Czada, Roland, and Schmidt, Manfred G. (eds.). *Verhandlungsdemokratie, Interessenvermittlung, Regierbarkeit*. Opladen: Westdeutscher Verlag 1993, pp. 191–212.

Wapshot, Nicholas, and Brock, George. *Thatcherism*. London: Fontana. 1983.

Weale, Albert. "Environmental Regulation and Administrative Reform in Britain." In: Majone, Giandomenico (ed.). *Regulating Europe*. London: Routledge, 1996, pp. 106–130.

Weale, Albert, Pridham, Geoffrey, Williams, Andrea, and Porter, Martin. "Environmental Administration in Six European States: Secular Convergence or National Distinctiveness?" *Public Administration*. 74. 1996, pp. 255–274.

Weber, Max. *From Max Weber. Essays in Sociology*. New York: Oxford University Press. 1958.

Weber, Max. *Gesammelte politische Schriften*. Tübingen: Mohr Siebeck. (1958) 1971. (English translation: *Political Writings*. Cambridge: Cambridge University Press. 1994.)

Weber, Max. *Wirtschaft und Gesellschaft. Grundrisse der verstehenden Soziologie*. Tübingen: Mohr Siebeck. 1972. (English translation: *Economy and Society: An Outline of Interpretive Sociology*. Berkeley: University of California Press. 1978.)

Weber, Max. *Gesammelte Aufsätze zur Wissenschaftslehre*. 4th ed. Tübingen: Mohr Siebeck. 1973.

Weidner, Helmut. *Clean Air Policy in Great Britain. Problem Shifting as Best Practicable Means.* Berlin: Edition Sigma. 1987.

Weidner, Helmut. "Umweltmediation: Entwicklungen und Erfahrungen im In- und Ausland." *Forum für Interdisziplinäre Forschung.* 17, 1996, pp. 137–168.

Weidner, Helmut, and Knoepfel, Peter. *Luftreinhaltung (stationäre Quellen) im internationalen Vergleich.* Vol. 2. *Bundesrepublik Deutschland.* Berlin: Edition Sigma. 1985.

Willke, Helmut. *Ironie des Staates. Grundlinien einer Staatstheorie polyzentrischer Gesellschaft.* Frankfurt a.M.: Suhrkamp. 1992a.

Willke, Helmut. "Prinzipien politischer Supervision." In: Bußhoff, Heinrich (ed.). *Politische Steuerung. Steuerbarkeit und Steuerungsfähigkeit. Beiträge zur Grundlagendiskussion.* Baden-Baden: Nomos. 1992b, pp. 51–80.

Wilsford, David. "Tactical Advantages vs. Administrative Heterogeneity: The Strengths and the Limits of the French State." *Comparative Political Studies.* 21/1. 1988, pp. 126–168.

Wilson, Frank. "French Interest Group Politics: Pluralist or Neocorporatist?" *American Political Science Review.* 77/4. 1983, pp. 895– 910.

Wilson, James Q. *Moral Judgment. Does the Abuse Excuse Threaten Our Legal System?* New York: Basic Books. 1997.

Windhoff-Héritier, Adrienne. *Policy Analyse. Eine Einführung.* Frankfurt a.M.: Campus. 1987.

Winthrop, John. "A Model of Christian Charity." In: Miller, Perry, and Johnson, Thomas. (eds.). *The Puritans.* New York: Harper and Row. 1963, pp. 195ff.

Wolf, Rainer. "Herrschaft kraft Wissen in der Risikogesellschaft." *Soziale Welt.* 39/2. 1988, pp. 164–187.

Wolfe, Willard. *From Radicalism to Socialism. Men and Ideas in the Formation of Fabian Socialist Doctrines, 1881–1889.* New Haven, Conn., and London: Yale University Press. 1975.

Wolff, Christian. "Vernünftige Gedanken von dem gesellschaftlichen Leben der Menschen und Insonderheit dem gemeinen Wesen." In: Wolff, Christian. *Gesammelte Werke.* Dept. 1. Deutsche Schriften. Vol. 3. Ed. J. Ecole. Hildensheim: Olms. (1736) 1975.

Wood, B. Dan. "Modeling Federal Implementation as a System: The Clean Air Case." *American Journal of Political Science.* 36/1. 1992, pp. 40–67.

Wood, Christopher. *Planning Pollution Prevention. A Comparison of Siting Controls over Air Pollution Sources in Great Britain and the U.S.A.* Oxford: Heineman and Newnes. 1989.

Wood, Gordon S. *The Creation of the American Republic, 1776–1787.* Chapel Hill: University of North Carolina Press. 1969.

Worms, Jean-Pierre. "Le préfet es ses notables." *Sociologie du travail.* 8/3. 1966. pp. 249–275.

Wynne, B. C. G. "Barkla and the J-Phenomenon: A Case Study on the Treatment of Deviance in Physics." *Social Studies of Science.* 6. 1976, pp. 307–347.

Wynne, B. "Between Orthodoxy and Oblivion: The Normalization of Deviance in

Science." In: Wallis, R. (ed.). *On the Margins of Science: The Social Construction of Rejected Knowledge.* Keele, Staffordshire: University of Keele Press. 1979, pp. 67–84.

Yearley, Steven. "Skills, Deals and Impartiality: The Sale of Environmental Consultancy Skills and Public Perceptions of Scientific Neutrality." *Social Studies of Science.* 22. 1992, pp. 435–453.

Zilleßen, Horst, and Barbian, Thomas. "Neue Formen der Konfliktregelung in der Umweltpolitik." *Aus Politik und Zeitgeschichte*, 39–40, 1992, pp. 14–23.

Zola, Émile. "J'accuse." *L'Aurore*, 13th January 1898.

Index

About the Contributors

CORNELIA BORGARDS works as an academic assistant at the Social Sciences Department at the University of Osnabrück. The focal areas of her work cover the sociology of the environment and the sociology of organization.

CLAUDIA JAUß holds a scholarship for postdoctoral lecturing qualification at Otto-Friedrich University in Bamberg. The focal areas of her work cover political theory, environmental policy, and European research. Her publications include *Politik als Verhandlungsmarathon. Immissionsschutz in der amerikanischen Wettbewerbsdemokratie* (1999), which was awarded the J. William Fulbright dissertation prize in 1999, as well as *Lobbying als Beruf. Interessengruppen in der Europäischen Union* (2000).

MARKUS KURTH focuses on international relations, political economy, and the sociology of technological change. From 1994 to 1997 he did research on British environmental policy at the Heinrich-Heine-University in Düsseldorf. He is currently working in Dortmund as a researcher and professional campaigner for a regional alliance of community groups, employment initiatives and scientists in the Ruhr-area. His research concentrates on the decision-making process for complex urban transformations with attention to conflicts of interest, political planning tools, participation, and social equity.

CHRISTIAN LAHUSEN is a member of the Department of Sociology at Otto-Friedrich-University in Bamberg. He has worked extensively in the realm of cultural and political sociology, with particular emphasis on social movements and political mobilization. He is the author of *The Rhetoric of Moral Protest. Public Campaigns, Celebrity Endorsement and Political Mobilization* (1996). He is currently working on cooperative politics in the realm of environmental regulation in France, Germany, Great Britain, and the United States.

RICHARD MÜNCH is professor for sociology at the University of Bamberg. His main field of research includes sociological theory, sociology of culture, and social integration with a particular emphasis on comparative sociology. He is the author of several books and numerous articles in these areas. Among his publications are *Sociological Theory 1–3* (1994) and *Globale Dynamik, lokale Lebenswelten* (1998).

CARSTEN STARK is sociologist and academic assistant at the Department of Sociology 2 of Otto-Friedrich University in Bamberg. The focal areas of his work cover sociological theory, political sociology, and sociology of the environment. He has published *Die blockierte Demokratie. Kulturelle Grenzen der Politik im deutschen Immissionsschutz* (1999).